HANDBOOKS

SAN MIGUEL DE ALLENDE
GUANAJUATO & THE BAJÍO

JULIE DOHERTY MEADE

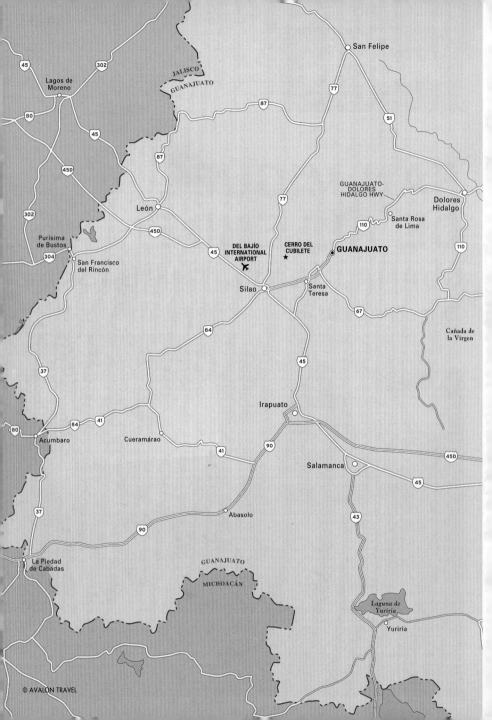

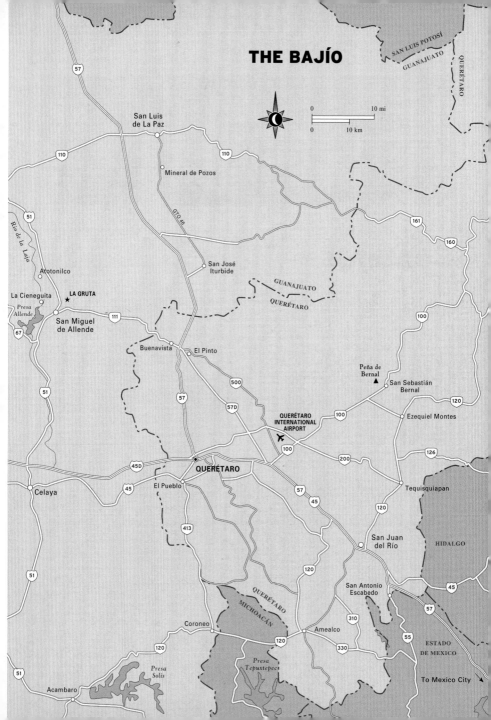

Contents

Discover
San Miguel de Allende

As evening falls across the Sierra de Guanajuato, the brilliant blue skies of the Bajío warm to rosy pink. Along the cobbled streets of San Miguel de Allende and Guanajuato, amber streetlights illuminate the sandstone domes of 18th-century churches, while clanging iron bells herald the end of another day. As the dry air drops to a pleasant chill, mariachis tune their instruments and sidewalks hum with diners, gallery-goers, and revelers. This is Mexico *mágico,* the mythic place of *corridos* (ballads) alive and thriving on the high plains.

Located in Mexico's semi-arid central highlands, the Bajío region is a gateway between the vast northern deserts and bustling southern states. Built with the spoils of the silver trade, its colonial cities are some of the country's most splendid, renowned for their fine Mexican baroque architecture and historic city centers. In San Miguel de Allende, you can stroll along cobbled streets barely wide enough for cars, flanked by crumbling walls and draping vines of bougainvillea. To the north, Guanajuato might be the world's most breathtaking university town, where boxy, jewel-colored houses rise above a maze-like *centro histórico* (historical district).

The Bajío is a quintessentially Mexican region, where tacos and tamales are standard fare, the midday siesta is still respected, and religious

festivals are frequent, ritualistic, and raucous. It was also the cradle of the independence movement; it was from the steps of the cathedral in Dolores that revolutionary hero Miguel Hidalgo raised his famous cry, *"¡Viva Mexico!"* Alongside legendary sights, you'll find artisan shops, several of Latin America's oldest art academies, and markets brimming with a bounty of produce, handmade tortillas, and local cheese.

Today, tradition and modernity are intertwined in the Bajío. The large expatriate population in San Miguel de Allende has added a new twist to the local culture, where gin martinis and hamburgers are as common as hot sauce and jalapeños. Here, fusion food is welcomed with the same enthusiasm as modern art, creating a unique mix of people and culture. This joyous conviviality is precisely what makes San Miguel de Allende, Guanajuato, and the surrounding region such an imminently rewarding place to visit, to spend a season, and to become a part of *la vida mexicana.*

Planning Your Trip

▶ WHERE TO GO

San Miguel de Allende

San Miguel de Allende is a small colonial city, known for its beautiful light, charming atmosphere, and artsy expatriate community. Irresistibly romantic yet surprisingly modern, San Miguel offers a little of something for everyone, whether you are an artist, a history buff, or just someone looking for a great place to relax. Tour colonial architecture, visit contemporary art galleries, shop for traditional crafts, or linger over coffee in a sidewalk café. While there, visit the hot springs for a relaxing afternoon in the desert or take a horseback ride through the desert chaparral.

Guanajuato

Guanajuato is one of Mexico's famous silver cities, built with the wealth of the colonial mineral mines. The city boasts a spectacular mix of baroque art and architecture, as well as an unusual urban map. It's built along the edge of a ravine, and automobile traffic passes through tunnels underground while pedestrians navigate a dizzying mess of alleyways along the hillside. Home to a large public university, Guanajuato is a spirited college town with a youthful atmosphere, plenty of inexpensive hangouts, and an active arts and theater scene.

The Bajío

The Bajío region is a large plain within Mexico's central plateau,

IF YOU HAVE . . .

- **A LONG WEEKEND:** Head straight to San Miguel de Allende and spend the weekend exploring the city's *centro histórico*.

- **ONE WEEK:** Follow the "Best of the Bajío" itinerary, allowing for a travel day at the beginning and end of the trip.

- **ONE MONTH:** Make San Miguel de Allende your home base and plan trips to the cities of Guanajuato, Mineral de Pozos, and Querétaro.

- **A WINTER:** With a season in San Miguel, you can do it all: make friends, take a class, attend concerts, soak in the hot springs, and plan day trips throughout the region.

sandstone sculpture adorning the Templo San Roque in Guanajuato

The Universidad de Guanajuato's massive main campus is located on a narrow street in the city center.

which encompasses the cities of San Miguel de Allende and Guanajuato. Located in the geographic center of Mexico, the Bajío was among the most populous and wealthy parts of New Spain, growing along with the silver trade. Today, the Bajío is an industrial and agricultural region, its open expanses dotted with cities and pueblos. Visit Querétaro to enjoy a unique mix of urban and colonial culture, or spend a day exploring the former mining camps in Mineral de Pozos, a glimpse into Mexico's past.

Paper flags fly in front of the Parroquia de San Miguel Arcángel during Día del los Muertos in San Miguel de Allende.

▶ WHEN TO GO

San Miguel de Allende, Guanajuato, and the Bajío are **year-round destinations,** though climate and costs vary depending on the season you choose to visit. North American winter is typically the tourist **high season** in San Miguel de Allende, when the region is cool, dry, and sunny. From **December through April,** large numbers of part-time residents from the United States and Canada arrive for their annual sojourn in San Miguel, while regular tourism surges throughout the region. If you plan to visit San Miguel de Allende between **November and April,** make your hotel reservations in advance.

Throughout the Bajío, the weather heats up significantly during the month of **May,** and tourism is generally sluggish until the **rainy season** begins, around mid-June. With the rains, the climate cools off pleasantly, making it a nice time to visit. Often, students and families take advantage of school vacations to visit Mexico during the summer. Although hotels and restaurants aren't as full during the summer as they are during the winter, there is still a pleasant buzz of international tourism. **Summer** is also a popular time for college students to take language classes or volunteer in San Miguel or Guanajuato.

One thing to keep in mind when planning your trip to San Miguel de Allende, Guanajuato, and the Bajío is that these destinations are popular with national tourists, as well as international tourists. During long weekends, San Miguel is often thronged with families from Querétaro and Mexico City, while big holidays, like Independence Day, can literally transform the city with crowds of revelers. You will need to make advance reservations in a hotel if you plan to visit the Bajío during **Holy Week** in the spring, **Independence Day** in September, or during the **Christmas season** in December, or if you plan to visit Guanajuato in **October,** when the city hosts the annual Festival Internacional Cervantino.

San Miguel abounds with quaint, picturesque alleys.

a colorful street in downtown Guanajuato

▶ BEFORE YOU GO

Passports and Visas

Since 2008, all foreign visitors must have a valid passport to enter Mexico. At the port of entry, immigration officials issue each visitor a six-month temporary tourist permit. You must keep your stamped permit and return it at the airport when you check in for your flight. If you enter by car, you must stop at an immigration office at the border to pick up your tourist card, and, likewise, return it to immigration officials on your way home.

Transportation

San Miguel de Allende and the Bajío region can be accessed by air via the León-Bajío International Airport (BJX) in the northern part of Guanajuato state and the Querétaro International Airport (QRO) in the southern Bajío. Most travelers arrive in León, which offers more international flights than Querétaro. From both of these airports, it takes about 90 minutes to get to San Miguel de Allende, and there are several tour operators who offer shuttle service to and from the airport. The city of Guanajuato is about a half hour from the BJX terminal. For some travelers, it is easiest to book flights to Mexico City and then use ground transportation to reach their destination in the Bajío.

There is plenty of bus service to and from the region, which is in the very center of Mexico, including frequent departures to San Miguel de Allende, Guanajuato, and Querétaro from Mexico City. There is also frequent service between Bajío cities, including hourly departures to Querétaro and Guanajuato from San Miguel.

What to Take

The Bajío has a year-round temperate climate, which doesn't call for any special clothing or

pomegranate seeds for sale in Querétaro

gear. The one exception is footwear. San Miguel de Allende and Guanajuato have colonial-era downtown districts, crisscrossed by uneven cobblestone streets. They can be quite slick, especially in the rain, and it is not unusual for visitors to slip or sprain an ankle while momentarily distracted by a beautiful 18th-century bell tower. For sightseeing, bring comfortable shoes that are good for walking.

When packing, keep in mind that the dry, semi-arid climate in the Bajío means that temperatures fluctuate significantly from morning to midday to evening. In the winter months, it can drop below freezing at night. Bring layers and, if you are visiting in the summer, an umbrella and waterproof shoes. Dress code is generally casual in the Bajío, even at the nicest establishments. At the same time, the Bajío is not the beach, so tourists in excessively summery outfits (shorts, bathing suits, sarongs, and the like) may stand out a bit.

If you plan on doing a little shopping in San Miguel de Allende, bring along your checkbook, in addition to bank cards and credit cards. Surprisingly, many small businesses will accept checks from U.S. banks, even if they don't accept credit cards.

Explore San Miguel de Allende, Guanajuato, and the Bajío

▶ THE BEST OF THE BAJÍO

San Miguel de Allende, Guanajuato, and the Bajío unite recreation, relaxation, and culture. If you want to see and do as much as possible, San Miguel makes a good home base, with interesting sights, a wide variety of hotels and restaurants, and plenty of tourist services.

In five days, you'll have time to visit most of the Bajío's famous sights, do some quality shopping, and eat well in a range of restaurants. However, the colonial cities of the Bajío are as much about atmosphere as attractions; you'll often find your most memorable moments were encountered by surprise. If time affords, space out your itinerary and take the time to simply enjoy life in Mexico's high plains.

Day 1

Every tour of San Miguel de Allende should begin at the *jardín,* the city's central square. The ever-busy plaza is quieter in the mornings, attended by flocks of pudgy pigeons. Sip a cup of coffee while admiring the pink sandstone arches of the Parroquia de San Miguel Arcángel, the city's unusual neo-Gothic church. Next, stop into the Museo de San Miguel, which offers a nice introduction to the city's history.

Tourists and residents enjoy a warm afternoon in San Miguel's *jardín.*

Revelers gather for a festival near the Parroquia de San Miguel Arcángel.

Day 2

Now that you've got the lay of the land, give yourself the luxury of a lazy morning, lingering over juice or coffee at Café de la Parroquia or one of the many other breakfast spots in town. When you are ready to get moving, take a taxi to El Charco del Ingenio, the botanical gardens and ecological preserve located just above the city center. Spend some time spotting cactus along El Charco's winding nature trails and enjoy the sweeping views of the city below.

Head back to town for a leisurely *comida* (the late lunch typically eaten in Mexico), then consider retiring for a well-earned siesta. After your nap (or in lieu of it), take a turn around the downtown district to browse the many beautiful shops, galleries, and boutiques in San Miguel.

In the evening, pick up a copy of *Atención San Miguel* and leaf through the pages to see what's going on around town; you may find some live music, theater, or film events that interest you. Snack on some tacos and head to a show, or simply linger over dinner alfresco at one of the restaurants downtown.

Now it's time to perfect the art of the not-totally-aimless wander. You might choose to begin at the Centro Cultural Ignacio Ramírez, an art school and gallery, or visit the adjoining Templo de la Inmaculada Concepción, San Miguel's largest domed church. Head east toward the Oratorio San Felipe Neri and the Templo de San Francisco, then stroll through the Mercado Ignacio Ramírez on the other side of the Plaza Cívica. Stop for a snack at La Colmena, a traditional Mexican bakery.

Eat lunch in one of the dozens of restaurants and cafés in downtown San Miguel, then continue south. Visit galleries in the Instituto Allende, the country's oldest art school, and scale the staircases of El Chorro, the site of San Miguel's founding. Enjoy a shady respite in Parque Juárez amid the cries of snowy egrets and the giggles of local children. As evening falls, relax in the *jardín* before heading out to dinner at one of San Miguel's casual Mexican eateries. If it's a Friday or Saturday night, join the locals at Bovedas for salsa dancing, or drop by Harry's New Orleans Café for a margarita at the bar.

The nature trails around El Charco del Ingenio will introduce you to native plants and animals.

SANDSTONE HEAVEN:
ARCHITECTURE IN THE BAJÍO

During the 17th and 18th centuries, the booming silver trade brought prosperity to the Bajío. Working with some of Mexico's most celebrated architects and artists, the region's wealthy families supplied funds for haciendas, churches, and other religious and civil buildings. Many of these architectural wonders can still be seen today.

MEXICAN BAROQUE

Downtown San Miguel de Allende and Guanajuato are often compared to the Old World, and for good reason: During the colonial era, Mexican architecture followed trends from Spain, where baroque architecture was the dominant aesthetic. An evolution of the classical style favored during the Renaissance, baroque is characterized by its elaborate ornamentation, dramatic use of light, and monumental facades.

Where to Find It
In Guanajuato, the **Templo San Roque** and the

Basílica de Nuestra Señora de Guanajuato are two beautiful representations. In San Miguel, the **Casa de Allende** was built in the 18th century by one of the city's prominent families.

CHURRIGUERESQUE

During the late 1600s, Spanish architect José Benito de Churriguera developed a style of ornamentation, called churrigueresque, that was a more-elaborate offshoot of baroque design. Influenced by Churriguera's florid aesthetic, Mexican architects began to incorporate more extravagant embellishments onto the facades of 18th-century churches.

Where to Find It
In San Miguel, visit the **Templo de San Francisco** for a fine example of early-18th-century churrigueresque ornamentation. You can see the direct influence of Churriguera's style in the elaborately carved sandstone columns. Near Guanajuato, the astonishingly detailed

The Templo de San Francisco is an 18th-century church with a hand-carved sandstone facade.

The columns and arches of the Alhóndiga de Granaditas exemplify neoclassical architecture.

sandstone relief on the **Templo de San Cayetano** is known throughout the country as one of the most beautiful representations of churrigueresque ornamentation.

GOTHIC REVIVAL

In Northern Europe, the mid-1700s saw a resurgent interest in Medieval architecture, known as the Gothic Revival. Gaining popularity in the New World in the 1800s, this style was borrowed from traditional Gothic design and aesthetics.

Where to Find It

In San Miguel, there is one unmistakable neo-Gothic structure: the pink sandstone facade on the famous **Parroquia de San Miguel Arcángel,** inspired by Gothic cathedrals in Europe. Its towering spires and pointed arches are distinct trademarks of the style.

NEOCLASSICAL

During the late 1700s, classical architecture also experienced a revival. Typified by its clean lines and symmetry, neoclassical architecture often employs large arches, columns, and pilasters.

Where to Find It

In Guanajuato, there are many striking neoclassical buildings downtown, from the austere **Alhóndiga de Granaditas** to the impressive columned facade of **Teatro Juárez.** Also note the massive neoclassical altarpieces in many of San Miguel's churches – including the **Templo de la Inmaculada Concepción** and the **Parroquia de San Miguel Arcángel.**

THE HACIENDA

The hacienda – a large estate overseen by a Spanish family – was a major influence on Bajío architecture. Throughout the region, small towns, such as Dolores Hidalgo, were often founded as haciendas, eventually growing large enough to become cities in their own right. In downtown San Miguel, many present-day individual homes were once a part of larger family estates.

Where to Find It

For a glimpse into the lifestyle of 17th- and 18th-century haciendas, visit the **Ex-Hacienda San Gabriel de Barrera** in Guanajuato.

The Templo San Roque in Guanajuato is an example of Mexican baroque architecture.

Day 3

It's worth getting an early start to visit the natural hot springs when the air is still cool and there aren't big crowds in the pools. Just 10 minutes from downtown San Miguel, La Gruta is the most well known bathing spot, but there are several other options along the highway to Dolores Hidalgo.

Post-soak, visit the village of Atotonilco, just down the road from La Gruta. Presiding over this small town, the massive Santuario de Jesús Nazareno de Atotonilco was constructed in the 18th century. Inside this spectacular church, take a look at the hand-painted walls depicting biblical scenes.

Travel back to San Miguel to watch the sunset from the rooftop bar at La Azotea or Mama Mia. Follow it up with a hearty dinner at one of San Miguel's wonderful Italian or international restaurants before crashing to sleep amid the clang of church bells.

Day 4

By the time you've spent a few days in San Miguel, you've likely fallen in step with the city's easygoing manner. Now it's time to pick up the pace in Querétaro, a medium-sized city just an hour southeast of San Miguel. From the bus station in Querétaro, take a taxi to the Plaza de Armas, located on the northern edge of the *centro histórico*. The adjoining tourist office can provide clear, annotated maps of the many sights downtown. You can start your day with a coffee in one of the shaded restaurants adjoining the plaza.

Wander down one of the pedestrian streets to the Plaza de la Corregidora and the Jardín Zenea. History buffs may want to stop into the Museo Regional, adjoining the Templo de San Francisco, while art lovers may head south to the Museo de Arte de Querétaro, a lovely fine-art museum housed in a gorgeous former convent.

ceiling frescoes in the Santuario de Jesús Nazareno de Atotonilco

The Museo de Arte de Querétaro is housed in a former Augustine convent.

PICTURE-PERFECT SAN MIGUEL

a panoramic view of San Miguel and the surrounding valley from El Mirador

San Miguel de Allende's colorful cityscapes and beautiful vistas are likely to inspire your inner photographer. Even snapshots of the city can be surprisingly stunning and colorful, which is auspicious for enthusiastic amateurs. If you want to bring home an impressive album of travel shots, here are some subjects to inspire point-and-shoot magic.

NIGHTTIME AT THE PARISH

Parroquia de San Miguel Arcángel is the most recognizable – and most frequently photographed – monument in town. Catching this unique church in the right light can be a bit of a challenge; for a shot worthy of any postcard, steady your hand and photograph the church at night, when its many arches are illuminated with floodlights.

COBBLESTONE STREETS

Calle Aldama extends from the central square to Parque Juárez; its cobblestones give way to an iconic vista of the painted domes of the *parroquia,* rising above the multicolor jumble of colonial mansions.

MARKET ROSES

At the **Mercado Ignacio Ramírez,** San Miguel de Allende's covered market, the heaps of roses, lilies, carnations, gladiolas, and gerberas add a colorful flourish to the Mexican market scene.

MARIACHIS

A picture of the *plaza principal* becomes all the more alluring when you capture a group of mariachi musicians mid-tune, dressed in the traditional *charro* costume and singing in unison.

DYNAMIC PANORAMAS

If you are willing to huff and puff for a photo op, head up to **El Mirador,** a small rest stop on the Salida a Querétaro, which offers sweeping views of the city center, the reservoir, and the valley below town.

PARADES AND FESTIVALS

From the explosion of fireworks over the *parroquia* on **Día de la Independencia** to the giant papier-mâché figures that dance outside the church at traditional weddings, there is no shortage of festivals, color, and pageantry around San Miguel de Allende.

DONKEYS

The image of a packed donkey walking down a picturesque residential street is classic San Miguel de Allende. If you see the donkey's owner, it's customary to offer a small tip after you snap a shot of the beast.

A gargoyle adorns the buttresses of the Ex-Convento de Santa Rosa de Viterbo in Querétaro.

one of the most impressive baroque structures in the Bajío. If you stay until evening, stop into **La Selva Taurina** for a beer in a classic cantina setting, or wander down Arteaga Street, where numerous small storefronts serve the traditional Mexican dinner of tamales and *atole*. Though it's tempting to stay, don't linger too long: The last buses leave for San Miguel around 10 P.M.

Day 5

Get up early and take off for **Guanajuato**, an hour's drive northwest of San Miguel. Start your tour in the Jardín de la Unión, the city's central plaza. After a turn around the garden, pay the admission fee for **Teatro Juárez**, a neoclassical performance space with an elaborate Moorish interior. Back outside, walk north toward the Plaza de la Paz, following Avenida Juárez until you arrive at the **Mercado Hidalgo**. Grab a snack in the market, then head to the

For lunch, stop at La Mariposa, where the atmosphere and food seem to have been frozen in time. Next, visit the **Templo y Ex-Convento de Santa Rosa de Viterbo**,

the main campus at the Universidad de Guanajuato

famous **Alhóndiga de Granaditas,** just a block away.

After touring the Alhóndiga, have a relaxing afternoon meal in the shaded Plaza San Fernando. Feel free to go big, as you can quickly burn off your lunch with a trek up the alleyways toward the monument to El Pípila, which towers over downtown. If your legs have had enough, take the funky little funicular up the hillside. After you've snapped some photos, spend the afternoon wandering along Calle Positos and the main campus of **Universidad de Guanajuato.**

Spend a night in Guanajuato to enjoy the convivial atmosphere (additionally, Guanajuato is much closer to the León airport, if your flight is in the morning). Start the evening by sipping a glass of top-shelf tequila at **Bar Tradicional Luna** in the Jardín de la Unión or enjoying the view of Teatro Juárez from the outdoor tables at El

the elaborate interior of Teatro Juárez in Guanajuato

Galería Café. If you want to make it a late night, head off to **Zilch Bar** or La Dama de las Camelias for a bohemian crowd, live music, and dancing.

one of the many bustling courtyards in Guanajuato's city center

THE HIGHLAND PALATE

Mexico's color and creativity are reflected in its culinary traditions. There are several traditional Mexican dishes and unusual ingredients that are frequent features of Bajío cuisine. If you want to get a taste of the highlands, here's what to order:

GORDITAS

Gorditas are thick corn flatbreads, grilled and stuffed with fillings like cheese, chile peppers, chicken, or beans. Gorditas are sold by street vendors and in market stalls throughout the region. For freshly made gorditas with a range of savory fillings, check out **El Comal de Doña Meche** in San Miguel de Allende.

A specialty of the Bajío, gorditas are made with both yellow and blue corn.

ENCHILADAS MINERAS

A hearty meal suited to a hungry miner, these cheese-stuffed enchiladas are bathed in *guajillo* chile sauce and topped with a generous serving of sautéed potatoes, carrots, and cheese. Fill your stomach with this regional specialty at **Tacos Don Felix** in San Miguel de Allende or **Truco 7** in Guanajuato.

NOPAL

Nopal, or prickly pear cactus, is a popular vegetable in the Bajío region, often served as a stuffing in gorditas or grilled whole and served beside a cut of meat. One tasty stew served throughout the Bajío features chopped nopal with garbanzo beans and cilantro. The best spots to find nopal in San Miguel are at the **Mercado Ignacio Ramírez,** where you can buy it both fresh and prepared, and at **Hecho en Mexico,** where you can order it as a grilled side dish.

XOCONOSTLE

Throughout Mexico, the tuna (prickly pear fruit) is consumed whole or blended into ice cream and *aguas*. In the Bajío, a type of sour tuna called *xoconostle* is used in regional dishes, such as chicken in *xoconostle* sauce. It is also commonly used in sweets, as its sour taste creates a pleasingly tart flavor. Buy some from Santa Rosa de Lima's **Conservas Santa Rosa,** or tip back a xoconoxtle margarita at

▶ ART LOVER'S TOUR

It's no wonder that San Miguel de Allende has been home to a prominent artist community since the early 20th century: Baroque architecture, saturated colors, contemporary art, and clear blue skies inundate the senses, inspiring artists and art lovers alike.

Day 1

Begin at the Centro Cultural Ignacio Ramírez, a visual arts and music school. In the galleries downstairs, you'll find rotating exhibitions of work by students and local artists, as well as an unfinished mural by Mexican master David Alfaro Siqueiros in one of back salons.

Grab a gallery guide (there are many free booklets published in town) and spend the morning wandering the many artist-owned

Pulque is made from the maguey plant.

nopal stew

Las Mercedes Banquetes y Restaurante in Guanajuato.

MIXIOTE

Popular in the Valley of Mexico as well as the Bajío, *mixiotes* are slow-cooked meats (typically rabbit, chicken, lamb, and pork) wrapped in maguey leaves and steamed in an underground pit. While in San Miguel, you can order mixiotes at the rooftop restaurant **La Posadita,** or try them in a casual setting at **El Pato.**

PULQUE DE TUNA

Pulque is a fermented, lightly alcoholic drink from the heart of the maguey, which has been produced in Mexico since the pre-Columbian era. During the Bajío's abundant prickly pear season, pulque is mixed with red tuna to create the flavorful, bright magenta beverage *pulque de tuna.* In late summer, you can track some down in the *plaza principal* in **Mineral de Pozos.**

QUESO RANCHERO

Called *queso fresco* in other parts of Mexico, the Bajío's delicious *queso ranchero* is a fresh, white, salty cheese, often crumbled atop enchiladas or guacamole. It is sold in marketplaces and supermarkets; look for *queso ranchero* at San Miguel's **Mercado de Martes** or drop by **Luna de Queso** for a large selection of Mexican cheese and dairy.

CAJETA

Caramelized milk candy *(cajeta)* is a specialty of Celaya, a small industrial city just an hour east of San Miguel. Created with a mix of scalded goat and cow milk, this *cajeta* sauce is served in crepes, on ice cream, or slathered onto wafers. You can also find *cajeta* candy rolled in nuts. Try some at Guanajuato's **La Catrina** sweet shop, or order a scoop of *cajeta*-flavored ice cream in the town square in **Dolores Hidalgo.**

collectives, contemporary exhibition spaces, and fancy design stores in the *centro histórico.* San Miguel is also a wonderful place to see popular art, with many well-curated shops that elevate craft to fine-art status. After lunch, visit the Casa del Mayorazgo de la Canal, a cultural center and exhibition space operated by the Banamex foundation.

Day 2

Tip back a *café con leche* in the *centro histórico,* then stroll to the Fábrica La Aurora, a large art and shopping center located in a converted turn-of-the-20th-century textile factory. Don't shy away from exploring the labyrinthine space: You'll find dozens of galleries, studios, and shops tucked into unexpected nooks and crannies.

You can nourish your soul and your stomach at one of the Aurora's restaurants, or head back downtown for a meal, soaking up the saturated colors of colonial Mexico. After lunch, drop into La Esquina: Museo del Jugete Popular Mexicano, a lovely little museum that showcases the fine craftsmanship and creativity behind traditional Mexican toys. Those interested in baroque painting may also want to visit the **Oratorio San Felipe Neri** and the adjoining **Iglesia de Nuestra Señora de la Salud;** both churches contain small but interesting oil paintings and retablos from the 18th century.

With so many artists in town, there is always an event to attend—a quintessential San Miguel experience. If you haven't been invited to an opening exhibition during your gallery tour around town, pick up a copy of *Atención San Miguel* to see if there are any that night. If a popular local artist is having a show, you can expect a flurry of attendees and little cups of cheap Chilean wine at the gallery. Join in the fun, but don't stay up too late. You have to catch an early bus to Guanajuato, where your tour continues.

Day 3

Head straight to the heart of Guanajuato, and make your first stop the **Templo de San Diego,** which has numerous large-format oil paintings from the 17th century through the post-independence era, many by anonymous artists. Next, travel to the university, where you can see the large collection of religious paintings at the **Templo de la Compañía de Jesús,** which includes work by master artist Miguel Cabrera. On the other side of the *centro histórico,* you can visit the lovely **Iglesia de San Francisco** to see numerous restored 18th-century oil paintings.

In the afternoon, take a bus or taxi up the hill to visit the **Templo de San Cayetano** to see the elaborate wood altarpieces. Hand-carved in the baroque style and then washed in gold leaf, these amazingly three-dimensional floor-to-ceiling altars are awe-inspiring.

Day 4

The must-see stop this morning is the **Museo y Casa de Diego Rivera,** located in the childhood home of the famous muralist.

Casa del Mayorazgo de la Canal in San Miguel

Within this surprisingly extensive museum, visitors can enjoy an interesting selection of Rivera's early work, as well as a collection of work by the artist's contemporaries.

Just down the road, it is worth the modest admission fee to visit the **Museo del Pueblo de Guanajuato,** which exhibits a nice collection of colonial artwork, as well as rotating exhibitions by contemporary artists. Keep walking down Calle Positos to visit the fine art galleries located in the Universidad de Guanajuato, including the unique **Galería El Atrio,** just beneath the Templo de la Compañía de Jesús. After your tour, rub shoulders with Guanajuato's arts-and-letters crowd with a meal or a coffee near the university.

handmade rocking horses on display at La Esquina: Museo del Jugete Popular Mexicano in San Miguel

▶ SPIRIT OF SAN MIGUEL

A trip to San Miguel de Allende can often inspire a journey within. From the clear mountain air to the warmth of its people, this small city has a way of provoking change and promoting self-discovery. For dharma bums or burgeoning artists, this is a wonderful place for a low-key retreat from real life, relaxing and reflecting beneath the sparkling skies of Mexico.

Heal

A multifaceted healing arts and wellness retreat, **LifePath Center** offers a range of therapies with local practitioners, including reiki, dream-work, psychological counseling, naturopathic medicine, and healing massage. There are also ongoing classes in yoga, tai chi, and art, all held in the lovely and leafy rooms of a colonial mansion.

Chill

Operated by the luxury hotel Casa de Sierra Nevada, **Laja Spa** lets you unwind with an aromatherapy massage or detoxifying herbal wrap in one of their serene private rooms. For a down-to-earth experience, check out **Jasmine Day Spa** on Calle Jesús, where you can get a pedicure or a massage in the colorfully decorated rooms on the second floor of a colonial home.

Soak

Spend a morning soaking in the covered pools at **La Gruta** and then sipping on juice in the flower-filled gardens. The natural warm water that fills La Gruta's pools is believed to have healing properties. Just down the road, **Escondido Place** has a series of progressively warmer pools, filled daily by natural springs, as well as cold-water pools in the expansive gardens.

Swim

Take a dip beneath the desert sky in the sparkling, spring-fed lap pool at **Taboada.** Bring a blanket to relax on the lawn after your workout. In town, head up to the Atascadero

The naturally heated lap pool at Taboada is great for a leisurely morning swim.

neighborhood for an early swim at the Santo Domingo Health Club.

Stretch

Yoga is a favorite San Miguel activity. You can take serene Hatha yoga classes at Centro Shakti Yoga or sweat through a session of Iyengar yoga at Yoga San Miguel.

Reflect

Participate in a little still and silent meditation at the friendly and low-key Meditation Center of San Miguel, tucked into a small alley downtown.

Express

Awaken your creativity by taking classes with local artists, photographers, or writers. Peruse listings in the local paper, *Atención San Miguel,* or check out The Little Schools (www.little-schoolssma.com) online for locations.

Listen

In addition to its movie series, the Teatro Santa Ana (inside the Biblioteca de San Miguel de Allende) hosts interesting and inspiring speakers. See local writers share their work or attend a lecture on Mexican culture.

Energize

El Charco del Ingenio, San Miguel's unique botanical gardens and nature preserve, has a special energy. You can visit El Charco to enjoy sweeping views of the canyon, or to attend the morning yoga sessions, wildlife workshops, and other special programs. On several occasions, the preserve has invited Tibetan monks to perform ceremonies in the main garden.

Explore

For gorgeous scenery and a glimpse into the past, plan a trip to the Cañada de la Virgen, San Miguel's recently inaugurated archaeological site and ecological reserve. The power of pre-Columbian monuments is reflected in the Cañada's largest pyramid structure, which is oriented toward the path of the rising sun.

SAN MIGUEL DE ALLENDE

San Miguel de Allende is a town of a thousand picture postcards, renowned for its Mexican baroque architecture and sparkling blue skies. You can hardly turn a corner without finding another splendid scene before you. On one block, there is a crumbling stone chapel, its four iron bells hanging crookedly in the belfry. On another, a flower seller stacks bushels of roses atop an 18th-century fountain. Along the winding streets of the *centro histórico* (historical district), vines of magenta bougainvillea spill over the earthy walls of colonial residences, each painted a different shade of ochre, brick red, cinnamon, or rust. The scene is made all the rosier by the setting sun, which throws a scarlet blanket across the sky throughout the winter and spring. It is precisely when everything seems too beautiful to believe that you stumble upon something new: an old wood doorway, a wedding party led by a flower-wreathed donkey, an unexpected burst of fireworks over the starlit skyline. Open and friendly yet never predictable, San Miguel is a town of no secrets, but many surprises.

Yet San Miguel is much more than a beautiful facade, as some cynics might claim. It is a place of living culture and community, where neighbors gladly greet each other in the streets, the arts are celebrated, and small family-run businesses are the heart and soul of downtown. Here, there is beauty in the mix of cultures and traditions: the modern art gallery and the antique apothecary, the French bistros and the buzzing taco stands. On the weekends, the sidewalks are pleasantly humming with diners, revelers, and families. Crowds spill from the

HIGHLIGHTS

◖ Parroquia de San Miguel Arcángel: San Miguel's iconic parish church is a symbol of the town and one of the most original architectural achievements in Mexico. In the evening, its multitiered pink towers are beautifully illuminated against the starry sky (page 34).

◖ El Jardín: Since the early 18th century, the central square, or *jardín*, has been the heart and soul of San Miguel de Allende. If you are new in town, this is the best place to relax with an ice cream and enjoy some quality people-watching (page 34).

◖ Parque Juárez: A lively urban park that has become a favorite nesting spot for egrets, this is a wonderful place to enjoy a peaceful afternoon in the shade of fan palms and jacarandas (page 39).

◖ El Chorro and the Casa de la Cultura: Located at the original site of San Miguel's founding, the cascading terraces of El Chorro and the Casa de la Cultura are among the most beautiful and most historic spots in town. Climb the winding stairs to see the old Capilla de la Santa Cruz, or listen in on a music class in the adjoining cultural center (page 39).

◖ Fábrica La Aurora: This former turn-of-the-20th-century textile factory has been refashioned as a cosmopolitan art and design center, with more than 35 galleries, shops, and studios, plus restaurants and a café. Spend an afternoon wandering around the cool corridors, peeking into artists' studios, or relaxing with a coffee on one of the lovely patios (page 40).

◖ El Charco del Ingenio: An expansive nature preserve and botanical garden, El Charco affords sweeping views of the city, charming nature trails, and satisfying bird-watching along a dramatic canyon ridge. In 2004, it was designated a Peace Zone by the Dalai Lama (page 41).

◖ Santuario de Jesús Nazareno de Atotonilco: One of the finest churches in all of Mexico, the enigmatic sanctuary in Atotonilco has been a site of religious retreat and refuge since the 18th century, as well as the permanent home of the much revered figure of El Señor de la Columna. In 2008, it was declared a World Heritage Site by the United Nations (page 100).

◖ La Gruta: Near the town of Atotonilco, volcanic activity beneath the Earth's surface has created a bank of clean, nonsulfurous thermal water. Don't miss the opportunity to soak at La Gruta, one of the many thermal pools near San Miguel de Allende, which many believe have healing properties (page 102).

Santuario de Jesús Nazareno de Atotonilco

La Gruta

0   1 mi
0   1 km

51

Fábrica La Aurora

El Charco del Ingenio

El Jardín

Parroquia de San Miguel Arcángel

San Miguel de Allende

111

Presa Allende

51

Parque Juárez

El Chorro and the Casa de la Cultura

© AVALON TRAVEL

LOOK FOR ◖ TO FIND RECOMMENDED SIGHTS, ACTIVITIES, DINING, AND LODGING.

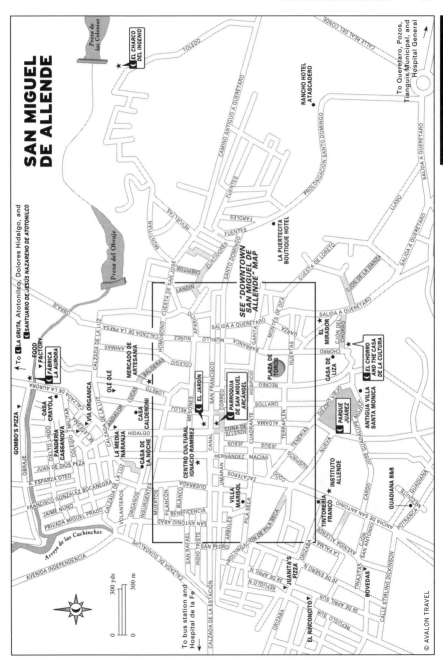

SAN MIGUEL DE ALLENDE

To **LA GRUTA**, Atotonilco, Dolores Hidalgo, and **SANTUARIO DE JESÚS NAZARENO DE ATOTONILCO**

To Querétaro, Pozos, Tianguis Municipal, and Hospital General

★ EL CHARCO DEL INGENIO

RANCHO HOTEL ATASCADERO

LA PUERTECITA BOUTIQUE HOTEL

SEE "DOWNTOWN SAN MIGUEL DE ALLENDE" MAP

★ EL MIRADOR

★ EL CHORRO AND THE CASA DE LA CULTURA

CASA DE LIZA

PLAZA DE TOROS

FOOD FACTORY ▼

FÁBRICA LA AURORA

MERCADO DE ARTESANÍA

OLÉ OLÉ ▼

VÍA ORGÁNICA ▼

GOMBO'S PIZZA ▶

CASA CRAYOLA

PANDERÍA CASSANOVA

CIELO LINDO

LA MEDIA NARANJA ▼

CASA CALDERONI

CASA DE LA NOCHE ▼

★ EL JARDÍN

★ PARROQUIA DE SAN MIGUEL ARCÁNGEL

CUNA DE ALLENDE

★ CENTRO CULTURAL IGNACIO RAMÍREZ

★ PARQUE JUÁREZ

ANTIGUA VILLA SANTA MÓNICA

INSTITUTO ALLENDE ★

GUADIANA B&B

VILLA MARISOL ▼

TINTORERÍA FRANCO ★

JUANITA'S PIZZA ▼

BÓVEDAS ▶

EL RINCONCITO ▼

To bus station and Hospital de la Fe

Presa de las Colonias

Presa del Obraje

Arroyo de las Cachinches

TOLEDO

CALLE REAL DEL CONDE

CAMINO ANTIGUO A QUERÉTARO

PROLONGACIÓN SANTO DOMINGO

SALIDA A QUERÉTARO

SALIDA A QUERÉTARO

SALIDA A QUERÉTARO

SALIDA A QUERÉTARO

FUENTES

FUENTES

REVUELTAS

MONTITLÁN

CURTIDORES

CHEPITOS

SANTO DOMINGO

FAROLES

CUESTA DE LORETO

CJÓN DE LA DANZA

CUESTA DE SALIDAS

LANDÍN

OJO

APARICIO

NÚÑEZ

MURILLO

MONTES DE OCA

GARZA

HUERTAS

BARRANCA

GARITA

RECREO

HOSPICIO

SOLLANO

ALDAMA

TERRAPLÉN

DIEZMO VIEJO

CUADRANTE

NUEVA

JOSÉ GUADALUPE MOJICA

CALZADA DE LA PRESA

HOMOBONO

ÁNIMAS

COLEGIO

BALDERAS

LORETO

RELOJ

MESONES

SAN FRANCISCO

CORREO

CANAL

HIDALGO

JESÚS

JESÚS

HERNÁNDEZ MACÍAS

ZACATEROS

SUSPIROS

TENERÍAS

JUMÁRAN

PILA SECA

BLANCO

QUEBRADA

BENEFICENCIA

PILANCÓN

SAN ANTONIO ABAD

ÁRBOLES

PROLONGACIÓN DE PILA SECA

ORIZABA

ORIZABA

ORIZABA

ANCHA DE SAN ANTONIO

AVENIDA ALTERNO

LA PALMA

TINAJITAS

CODO

PROLONGACIÓN DE LA LUZ

CALZADA DE LA LUZ

CALZADA DE LA AURORA

CALZADA DE GUADALUPE

CALZADA DE LA ESTACIÓN

AVENIDA INDEPENDENCIA

OBRAJE

A ESPARZA OTEO

JUAN DE DIOS PEZA

FRANCISCO GONZÁLEZ BOCANEGRA

JAIME NUNO

PRIVADA MIGUEL PRADO

SAN RAFAEL

INDIO TRISTE

SAN PEDRO

REFUGIO N.

28 DE ABRIL N.

20 DE ENERO N.

28 DE ABRIL SUR

REFUGIO SUR

CALLE STIRLING DICKINSON

CJÓN SAN ANTONIO

CARDO

POTRANCA

POTRANCA

MAGUEY

CJÓN GUADIANA

VOLANTEROS

ÓRGANOS

INSURGENTES

MUERTOS

COLEGIO MILITAR

ENSEÑANZA

ANDALÓN

MONTIJAN

MONTES DE OCA

CHORRO

EL CHORRO

SALIDA A QUERÉTARO

GARZA

DEL

SALIDA A QUERÉTARO

CJÓN DEL CHORRO

SAN MIGUEL DE ALLENDE

0   300 yds
0   300 m

© AVALON TRAVEL

doors of overstuffed galleries, where local artists host exhibitions fueled by glasses of cheap *vino tinto* (red wine). Join the crowd and you'll quickly learn that there are no tourists in San Miguel. Everyone's a local in this convivial city, where cultures and people mix as easily as lime juice and tequila.

Since the 1940s, San Miguel has been home to a well-known expatriate community. Many of the city's first foreign residents came to study art at the Instituto Allende, but ended up making San Miguel their permanent home. Once home to a largely bohemian crowd, the city now attracts foreigners of every ilk, creating an increasingly diverse and international society. A passion for art and culture still unites the community, but people come here to live dreams of every type. In San Miguel, you can hear live chamber music, take Qigong classes, or practice your backhand in tennis. For some, it is place to relax, read, and travel, while others come to start a new career or open a business. The city seems ripe for personal invention, and even tourists may find themselves surprisingly inspired by the magical environment.

Every year, San Miguel becomes a bit bigger and more cosmopolitan. Restaurants cater to sophisticated customers with international fare, like Vietnamese spring rolls, Texas chili, curried chicken, and, of course, *enchiladas verdes* (green salsa enchiladas). Chic nightclubs and luxury hotels, once largely unheard of, have cropped up around the city center. Yet pretension is mellowed by the pervasively friendly atmosphere. In fact, what makes San Miguel so remarkable is its capacity to accept change yet never lose hold on its character. Even as the suburbs expand, prices rise, and gluten-free cooking seems as traditional as tamales, San Miguel remains close to its history. Throughout the city center, old friends convene outside 18th-century chapels, and mariachi musicians gather in the central square every evening. During one of San Miguel's municipal festivals, the city becomes all the more splendid, a wash of brilliant colors and pageantry.

Two donkeys take off down a San Miguel street, with no regard for traffic.

© ARTURO MEADE

HISTORY

When the Spanish arrived on the North American continent, the semi-arid plains of the Bajío were sparsely populated by nomadic tribes from Northern Mexico. It was part of a larger cultural region, known to the Spanish as El Gran Chichimeca. There was a mix of cultures living around modern-day San Miguel de Allende, including the Purépecha people from Michoacán and the Otomí. Having heard news of the conquest, many indigenous inhabitants fled the Bajío when Spanish settlers appeared.

In 1542, a Franciscan friar, Fray Juan de San Miguel, arrived in the Laja River valley from his missionary post in Michoacán. He founded the native settlement of San Miguel de los Chichimecas along the banks of the river, in what is now the municipality of San Miguel El Viejo. Somewhere between 1548 and 1549, Fray Juan's successor, French friar Bernardo Cossin, moved the settlement to the hill of Izcuinapan, site of a copious natural spring, known then as today as El Chorro.

During the mid-16th century, the discovery of large silver veins near the cities of Zacatecas and Guanajuato changed the course of history for this small settlement. Propitiously located between the northern mines and Mexico City, San Miguel became a strategic stopping point for traders on the silver route. At the same time, tensions grew between the Spanish settlers and indigenous inhabitants of the region. San Miguel de los Chichimecas was temporarily abandoned during a period of violent clashes between 1551 and 1554.

In 1555, by order of the Spanish viceroy, the settlement was re-established as a protective town on the Camino Real de Tierra Adentro (Royal Inland Route) and renamed San Miguel el Grande. Though not a mining town, San Miguel el Grande's association with the booming silver trade stimulated tremendous prosperity and growth. By 1560, the town already had its first fulling mill, and four years later, the bishop of Michoacán established a parish in San Miguel. Catering to the exhaustive needs of the silver cities, San Miguel developed many lucrative industries. Through livestock

The Parroquia de San Miguel Arcángel was built at the end of the 17th century.

farming, its ranches became major producers of wool, leather, and meat, as well as artisan products like soap, candles, and saddles. San Miguel also specialized in forged ironware, like knives, keys, scissors, branding irons, spurs, and machetes, as well as utilitarian and decorative textiles. According to some historians, the design for the colorful Mexican serape was based on the beautiful blankets produced by the Otomí weavers in San Miguel el Grande.

During the course of the 17th century, San Miguel el Grande grew from a tiny settlement of just a few hundred to a small city of about 15,000 inhabitants. It was now a wealthy town, and the people of San Miguel commissioned architect Marcos Antonio Sobrarías to build a new parish church in 1683, the Parroquia de San Miguel Arcángel. With the exception of the neo-Gothic facade (added in the 19th century), the church still stands in San Miguel's central plaza, the *jardín*, today. By the early 18th century, wealthy criollo (Spanish American) families had begun to build luxurious homes around the town's main plaza.

These same families also contributed extravagant funds to erect churches and monuments throughout the city. The opulence attracted some of Mexico's best architects to the region, as well as many of the country's most celebrated painters. Then, as today, San Miguel el Grande was considered one of the most beautiful places in New Spain.

The 18th century also brought about important changes in the Spanish governance of their New World territories, as the Bourbon kings began to exert more control over Mexico's land and its industries. As a result of these governmental changes, as well as a devastating famine in 1785, San Miguel began to lose hold of its wealth and privilege. Around 1780, silver production had also reached a peak, though the industry would continue to fruitfully produce for another decade.

In the meantime, the seeds of independence from Spain were being sown across the Bajío region. In San Miguel el Grande, Ignacio Allende was one of the chief opponents of Spanish rule, and he organized secret meetings with co-conspirators in his home on San Miguel's town square. When the fighting began in 1810, San Miguel was one of the first places to fall to the newly formed Mexican army. There was no violent conflict in San Miguel, but the town was ruinously sacked and looted after its surrender. A year later, Ignacio Allende was captured by the Spanish forces and executed for treason.

While Allende is the city's most celebrated name, San Miguel was the birthplace of many of Mexico's independence heroes, including Juan Aldama, the Malo and Lanzagorta brothers, and Juan José de los Reyes Martínez, or El Pípila, who would become famous for his role at the Alhóndiga de Granaditas in Guanajuato. After the protracted War of Independence finally drew to a close, San Miguel was largely destroyed, and many of its most prominent families had lost their heirs in battle. The royal government was no longer sufficiently organized to oversee the silver mines; production dropped, and San Miguel went into decline. By 1821, there were only 5,000 people living

in town, which was renamed San Miguel de Allende in 1826.

Although San Miguel's industries began to recuperate in the late 19th century, it remained sleepy, rural, and largely forgotten until the early 20th century. Despite ruin, it was still an incredibly beautiful place, and it was declared a national monument by the Mexican government in 1926. Shortly thereafter, Latin America's first art school, La Escuela Universitaria de Bellas Artes, opened in a former 18th-century cloister in downtown San Miguel de Allende. The school attracted intellectuals and artists from Mexico and abroad, as it was accredited in the United States. After World War II, a handful of Americans came to study in San Miguel under the GI Bill. Many never left. Since those days, the expatriate community in San Miguel has continued to grow, with a new crop of creative-minded individuals arriving in town each year. Today, it is known throughout Mexico as an artists' enclave, as well as a tourist center and major expatriate community. In 2008, the United Nations Educational, Scientific and Cultural Organization named the entire downtown district of San Miguel de Allende a World Heritage Site.

PLANNING YOUR TIME

Almost everything there is to do, see, eat, and experience happens in the 10 square blocks around San Miguel de Allende's central square. If you have just a day or two in town, you should plan to spend your time in the *centro histórico*. In a couple of easy days, you can visit many of the beautiful monuments that have made San Miguel famous, fit in some quality shopping, and eat in a few of the city's nice restaurants. If your time is short, a guided walking tour can provide an interesting introduction to San Miguel's sights and history, leaving the afternoon free for an independent ramble. No matter how long you are in San Miguel, you should definitely take the opportunity to spend a few hours wandering the town, no destination in mind. Strolling around the *centro,* you will stumble upon little

© ARTURO MEADE

the Templo de la Inmaculada Concepción, in San Miguel's *centro histórico*

arrive in town, pick up a copy of *Atención San Miguel,* an English-language newspaper. The weekly *Que Pasa* insert lists artistic and cultural events going on throughout the week, as well as classes and tours. Attending a lecture or an art opening is a quintessential San Miguel experience, and the best way to get a taste of the very particular social scene in this friendly little community.

As many residents of San Miguel will tell you, the longer you stay, the better it gets. If you come to town for a longer sojourn, there are plenty of off-the-beaten-track places to visit, enough restaurants to fill up weeks, and a seemingly endless array of classes, educational opportunities, and cultural events. On that note, the best advice to anyone coming to San Miguel for an extended visit is to get involved. Consider enrolling in an art or Spanish-language class, joining a yoga group, or volunteering with a local organization. Many visitors are surprised to see how quickly they make friends and connect with the community. In fact, many come to visit and find they never want leave.

ORIENTATION

Like most Mexican cities, San Miguel de Allende is organized around a town square—the *plaza principal* or, as it is known to most residents, the *jardín.* Today, as in the 17th century, the blocks surrounding the town square comprise the busiest and most important district in the city. Here, you'll find government buildings, banks, and the highest concentration of shops and restaurants. You will also find most of San Miguel's most interesting sights just a stone's throw away from each other.

Although city streets form a loose grid around the *jardín,* the names of these streets often change as they cross the plaza from east to west or north to south. For example, Calle San Francisco runs directly into the plaza from the east, changing its name to Canal as it exits to the west. Even streets that don't run directly through the plaza will often take new names as they change latitude. One major street changes its name four times as it crosses downtown:

alleyways unfit for cars, gurgling fountains, and small stone chapels—old but not forgotten. Even the quiet residential streets can be surprisingly charming, with rows of rust-colored houses draped with flowers and decorated with rooftop gardens.

If you plan to spend more than a couple days in San Miguel, you will have time to visit the botanical gardens, take a trip to the hot springs, or make a jaunt to the countryside for horseback riding or hiking. You can eat in a few more restaurants, visit the markets, and, just as importantly, relax. For many visitors, San Miguel de Allende is just as much about down time as it is about sightseeing. With a friendly small-town atmosphere and year-round sunny weather, San Miguel is the perfect place to unwind, either on a bench in the town square or on the patio of your bed and breakfast. Visitors should also take advantage of San Miguel de Allende's surprisingly robust art and cultural scene. When you

charra **(cowgirl) on horseback in San Miguel's town square**

from Pila Seca to Cuadrante to Hospicio to Garita.

To make everything more complicated, many of these streets have changed their names during the course of history. In many cases, the former street name is still posted on the corner! For the San Miguel novice, navigation can be a bit frustrating, if also a bit amusing and folkloric. When in doubt, look for the spires of the *parroquia* (church) in the town square, or just ask a local for directions. People in San Miguel are famously friendly, and most will gladly help you find what you are looking for.

There are some sights, restaurants, and accommodations in the residential neighborhoods that surround the city center. The San Antonio and Guadiana neighborhoods to the south, as well as the Guadalupe and Aurora neighborhoods to the north, are accessible on foot, or, more quickly, by taxi. Beyond these central neighborhoods, San Miguel de Allende is ringed by residential communities, predominantly inhabited by Mexican families and a smattering of expatriates.

Sights

Located on the Camino Real de Tierra Adentro (Royal Inland Route), San Miguel de Allende grew rapidly during the silver trade of 17th and 18th centuries. Today, San Miguel's *centro histórico* is a unique example of city planning from that era, with an unusual mix of architectural styles. In particular, the town is recognized for its fine 18th-century Mexican baroque buildings. In 1926, San Miguel de Allende was declared a national monument by the Mexican government, a designation that, among other things, prohibits the construction of tall buildings or other structures that would compromise the city's historic downtown. As a result, the center of San Miguel de Allende has been remarkably well preserved, even as the city expands around it.

Not unusual for the period, most of San Miguel de Allende's historic architecture is religious, with many beautiful churches, chapels, and convents crammed into the narrow streets of the *centro histórico*. Many of these old churches are still used for religious services, though visitors and tourists are welcome to go inside. When entering a church, be respectful by speaking in a low voice and not using flash on your camera. If a mass or ceremony is in progress, observe before entering. Tourists sometimes wander into churches during more personal events, like funerals, which are best left to the family. If you would like to avoid religious services altogether, most churches do not hold mass 1–5 P.M.

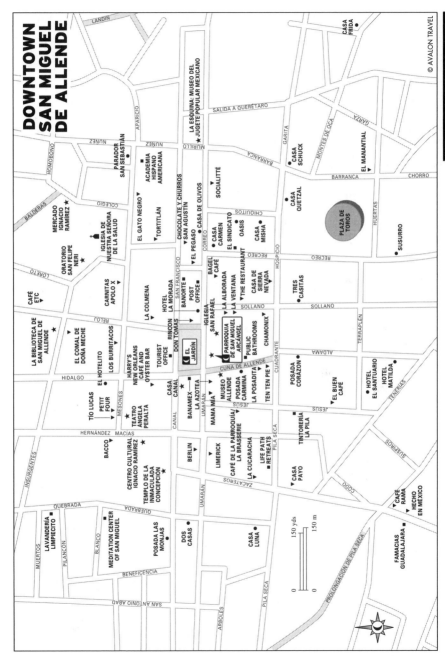

DOWNTOWN SAN MIGUEL DE ALLENDE

© AVALON TRAVEL

CASA FRIDA

LANDIN

LA ESQUINA: MUSEO DEL JUGETE POPULAR MEXICANO

SALIDA A QUERÉTARO

APARICIO

NÚÑEZ

MURILLO

PARADOR SAN SEBASTIÁN

ACADEMIA HISPANO AMERICANA

HOMOBONO

NÚÑEZ

CASA SCHUCK

GARITA

MONTES DE OCA

GARZA

EL MANANTIAL

BALDERAS

MERCADO IGNACIO RAMÍREZ

CHOCOLATE Y CHURROS

CASA DE OLIVOS

SOCIALITTÉ

BARRANCA

BARRANCA

CHORRO

COLEGIO

ORATORIO SAN FELIPE NERI

IGLESIA DE NUESTRA SEÑORA DE LA SALUD

EL GATO NEGRO

TORTITLÁN

SAN AGUSTÍN

EL PEGASO

CORREO

CHIQUITOS

CASA CARMEN

EL SINDICATO

OASIS

CASA MISHA

CASA QUETZAL

HUERTAS

PLAZA DE TOROS

SUSURRO

LORETO

CAFÉ ETC

CARNITAS APOLO X

LA COLMENA

SAN FRANCISCO

BANORTE

POST OFFICE

HOTEL LA MORADA

BAGEL CAFÉ

LA ALBORADA

LA VENTANA

THE RESTAURANT

CASA DE SIERRA NEVADA

RECREO

HOSPICIO

RECREO

RELOJ

LA BIBLIOTECA DE SAN MIGUEL DE ALLENDE

EL COMAL DE DOÑA MECHE

EL HOTELITO

LOS BURRITACOS

HARRY'S NEW ORLEANS CAFÉ AND OYSTER BAR

RINCÓN DON TOMÁS

TOURIST OFFICE

EL JARDÍN

IGLESIA SAN RAFAEL

PARROQUIA DE SAN MIGUEL ARCÁNGEL

PUBLIC BATHROOMS

CHAMONIX

SOLLANO

SOLLANO

TRES CASITAS

TERRAPLEN

HIDALGO

TÍO LUCAS

PETIT FOUR

MESONES

TEATRO ÁNGELA PERALTA

CASA CANAL

BANAMEX

LA AZOTEA

MAMA MÍA

MUSEO ALLENDE

POSADA CARMINA

LA POSADITA

TEN TEN PIE

CUNA DE ALLENDE

CUADRANTE

POSADA CORAZÓN

ALDAMA

EL BUEN CAFÉ

HOTEL EL SANTUARIO

HOTEL MATILDA

TENERÍAS

HERNÁNDEZ MACÍAS

BACCO

CENTRO CULTURAL IGNACIO RAMÍREZ

TEMPLO DE LA INMACULADA CONCEPCIÓN

CANAL

UMARÁN

BERLIN

LIMERICK

CAFÉ DE LA PARROQUIA/ LA BRASSERIE

LA CUCARACHA

LIFE PATH RETREATS

JESÚS

PILA SECA

TINTORERÍA LA PILA

INSURGENTES

QUEBRADA

LAVANDERÍA LIMPIECITO

MEDITATION CENTER OF SAN MIGUEL

POSADA LAS MONJAS

QUEBRADA

BLANCO

PILANCÓN

MUERTOS

BENEFICENCIA

DOS CASAS

UMARÁN

ZACATEROS

CASA PAYO

CASA LUNA

PILA SECA

SUSPIROS

CÓDO

CAFÉ RAMA

HECHO EN MÉXICO

SAN ANTONIO ABAD

ARBOLES

PROLONGACIÓN DE PILA SECA

FAMACIAS GUADALAJARA

0   150 yds

0   150 m

CENTRO HISTÓRICO
◖ Parroquia de San Miguel Arcángel

The neo-Gothic sandstone towers of the Parroquia de San Miguel Arcángel (Plaza Principal s/n, tel. 415/152-4197, generally 8 A.M.–8 P.M. daily) are the rosy crown of the city, presiding over San Miguel both day and night. The building itself was constructed in the 16th century and, as old photographs corroborate, was large but rather unspectacular. In the 19th century, the church's facade received a complete renovation at the hands of an imaginative architect, Zeferino Gutiérrez. According to local history, this self-taught draftsman based his design for the parish on a postcard depicting a French Gothic cathedral. No matter what Gutiérrez had in mind, the results are entirely original, with cascading bricks of pink sandstone surrounding the peaked archways of the parish, concluding in three pointed bell towers.

While the exterior of the *parroquia* is elaborate, the interior's design is spare neoclassical, with towering stone columns flanking the altar and chapels, some gilded. There is a carved statue of the eponymous San Miguel Arcángel on the altar; however, there is a more notable sculpture of Jesus in the east transept, carved from cane bark and highlighted by a backdrop of turquoise Byzantine mosaic and aging murals. Today, the Parroquia de San Miguel Arcángel is still the parish seat and mass is held daily. On days of celebration, the four iron bells of the *parroquia* are manually rung from the towers. When you hear their merry cacophony, look for the figures between the narrow arches, spinning the bells in circles.

Iglesia de San Rafael

Also known as the **Santa Escuela,** the small and often overlooked Iglesia de San Rafael (Plaza Principal s/n, tel. 415/152-4197, generally 8 A.M.–8 P.M. daily) shares its courtyard entrance with the *parroquia.* Inside, the church is a wash of aqua, with turquoise tile floors and painted blue ceilings. Large oil paintings and wooden saints line the walls, some in rather dramatic dioramas. There is a particularly nice oil painting to the left of the neoclassical altar depicting San Miguel. Above the Iglesia de San Rafael, the brick bell tower rings out the time every 15 minutes.

◖ El Jardín

The town square—officially called the **plaza principal,** but known to all as the *jardín*—is the heart and soul of San Miguel de Allende. From dawn to dusk, the *jardín* is filled with a pleasant crowd of locals and tourists resting their legs on iron benches, walking their dogs, or stopping for a chat in the shade of the well-manicured laurel trees. Above them, hundreds of happy birds tweet away the afternoon, while balloon sellers and fruit vendors make a slow turn through the crowds, tempting the children who've come to play on the flat stone floor. Sit on a bench to soak up the sun with an ice cream, or pretend to read the paper while you watch people go by.

Those who've traveled in other parts of Mexico often wonder why San Miguel's square is referred to as the *jardín,* not the *zócalo.* The term *zócalo* refers to a central plaza adjoining a cathedral. Despite its multi-tiered opulence, San Miguel's *parroquia* is not a cathedral but, in direct translation, a parish. The cathedral and the seat of the bishop overseeing San Miguel de Allende's parish are in the city of Celaya.

Casa de Allende

A famous hero in Mexico's War of Independence from Spain, Ignacio Allende was born to a prominent family of San Miguel el Grande in 1769. His family's home, an opulent colonial-era mansion on the southeast corner of the central square, is now the **Museo de San Miguel** (Cuna de Allende 1, tel. 415/152-2499, www.inah.gob.mx, 9 A.M.–5 P.M. Tues.–Sun., US$3). The museum is commonly known as Casa de Allende. Today, the space is dedicated to the history of the town and to the life of its most famous former resident.

During the 17th century, the first floor of a colonial mansion was generally reserved for servants' activities and quarters. Here, the museum dedicates these rooms to the history of San Miguel de Allende, from its founding through the independence. The rooms contain a few nice artifacts from the colonial era and a surprising number of informational videos, all in Spanish. Upstairs, the Allende family's living quarters have been restored and recreated. The replica of the kitchen is particularly interesting, since it deviates so greatly from the modern version. It is also worth noting that there were no bathrooms in the opulent Allende home, though a toilet did exist near the horse stables in the home's pretty back patio.

Casa del Mayorazgo de la Canal

A wealthy businessman from Mexico City, Don Manuel Tomás de Canal, moved to San Miguel in 1732. He bought numerous haciendas in the region, took control of San Miguel's textile industry, and made major investments in buildings and infrastructure throughout the city. He is remembered as one of San Miguel's most generous benefactors. In addition to the money that Canal spent on religious and municipal projects, he spent thousands of pesos lavishly refurbishing his magnificent mansion, which still stands on the corner of Canal and Hidalgo on San Miguel's central square. His home, the Casa del Mayorazgo de la Canal, officially called the **Casa de Cultura Banamex** (Canal 4, tel. 55/1226-0256, www.casadelacanal.com, 9 A.M.–2 P.M. daily, free), is one of the most spectacular examples of 17th-century civil architecture in the region. Its massive red facade runs along the side of the *jardín,* where a row of balcony windows from the family's living quarters overlook the *parroquia.* Take note of the elaborately carved wooden doorways on the north side of the building, flanked by towering stone columns. The niche above them holds a stone figure of Our Lady of Loreto and the family coat of arms.

Today, the Casa del Mayorazgo de la Canal is owned and operated by Banamex's Cultural Foundation, and it is open to the public as a part of their Casas Señoriales program. Visitors can peek inside the home's incredible inner courtyard and back patio, where soaring archways separate the first floor from the second. Banamex has also installed several exhibition spaces for rotating art shows. Upstairs, the house is reserved for bank executives.

Oratorio San Felipe Neri

During the 18th century, the congregation of San Felipe Neri was rapidly gaining popularity throughout New Spain. In San Miguel de Allende, the congregation constructed the beautiful Oratorio San Felipe Neri (Insurgentes s/n, tel. 415/152-0521, http://oratoriosma.congregacion.org, generally 9 A.M.–6 P.M. daily) in 1714, along with the school, Colegio San Francisco de Sales. The pink sandstone facade of the *oratorio* is delicately carved and represents the beginning of a shift in architectural aesthetic, from baroque to churrigueresque. Above the facade, the church has five beautiful bell towers, which were recently restored. The unpainted pink sandstone tower to the northwest of the church is particularly lovely.

© ARTURO MEADE

The facade of the Oratorio San Felipe Neri represents a transition from classic baroque to churrigueresque aesthetic.

Inside the oratory, delicate pink frescos on the ceiling, old tiled walls, and worn floors reflect the church's long history. As in the majority of baroque churches in San Miguel, most of the original paintings and altarpieces in the *oratorio* were lost or looted; however, there are still several of the original 18th-century wood saints and retablos on the walls of the nave. In the 19th century, the famous architect of the *parroquia,* Zeferino Gutiérrez, designed the building's neoclassical altar. As you walk out, look up at the beautiful gilded organ above the entryway. On occasion, the oratory will host organ concerts with this unique instrument.

You will have to make an extra effort if you want to visit the spectacular chapel, **Santa Casa de Loreto,** and the adjoining **Camarín de la Virgen,** a jewel of colonial architecture located in the precept to the left of the oratory's altar. Commissioned and paid for by Don Manuel Tomás de Canal in the 18th century, this elaborate gilded chapel is possibly San Miguel's finest historic structure. The chapel is not normally open to the public. However, the priests do unlock the chapel's old iron doors during morning and evening masses (though they do so inconsistently), which are held at 8 A.M. and 6 P.M.

Iglesia de Nuestra Señora de la Salud

Just to the east of the *oratorio* and overlooking the Plaza Cívica, the Iglesia de Nuestra Señora de la Salud (Church of Our Lady of Health, Plaza Cívica s/n, no tel., generally 9 A.M.–6 P.M. daily) is distinguished by the scalloped stone dome that presides over the church's curved entryway. An influential figure in San Miguel de Allende, Father Luis Felipe Neri de Alfaro erected this church in the 17th century as an accompaniment to the adjoining school, San Francisco de Sales. The school was also an important institution in San Miguel de Allende, teaching philosophical thought to many of the young criollo heirs who would oversee the town and, eventually, instigate the independence movement.

Inside the Iglesia de Nuestra Señora de la Salud, the altar surrounds an azure-dressed Virgin Mary in a gilded glass box. Like the oratory, this small church was looted, and most of its original pieces were destroyed. However, to the right of the altar, there is still a beautiful collection of 17th-century oil paintings depicting the Stations of the Cross, some punctured or damaged.

Outside, the **Plaza Cívica** is a popular place to sit in the shade, and it is occasionally the site of crafts or book fairs (during late October, there is a large market selling crafts, candies, and candles for Día de los Muertos altarpieces). For many years, the Plaza Cívica was also the site of San Miguel de Allende's municipal market.

Templo de San Francisco

The many pigeons perched on the stone facade of the Templo de San Francisco (San Francisco s/n, esq. con Juárez, tel. 415/152-0947, 8 A.M.–2 P.M. Mon.–Sat., hours vary Sun.)—despite the city's attempts to ward them off with chicken wire—have found plenty of places to nest amid the ornate carvings of this church's churrigueresque entryway. A fine example of Mexican baroque architecture, this church was constructed at the end of the 18th century. The principal facade is the site's most striking feature, with cascading sandstone columns carefully carved with saints and figures. Walk east around the church to get a sense of its size and grandeur. There is another less ornate but beautiful facade on its eastern wall. Above it, the church's large dome towers over Calle Mesones. In contrast to its ornate exterior, the Templo de San Francisco's interior is austere, with very high ceilings and glass chandeliers, a neoclassical altar, and walls lined with rows of wood saints and dark retablos.

Directly to the east and adjoining the same small plaza as the Templo de San Francisco, the **Capilla de la Tercera Orden** is a far simpler Franciscan church. Like its neighbor, it was constructed in the 18th century, though it appears much older. The lovely, crumbling belfry that tops this old stone building has recently

© ARTURO MEADE

The east facade of the Templo de San Francisco overlooks Calle Juárez below.

been restored and repainted, and it wears its age handsomely.

Teatro Ángela Peralta

The neoclassical Teatro Ángela Peralta (Hernández Macías 82, tel. 415/152-2200, open only during events) was built at the end of the 19th century. The sandstone facade was restored during the 1980s, but the building is basically unchanged since its construction. Its namesake, Ángela Peralta, was a famous opera singer of her day, and she personally inaugurated the theater with a concert on May 20, 1873. Since its inauguration, the theater has been, and continues to be, one of San Miguel's most important venues for music and performance. Though not open to the public on a regular basis, the theater opens its doors frequently for concerts and events.

Templo de la Inmaculada Concepción

The massive dome that dominates San Miguel's skyline belongs to the Templo de la Inmaculada Concepción, and is most widely known as **Las Monjas** (esq. Canal y Hernández Macías s/n, tel. 415/152-0688, generally 9 A.M.–6 P.M. daily). Originally commissioned and funded by a young nun and heiress, Josefina Lina de la Canal y Hervas, it was founded as a church and nunnery (hence its popular name, Las Monjas, which means "the nuns"). The first child of Manuel Tomás de Canal, Josefa was a devout Catholic and a close confidante of Father Luis Felipe Neri de Alfaro. After spending a week at his religious retreat in Atotonilco, Josefa decided to spend her entire inherited fortune building a lavish new temple and religious convent for an order of nuns in San Miguel. Construction on the massive building began in 1755, though funds ran out before its conclusion. Josefa herself died in 1770.

Today, this massive church is one of San Miguel's most iconic structures. Although the temple's architect is unknown, the dome was said to be a copy of Les Invalides in Paris. At night, this massive structure often out-glitters the Parroquia de San Miguel Arcángel, with

© ARTURO MEADE

The Templo de la Inmaculada Concepción was originally constructed in the 18th century as a convent; its large dome was added in the next century.

a ring of bright lights illuminating the dome and the parade of stone saints that surround it. Pass through the worn wooden doors of the church to admire the massive dome from the inside, where it illuminates a towering neoclassical altar, with numerous niches containing life-size statues of saints. On your way out, note the large conch shell that is embedded into the stone column as a receptacle for holy water.

Centro Cultural Ignacio Ramírez

The large stone building adjoining the Templo de la Inmaculada Concepción was once the cloister for the temple's order of nuns. Today, it is the Centro Cultural Ignacio Ramírez (Hernández Macías 75, tel. 415/152-0289, 10 A.M.–7:30 P.M. Mon.–Sat., 10 A.M.–2 P.M. Sun., free), popularly known as **Bellas Artes.** Owned and managed by Mexico's Instituto Nacional de Bellas Artes (National Fine Arts Institute), Bellas Artes is both an art school and cultural center. Although this building

was constructed for religious purposes, the center's namesake, Ignacio Ramírez, was a famous writer, thinker, and outspoken atheist, born in San Miguel de Allende during the early 19th century.

In 2011, the building suffered some serious damage and at press time was closed indefinitely for repairs. When open to the public, Bellas Artes is one of the most peaceful places in downtown San Miguel. The school's lovely courtyard is filled with swaying reeds of bamboo, blooming orange trees, and a lovely old stone fountain. Beneath the arcades that surround the courtyard, there are several exhibition spaces open to the public, showing work by local artists as well as itinerant exhibitions from across the country. Notably, one of the back salons contains an incomplete mural by famous post-revolutionary artist David Alfaro Siqueiros. On the second floor, the school's enchanting classrooms are housed in the tiny rooms of the former cloister, each dedicated to a discipline, such as puppetry, etching, weaving, oil painting, guitar, and piano. The old textile looms are particularly impressive.

Biblioteca de San Miguel de Allende

A nonprofit, nongovernmental organization, the Biblioteca de San Miguel de Allende (Insurgentes 25, tel. 415/152-0293, www.bibliotecasma.com, 10 A.M.–7 P.M. Mon.–Fri., 10 A.M.–2 P.M. Sat.), formerly known as the Biblioteca Pública, is home to a bilingual lending library, a nice café, and a small theater. As a part of its mission to serve the community, the *biblioteca* manages a scholarship program for local children, as well as free art and music classes, a language exchange program, and other educational opportunities. For many expatriates, the library is something of a social hub, where people come together to lend a hand, have a cappuccino, or see an English-language movie in the Teatro Santa Ana. The newspaper *Atención San Miguel* supports the library's social programs, as do frequent book sales, fundraising events, and the weekly House and Garden Tour. Check the library's corkboard for information about upcoming programs, or pick up a copy of *Atención San Miguel* for the full list of events, movies, and volunteer opportunities.

◖ Parque Juárez

A few blocks south of the central square, the beloved Parque Juárez (between Aldama and Diezmo Viejo) is one of the freshest and greenest spots in San Miguel de Allende. At this well-utilized urban park, there is always a game on the basketball courts and the playground is never empty. Take a stroll through the park's curving walkways, admiring the old stone fountains and wild, tropical gardens. Throughout the day, you'll find teenage couples holding hands, ambitious joggers, exuberant Zumba classes, or dogs and their owners wandering along the shaded path. Bring a book and stake out a spot on one of the weathered stone benches, or simply enjoy the people-watching. The park is also a favorite nesting spot for white egrets, and the

birds in the trees above the park can become surprisingly noisy.

◖ El Chorro and the Casa de la Cultura

After its founding on the banks of the Río Laja, the native settlement of San Miguel de los Chichimecas moved to the hill of Izcuinapan, site of a copious natural spring. According to local legend, the Purépecha people from Michoacán had originally discovered the spring after their *xoloitzcuintle* dogs dug up water along the hillside. Today, the site of San Miguel's founding is a verdant corner of the city, known as El Chorro (the spring). In an arcaded colonial building, the site is graced by the Casa de la Cultura (Bajada del Chorro 4, tel. 415/154-5670, 9 A.M.–7 P.M. Mon.–Fri., 9 A.M.–1 P.M. Sat.), a cultural center that offers art, dance, and music classes to local children.

In the shade of breezy trees, El Chorro is among the most beautiful spots in town. The steep hill leading up to the Casa de la Cultura

Children can take art, dance, and music classes at the Casa de la Cultura.

is lined with cascading patios and winding staircases, a lovely place to rest amid the lush foliage and the sound of squabbling egrets. Just to the north of the Casa de la Cultura, a stone staircase leads you to a pretty plaza and **La Capilla de Santa Cruz del Chorro,** a 16th-century church and one of the oldest structures in San Miguel de Allende. From there, you can huff and puff up the tiny pedestrian alleyway La Bajada del Chorro, an enchanting, if challenging, hike up to the Salida a Querétaro.

Just below El Chorro, take special notice of the row of red *lavaderos públicos* (public washtubs), which surround a small plaza below the hillside. For years, the natural spring fed water into these washtubs, where local families came to wash their laundry. According to some historians, these washtubs were among the municipal projects financed by Manuel Canal in the 18th century. Even today, some San Miguel residents will wash their clothes and linens in the *lavaderos,* and, on the weekends, there is a casual art market in the plaza they adjoin.

Instituto Allende

Home to the oldest art academy in the Americas, the Instituto Allende (Ancha de San Antonio 20, tel. 415/152-0226, www.institutoallende.com.mx, 11 A.M.–6 P.M. Mon.–Sat.) has a huge stone facade that dominates the busy avenue below. Originally built by the wealthy Canal family as a country residence, this massive building became an art school in the 1950s, when Cossío de Pomar moved his academy from the ex-convent at the Templo de la Inmaculada Concepción to its current home. (The Centro Cultural Ignacio Ramírez is now located in the ex-convent of the Inmaculada Concepción, but that school is under the direction of the Mexican government.)

Today, the institute is divided into two parts. In the back, the buildings and gardens continue to function as an art college, offering an undergraduate program for Mexican students, an international Master of Fine Art (MFA) program, and noncredit public classes for tourists and residents. The front of the building is a nice commercial plaza with a comfortable café and several good galleries. Every few months, the central plaza of the *instituto* is the site of the **Feria de Lana y Latón,** a large crafts fair that draws crafts vendors from around Mexico.

NORTH OF THE *CENTRO*
◖ Fábrica La Aurora

Many longtime residents of San Miguel remember the cry of the steam-generated whistle that sounded every morning from Fábrica La Aurora (Calzada de la Aurora s/n, Col. Aurora, tel. 415/152-1012, www.fabricalaaurora.com, generally 9 A.M.–11 P.M. Mon.–Sat., 10 A.M.–5 P.M. Sun., hours vary by shop). Until the early 1990s, La Aurora was one of Mexico's largest textile factories and the single biggest employer in the town of San Miguel. After cotton imports began flooding the Mexican market, domestic production was greatly affected. The factory closed in 1991 and the space was converted to a warehouse. A few years later, some local artists and designers began to express interest in renting the old factory rooms as studios and workspaces. The first shops and studios opened in 2001. Since then, the project quickly grew, and today, the former factory houses more than 35 studios, galleries, and design shops, as well as a bookstore, restaurants, and a café. Many of San Miguel's most beloved artists and exhibition spaces are located in the Aurora, so it's a required stop for anyone with an interest in the visual arts. From massive sculptural pieces to delicate jewelry, you could spend a full day exploring the Aurora.

Typical of turn-of-the-20th-century constructions, the factory's long sandstone facade, concrete floors, and industrial architecture provide a contrasting (yet complementary) backdrop to modern art and design. Wandering around the corridors, you can see some of the old equipment from the factory's former days in textile production, and old photographs of the space line the walls of the principal hallway. Hours vary by shop, so visit during the morning or early afternoon to see the most spaces open.

© ARTURO MEADE

Fábrica La Aurora is an art and design center located in a former cotton factory.

EAST OF THE *CENTRO*
El Mirador

If you have a set of wheels or strong legs for walking, you can follow the Salida a Querétaro up the hill to El Mirador, a small outlook, with panoramic views of the city below. From here, you can see the river valley stretching beyond the town, including the large reservoir beyond the city and the distant Sierra de Guanajuato. The bust of Pedro Vargas, a famous singer and actor from Mexico's golden age of cinema, presides over the *mirador*. Vargas was born in San Miguel; his former home adjoins this small plaza and outlook.

◖ El Charco del Ingenio

San Miguel de Allende's unique botanical garden, El Charco del Ingenio (Paloma s/n, tel. 415/154-4715 or 415/154-8838, www.el-charco.org.mx, dawn–dusk daily, US$3) is located along the ridge of a canyon overlooking the city center. Bring a hat and good walking shoes to explore the rustic and meandering footpaths within this ecological preserve, which covers more than 100 acres of natural habitat along the canyon's edge and the shores

of a small reservoir. With admission, staffers will give you a map to the grounds; a highlight is the covered conservatory, which houses a rare and weird collection of cactus and succulents. El Charco del Ingenio frequently hosts special events, such as full moon ceremonies, nature talks, yoga classes, or traditional *temazcal* steam baths. There is also a small coffee shop and gift store at the entrance, where visitors can support the project by purchasing a live cactus, books, or handicrafts made in local villages.

Mercado de Martes

The weekly municipal market, casually referred to as the Mercado de Martes (Plaza Municipal, no tel., 8 A.M.–5 P.M. Tues.), descends upon San Miguel's upper plaza once a week. You can find almost anything you're looking for at this busy open-air marketplace, whether it's blender parts, new Converse sneakers, drill bits, or a birdcage. For food shopping, this is the best deal in town. Fruits and vegetables in season often come at rock-bottom prices—think kilos of mangos for a dollar. There are also plenty of little places where you can grab a bite to eat, though strong stomachs are best for those who want to dig into the delicious green chorizo tacos or deep-fried fish plates. Come prepared for dust and bustle, and bring a shopping bag, if you plan to buy. Located on the plains above town, the market is too far to comfortably walk to from downtown, but a taxi will get you there in five minutes.

SIGHTSEEING AND CULTURAL TOURS

A local nonprofit organization, **Patronato Pro Niños** (tel. 415/152-7796, www.patronatoproninos.org, US$15), offers cultural walking tours of San Miguel de Allende's historic center with knowledgeable English-speaking tour guides. Tours depart from the *jardín* every Monday, Wednesday, and Friday at 9:45 A.M., cover about 10 blocks, and last about 2.5 hours. The proceeds from the tour benefit Patronato Pro Niños' medical and dental services program, which serves local children.

Ever wondered what's behind those old wooden doors and big stucco facades? You're not alone. One of the most popular gigs in town, the weekly **House and Garden Tour** (Biblioteca Pública, Insurgentes 25, tel. 415/152-0293, sandra@bibliotecasma.com) gives participants a chance to peek inside several historic and lavishly decorated homes in San Miguel de Allende. Drawing from a roster of over 300 historic homes in San Miguel, the lineup changes week to week, but usually includes at least four properties. The tour departs from the *biblioteca* every Sunday in large buses. You can buy tickets ahead of time at the gift shop, which is open 10 A.M.–2 P.M. and 3–6 P.M. Monday–Friday, though you can also just show up on Sunday morning.

Helene Kahn's tour group **And You Thought You'd Seen Everything . . .** (Apartado/P.O. Box 98, tel. 415/152-0849, cell tel. 415/153-5944, www.helenekahn.com) offers informative walking tours of downtown San Miguel de Allende for individuals and private groups. A guided introduction to the city's major sights usually takes about an hour or two, and the route can be tailored depending on your interests (and how many hills you are willing to climb). Helene has spent many years in Mexico, and she can offer tips on where to eat, where to shop, and what to do around San Miguel, so one of her walking tours can be a nice way to kick off your trip to town. In addition, the group offers day trips to various destinations in the Bajío, like Dolores Hidalgo, Guanajuato, Pozos, and Querétaro, with optional excursions to artist workshops for those interested in crafts or ceramics.

Arts and Entertainment

San Miguel de Allende is a small town, but it is also a lively one. It is a place where different people and cultures mix comfortably, and where tradition and experimentation coexist without friction. Since the early 20th century, San Miguel has been home to a cozy community of artists and writers, both national and international. Today, there are a slew of galleries which are known to inaugurate new exhibitions every weekend, many drawing crowds so large they can't squeeze inside. Music, dance, and even live theater are common throughout the town, jazz music is universally popular, and cool nightclubs make San Miguel a semi-chic destination for Mexico City weekenders.

Despite the modern vibe, local tradition and culture continue to play a large role in daily life in San Miguel. There are plenty of old cantinas where you can tip back a glass of tequila, and the traditional festivities during Holy Week are among Mexico's most splendid. The resulting blend of tradition and modernity is exhilarating and unique.

NIGHTLIFE

When it comes to nightlife, San Miguel is a relatively quiet town. For most visitors and

© ARTURO MEADE

evening in the *jardín*

residents, evenings are best enjoyed in the company of friends, kicking back with a book, or lingering over a good meal. During the week, nightlife is limited to a few old standbys, where locals convene for drinks and conversation. Weekends are much livelier, when large crowds of tourists or day-trippers arrive from Mexico City, Querétaro, and beyond. On Friday and Saturday nights, San Miguel's bars extend their hours, and a good party can be found throughout the *centro histórico*. Though not a major city, San Miguel offers just enough style to feel cosmopolitan, and just enough folklore to feel like Mexico.

Right beneath the spires of the *parroquia* and overlooking the dome of Las Monjas, **La Azotea** (Umarán 6, tel. 415/152-4977, http:// azoteasanmiguel.com, 1 P.M.–midnight Sun.– Thurs., 1 P.M.–2 A.M. Fri.–Sat.) has one of the prettiest views in San Miguel. This chic rooftop bar is a good choice for a pleasant drink in the early evening, as the sun sinks behind the distant mountains, bathing the town in a rosy glow. Here, you can lounge on a couch, order some tapas, and watch as flocks of birds flitter across the sky. For more excitement, hang around a little longer. As the evening wears on, the crowd swells and the music gets louder. On Friday and Saturday nights, La Azotea draws a trendy crowd of locals and weekenders, and there is often a live DJ. There is no sign for La Azotea from the street. To get there, enter through the Pueblo Viejo restaurant (once you're inside, the host will direct you to the bar) and take the stairs to the top floor.

Just a block from the main plaza, **Berlin** (Umarán 19, tel. 415/154-9432, 4:30 P.M.–midnight daily) is a small bar and restaurant that serves well-prepared German and continental food, like roast chicken and savory crepes, as well as oft-praised hamburgers. While the restaurant has many loyal patrons, the bar is the true locus of this convivial joint. Any evening at Berlin, you're likely to find a crowd of graying expatriates nursing inexpensive cocktails and chatting with the wait staff. You can do like the locals and order dinner or appetizers at the bar while eavesdropping on the night's voluble conversations.

It's hard to miss the bustle at **Harry's New Orleans Café and Oyster Bar** (Hidalgo 12, tel. 415/152-2645, www.harrysneworleanscafe. com, noon–1 A.M. Mon.–Thurs., noon–2 A.M. Fri., 10 A.M.–2 A.M. Sat., noon–10 P.M. Sun.), especially when there is a two-for-one drinks special at the bar. On the weekly martini or margarita night, the elegant and well-stocked bar is packed to the gills with merry expatriates soaking up drinks and gobbling up appetizers. Harry's stocks an impressive range of imported liquors, many of which are hard to find in Mexico, even in an upscale liquor store. If you order something special, the bartenders use a sliding ladder to retrieve bottles from the top shelf. The adjoining restaurant serves Cajun-inspired food, and, with nice plates of fresh and well-prepared seafood, is just as popular as the bar.

The younger and rowdier crowd gathers at **Limerick Irish Pub** (Umarán 24, tel. 415/154-8642, 6 P.M.–1:30 A.M. Tues.–Thurs. and Sun., 6 P.M.–3 A.M. Fri.–Sat.), an expansive Irish-inspired bar with a billiard table, cheap beer, and loud music. This casual pub is a longtime favorite with locals, and it is filled to the brim on the weekends, when there is often a live band or DJ in addition to the big crowds. So many of the Limerick's clients know each other from around town that the atmosphere resembles a giant, raucous house party. On Saturday nights, the staff eventually turns off the lights to force revelers out the door.

One of San Miguel de Allende's oldest watering holes, **El Manantial** (Barranca 78, tel. 415/110-0007, 1 P.M.–midnight Tues.–Sun.) has changed ownership several times in the past few years but remains one of the most pleasant places to tip back a drink in a low-key, historic setting. Officially operating under the name La Sirena Gorda, the lovely old building has thick adobe walls and old wood beams crossing its incredibly high ceiling. Locals flock here for inexpensive drinks, jovial company, and the delicious menu of fish tacos and tostadas. Here, many classic Mexican dishes

are prepared with fish rather than meat, so tacos *al pastor, chilorio,* and *carnitas* take on a new, delicious twist. The bar's owner benevolently oversees the dinner crowd and friendly team of servers until closing.

For a more gritty cantina experience, **El Gato Negro** (Mesones 12, tel. 415/152-6544, 11:30 A.M.–11 P.M. daily) is an old, multistory cantina with some of the cheapest drinks downtown. Push through the swinging wooden doors and into the small bar, where they have been serving drinks for decades. Those in the know take their beers up to the teensy rooftop terrace, where a few plastic chairs overlook the historic sandstone towers of San Miguel de Allende. It's a million-dollar view at a discount price.

Of all the cantinas in San Miguel de Allende, **La Cucaracha** (Zacateros 22, tel. 415/152-0196, 7 P.M.–5 A.M. daily) is clearly the granddaddy of them all. This incredibly cheap and often rowdy dive bar is a favorite of students, youthful expatriates, old-timers, riff-raff, and young ranchers from the towns surrounding San Miguel. Opened in the 1940s, this historic bar was located in the Casa del Mayorazgo de la Canal on San Miguel's central square—today, a Banamex branch. At the current location on Zacateros, the walls are decorated with original artwork from local artists (in the true spirit of San Miguel, La Cucaracha will occasionally host an art exhibition). Bathrooms leave something to be desired (and may house a few of the bar's namesake critters), but beers are among the cheapest in town and the laid-back vibe will appeal to dive-bar aficionados. The booming jukebox often determines the humor of the evening, depending on who's controlling the shuffle. Late at night, the atmosphere can be jovial or aggressive. Use your judgment if you stay into the wee hours.

If you want to shake your booty to some Latin rhythms, head to **Bovedas** (Tinajitas 24, Col. San Antonio, tel. 415/152-0538, 7 P.M.–3 A.M. Thurs.–Sat.), a dance hall dedicated to salsa, cha cha cha, mambo, and other Latin dances. Located in the San Antonio neighborhood to the southwest of the *centro histórico,* this popular club is only open on the weekends, when it is packed with dance lovers. Beginners are welcome here, but you'll also have a chance to see some very impressive and passionate dancers on the floor. If you don't know the steps, Bovedas has got that covered, too: On the weekends, there are twice-nightly dance classes at 7 P.M. and 9 P.M.

LIVE MUSIC

Live music plays an important role in Mexican culture and celebration. In San Miguel de Allende, marimba musicians play jubilantly on busy avenues for tips from passersby, while merry marching bands accompany wedding parties as they make their way out of the chapel. Roving guitarists play songs by request in San Miguel's fancy restaurants, and *norteño* trios entertain the taco rush at the weekly Mercado de Martes. Every night, the strains of mariachi float over the town square, as these traditional Mexican musicians play songs to a crowd of friends and family.

Many of San Miguel de Allende's popular restaurants hire live musicians to accompany the nightly dinner crowd. There are several good jazz ensembles that perform in San Miguel's bars and restaurants, excellent classical guitarists, as well as some rockers like Vudu Chile and The Sharpies, for those who want to dance. The violin and guitar ensemble Gil y Cartas is one of San Miguel's most talented and popular acts, often employed in fine local restaurants when they aren't on international tour. Jazz trumpeter Doc Severinsen of *Tonight Show* fame is a San Miguel resident, and he often plays at local venues. As always, you can see what's going on in *Atención San Miguel,* or just follow your ears to the party.

Throughout the year, there are frequent live music and dance performances in the *jardín,* sponsored by the municipal and state government. These free concerts really run the gamut, from lively traditional dance performances to wailing rock shows by San Miguel teenagers. Sometimes wonderful, sometimes painful, most performances in the town square draw a

Mariachi music can often be heard throughout the *jardín.*

multigenerational crowd. To see what's coming up, you can check the monthly schedule in the *jardín,* which is usually posted beneath the arcades on all four corners of the square.

For a formal concert, the historic **Teatro Ángela Peralta** (Hernández Macías 82, tel. 415/152-2200) presents an ongoing program of live music, film, dance, theater, and other performances. It is one of the major venues for the annual San Miguel de Allende Chamber Music Festival in July, which features a wonderful two-week program of classical music ensembles. To see what's playing while you are in San Miguel, check the newspaper, *Atención San Miguel,* or drop by the Ángela Peralta box office, a cubbyhole on the west side of the theater.

ART

For a town of its size, San Miguel has built a strong reputation for its commitment to the visual arts, boasting numerous art schools, a surprising number of galleries, and a slew of

EXPATRIATE ART

In addition to its colonial art and architecture, San Miguel de Allende is well known for its large expatriate and artistic community. At first glance, the prevalence of creative-minded foreigners seems easy enough to explain: the low cost of living, the lovely natural light, and the imaginative architecture all make San Miguel a perfect place for an artistic sojourn. While the appealing environment certainly plays its part, there is more to the story. In fact, San Miguel has a long and important history in the visual arts, dating back to the early 20th century.

At one time, San Miguel was a relatively forgotten place. After the decline of the silver trade and the end of the War of Independence, the town was largely abandoned and its many industries declined. By the end of the 19th century, San Miguel was little more than a tiny outpost at the end of a dusty road, principally accessible by train. Still, its beauty was legendary, and the romantic atmosphere began to attract artists and thinkers. During the early 1930s, the famous bullfighter, Pepe Ortiz, along with opera singer José Mojica, arrived in San Miguel de Allende. They were quickly enamored of its ruined charms and abandoned orchards; Ortiz bought a ranch on the outskirts of town, which is today the Rancho Hotel Atascadero. Here, they invited other intellectuals and artists to town for readings and parties, and they formed the Sociedad Amigos de San Miguel (Society of Friends of San Miguel). In this context, San Miguel's reputation as an artist's haven began to flourish. Mexican scholar Alfonso Reyes came to visit the tiny town, as did the celebrated Chilean poets Gabriela Mistral and Pablo Neruda. Oaxacan painter Rufino Tamayo and his wife, Olga, were among the city's most famous fans.

In 1938, Felipe Cossío del Pomar, a Peruvian artist and art historian, followed their footsteps to San Miguel de Allende. It was a time of great intellectual and artistic achievement in Mexico. In the wake of the Revolution of 1910, writers and artists were refashioning Mexico's cultural identity through government-backed programs spearheaded by the former Minister of Education, José Vasconcelos, among others.

Cossío was not only a historian, but a political activist with ties to many of Mexico's prominent thinkers and artists. In the late 1930s, the Mexican government granted Cossío the former convent at the Templo de la Inmaculada Concepción in San Miguel's *centro histórico* – at that time, little more than a ruin. There, Cossío founded the Escuela Universi-

working artists, both newbies and professionals. Notably, there is great interest in the visual arts throughout every sector of the community. Here, even coffee shops, dive bars, and real estate offices are known to host an exhibition or two.

The majority of local artists show their work in private galleries; however, there are several public exhibition spaces on the first floor of the **Centro Cultural Ignacio Ramírez** (Hernández Macías 75, tel. 415/152-0289, 10 A.M.–7:30 P.M. Mon.–Sat., 10 A.M.–2 P.M. Sun.). Often, these spaces are dedicated to work by local artists who have studied or are studying at the school, and opening events are usually loud and well attended. Throughout the year, the school hosts several new and itinerant exhibitions by Mexican artists outside of San Miguel. The galleries are free and open to the public. Wander in to see what's been hung, or check *Atención San Miguel* to see if a new show is being inaugurated while you are in town.

Located in the bottom floor of the Casa del Mayorazgo de la Canal, the **Casa de Cultura Banamex** (Canal 4, tel. 55/1226-0256, www. casadelacanal.com, 9 A.M.–2 P.M. daily, free) has several small and nicely renovated exhibition spaces, dedicated to rotating exhibitions of work by important Mexican and international artists. In tandem with Mexico's bicentennial celebrations, Banamex inaugurated the space in September 2010 with an exhibition of

taria de Bellas Artes, San Miguel's first fine art school. (Later, the school would move to a new facility on the Ancha de San Antonio and, in 1950, was renamed the Instituto Allende.)

Cossío de Pomar's arrival in San Miguel coincided with the appearance of another important expatriate, Stirling Dickinson of Chicago. Ivy-educated but rather shy, Dickinson became the first art director of Cossío's new school. Dickinson helped Cossío to promote the school in the United States, luring a few American students down to study in San Miguel. His efforts got a major boost with the passage of the GI Bill, which granted World War II veterans a free college education. San Miguel's art school was accredited in the U.S., and by 1946, a few GIs had arrived to study at the *escuela*.

By 1948, the word had gotten out about San Miguel de Allende and the GI presence had grown. *Life* magazine ran an article and photo spread depicting the carefree life of art students in Mexico's inexpensive paradise. The article inspired thousands more GIs to apply to the art school; many more Americans came down on their own. This community of students and artists laid the foundation for the large expatriate community in San Miguel today.

In addition to Americans, the establishment of an art college in San Miguel drew many colorful personalities to town. In the late 1940s, David Alfaro Siqueiros, an icon of the Mexican mural movement and a vocal member of the Communist Party, was hired as a guest lecturer. Siqueiros also agreed to work with students on a mural depicting the achievements of Ignacio Allende. In a story now famous throughout San Miguel, Siqueiros had a violent argument with the art school's director, Alfredo Campanella, and threw him down a flight of stairs. The faculty and the majority of the students then walked out in support of Siqueiros.

Since those days, San Miguel de Allende has continued to build its reputation as an artist community. Today, expatriates compose an estimated 10 percent of the town's population, and there are more galleries and international restaurants than you can throw a bagel at. The large community of foreign residents is integral to San Miguel's identity and modern culture, as well as a large part of this small town's history. Stirling Dickinson would eventually become known as one of San Miguel's most influential citizens, as well as one of its greatest benefactors. He died in San Miguel de Allende in 1998.

work by the early 20th-century Mexican master, Juan O'Gorman. Exhibitions are ongoing, free, and open to the public.

An enchanting little museum located in a beautifully renovated colonial home, **La Esquina: Museo del Juguete Popular Mexicano** (Nuñez 40, tel. 415/152-2602, www.museolaesquina.org.mx, 10 A.M.–6 P.M. Wed.–Sat., 1–3 P.M. Sun., US$2.50 adults, US$1.50 kids, seniors, and students) has three show rooms dedicated entirely to traditional Mexican toys. Behind the museum's glass display cases, the permanent collection includes a wide range of antique toys, including painted papier-mâché dolls, corn-husk figurines, clay whistles, little wooden chairs, toy planes and

automobiles, wool stuffed animals, toy instruments, and many other lovely and imaginative designs. There are also changing exhibitions on the top floor, dedicated to regional toy designs from different Mexican states. The light and colorful space is appropriate for kids (plus they get a discount on the admission cost), but visitors of any age will enjoy the diversity and imagination of traditional toy design from across Mexico. If the project inspires you, there is also a small gift shop where you can pick up your own *juguetes*.

FESTIVALS AND EVENTS

Many people in San Miguel de Allende claim that this small town has more municipal festivals than any other city in Mexico. While that may or may not be true, it is easy enough to believe. In San Miguel, barely a day goes by that does not celebrate a patron saint, a beloved chapel, or a revolutionary hero. Every neighborhood has its own annual party, and on any given night loud fireworks crackle through the sky in celebration.

In addition to the near-constant festivities rumbling through San Miguel's neighborhoods, there are several important events that take place every year, with much anticipation and fanfare. Visiting during one of the San Miguel's festivals can be a memorable experience; however, you should plan ahead if you want to visit during the most popular dates, especially the weeks around Semana Santa and Día de la Independencia.

La Candelaria

On El Día de los Reyes Magos (Three Kings' Day, celebrated annually on January 6), Mexican families get together to exchange gifts and share a *rosca de reyes,* a wreath-shaped sweet bread topped with crystallized fruit. The person who finds a figurine baked inside their slice of cake is appointed godmother or godfather to the baby Jesus in the family's nativity scene. The godparent is responsible for dressing baby Jesus and taking him to the church for blessing on February 2, the day of La Candelaria. On the same day, the godparent must also invite friends and family to their home for a traditional dinner of tamales, *atole,* and hot chocolate. While La Candelaria is a Catholic tradition, the tamales and *atole* may have derived from a pre-Hispanic tradition in honor of the rain god, Tlaloc.

In addition to the family gatherings throughout town, San Miguel de Allende celebrates La Candelaria with the opening of the annual plant and flower sale at Parque Juárez. This lovely and aromatic market fills the winding walkways of the already-verdant park with an impressive array of plants, flowers, hanging vines, trees, fresh herbs, cactus, and succulents. Vendors come from as far away as Veracruz and Puebla, and many set up tents

to camp in during the 10 market days. If you are on an extended sojourn in San Miguel de Allende, La Candelaria is an excellent place to buy well-priced plants and flowers. If you are just visiting, be sure to stop by the park to see the many exotic plants and cactus on sale.

San Miguel Writers Conference

Just as it has attracted many visual artists, San Miguel de Allende is home to writers of every stripe, from memoirists to poets. Organized by the English-language writers' group, the San Miguel Literary Sala, the annual San Miguel Writers Conference (La Conexión, Aldama 3, tel. 415/185-2225, U.S. tel. 510/295-4097, www.sanmiguelwritersconference.org) is a high-quality and well-organized five-day event that invites editors, publishers, literary agents, and published authors to give talks and workshops to conference participants. Throughout the long weekend, there is a full schedule of panel discussions, readings, classes, and parties. Programs range from practical advice on getting published to fiction and memoir writing workshops. For those visiting San Miguel for the first time, the Writers Conference also organizes cultural tours of the city. Past keynote speakers include such famous names as Barbara Kingsolver, Sandra Cisneros, and Tom Robbins. Admission costs include meals.

Semana Santa

San Miguel de Allende is well known for its beautiful Semana Santa (Easter week) celebrations. There is amazing color and pageantry throughout the week, with major events drawing thousands of spectators. Most Mexican schools break in the week preceding and following Easter Sunday, bringing a flood of national tourism to town. If you are planning a visit, make hotel reservations in advance and be prepared to experience a more bustling version of the city. Once you touch down, be sure to pick up a copy of *Atención San Miguel,* which always publishes a detailed list of Semana Santa events. Alternatively, you can look over the week's schedule on the municipal message boards in the town square.

ON INTRIGUES AND THE BEAT GENERATION

Like a fictional town from a Gabriel García Márquez novel, San Miguel de Allende is a place of myth and magic. Rumors abound, unsubstantiated but often alluring. According to many locals, Fray Juan de San Miguel's dog was the true founder of the town, independently discovering the natural spring at El Chorro and leading his master to the water source. Others claim they have discovered hidden treasures from the 18th century, plastered within the walls of San Miguel's colonial mansions and chapels. When trying to explain San Miguel's ineffable allure, many point to quartz deposits buried beneath the city. All these stories are based on fact but embellished with imagination.

One of San Miguel's most alluring modern legends is also the most elusive. According to local rumors, Beat Generation writers Jack Kerouac, William Burroughs, and Allen Ginsberg all visited San Miguel de Allende, possibly all at the same time. Given the time and context, the possibility doesn't seem far-fetched. During the 1950s and 1960s, Mexico was a politically active and leftist country, attracting plenty of artists and bohemians from Europe and the United States. Famously, Jack Kerouac wrote *Mexico City Blues* during a long sojourn in the capital. Allen Ginsberg came to visit him, and the two were photographed in front of one of the city's fountains in 1956.

In those years, San Miguel had already gained notoriety as an artists' enclave, and plenty of counterculture's less famous names had already found their way here. The legendary dive bar, La Cucaracha, was known as a gathering place for tough townsfolk and leftist writers. Some San Miguel old-timers remember the poets gathering in town, and some even say they met Kerouac. As appealing as the rumors may sound, other literary buffs insist that these legendary writers never made their way to San Miguel; timelines of their lives don't leave room for their visiting the town – especially not the appealing yet improbable triumvirate of Kerouac, Burroughs, and Ginsberg visiting San Miguel together.

A mythical figure himself, Neal Cassady is one of the few great counterculture personalities whose presence in San Miguel is never debated. The inspiration for the character of Dean Moriarty in Kerouac's *On the Road,* Neal Cassady died in San Miguel de Allende in 1968. His body was found beside the train tracks to Celaya after a late-night party. He had died of exposure.

Though some of San Miguel's literary myths are sure to be exaggerations, there's no denying that they've left a palpable magic in the city. Writers and other creative types flock here from around the world, trying to nab a little piece of that magic for themselves.

One of the first major events related to Holy Week actually takes place two weeks before Easter. On the fifth Sunday of Lent, a massive pilgrimage departs from the Santuario de Jesús Nazareno, as the sacred figure of the **Señor de la Columna** is carried, along with La Virgen de Dolores and the Señor de San Juan, from Atotonilco to San Miguel de Allende. The journey is made slowly and in silence, with a mass held at the midpoint. Just before daybreak, the procession passes through San Miguel de Allende via the Avenida Independencia, where families have lined the streets with palm leaves, balloons, and flowers. With much fanfare, the figure of El Señor de la Columna is carried to the church of San Juan de Dios, where it will stay until Easter Sunday.

A lovely local tradition, **Viernes de Dolores** is celebrated on the final Friday of Lent, two days before Palm Sunday. This holiday is dedicated to La Virgen de Dolores (Our Lady of Sorrows), who is remembered with special masses in the town's church, fresh flowers in the city fountains, and the distribution of *aguas de fruta* in the local community. At the workplace, employers will often provide *aguas* or ice cream to their employees, and some will also give out miniature popsicles to clients and passersby. The *aguas* are said to be symbolic of the virgin's tears.

The same evening, Our Lady of Sorrows is honored with hundreds of small home-built altars, erected in the windows and doorways of family homes throughout San Miguel de Allende. These altars are traditionally adorned with a statue or image of the virgin, chamomile, purple flowers, and little parcels of green wheat sprouts. All the town's lovely altars are open to the public, so there is quite a buzz on the street. As children go from house to house visiting with their neighbors, they are served hibiscus juice, ice cream, and popsicles.

Two days later, **Domingo de Ramos** (Palm Sunday) officially begins the Holy Week festivities. All day long, beautifully woven palm crosses and other palm adornments are sold outside every church in San Miguel. Local families buy their palms and take them to the church for blessings. There are also several religious processions on Palm Sunday, commemorating Jesus's arrival in Jerusalem.

Viernes Santo (Good Friday), is the single most important day during Semana Santa. In fact, it is more likely that a shop or restaurant will close to business on Good Friday than on Easter Sunday. Good Friday is not a day of celebration, so much as a day of mourning, with solemn processions throughout the town. The *jardín* is the locus of activity, with huge crowds gathered there from morning until evening.

The events of Viernes Santo begin when the cross from Atotonilco is carried to the *parroquia,* followed shortly thereafter by El Señor de la Columna. The revered statue will spend the weekend in the *parroquia* before being returned to Atotonilco on the following Wednesday. Around midday, there is a live and unflinching reenactment of the Stations of the Cross, which concludes with Jesus's trial by Pontius Pilate in the esplanade of the *parroquia.* In preparation, a slow and serious procession weaves through town, carrying statues of Jesus and the saints aloft. Men are dressed in dark suits, and the women, or the *mujeres dolientes,* are dressed in mourning attire. Among them, young girls in white dresses

with bright purple sashes drop chamomile along the path to the *parroquia.* As evening falls, another mournful parade, the **Procesión del Silencio,** weaves through town toward the *parroquia.* For this beautiful and solemn event, capped men and women dressed in black proceed slowly and silently to the *jardín,* holding flickering candles.

In the days before Easter Sunday, or **Domingo de Pascua,** colorful papier-mâché Judas figures are hung over the *plaza principal,* between the Presidencia Municipal and the *jardín.* Just after Easter mass, a crowd gathers to burn the Judases, which have been rigged with explosives. One at a time, these paper giants spin in circles until they burst into flame, to the delight and applause of onlookers. Today, many of the Judas figures are fashioned to look like politicians or other famous (but controversial) figures. Other than this colorful event, Easter Sunday is generally a quieter day, spent with family and attending mass.

San Antonio de Padua: Fiesta de Los Locos

Saint Anthony is one of San Miguel's most popular saints, as well as the namesake for one of the city's biggest neighborhoods. On the Sunday after Saint Anthony's feast day, June 13, San Miguel has a very particular way of feting this favored figure. On this auspicious day—also dubbed Los Locos—thousands of San Miguel residents march through the streets in silly and sometimes provocative costumes, from political masks to gorilla suits. The prevalence of cross-dressing is a particularly noticeable aspect of this parade, as many of San Miguel's mustachioed *señores* don dresses, lipstick, and wigs for the tour around town. Ogle all you want, but remember that onlookers are routinely pegged (and with gusto!) by handfuls of hard candy from the marchers. After the parade ends, the party continues well into the evening. From morning, to afternoon, to the wee hours of the night, wigged and costumed revelers dance ceaselessly, until they finally run out of steam the following morning.

Expresión en Corto

San Miguel de Allende and Guanajuato co-host the annual Expresión en Corto short film festival (Fábrica La Aurora, Local 5-B, tel. 415/152-7264, www.expresionencorto.com) during the final week of July. During the festival, films selected from thousands of international entries are shown in more than 20 different venues. The festival's complex, color-coded program groups screenings by category, such as short documentary, short animation, and others. For film buffs, this long weekend is a morning-to-evening commitment. While the festival is specifically dedicated to shorts (as indicated by its name), there are numerous feature-length films included in the program, some of which are making their debut at the festival. In San Miguel de Allende, movies are shown in the *jardín* and in the Centro Cultural Ignacio Ramírez, among other venues. Many films are in Spanish—though, in most cases, international selections are subtitled in both Spanish and English (language is indicated in the program). All screenings are free and open to the public.

San Miguel de Allende Chamber Music Festival

Every summer, the **Festival Internacional de Música de Cámara** (International Chamber Music Festival, Hernández Macías 75, tel. 415/154-8722 www.festivalsanmiguel.com) invites renowned quartets and soloists from across the world to play in a series of concerts in San Miguel de Allende. Often excellent, concerts take place in a variety of venues and vary in price, though there are always several free events included in the annual program. Proceeds from this not-for-profit festival benefit the Advanced Music Student Program, through which promising young musicians from across Mexico are invited to San Miguel to work directly with acclaimed international musicians.

Independence Celebrations and El Grito

San Miguel de Allende is often described as the cradle of independence, so it is no surprise

Even pets participate in Independence Day celebrations.

© ARTURO MEADE

that this party-loving town is a major destination for the national Día de la Independencia de México (Independence Day) celebrations. In the weeks leading up to the festivities, public spaces are festooned with tri-color decorations, local families hang Mexican flags outside their windows, and vendors appear in the streets with every manner of patriotic kitsch. Festivities technically begin on the night of September 15 with the traditional cry *"¡Viva Mexico!,"* delivered in the *jardín* by the town's mayor. After the crowd is riled up, fireworks explode over the *parroquia* and spindly towers of pyrotechnics burst into multicolored flame. Quite seriously, you must watch out that your hair does not catch on fire.

During the independence celebrations, the town is flooded with national tourism, including the inevitable and noisy crowd of youngsters who've come to party in San Miguel's nightclubs. After the pyrotechnics, Independence Day is a big night out. Bars and clubs are packed and riotous until daybreak, with numerous new storefronts opening just for the week's festivities. Those who know San Miguel de Allende well will see the town center transformed. While September 15 is the biggest party, the anniversary of the independence movement is actually September 16, a national holiday, with banks and most business closed. Needless to say, the parties continue.

Día de San Miguel Arcángel

The widespread city festivals in honor of its patron saint begin almost immediately after the Independence Day parties end. Saint Michael's feast day is technically September 29. However, if the 29th falls on a weekday, the festivities are pushed back to the following weekend, culminating with the largest and most well attended *fiestas* on Sunday.

The festivities in honor of San Miguel actually begin with a novena, nine days of prayer and celebration leading up to the saint's feast day. During each of these nine days, one of the city's neighborhoods, along with various

Dancers from throughout the country arrive to pay tribute to Saint Michael during the Día de San Miguel Arcángel.

© ARTURO MEADE

civil and religious groups, organizes processions around the city. The sounds of drums or marching bands echo through the narrow streets as the processionists dance through town, eventually arriving at the Parroquia de San Miguel Arcángel, where the festivities often continue.

On Friday afternoon (two days before the official feast day celebrations), a procession departs from the Aurora neighborhood, accompanied by the Aguascalientes Brothers band. They arrive at the *parroquia* at dusk, just as vendors are setting up hot punch and taco stands in preparation for the night ahead. At this point, marching bands, dancers, and devotees of Saint Michael have begun to arrive from across Mexico—some coming from as far as the United States. At 4 A.M. on Saturday morning, the festivities officially begin with the traditional **La Alborada,** an astonishing hour-long fireworks display over the *jardín*. During this endless spray of pyrotechnics, the town square is filled with smoke, and the sound of explosions is almost deafening. The party continues until 6 A.M., when the revelers sing *Las Mañanitas* (Mexico's birthday song) to San Miguel, and then attend mass.

The weekend continues with dances, masses, and celebration. On Saturday afternoon, a long and beautiful procession of dancers and indigenous groups heads up Canal Street to the *parroquia*. When they arrive, they decorate the *parroquia* with flowers and banners. The beautiful **Voladores de Papantla** from Veracruz perform their unique tree-top ceremony as the dancing continues, and inevitably, there are more fireworks. The party continues through Sunday, with another procession of dancers up Zacateros street to the *jardín*. The fireworks and dancing don't stop until late Sunday night.

Día de los Muertos

Día de los Muertos (Day of the Dead), is one of Mexico's most well known holidays. The name is a bit of a misnomer, as the holiday is actually celebrated during two days, November 1 and November 2. In San Miguel de Allende, like everywhere in Mexico, regional traditions distinguish local Day of the Dead festivities. In the week leading up to November, San Miguel families and prominent organizations build traditional altars in the town square using sugar skulls, *pan de muerto,* gourds and jicama, colored sand, and marigolds *(cempasuchil),* the flower of the dead. You may notice that traditional altar design in this region tends to be neater and more geometrical than in other parts of Mexico.

Throughout the two-day holiday, the municipal cemetery (behind the Real de Minas hotel on the Salida a Celaya) is packed with families who have come to leave flowers and treats on the graves of loved ones. Many families spend the entire day there, cleaning the gravesite, laying flowers, offering food and drink to their ancestors, or eating a picnic lunch together. By the evening, the crowds are so dense that it can take several hours to get into the cemetery.

Christmas and New Year's Eve

With a chill in the air and a new year about to begin, the Christmas holidays are a beautiful time of year in San Miguel de Allende. By the end of November, Christmas decorations begin to appear around town, often in the form of colorful *papel picado* (decorative cut-paper adornments) and piñatas strung between buildings. In the town square, a large nativity with live farm animals is installed in front of the *parroquia.* Many of the female animals are pregnant and will give birth in the *jardín* during the Christmas season.

Preparations for Christmas begin in November, but the season really kicks off on December 12, the day of La Virgen de Guadalupe. Although December 12 is not a recognized national holiday, it is widely celebrated throughout Mexico. In San Miguel de Allende, you can expect to hear loud fireworks exploding throughout the night in the virgin's honor. Shortly thereafter, local families gather for posadas, which are performed during the nine days leading up to Christmas. On the night of a posada, guests gather at a neighbor's house with candles and costumes,

asking the host family for shelter (and thereby reenacting Mary and Joseph's search for shelter on the night that Jesus was born). Once they have gone inside, the families say a rosary and sing Christmas songs. Then children may break a piñata while adults sip on punch. Posadas conclude on December 24, the most important night of the season. Traditionally, Mexican families gather for a late dinner on the 24th, attending midnight mass afterward. December 25 is a quiet day, usually spent relaxing with family—and usually accompanied by copious leftovers.

In San Miguel de Allende, New Year's Eve is similar to what you'd find in most cities: lots of parties, people, and bubbly. There are often live music performances in the town square and, at midnight, a large fireworks display over the Parroquia de San Miguel Arcángel. For anyone who hasn't seen an explosion of lights over San Miguel's iconic church, here's your chance for that postcard-perfect photo. If you want to follow Mexican tradition, eat 12 grapes for good luck when the clock strikes midnight—one grape for each month of the year. But be aware that the price of grapes in the market is always much higher on December 31!

Other Festivals and Events

If you hear fireworks exploding outside your window at four o'clock in the morning, it's likely that something or someone is being feted in your neighborhood. In addition to San Miguel's major festivals and events, there are dozens of other popular celebrations, smaller than the town-wide events but no less enthusiastic.

While not a national holiday, **Ignacio Allende's birthday** is celebrated in San Miguel on January 21. The life and achievements of San Miguel's native son are recognized with a parade downtown, put on by local schoolchildren.

For the ultimate cute fix, don't miss the parade on March 20, heralding the **first day of spring.** Just as San Miguel's many jacaranda trees begin to bloom, all the town's children dress up as flowers, bumblebees, butterflies, and bunnies, then proceed through the streets of downtown as their proud parents snap photos of the parade.

During May, four historic neighborhoods in San Miguel de Allende hold their annual celebrations. On the fourth Sunday in May, the most raucous of these celebrations, the **Fiesta de la Santa Cruz,** is held in the Valle del Maíz. This major block party has roots dating back to the 16th century and includes live music, pageantry, and plenty of libations.

In addition to regional festivals, San Miguel enthusiastically participates in every national holiday, from Cinco de Mayo to Constitution Day. You'll also see plenty of festivities during the numerous unofficial but incredibly important holidays like May 10— Mother's Day.

Shopping

With a slew of unique stores and many creative minds at work, San Miguel de Allende is a wonderful place to shop. Although there are a few chain supermarkets and large department stores in San Miguel's suburbs, the *centro histórico* is still largely populated by mom-'n'-pop bakeries, corner stores, specialty boutiques, and artist-owned galleries. Here, local proprietors usually tend their own shops, and many are on a first-name basis with their clients.

San Miguel excels in everything related to art, design, craft, and interiors. There is quite a bit of diversity for a town of its size, as a few hours of window-shopping will quickly reveal. From small gifts and contemporary art, a unique piece of jewelry or even a new couch for your living room, San Miguel's creative climate is reflected in the many unique and local products it sells.

TRADITIONAL CRAFTS

From elaborately woven textiles to simple palm baskets, Mexico's rich traditions in art and handicrafts are amply represented in San Miguel de Allende. The Bajío region is known for stamped tin, copper, and aluminum, forged iron, glass boxes, decorative and carved wood figurines, leather goods, and hand-painted majolica-style ceramics, all of which can be found in shops around San Miguel de Allende. In addition to local products, San Miguel's best craft shops show the work of master artisans from across Mexico. In many cases, shop owners are knowledgeable about the traditional art they

sell and can give you insight into a piece's origins or the artist's technique.

For a large selection of inexpensive and predominantly regional handicrafts, check out the **Mercado de Artesanía** (Andador Lucas Balderas, tel. 415/152-2844, hours vary by shop daily), located in a descending alleyway between the Mercado Ignacio Ramírez and Calle Loreto. Here, you'll find painted tin

© ARTURO MEADE

a variety of hats on sale outside the Mercado de Artesanía in the *centro historico*

RESPECT THE SIESTA!

The famous siesta, or midafternoon nap, has practically become a symbol of living the good life in Mexico. In every tourist resort or border town, you can buy a ceramic figurine or a hand-painted shot glass depicting a Mexican *muchacho* asleep against a cactus, sombrero pulled over his eyes. The siesta, it seems to tell us, is Mexico's way to relax.

In reality, the siesta is an important part of family life in many parts of Mexico, including San Miguel de Allende. Here, the midday meal, known as the *comida*, is the biggest and most important meal of the day. Traditionally eaten at 2 P.M., the *comida* is a time that families spend together, just after children return home from school. Often, people take a short nap after lunching; hence, the entire midday break is often referred to as the siesta.

Although the traditional siesta is losing is prevalence in big cities, it continues to be very much a part of daily life in smaller towns like San Miguel de Allende. Notice the operating hours at many small businesses, like pottery shops, galleries, or real estate offices. They usually close 2-4 P.M., a time during which the shop's proprietors will go home for lunch and relaxation. For tourists, the siesta can be a bit of a nuisance, since few expect to find a gift shop or clothing boutique closed during the bright light of day. Most, however, learn to do like the locals and enjoy a long and leisurely lunch.

Like the siesta, Sundays are an important family day in Mexico, often undisturbed by the necessity of running a business. You will find that if you ask a shop's hours, they will tell you they are open every day. Frequently, when the proprietors say every day, they are automatically excluding Sunday. It can be very surprising to learn that the majority of shops – and even restaurants – are closed all day on Sunday, when tourists flock to San Miguel from nearby towns like Celaya and Querétaro. Yet personal time, family, and tradition are still a priority in this small Mexican town.

ornaments, *milagritos,* and other metalwork, as well as wooden utensils, ceramics, beaded jewelry, papier-mâché, and textiles. A few shops specialize in art and crafts from Oaxaca and Michoacán, as well as clay miniatures. There is some good work here, but it also takes a good eye to find the best pieces amidst the jumble of storefronts. Along the exit of the *mercado* on Calle Loreto, there are many more small shops selling craft work from across Mexico.

Right on the main plaza, **Ono** (Plaza Principal 20-A, tel. 415/151-1182, 9 A.M.–8 P.M. Mon.–Fri., 10 A.M.–9 P.M. Sat.–Sun.) sells traditional Mexican handicrafts, with an emphasis on clothing and textiles. They stock a wide range of rebozos and shawls, cotton dresses, sweaters, embroidered shirts, and huipiles, as well as panama hats, painted wood toys, and some contemporary wood-and-silver jewelry. When shopping for textiles, the staff can explain the difference in materials, quality, and cost.

A delightful shop across the street from the Capilla de la Tercera Orden, **El Nuevo Mundo** (San Francisco 17, tel. 415/152-6108, 9 A.M.–8 P.M. Mon.–Fri., 10 A.M.–9 P.M. Sat.–Sun.) sells a bright and colorful range of crafts from central and southern Mexico. Handmade clothing and textiles are a specialty here, including beautiful hand-embroidered shirts, huipiles, rebozos, shawls, woven bags, tablecloths, bedspreads, and scarves. Also an excellent place to pick up a small gift for a friend at home, El Nuevo Mundo has an assortment of tin ornaments and boxes, miniatures, painted wooden animals, and other well-selected curiosities and trinkets. The friendly staff is knowledgeable about their products, and patient if you'd like to try on a piece of clothing or two.

Galería Tesoros (Recreo 8B, tel. 415/154-4838, galeriatesoros@yahoo.com, 9:30 A.M.–8 P.M. Mon.–Sat., 9:30 A.M.–6 P.M. Sun.) has a large collection of arts and crafts from varied traditions across Mexico. When entering this spacious gallery, the first thing that

ARTESANÍA

Mexico is well known for its unique traditional handicrafts *(artesanía)*, which often fuse pre-Hispanic artisan techniques with Spanish aesthetics. Like food, drink, and religious festivities, traditional handicrafts are highly specific to the region in which they are produced. Throughout Mexico, crafts have the definitive stamp of their home and the personal touch of the artisan who made them.

Learning about and shopping for *artesanía* is one of the great pleasures of a trip to Mexico, and it is also an important way to support the ongoing artistic traditions in rural Mexico. Understanding a piece's origins, as well as the technique behind its production, can make the experience all the more rewarding.

CERAMICS

Long before the arrival of the Spanish settlers, decorative and utilitarian clay vessels were produced throughout Mesoamerica. After the conquest, Spaniards introduced kiln firing and ceramic glazes to Mexico's artisans. Since the 16th century, the states of Puebla and Guanajuato have been major producers of tin-glazed **majolica-style ceramics,** with the finest and most expensive ceramics produced in Puebla. Puebla's pottery is generally referred to as **talavera,** a traditionally Spanish subset of majolica.

You can find Puebla's delicately painted ceramic work in many of San Miguel's craft shops; however, the vast majority of majolica-inspired ceramics in town come from nearby Dolores Hidalgo, one of the country's largest producers of hand-painted clay tiles and flatware. In Dolores, pottery is more loosely painted and more brightly colored than with the painstaking ceramic technique introduced by the Spanish. In fact, many of Dolores's ceramics are produced in great quantities and are far more inexpensive than true majolica. At the same time, the whimsy, color, and spontaneity of Dolores Hidalgo's ceramic work can often be just as charming, unique, and decorative as the famed ceramic work from Puebla. When shopping for ceramics, seek out individual quality in each piece. Although there may be 25 ceramic plates of the same general design, you will often find some are, by luck, more beautifully painted than others.

The state of Michoacán is Guanajuato's neighbor to the west, and home to many of the most prolific and important craft traditions in Mexico. Because of the proximity and quality of Michoacán's artisans, crafts from this region are well represented in San Miguel de Allende. Here, you can find the shiny and elaborate **ceramic pineapples** from the tiny towns of Patamban and San José de Gracia, where potters produce their wares without the use of a potter's wheel. Burnished clay pottery is also a technique commonly found in Michoacán, specifically from the town of Capula. Capula pottery is durable and beautiful, easily recognizable because it is painted with hundreds of white dots. Also look for the shiny glazed platters, plates, and pots from Huancito, and the typical green and black pottery from Tzintzuntzan, among others.

In addition to use as pots and housewares, ceramics are often used in decorative sculpture. *Árboles de la vida* (trees of life) are highly elaborate sculptural pieces depicting a leafy tree filled with birds and figurines. In San Miguel, you will find *árboles* from the state of Mexico as well as from Michoacán.

TEXTILES

Chales, **rebozos,** and **mantillas** are three types of wraps or shawls, which are produced throughout Mexico but differ in design and style. As with all textile work, the best (and priciest) shawls are made with natural fibers, usually silk or cotton. The famous silk rebozos of Santa María del Río can be found in a few shops in San Miguel, and are so finely woven that, despite their large size, they can pass through a woman's ring.

Manta, light cotton muslin, was mass-produced throughout Mexico and has long been the base for traditional Mexican clothing. Today, the majority of manta in Mexico is

© ARTURO MEADE

This close-up of a traditional dancer's tunic shows off its artisan's techniques.

imported from China, but clothing made from this lightweight fabric is produced throughout the country. Throughout town, you can find beautiful embroidered manta tunics and huipiles from the state of Oaxaca, as well as the geometrically stitched Magdalena huipiles from Chiapas. In addition to manta, Oaxaca is a major producer of beautiful textiles and clothing, much of which is hand-loomed and colored with natural dye.

Although they were once abundant, there are few local producers of **wool rugs** in the state of Guanajuato today. However, you will occasionally find these, as well as the famous wool rugs from Oaxaca, in and around the Mercado de Artesanías. The most famous rugs in Mexico come from Teotitlán del Valle in Oaxaca, which are woven with natural-dyed wool and often depict pre-Hispanic designs or concepts. The best and most expensive rugs

are always made with natural fibers. However, acrylic thread is often used in rugs today. To test for acrylic, take a rug out into the sun. Unlike wool, acrylic will shine.

METALWORK

You can see the work of San Miguel's colonial-era artisans on the aging balconies, window grates, and antique locks of homes throughout the city center. Today, San Miguel is still home to many skilled metalworkers, and **forged iron** is one of the true specialties of this region.

Hojalatería (tin products) are also a craft specialty in San Miguel de Allende, where you'll find every manner of stamped tin lamps and candelabras, wastepaper baskets, mirrors, and frames. San Miguel also has a long tradition of creating delicate blown glass lanterns and boxes, fused with iron; this tradition is far less prevalent than it was in the past, though these products have been produced here since the colonial era.

In addition to locally produced metalwork, San Miguel's shops may also carry the shiny stamped copper pots, vases, and candlesticks from Santa Clara del Cobre in Michoacán.

WOOD

Whittled wood toys and figurines are produced locally and sold in many of the older craft shops in San Miguel de Allende. Made from the wood of the copal tree, *alebrijes* are delicately carved and brightly painted animals and figurines, principally produced in San Antonio Arrazola, Oaxaca. Some of the more elaborate *alebrijes* can take an artisan weeks to carve and paint. Prices for these individually created crafts can run the gamut.

Wooden masks are often used in traditional ceremonies throughout Mexico, principally in the states of Oaxaca, Michoacán, and Guerrero. The highly original designs can range from saints and devils to animals and angels. Masks are very individual artisan products, and they carry more significance if they have already been used in a ceremony.

catches your eye is the beautiful ceramic work from Tzintzuntzan, Capula, and Tlaquepaque, among other regions, as well as the large collection of ceramic *catrinas,* grouped together in the store's foyer. Tesoros is one of the few places in San Miguel that sells the delicate Mata Ortiz pottery from the state of Chihuahua, which resembles the design aesthetic of the Indians of the American Southwest. On the livelier side, Tesoros stocks the famous lewd figurines from Ocumicho, Michoacán, genuine hammocks from the Yucatán Peninsula, decorative Huichol wall art, and elaborate *alebrijes* from Oaxaca. With one of the most diverse selections in San Miguel, it can be easy to breeze through this big store too quickly. Slow down and look closely at these high-quality pieces.

Zócalo (Hernández Macías 110, tel. 415/152-0663, www.zocalofolkart.com, 10 A.M.–7 P.M. Mon.–Sat., 10 A.M.–3 P.M. Sun.) has a spirited collection of clay figurines, elaborate trees of life, candlesticks, decorative platters, and other ceramic art from Michoacán, Puebla, Oaxaca, and elsewhere in Mexico. Here, craft leans toward fine art; many pieces are elaborate, highly original, and signed by their author. On the back wall, Zócalo also maintains an excellent collection of ceremonial masks from various small towns throughout central and southern Mexico; ask the salesperson to identify their origin.

A tiny storefront with over 75 years in operation, the small but adorable **La Casa** (Pepe Llanos 11, tel. 415/152-1027, 10 A.M.–3 P.M. and 5–8 P.M. Mon.–Sat.) sells a variety of natural wicker baskets, plaited fans, and tortilla holders, as well as a zoo full of unpainted hand-carved wooden animals and statues. It is a shoebox of a space, with everything stacked in pleasing disorder and smelling of fresh wood. The store's elderly owner is a bit hard-of-hearing, but she'll happily do her best to understand your questions.

Around the corner from La Casa, **Jarciería San José** (Mesones 36, tel. 415/152-1424, 11 A.M.–7 P.M. daily) is another tiny shop with a long history in San Miguel de Allende. Just across from the Plaza Cívica, the *jarciería* sells

wood cooking utensils and spatulas, carved wood animals, wood trivets, wicker baskets, and rustic wooden tortilla presses. They also sell *petates,* woven rush mats with a wonderful fresh smell. In this small and jumbled store, the simple wood and palm products feel as timeless as the place itself, which has been in business for more than 60 years.

Artes de Mexico (Calzada de la Aurora 47, tel. 415/152-0764, artesdemexicosma@ gmail.com, 9:30 A.M.–7:30 P.M. Mon.–Fri., 9:30 A.M.–6 P.M. Sat.) has a large, diverse, and yet well-selected stock of furniture, lamps, blown glass, framed mirrors, ceramics, papier-mâché, and other crafts. With such a huge variety, this store can feel like a small *artesanía* warehouse, yet quality is very good. Of particular note, Artes de Mexico stocks a range of *equipales:* large chairs, couches, and round tables made of lightweight natural wood and pigskin. Based on pre-Hispanic designs, *equipales* are comfortable and inexpensive traditional furniture from Jalisco.

A small and stylish shop in the Fábrica La Aurora, **Hilo Negro** (Local 3D, Fábrica La Aurora, Calzada de la Aurora, tel. 415/152-4835, www.hilo-negro.com, 10 A.M.–6 P.M. Mon.–Sat., 11 A.M.–3 A.M. Sun.) features beautiful traditional crafts, as well as imaginative decorative pieces by the shop's owner, Ricardo Garcia. Garcia's interest in traditional Mexican games, like *lotería* and *pissota,* often inspires his work, which is playful yet stately, and often elaborated with a mix of materials like wood, burnished clay, and antique coins. Though inspired by *artesanías,* Garcia's pieces are more akin to fine art, with the prices to match. In addition, the store has a fine collection of hand-painted majolica platters.

Galería Quinta Irma (Hernández Macías 56A, tel. 415/154-5694, and Zacateros 15, tel. 415/154-8917, www.galeriaquintairma.com, 10 A.M.–5 P.M. Mon.–Sat.) has two locations downtown. One corner shop exclusively features their ceramic designs, while the other shop also exhibits large-format oil paintings. Whichever location you run across first, the majolica-style ceramics are definitely the standout. At Quinta Irma, the beautiful hand-painted tiles, platters, vases, and sinks have an Old World quality, with the bright colors and charming figures that typify Mexican craft.

CLOTHING AND JEWELRY

For a bit of modern luxury, **Pepe Cerroblanco Joyería** (Centro Canal 17, tel. 415/152-0502, Fábrica la Aurora, tel. 415/154-9501, cerroblancojoyerias@prodigy.net, 11 A.M.–6 P.M. Mon.–Sat.) is an upscale boutique that sells a proprietary line of silver jewelry. Not for the fainthearted, Pepe Cerroblanco's designs are large and structural statement pieces, which often incorporate precious and semiprecious stones, turquoise, or amber. Everything here is expertly crafted in Pepe Cerroblanco's San Miguel de Allende studio, which has been in the family for three generations. Jewelry is displayed on black velvet stands and locked within delicate glass cases. Prices match the upscale atmosphere.

Inside the Plaza Vista Hermosa, **Mekishiko Designs** (Cuna de Allende 11, Int. 3, tel. 415/152-0888, mekishikodesigns@yahoo.com, 10:30 A.M.–7 P.M. Mon.–Sat., 10:30 A.M.–4 P.M. Sun.) represents a range of different jewelers, many from the local community. Predominantly showcasing work in silver, pieces are well selected and displayed with care; the store's clean, modern layout allows you to really observe each piece of jewelry, rather than creating the feeling of a jewelry clearing house. Diverse designers each bring a special touch. Some work is incredibly contemporary while other work has a homemade feeling. With a range of prices and styles, there's something here for varying tastes or budgets.

Owned by a family of well-known Oaxacan craft experts, **Juana Cata** (Recreo 5A tel. 415/152-6417, cbram@prodigy.net.mx, 10 A.M.–6 P.M. Wed. and Sun., 10 A.M.–8 P.M. Mon.–Tues. and Thurs.–Sat.) sells gorgeous handmade clothing and textiles from the state of Oaxaca. Take your time perusing the stacks of expertly woven shawls, thick hand-dyed cotton fabrics, and lovely velvet huipiles, lavishly embroidered with colorful flowers in the Isthmus of Tehuantepec. Here, every piece is painstakingly created and expertly selected. For those interested in Mexican textiles and weaving traditions, this shop is essential. In addition to textiles, Juana Cata has a nice collection of Oaxacan silver jewelry, known for its delicate filigree details.

There is a hip mix of crafts, collectibles, and clothes at **Mixta** (Pila Seca 16A, tel. 415/152-7343, 11 A.M.–7 P.M. Mon.–Sat., 10 A.M.–4 P.M. Sun.), a colorful little boutique on busy Calle Pila Seca. Those who love quirky gifts or souvenirs should be prepared to spend some time picking through Mixta's funky selection of crocheted earrings, bangles, beaded necklaces, greeting cards, scarves, totes, oilcloth wallets, votive candles, throw pillows, and photographs. The shop's warm Australian owner is often behind the register; she selects all the work for the shop, looking far and wide for unusual items you won't find in elsewhere in San Miguel.

The blast of color at **Abrazos** (Zacateros 24, tel. 415/154-8580, info@sanmigueldesigns.com, 10 A.M.–7 P.M. Mon.–Sat., 10 A.M.–4 P.M. Sun.) comes from the light-hearted, Mexican-themed cotton fabrics that form the base of the store's product line. A great place to pick up a gift for yourself or someone at home, Abrazos has a range of cute and colorful aprons, handbags, kimonos, pajamas, and men's ties, as well as funky jewelry, buttons, and notebooks. All the shop's products are handmade in San Miguel de Allende by a cooperative of local seamstresses. In addition to the store's original collection of clothes and fabrics, Abrazos stocks some funky tin adornments and kitschy souvenirs, like Pedro Infante paper dolls.

Located in the Fábrica La Aurora, **Alquimia4** (Local 16A, Fábrica La Aurora, Calzada de la Aurora s/n, tel. 415/152-6012, 10 A.M.–6 P.M. Mon.–Sat., 11 A.M.–3 P.M. Sun.) is a gallery and jewelry shop. Large stone, metal, and clay sculptures by Victor Hugo Nuñez dominate the space. However, you should also seek out the various display cases with Lila Parilla's original and highly varied jewelry designs. Parilla works in silver, but pieces often incorporate precious and semiprecious stones, leather, and pearls.

Some of her recent collections are inspired by pre-Hispanic art and architecture, while others take their designs from natural forms.

HOME AND FURNITURE

Decorating a colonial mansion calls for some serious furnishings, but **Casa Maria Luisa** (Canal 40, tel. 415/152-0130 or 415/152-8965, casamarialuisa@prodigy.net, 10 A.M.–7 P.M. Mon.–Sat., 10 A.M.–4 P.M. Sun.) has all the iron fixtures and monumental accessories that an 18th-century home deserves. The ceilings of this shop's large showrooms are filled with tin lamps and chandeliers of every conceivable design, while metal candlesticks, vintage-style furniture, tableware, elaborate mirrors, stately clay urns, picture frames, and other housewares cram the floor space. Impressive home accessories blend old San Miguel style with the polish of contemporary design. On the outdoor patio, there is also a selection of iron tables and chairs, along with concrete fountains.

If you've been envying your neighbor's heavy brass door knocker, it's time for a trip to **Productos Herco** (Relox 12, tel. 415/152-1434, 9 A.M.–2 P.M. and 4–7 P.M. Mon.–Sat.) at the Casa Cohen. This old store sells handmade brass, aluminum, and iron accessories for the bathroom, kitchen, and home. Come here if you are looking for handmade iron water spigots, fancy doorknobs, or an ornate lock for your patio. Casa Cohen has been in business since 1930, and many of their designs are as classic as the place itself.

A charming little shop selling luxury home accessories, **La Bottega di Casa** (Local 17A, Fábrica La Aurora, Calzada de la Aurora s/n, Local, tel. 415/152-8636, www.labottegadicasa. com, 10 A.M.–6 P.M. Mon.–Sat., 11 A.M.–3 P.M. Sun.) specializes in fine bed linens, tablecloths, and other textiles from Italy and France, all specially selected by the store's sophisticated Italian owner. La Bottega di Casa also sells posh silver, copper, glass, and ceramics from Europe, like Merino vases and 19th-century lithographs. In addition to imported items, the store has a proprietary collection of beautiful, locally made products, which are based

on European designs but created by Mexican artisans. Here, you can find unique blown glass pitchers and drinking glasses, hammered copper lamps, and white-glazed ceramic table settings, elegantly produced and presented.

Also in the Fábrica La Aurora, **Sisal** (Local 2A, Fábrica La Aurora, Calzada de la Aurora s/n, www.sisal.com.mx, tel. 415/152-0338, 10 A.M.–7 P.M. Mon.–Sat.) sells an eclectic yet tasteful mix of modern furniture, imported Asian antiques, Mexican rugs, and contemporary art. The store's owner, a Querétaro businesswoman with a flair for design, is constantly seeking out new merchandise; every time you go back, there's something different on the floor. Sisal also carries accessories, like colorful throw pillows, baskets, onyx lamps and accessories, bath products, and mirrors.

Located on a busy street, just outside the *centro histórico*, **Los Botes Chilo** (Prol. Calzada de la Luz 51-B, tel. 415/152-2789, aresaniaslos-botes@hotmail.com, 10 A.M.–6 P.M. Mon.–Sat., 11 A.M.–3 P.M. Sun.) produces decorative tin accessories, an artisan specialty of the San Miguel de Allende region. Here, you'll find both readymade and custom tin lamps, mirrors, and frames. The tiny showroom is packed with examples of their work, some quite original. Although you can buy directly, Chilo specializes in custom-designed products for San Miguel de Allende homeowners.

ART GALLERIES

Blessed with ornate architecture and lovely natural light, San Miguel de Allende is a feast for the eyes. As such, it is hardly surprising that this small town has been home to a cozy community of artists since the early 20th century. Free of the pretension you'd find in major cities, San Miguel is a welcoming place to see, make, or buy art. Here, amateurs and art students can quickly find a place to show their work, and opening events feel like lighthearted social gatherings among a group of friends. Every weekend, new exhibitions are inaugurated in San Miguel's galleries, or an Art Walk is hosted by a group of exhibitors and studios. Visiting these spaces is a quintessential part of visiting San Miguel.

Right next to the Teatro Ángela Peralta, **Galería Izamal** (Mesones 80, tel. 415/154-5409, www.galeriaizamal.com, 11 A.M.–3 P.M. and 4–8 P.M. daily) is one of the longest-running artist-owned collective galleries in town. This tiny overstuffed storefront features diverse drawings, paintings, and jewelry by the exhibiting artists and co-owners, who each work a weekly shift in the gallery. Their techniques vary, but all are good quality artists with many years of recognition in San Miguel. Two of the gallery's artists also give informal drawing and creativity workshops behind the gallery; inquire in the shop for more information. Depending on when you stop in, you may have the opportunity to chat with one of the creative folks behind the space.

Just a few steps from Izamal, **Galería Indigo** (Mesones 76, tel. 415/152-2749, www.indigomx.com, 11 A.M.–2:30 P.M. and 5:30–8:30 P.M. Mon.–Sat., 11 A.M.–4 P.M. Sun.) carries fine art by numerous well-known Oaxacan artists, from contemporary painters, like Guillermo Olguin, to masters, like Rodolfo Nieto. Often showing large-format pieces, Indigo's collection of paintings can be a bit difficult to appreciate in the low-ceilinged showrooms (the store has been divided into two stories with a wooden loft, truncating the wall space). However, if you take a moment to look closely, much of the work is wonderful. In addition to fine art, Galería Indigo carries a changing selection of elaborate and high-quality popular art from the states of Oaxaca, Michoacán, and Mexico.

On the charming back patio of the Instituto Allende, **Galería La Pérgola** (Instituto Allende, Ancha de San Antonio 20, tel. 415/154-5595, www.galeriapergola.com, 10 A.M.–6 P.M. Mon.–Sat.) is a lovely, light-filled gallery, which hosts rotating exhibitions by Mexican contemporary artists. Galería Pérgola's curved ceilings, thick white walls, and polished wood floors provide a sophisticated backdrop to the often colorful and largely abstract work the gallery favors. With a commitment to promoting Mexican contemporary painting and printmaking, Galería La Pérgola also hosts an annual exhibition entitled "Modern Mexican Masters," which showcases the work of celebrated national artists like Rufino Tamayo and Pedro Coronel.

Occupying the southeast corner of the Instituto Allende, **Yam Gallery** (Instituto Allende, Ancha de San Antonio 20, Int. 1, tel. 415/150-6052, http://yamgallery.com, 11 A.M.–5 P.M. Mon.–Sat.) is a unique space that has distinguished itself through a series of original (and even controversial) contemporary exhibitions. In 2006, Yam made international news for exhibiting 20 works on paper by Donald Johnson, a prisoner in solitary confinement at Pelican Bay State Prison in California. More recently, the gallery has shown work by emerging Mexico City artists, Chilean masters, and experimental photographers. One the town's most popular galleries, Yam's opening events are packed and raucous. In addition to artwork, Yam Gallery represents a prestigious collection of silver jewelry from the hands and workshop of Taxco master William Spratling.

Born in Florence, Italy, but raised in Mexico, artist and architect Pedro Friedeberg was one of the country's most prominent artists of the 20th century. When Friedeberg moved to San Miguel de Allende, he redecorated the colonial interior of **Casa Diana** (Recreo 48, tel. 415/152-0885, www.casa-diana.com, 10 A.M.–2 P.M. and 4–7 P.M. daily, closed Wednesday and Sunday afternoons), which now houses an art gallery in the downstairs living spaces. The gallery is open to the public and hosts rotating exhibitions of local artwork, with an emphasis on sculpture. Friedeberg is one of the gallery's permanent artists. Needless to say, Friedeberg's unique decoration is one of the main reasons to visit Casa Diana, where you can see his imagination at work, as well as some of his iconic hand-chairs.

One of the first spaces to open in the Fábrica La Aurora, **Galería/Atelier** (Fábrica La Aurora, Calzada de la Aurora s/n, cell tel. 415/151-8665, U.S. tel. 917/720-8377, http://galeriaatelier.com, 11 A.M.–6 P.M. Mon.–Fri., 11 A.M.–4 P.M. Sat.) is a small but gracious contemporary art gallery, representing painters, sculptors, jewelers, and printmakers from the greater San Miguel area, as well as work by American, Japanese, French, and Chilean artists. Like many exhibition spaces in the Fábrica La Aurora, Galería/Atelier retains the rustic charms of the factory's former days, with substantial stone floors and high ceilings that make a nice backdrop for the gallery's collection of contemporary art. Large barrel drums that once held spindles of fabric now serve as display cases for sculpture and jewelry. The gallery's exhibition schedule is ambitious, with new individual or collective exhibitions every month or two. Openings often coincide with the monthly Art Walk at La Aurora, and are always well attended.

Right across from Galería/Atelier, the **Generator Gallery** (Fábrica La Aurora, Calzada de la Aurora s/n, Local 14A, tel. 415/154-9588, www.generatorgallery.org, 10 A.M.–6 P.M. Mon.–Sat., 11 A.M.–3 P.M. Sun.) is one of the largest artist-owned cooperative spaces in San Miguel de Allende. Featuring the work of more than 25 painters, sculptors, ceramicists, and jewelers, the work at Generator is very diverse. The gallery itself is divided into two spaces: a long, white-walled room exhibits large-format paintings and ceramics, while a smaller and funkier room shows jewelry design, smaller sculpture, and drawing. The smaller room once held the Fábrica's power generator—hence the gallery's name.

In addition to galleries, numerous working artists have studio space in the **Fábrica La Aurora,** many of which are open to the public. While their hours vary, most of the Aurora's artists hold open studios 10 A.M.–5 P.M. on Thursday. If you'd prefer to view artwork accompanied by a glass of wine, the Fábrica La Aurora also hosts an Art Walk on the first Friday of each month.

ANTIQUES

The opulence of 17th and 18th century San Miguel left behind its share of spoils. Today, the former finery from old haciendas and colonial mansions often turns up in dusty antique

shops around town. While the number of antiques is beginning to dwindle, those interested in vintage wares will find good places to buy them in town, in addition to antique popular art and pottery.

Bazaar is an apt description of the atmosphere at **Bazaar Unicornio** (Hernández Macías 80, tel. 415/152-1306, 11 A.M.–7 P.M. Mon.–Sat.), a big and rambling store with dusty antiques and popular crafts. Perhaps the store's most impressive feature is the large collection of old ceremonial masks covering an entire wall of the covered patio. Sought out in small towns from Guerrero to Chiapas, these masks are remarkably diverse, at times comic, and incredibly original. There is also a nice collection of new ceremonial masks in one of the adjoining rooms (however, an older mask that has been used in a ceremony generally has a greater emotional significance and higher market value than a new piece). Beyond the masks, the store has a quirky collection of vintage furniture, old wood toys, trinkets, and silver jewelry. There is absolutely no artfulness in the presentation, but dedicated antiques hunters will certainly find some treasures here.

It is easy to walk right past the little storefront, so keep an eye out for **La Calaca** (Mesones 93, tel. 415/152-3954, 11 A.M.–2 P.M. and 4–6:30 P.M. Mon.–Sat.), which specializes in antique popular and ceremonial art from around Mexico. The store's owner, Evita, has been trading *artesanías* for more than 25 years, and her experience has helped compile a lovely collection of masks, platters, ceramics, textiles, and other special objects that wear their age with dignity. A dim little spot on a bustling street, this tiny store is a good place to find a special piece for your home and to hear a little bit about its history from Evita.

Stepping through the door of **La Buhardilla** (Local 4A, Fábrica La Aurora, Calzada de la Aurora s/n, tel. 415/154-9911, 10 A.M.–6 P.M. Mon.–Sat., 11 A.M.–3 P.M. Sun.) is almost like stepping into another world. Inside this vast and artful shop in the Fábrica La Aurora, the walls are covered with antique masks and old oil paintings, vintage lamps swing from the ceiling, and worn but beautiful carpets cover the floors. Owned by experienced antiques dealers and restoration experts from Monterrey, Mexico, La Buhardilla is one of the best places to browse fine Mexican antiques in town. In recent years, the shop has also been at the center of an international controversy, after it announced the possession of a chest full of artifacts from artist Frida Kahlo's home, a collection that is yet unrecognized by Kahlo experts.

Also in the Fábrica La Aurora, **Cantadora** (Local 3A, Fábrica La Aurora, Calzada de la Aurora s/n, tel. 415/154-8302, www.cantadorasma.com, 10 A.M.–6 P.M. Mon.–Sat.) has some antiques of the monumental variety, like old stone urns, decorative pillars, and large wooden saints. They also carry antique ceramics, toys, chests, and ceremonial masks. One of the first shops you'll see inside the Fábrica La Aurora, Cantadora uses the factory's former architecture to its advantage. Soaring ceilings and bright but indirect light make this showroom particularly lovely.

ART SUPPLIES

For paints, brushes, canvases, colored pencils, drawing paper, notebooks, and other artistic necessities, head to **Lagundi's: La Esquina de Arte** (Umarán 17, tel. 415/152-0830, 10 A.M.–2 P.M. and 4–8 P.M. Mon.–Sat.). In addition to art supplies, Lagundi's also mats and frames artwork at a reasonable cost. If you are desperate for a copy of *Vanity Fair* or the *New Yorker,* Lagundi's has a large newsstand, with a pricey but impressive assortment of international magazines.

A favorite with locals for its good selection and low prices, **El Pato** (Margarito Ledesma 19, Col. Guadalupe, tel. 415/152-1543, Pato199@prodigy.net.mx, 9 A.M.–3 P.M. and 4–8 P.M. Mon.–Sat.) is a well-stocked art supply store in the Guadalupe neighborhood, about a 10-minute walk from the central square. Here, you can stock up on inexpensive national and imported oil, acrylic, and watercolor paint, a variety of natural bristle and synthetic brushes, canvases and frames, notebooks, drawing pads, pencils, pastels, linseed oil, and other essential art supplies. El Pato also has a small but good selection of heavy stock paper, sold by the sheet.

BOOKSTORES

For artistic inspiration, **Librería La Deriva** (Local 6A, Fábrica La Aurora, Calzada de la Aurora s/n, tel. 415/154-5076, libreriaderiva@yahoo.com, 10 A.M.–6 P.M. Mon.–Sat., 11 A.M.–3 P.M. Sun., and Correo 24, tel. 415/152-8809, 11 A.M.–7 P.M. Mon.–Sat.) has a large and well-chosen selection of glossy art books, with a strong focus on Mexican and Latin American artists. They also carry colorful children's books in Spanish. Though visual art is the bookstore's specialty, there is also a very nice selection of literature in Spanish. Ask the store's friendly owners, who often tend the shops, if you'd like a recommendation. If you already have plenty of reading material, La Deriva is also a nice place to pick up a paper gift, like a flipbook, calendar, or handmade journal.

El Tecolote (Jesús 11, tel. 415/152-7395, tecolotebooks@yahoo.com, 10 A.M.–6 P.M. Tues.–Sat., 10 A.M.–2 P.M. Sun.) has the largest selection of English-language books in San Miguel de Allende, with a good collection of contemporary literary fiction and popular fiction, as well as books on home design and interiors, Mexican history and culture, and spirituality. There is also a small collection of literature in Spanish and some good children's books. You can buy the newspaper, *Atención San Miguel,* at El Tecolote on Friday mornings, which often draws a large crowd of expatriates.

Located in the Centro Cultural El Nigromante (Bellas Artes), the bookstore **Educal** (Hernández Macías 75, tel. 415/154-9179, www.educal.com.mx, 9 A.M.–7 P.M. Mon.–Sat., 10 A.M.–2 P.M. Sun.) is operated by CONACULTA, the Mexican government's department of art and culture. This small store sells numerous titles from CONACULTA's own press, principally covering art and international literature, written in or translated into Spanish (almost all titles at this small but well-stocked bookstore are in Spanish). There is also a small collection of world music for sale.

Sports and Recreation

With its leisurely pace, near-perfect climate, and breathtaking architecture, it is easy to give in to San Miguel's relaxing atmosphere—except that it's so hard to sit still! There is always something to do in San Miguel, whether it's horseback riding through desert canyons or relaxing away the morning in natural hot springs. It' not a place for adventure sports or extreme activities; many folks choose to while away their vacation with a book and a margarita, while others spend their days on the golf course or the tennis court.

If you don't mind traveling a bit outside of San Miguel for the sake of soaking away the day, head about 13 kilometers (eight miles) north from San Miguel, to the town of Atotonilco. The surrounding region is famous for its natural, nonsulfurous hot springs.

YOGA AND MEDITATION

LifePath Center (Pila Seca 11, tel. 415/154-8465, U.S. tel. 214/432-5711, www.lifepathretreats.com) is a multifaceted center for wellness, healing, and personal growth, owned and operated by a collective of alternative practitioners. Located in a quirky colonial home, the center has many comfortable consult and massage rooms, where a range of therapists offer counseling, body work, and alternative therapies, like acupuncture, craniosacral therapy, massage, naturopathy, counseling, and reflexology. The good vibes begin as soon as Sophie, the sweet cocker spaniel on-site, greets you at the door. Classes and therapies are open to visitors, and there is a large, peaceful room for yoga, Pilates, and Qigong classes. In addition, LifePath welcomes people to plan a retreat at their center; they have three pretty guest rooms that are designed for people who would like to participate in or give classes or workshops.

At **Centro Shakti Yoga** (Ancha de San Antonio 9, 2nd floor, cell tel. 415/113-7061, www.yogasanmiguel.com.mx), Rodney Yee–certified teacher Tanya Kawan teaches Hatha Vinyasa and Power Yoga several times a week,

with both morning and evening classes. Tanya's serene nature and flowing breath-oriented classes are a favorite with many expatriates. Classes cost about US$7 for drop-ins, but multiple classes can be purchased at a discount.

Yoga San Miguel (Terraplén 34, tel. 415/119-1808, www.yogasanmiguel.com) offers beginning and intermediate yoga classes in the Iyengar tradition. In addition to classes by Yoga San Miguel's regular teacher, Margaretta, there are occasionally guest-taught workshops at the school's small studio on Terraplén. Yoga San Miguel shares a very similar website address to Centro Shakti Yoga, but they are two different studios. For drop-ins, classes cost about US$8.

The friendly **Meditation Center of San Miguel** (Callejón Blanco 4, www.meditationsma.org) provides three sitting meditation sessions Monday–Friday, at 8 A.M., 8:50 A.M., and 5 P.M., plus a single session on Saturday at 10 A.M. There are also several weekly yoga classes offered in the center's mellow main room. The center is Buddhist-oriented though non-denominational, and participants are welcome to practice any form of still, silent mediation. There is also a simple, inexpensive guesthouse behind the meditation room, which is open to guests who wish to visit San Miguel and participate in the Meditation Center's programs.

SPAS

San Miguel de Allende begs you to relax. But if stress persists, despite the soothing sunlight and strong margaritas, it may be time to visit one of the many day spas in San Miguel de Allende.

You do not have to stay at the Casa de Sierra Nevada to enjoy a bit of its luxury. The lovely little **Laja Spa** (Hospicio 13, tel. 415/154-4338, www.casadesierranevada.com) is in yet another colonial property owned by the hotel. The spa offers facials, manicures and pedicures, massages, and body treatments, like herbal body wraps. In line with San Miguel's rather new-agey outlook, they also offer reiki and reflexology treatments, as well as massage packages incorporating aromatherapy. The atmosphere is comfortable and attractive; treatments are given in cozy little rooms with low lighting, warm ceramic tile floors, and air-conditioning, and all are stocked with clean linens and fresh white towels.

The low-key atmosphere at **Jasmine Day Spa** (Jesús 25A, tel. 415/152-7973, www.jasminedayspasma.com, 10 A.M.–6 P.M. Mon.–Sat.) feels pleasantly in tune with the casual vibe of San Miguel de Allende. The simple spa rooms are cozy and painted bright colors, comfortable though nothing fancy. Treatments include Swedish, shiatsu, and deep-tissue massage, manicures and pedicures, facials, and body scrubs. Deep-tissue massage is a particular specialty of the spa. For a single treatment, prices are very reasonable.

At the very back of the Plaza Vista Hermosa, **Vital** (Cuna Allende 11, tel. 415/154-5167, 10 A.M.–6 P.M. Mon., Tues., and Thurs.–Sun., 10 A.M.–3 P.M. Wed.) offers beauty and health treatments in their small spa facilities, including facials, massage, manicures, pedicures, and body wraps, all at reasonable prices. The spa specializes in facials and massage, which they can combine with more unusual services, like chakra alignment and hot rock treatments. In all treatments, Vital uses a Mexican product line made from natural and some organic ingredients. The staff is friendly, though hours can be a bit inconsistent.

For manicures and pedicures, San Miguel's ladies love **Esteto Clínica María Ofelia** (Zacateros 50, tel. 415/152-2935, 10 A.M.–6 P.M. Mon.–Sat.), a small and cozy but highly professional salon, which offers waxing, facials, and reflexology treatments, in addition to attending your fingers and toes. A friendly businesswoman, María Ofelia oversees a small team of professional estheticians.

In addition to their other services, **LifePath Center** (Pila Seca 11, tel. 415/154-8465) has four massage therapists, each with different specialties. Treatments are given in a lovely and private massage room, with glass doors shaded by a leafy courtyard.

GYMS AND FITNESS

For a workout, **San Miguel Health & Fitness Center** (Plaza Pueblito, Stirling Dickinson 28, tel. 415/154-8395, 6:30 A.M.–9 P.M. Mon.–Fri., 8 A.M.–2 P.M. Sat.) is a small but well-equipped gym with weights and aerobic machines, plus steam bath and shower facilities. Check with the front desk for their schedule of classes, which includes Pilates, yoga, and zumba. Membership costs about US$40 per month.

Located in the Atascadero neighborhood, the friendly **Santa Domingo Health Club** (Santo Domingo 55, tel. 415/154-7545, 7 A.M.–2 P.M. and 4–8 P.M. Mon.–Fri., 7 A.M.–2 P.M. Sat.) has a well-stocked gym with aerobic and weight machines, plus a lightly heated 25-meter pool. They offer swimming classes for adults and children in the afternoons. Monthly membership is about US$50, but you can also join for a single day for about US$5.

Upbeat, positive, and a bit of a task master, **Sue Lawrence** (Guadiana 21, Col. Guadiana, tel. 415/152-2969, cell tel. 415/149-0176) is a certified Pilates instructor offering one- and two-person classes in her private studio. She also will also make house calls at a slightly higher cost.

TENNIS

Weber Tennis Courts (Callejón de San Antonio 12, Col. San Antonio, tel. 415/152-0659 www.sanmigueltennis.com, sunrise–sunset daily) has three clay tennis courts, popular with locals, both Mexican and expatriate. Courts are open to the public by reservation (though walk-ins are also welcome). If you want to improve your backhand, Weber's will also help set up private lessons.

A large inn on the Ancha de San Antonio, **Hotel Posada La Aldea** (Ancha de San Antonio 15, tel. 415/152-1022, cell tel. 415/109-1754, 8 A.M.–7 P.M. Mon.–Sat.) rents clay tennis courts by the hour. In addition, there are three tennis professionals who give private lessons at the hotel.

GOLF

San Miguel's oldest course, **Club de Golf Malanquín** (Carretera San Miguel-Celaya, Km 3, tel. 415/152-0516 or 415/154-8210, www.malanquin.com.mx) maintains a lovely and well-groomed nine-hole golf course, right on the edge of town. During the weekdays, greens fees are inexpensive, with additional discounts after 2 P.M. If you want to practice your stroke, the club's two excellent golf pros offer beginning, intermediate, and advanced golf clinics throughout the week. Membership will give you access to the club's tennis courts, swimming pool, steam bath, clubhouse, restaurant, and coffee shop. For tennis players, the club also rents courts by the hour.

The newer **Ventanas de San Miguel Golf & Resort** (Carretera Dolores-San Miguel, Km 1.5, tel. 415/154-9394, www.ventanasdesanmiguel.net) has a large 18-hole Nick Faldo Championship Course, plus a number of lots and residences for sale. The course is open and has hosted several golf tournaments, but the resort's development is still in process. To date, there is no clubhouse or other facilities.

BULLFIGHTS

Bullfighting originally came to Mexico with the Spanish settlers, though it did not gain popularity throughout all of New Spain. In the Bajío region, however, there is long tradition of bullfighting, dating back to the 17th and 18th centuries. According to local history, Ignacio Allende was a fan of the bullfights and even confronted the beasts himself.

For those interested in attending a *corrida de toros* (bullfight), San Miguel de Allende's centrally located **Plaza de Toros** (Recreo 52, no tel.) hosts live bullfights annually, sometimes bringing well-known matadors to the arena. If you have never been to a bullfight before, this plaza will provide a rather intense introduction. With a capacity of just 3,000, this bullring is rather small, so the battle is up close and personal. Here, bullfighting season is generally confined to the months of September, November, December, and January. Look for the large posters announcing the upcoming

corrida de toros. Events rarely sell out; you can buy tickets at the door.

ORGANIZED TOURS
Hiking, Biking, and Horseback Riding

A friendly, family-run tour group, **Coyote Canyon Adventures** (tel. 415/154-4193, cell 415/153-5005, www.coyotecanyonadventures.com) leads half-day and full-day horseback riding tours in the beautiful ranchland around the Cañada de la Virgen ecological preserve. The day of your scheduled outing, someone from the team will pick you and your group up in San Miguel and take you out to the country. Beautiful scenery and fun but manageable rides characterize this tour group. These country trips are suitable for children, and one of the lead cowboy's daughters will often accompany the tour. While horseback riding is Coyote Canyon's specialty, they also offer hiking and camping tours, biking, and nature walks. Prices range from US$85 per person for a half-day tour to around US$200 for an overnight trip.

Bici-Burro (Hospicio 1, tel. 415/152-1526, www.bici-burro.com, 9 A.M.–2 P.M. and 4–7 P.M. Mon.–Fri., 9 A.M.–2 P.M. Sat.) is a family-run bike shop and tour operator, leading both hiking and off-road biking trips in the countryside around San Miguel de Allende. Some of the bicycle tours will take you along the former silver route (which was used to bring goods to and from San Miguel during the colonial era) and out to the beautiful Santuario de Atotonilco. It is a great way to see the countryside while also checking out some of San Miguel's cultural sights. A six-hour tour runs about US$65 per person, including the rental of an aluminum mountain bike, helmet, gloves, and tour guide.

Friendly **Aventuras Sol y Luna** (Hospicio 10, tel. 415/154-8599, aventurasolyluna@hotmail.com, 10 A.M.–7 P.M. Mon.–Sat.) runs full-day horseback riding and mountain biking excursions to the countryside around San Miguel de Allende for about US$50–55 per person. They also run ATV tours for about

Horseback riding tours are a fun way to explore the Bajío.

double that price. If you want to go farther afield, Aventuras Sol y Luna will arrange tours to the neighboring towns of Guanajuato or Pozos, or farther away to Oaxaca—or even Guatemala or Cuba! Stop by their office on Hospicio for more information about their guided tours.

Bird-Watching

Mexico's only Audubon chapter, **Sociedad Audubon de México** (Box 414B c/o La Conexión, Aldama 3, www.audubonmex. org) runs an ongoing series of bird walks around San Miguel de Allende, El Charco del Ingenio, and the area around the Allende dam, where you can spot ducks, shovelers, hawks, kites, egrets, and many other beautiful bird species. If you have a little more time, the Audubon Society also leads hiking trips to ecological reserves near San Miguel de Allende, a great way to see the countryside and learn more about the region's feathered friends. If you are going to be in Mexico for an extended stay, check with the Audubon Society about longer trips to see the monarch butterfly migration in Michoacán or bird-watching on the Mexican coast.

Hot-Air Ballooning

You can get a whole new perspective on San Miguel's sandstone domes and winding streets from the air above. The fortunate folks who've taken a hot-air balloon ride with **Jay Kimball** (cell tel. 415/114-2174, US$185 pp) always come back giddy with exhilaration. You must book ahead to save the date; Kimball will notify you where to meet him on the morning of your tour. The balloon's course and its launch point depend on the day's winds, so prepare to be flexible. The balloon can take as few as two and as many as twelve people in its flying basket. Bring your camera!

Language and Education

San Miguel de Allende is a friendly and livable town, making it an excellent place to spend a few weeks, a few months, or even a few years studying language and arts, or pursuing new hobbies.

SPANISH LANGUAGE

Serious students should take a look at the excellent and centrally located **Academia Hispano Americana** (AHA, Mesones 4, tel. 415/152-0349, www.ahaspeakspanish.com), the oldest Spanish school in San Miguel de Allende and one of the best. Throughout the year, AHA offers intensive and semi-intensive Spanish curricula, which include grammar, pronunciation, and Spanish-language lectures on Mexican culture. New sessions begin each month, and class size is capped at 12. The school will also arrange for students to stay in the homes of local families, where they can eat, sleep, and keep practicing their Spanish. Each season, AHA also runs a series of informative cultural field trips to nearby towns like Querétaro and Guanajuato. College students can earn credit at AHA, which is associated with the University of Guanajuato.

A popular and effective language school with a proprietary system of Spanish instruction, **Warren Hardy Spanish School** (San Rafael 6, tel. 415/154-4017, warrenhardy.com) offers intensive, half-day courses, which are designed to ramp up your Spanish as quickly as possible. Students must purchase the series of Warren Hardy books and CDs, which complement in-class work. Classes start continuously throughout the year and are very popular with American and Canadian expatriates. This school is not only a great place to brush up your *español*, it is also a great place to make new friends in San Miguel.

A family-run language school, **Instituto Habla Hispana** (Calzada de la Luz 25, tel. 415/152-0713, www.mexicospanish.com) offers month-long intensive language programs throughout the year. Typically, Spanish programs include 20 hours of classroom instruction per week with cultural activities, like walking tours and cooking classes, during the afternoon. Upon arrival, students are tested and placed at a class appropriate to their level. While studying at Habla Hispana, students may choose to stay in the simple, inexpensive accommodations on the school's campus, or the school can arrange for students to stay with a local family. Most of the year, Habla Hispana's students are principally adults and seniors; however, in the summer months, the school enrolls a range of ages.

ART, PHOTOGRAPHY, AND JEWELRY

The historic art school at the **Centro Cultural Ignacio Ramírez** (Hernández Macías 75, tel. 415/152-0289) offers instruction in painting, printmaking, puppetry, ceramics, and loom weaving, among other disciplines. Run by the Mexican government's Instituto Nacional de Bellas Artes (National Fine Arts Institute), classes are high quality and tuition is incredibly reasonable. Here, the tiny classrooms were once nuns' cloisters, and the quirky atmosphere adds to the charm. Note: In 2011, the Centro Cultural Ignacio Ramírez suffered serious structural damage. As of press time, it is closed indefinitely for repairs and no date of reopening has been announced. When the center is open, registration is done in person. Often the most popular disciplines, like loom weaving and ceramics, have a waiting list.

The **Instituto Allende** (Ancha de San Antonio 22, tel. 415/152-4538, www.instituto-allende.edu.mx) is one of the country's oldest art academies, and many of San Miguel's artists have taken (or taught) a class or two there. Many well-loved teachers have left the school in recent years, but the Instituto Allende continues to offer short-term classes to visitors through the School of Arts and Handcrafts, including jewelry-making, digital photography, drawing, and painting.

The Instituto Allende is one of the oldest art academies in Mexico.

For serious instruction in jewelry creation and design, **Sterling Quest** (Guty Cardenas 3, Col. Guadalupe, tel. 415/100-8948, sterling-questschool.com) offers three ongoing small-group workshops, with class size capped at six. Spirited instructor Billy King has been teaching silverwork for more than 20 years, and he is a talented jeweler himself. His exacting style receives high praise from former students, many of whom later become professional jewelers themselves.

Run by a local artist, the **Ana Julia Aguado Gallery** (Plaza Principal 18, tel. 415/103-0228, galeriaanajuliaaguado@gmail.com) offers evening life-drawing sessions (sometimes with wine!) on her second-floor gallery overlooking the town square. There is no drawing instruction per se, but attendees have access to several hours with a live model for a reasonable price. Stop by the gallery to ask for details, or look for advertisements in the newspaper, *Atención San Miguel.* An associate at Galería Izamal, **Henry Vermillon** (Calle Atascadero, Callejón Sin Salida 14, tel. 415/152-6171, henryavermillon@yahoo.com), also offers drop-in life drawing classes on Thursday nights, as well as private classes on the fundamentals of drawing, per request.

Author and photographer of the well-loved books, *The Doors of San Miguel* and *Behind the Doors of San Miguel,* **Robert de Gast** (tel. 415/152-7396 or 443/321-8727, www.robertde-gast.com) gives private workshops and full-day photo tours, teaching both the technical and creative aspects of photography. De Gast is also a history buff, so his photo workshops double as historical tours of the region. They can be a great way to explore a small town like Mineral de Pozos. The classes are suitable for both digital and point-and-shoot cameras, amateur and seasoned photographers.

In her small **Atelier** (Tatanacho 8, Col. Guadalupe, tel. 415/154-5953, atelierdeflora-costa.blogspot.com) in the Guadalupe neighborhood, photographer Flor Acosta gives individual workshops in photography technique. An expert in the medium, she will tailor classes to fit a student's interests and experience. She also presents occasional photography exhibitions in the small gallery space downstairs.

In a spacious house adjoining the Fábrica La Aurora, **Gerardo Ruiz** (Casa 4, Fábrica La Aurora, tel. 415/152-6110, www.gerardoruiz.com) gives printmaking, etching, painting, and drawing courses in his large working studio. Students get plenty of individual attention, yet the environment is laid-back and casual. A master printer and a bit of a character, Ruiz has many students who return to work with him year after year. Those with no printmaking experience can get started here, though Ruiz can mentor more experienced printers as well.

German-born artist **Edina Sagert** (Local 8A, Fábrica La Aurora, tel. 415/120-8088, http://edinasagert.com) offers year-round watercolor workshops in her studio at the Fábrica La Aurora, as well as a series of drawing and creativity workshops with her partner, artist **Brian Care** (Local 8A, Fábrica La Aurora, http://briancare.com). Sagert has years of experience teaching watercolor, so these popular small-group classes are appropriate for students of any level. Many return to work with Sagert again. In addition to Sagert and Care's classes, check the Fábrica La Aurora website for a full list of artists offering individual classes.

MUSIC AND DANCE

A multipurpose community and cultural center, **El Sindicato: Casa de Las Artes Éscenicas** (Recreo 4, tel. 415/152-0131, cescenicas@hotmail.com) offers a variety of dance and workout classes at very reasonable prices. Swing by to check the upcoming schedule. Recent classes have included ballet, belly dancing, *danza conchera,* and traditional Mexican dance. For most classes, instruction is in Spanish. Zumba, an energetic aerobic dance class, is particularly popular at El Sindicato.

For instruction in salsa, swing, tango, mambo, foxtrot, waltz, and other classic ballroom dances, the popular **Arthur Murray** (Hernández Macías 68, tel. 415/152-0095, U.S. tel. 302/420-6429, www.arthurmurray.com.mx) will have you up and dancing in the first class. A part of the larger Arthur Murray franchise, this studio draws a consistent crowd of silver foxes and their chic partners for early evening dance instruction and maybe a cocktail. These social dances are all performed in couples, though solo students can sign up and dance with instructors or others sans partner. In addition, the studio offers private dance lessons.

A cultural immersion program for teenagers, **MexArt** (Calzada de la Aurora 48, tel. 415/152-8900, U.S. tel. 202/391-0004, www.gomexart.com) offers three month-long residential summer sessions with an emphasis in visual arts or dance. Art students choose an area of concentration, like painting or ceramics, while dance students take a mix of jazz, modern, and other dance styles. Campers also take conversational Spanish classes every day throughout the summer. Students live at the colorful and comfortable Casa Crayola, a lovely guesthouse that is temporarily refashioned into cozy dormitories. In addition to their studies in art and Spanish, students have the opportunity to take

day trips around Mexico, go horseback riding, and participate in various cultural events in San Miguel de Allende.

COOKING

Many believe that the best Mexican food is homemade. Throughout Mexico, heirloom recipes are passed down through families from generation to generation, and every cook has a slightly different approach to creating a traditional dish. With that in mind, **Marilau Traditional Mexican Cooking School** (Calle de La Luz 12, Col. San Antonio, tel. 415/152-4376, www.traditionalmexicancooking.com.mx) offers Mexican cooking classes to groups of up to 10 people, all taught by the talented Marilau herself. Depending on your interests, Marilau can organize classes based on a menu or based around a theme like salsa, tamales, or soups. With a long culinary tradition in her own family, Marilau shares her own family recipes from central Mexico. Knowledgeable, friendly, and English speaking, she is enthusiastic about sharing Mexican cuisine and culture with those visiting San Miguel.

There are cooking classes every Thursday afternoon at **La Cocina** (El Buen Café, Jesús 36, tel. 415/154-4825, www.mexicocooks.com). Run by Kris Rudolph, cookbook author and chef at the El Buen Café, these weekly culinary classes can accept up to 14 students in a large home kitchen. Classes emphasize innovative new recipes in Mexican cooking, as well as lean and healthy preparations of traditional Mexican foods. Dinner or lunch, margaritas, and copies of the recipes are included in most classes. In addition to the standard class schedule, La Cocina invites guest chefs to give courses on special topics, like chiles rellenos, moles, and *adobados.* This school also offers weeklong culinary tours in Mexico. Three- to four-hour sessions cost US$45–55.

The Casa de Sierra Nevada's beautiful kitchen and gift shop, **Sazón** (Correo 22, tel. 415/154-7671, www.sazon.com), operates ongoing Mexican cooking classes and market tours. Some courses are demonstration only, while others are hands-on (inquire when signing up).

Upcoming classes are announced on their website, or on the small chalkboard in the shop's entryway. Among others, Paco Cardenas and Norma Guerrero, co-owners and pastry chefs at the Petit Four bakery, are among the school's charismatic teachers. The pretty chef's kitchen is right behind the store, overlooking a courtyard with an old stone fountain and creeping vines.

An excellent cook and well-known local personality, Gabriela Green of **La Fonda Rosa** (tel. 415/150-7387, cell tel. 415/119-2195, www.lafondarosa.com), offers Mexican cooking classes with a changing lineup of dishes and menus. For those interested in exploring more unusual recipes, these classes can go beyond basics. Gaby can teach you to make salsa, but she can also instruct you in more unusual

fare, like *huazontle en chile pasilla* (traditional Mexican vegetable stewed in pasilla chili sauce) or *cochinita pibil* (Yucatán-style pulled pork). Classes are three to five hours long, and can be preceded by a market tour on request.

WRITING

Many published and aspiring writers live in San Miguel de Allende. The well-organized **San Miguel Literary Sala** (c/o La Conexión, Aldama 3, tel. 415/185-2225, www.sanmiguelliterarysala.org) offers monthly literary readings, a book discussion group, and a summer literary festival. The Literary Sala also organizes the annual writers conference each winter, which brings big names in fiction to speak to the San Miguel community.

Accommodations

There is a wide range of accommodations in San Miguel de Allende, with something to fit every style and budget. Visiting San Miguel is very much about relaxing, and hotels in almost every price range will cater to the laid-back atmosphere with lovely gardens and comfortable common spaces. You don't have to pay a bundle to get warm service or a good location near the town square. Not surprisingly, however, the more money you spend, the more luxurious your hotel will be. In fact, some of San Miguel's beautiful boutique hotels are a destination in and of themselves.

San Miguel has a tendency to attract creative minds, and as such, every bed-and-breakfast, posada, or hotel has its own individual character. For romantic travelers, San Miguel has its share of dark and creaky ex-haciendas, while modern junkies can sleep in sleek accommodations with iPod docks and flat-screen TVs. Some hotels are decorated with original art and traditional *artesanía,* while others are decked out with vintage furnishings and hand-painted tile.

San Miguel attracts tourists throughout the year, with the largest number of foreign

visitors coming to town between December and April, its high season. There is also a great deal of national tourism during Holy Week, Independence Day, and during the Christmas holidays. In some cases, hotels may raise their rates 10–15 percent during the winter months or during holidays, though the majority maintain the same rates year-round. Prices listed below are typical for a double room during San Miguel's high season.

UNDER US$50

In the blocks surrounding the town square, there are numerous casual hotels that cater to budget travelers. For a very low price, you can find a clean and centrally located crash pad, sometimes just a block or two from the *jardín.* While budget accommodations may not be the most luxurious, some are surprisingly pleasant, boasting roof decks or common courtyards, as well as excellent central locations. In almost every budget hotel, some bedrooms are nicer, lighter, or quieter than others. When you check in, ask to see a few different options.

Popular with young backpackers and solo travelers, the centrally located **Hostal Alcatraz**

(Relox 54, tel. 415/152-8543, US$11 pp) is one of the few youth hostels in San Miguel de Allende. Single-sex dorm rooms are clean, though a bit cramped, and bathrooms are shared. Guests can also make use of the communal kitchen downstairs, lockers, and the computers with Internet access. The friendly owners are happy to give tips about the town, and the location is excellent. Just five minutes away, the same family manages the **Hostel Inn** (Calzada de la Luz 31A, tel. 415/154-6727, hotelinnmexico@yahoo.com, US$32), which has both shared and private rooms for two, three, or four people. The accommodations here are simple and utilitarian—and even if you rent a double, it's still outfitted like a dorm room with three or four beds to choose from! However, the hotel is very clean, the staff is warm and friendly, and there are lots of shared facilities to make your trip to San Miguel easy and inexpensive, including free wireless Internet, a shared kitchen, a washing machine, and a living area to lounge in.

The small rooms at **El Hotelito** (Hidalgo 18, tel. 415/152-7711, US$25) are not particularly beautiful, but they are just cozy and comfortable enough to make this place a great value. Private bedrooms are decorated with thick curtains and aging cotton bedspreads, but each has a private bath and shower, a television, and big closets. Downstairs, rooms are rather dark. However, the hotel's upper floors are actually quite pretty, with nice terraces overlooking the surrounding rooftops. You can hardly get a better location than El Hotelito, just a few blocks from the *jardín* on Hidalgo, but set back from the noise and bustle of the street.

A great option in the lowest price range, **Parador San Sebastián de Aparicio** (Mesones 7, tel. 415/152-7084, US$28) is located on the most easterly block of Mesones, right past the Plaza Cívica and around the corner from the municipal market. The hotel's 30 guest rooms are nothing fancy but they are nonetheless spacious and clean, with old wooden furnishings and small private bathrooms with showers. Bottom-floor rooms are a bit dark but have windows overlooking the

hotel's sunny courtyard, surrounded by archways and hanging vines. Ask to see more than one room at check-in and then pick the best available. The reception desk can be a bit lackadaisical, but for this price, it's easy to overlook the drawbacks of this budget hotel. Parking is included in the cost.

Located on a small and dusty street in the residential Allende neighborhood, **Casita de las Flores** (Calle de las Flores, Col. Allende, tel. 415/117-7223, www.casitadelasflores.com, US$50) has five small guest rooms with shared bath surrounding a tranquil central courtyard. It can be a challenge to find this place the first time around, but once you make your reservations, the managers will send you a map with detailed directions. Rooms are small but clean and comfortable, with painted walls, tin-framed mirrors, and Mexican bedspreads. In the small communal kitchen, each guest has their own basket to store food, as well as their own shelf in the refrigerator. Though the managers are friendly, the guesthouse is rather self-service and 20 minutes from the *centro histórico*; it is best for fairly independent travelers.

US$50-100

With a little more cash, you can buy a lot more charm. While still relatively inexpensive, hotels in this price range offer more than just a place to rest your head. Downtown, the historic **Hotel Posada de las Monjas** (Canal 37, tel. 415/152-0171, www.posadalasmonjas.com, US$48–62) does not offer San Miguel's most luxurious accommodations, but it is certainly among the town's best values. This sprawling ex-convent presides over lower Canal Street, ideally located just a block and a half from the main plaza. Carpeted rooms are minimally decorated—they were once the residence of nuns, after all—but they are comfortable enough to crash in. When you arrive, ask to see a few available rooms: Some have beautiful views of the *parroquia* and semiprivate balconies. The nightly price includes a basic breakfast and, for those with wheels, parking.

In a quiet residential neighborhood not far from the *centro histórico,* the **Guadiana Bed** and **Breakfast** (Mezquite 11, Col. Guadiana, tel. 415/152-5171, US$48–52) is a friendly and reasonably priced place to call home. Spacious guest rooms have big windows, queen beds, and plenty of light. For US$5 extra, you can request a room with a king-sized bed. Rooms surround a central atrium, and guest room windows overlook a quiet street or a small park behind the hotel. This low-key neighborhood is one of the quietest in town, and a relatively easy walk to Parque Juárez and the *centro histórico*. Rates for a double may go up to about US$65 during the Christmas holidays or during other important festivals; however, they also may drop during the low season. Hotel staff is incredibly friendly, and the nightly price includes a small continental breakfast.

Unless you are rather spry, getting to and from **Casa Frida** (Cuesta de Loreto 24, tel. 415/152-7518, www.casafrida2.net, US$65–80) can be a bit of a challenge. However, if you don't mind making use of San Miguel's many taxis, the rooms at this hilltop bed-and-breakfast are very spacious, clean, comfortable, and reasonably priced. Accompanying bathrooms are decorated with pretty colored tiles, and some have tubs. The Matisse room is particularly nice, with a private balcony and a pretty view of the city below. Downstairs, breakfast is served in the shared dining room (it's included in the price), and there are several common areas for relaxing. The largest suite also has a private sitting area with a table and chairs. However, given its location, Casa Frida is best for visitors who plan to spend most of their days in town, heading back to the hotel for a good night's rest.

At **C Casa Crayola** (Calzada de la Aurora 48, tel. 415/152-8900, U.S. tel. 202/391-0004, casacrayolasanmiguel.com, US$75), proprietor Carly Cross says that she designed her bed-and-breakfast to feel like the places she likes to stay when she travels, at the prices she wants to pay. The result is spacious and comfortable guest rooms at surprisingly low rates. Here, seven large suites (casitas) surround a pretty courtyard with a stone fountain, leafy trees, and a fishpond. Large, comfortable, and cheerfully

decorated, each suite is painted with bright colors and adorned with Mexican crafts. They are all illuminated by ample windows and fully equipped with comfy beds and a small kitchen. The location on the Calzada de la Aurora is a few steps farther from the town square, but right across the street from the Fábrica La Aurora Art and Design Center.

On the eastern edge of San Miguel de Allende, the historic **Rancho Hotel Atascadero** (Prol. Santo Domingo s/n, tel. 415/152-0206 or toll-free Mex. tel. 800/466-0000, www.hotelatascadero.com, US$95–120) is on the grounds of a sprawling ex-hacienda, originally constructed in the 1880s. The property has changed hands many times, belonging once to a famous bullfighter, Pepe Ortiz, and later to a Peruvian scholar (and founder of the Instituto Allende), Felipe Cossío de Pomar. As a hotel, the Rancho Atascadero has been in business for more than 60 years, and it retains the distinct feeling of a 1950s family-style resort. Rooms are simple affairs, with old, oversized colonial furniture, red tile floors, and woven Mexican bedspreads. They are all equipped with chimneys and televisions, and many have little private balconies that overlook the hotel's verdant gardens. Amid stone fountains and pomegranate trees, the grounds boast a swimming pool, tennis courts, and racquetball for guests. Despite the vintage atmosphere and peaceful setting, the hotel also offers modern amenities like wireless Internet, as well as a shuttle to take guests into the center of San Miguel.

US$100-150

The paradigm of a successful bed-and-breakfast, **C Casa Calderoni** (Callejón del Pueblito 4, tel. 415/154-6005, www.casacalderoni.com, US$110–140) is a cute, centrally located, and reasonably priced place to stay, with comfortable rooms, friendly proprietors, and delicious made-to-order breakfasts. At Casa Calderoni, each bedroom is named after a famous artist, and the decor subtly reflects its namesake. The Diego Rivera room, for example, is gussied up with colorful textiles and serapes, and decorated with several Rivera posters on the wall. No matter which artist you call home, the cozy rooms are all brightly painted and have large beds with fluffy comforters, cute tiled bathrooms with brass sinks, cable TV, and special touches like painted desk lamps and skylights. The hotel's gregarious owners are meticulous about keeping the lodging clean and up-to-date, and the service is friendly and attentive.

A wonderful find just a bit off the beaten path, **Casa de la Noche** (Organos 19, www.casadelanoche.com, US$40–70 double, US$100–140 suites) was once a bordello; today, it is a charming guest house with 14 sunny rooms of varying size and amenities. Working with the unusual structure of the original house and its many nooks and crannies, the proprietor redesigned all the guest rooms with a delightfully colorful touch. For those on a budget, smaller rooms can accommodate two people in a double bed for a very reasonable price. Suites are spacious and have lovely tiled kitchens, comfortable sitting areas, and, often, small patios and pretty views. All rooms are impeccably clean, sunny, and have cute private bathrooms. It is easy to imagine settling in for a long stay in these cozy accommodations and, fortunately, Casa de la Noche offers discounted weekly and monthly rates.

Just a block from the town square, **Casa Carmen** (Correo 31, tel. 415/152-0844, cell tel. 415/103-4066, U.S. tel. 707/799-0083, www.casacarmenhotel.com, US$126–149) is one of San Miguel de Allende's oldest bed-and-breakfasts. With over 50 years in operation, this friendly family establishment makes it easy to imagine the quiet days before San Miguel was a tourist town. The hotel's 10 guest rooms are simple yet charming, with creaky high ceilings, clean bathrooms, and some vintage accessories, like old wood armoires and little glass chandeliers. Suites are more spacious and some are two-story, with a spiral staircase leading up to a creaky loft bed. The pretty Caballeriza Suite in the back patio is housed in the home's former stables. Unique in San Miguel, the cost of the room at Casa Carmen includes both breakfast and a three-course lunch in the hotel's airy dining room. Guests can also relax in the small sitting room or the sunny courtyard.

Located on a quiet corner, **Hotel Hacienda El Santuario** (Terraplén 42, tel. 415/152-1042, www.haciendaelsantuario.com, US$120–138) is a nice choice in its price range. Rooms are large and comfortable, with big white beds, carpeted floors, and chimneys, each surrounding the hotel's sunny and rather unembellished central courtyard. Rooms upstairs receive more light than those downstairs, but otherwise, most offer roughly the same atmosphere. Service is minimal, the courtyard is the only common area, and breakfast, though included, is continental. However, the spacious rooms and quiet yet central location make up for the lack of amenities.

The quirky-creative style at **Casa Luna** (Quebrada 117, tel. 415/152-1117, U.S. tel. 210/200-8758, www.casaluna.com, US$140–175) is quintessential San Miguel. Behind the unassuming door of this brick-red colonial house, there is a charming maze of 14 individually decorated guest rooms, each equipped with a private bath and a chimney for cool winter nights. Many rooms also open onto small private balconies. The decor is warm and eclectic, with lots of traditional Mexican touches, like embroidered textiles and hand-painted wooden chests. Downstairs, an old pepper tree keeps the house shady and cool. Full breakfasts are included in the price and served in the downstairs dining rooms. Common areas are comfortable and attended to by the innkeeper's fuzzy dogs.

Staying in a bed-and-breakfast becomes an experience in itself at **Casa de la Cuesta** (Cuesta de San José, tel. 415/154-4324, www.casadelacuesta.com, US$165), on a bustling residential street above the Mercado Ignacio Ramírez. Entering the house is like entering an oasis of calm, with plant-fringed courtyards and comfortable common areas. Throughout this colonial home, the owners' passion for traditional Mexican craft is amply reflected in the decoration, where clay figurines, ceremonial masks, and ceramic urns artfully complement the cozy atmosphere. From many of the shared spaces, as well as some of the guest rooms, there are views of downtown. Guest rooms are decorated with crafts and traditional textiles, painted in bright colors, and equipped with king-sized beds. Private baths are decorated with hand-painted tile. Breakfast is served in a traditional Mexican kitchen downstairs, adjoined by a common dining area, and guests are attended by the inn's charming and gracious owners, who take a personal interest in each visitor's San Miguel experience.

The large 18th-century mansion that houses the **Hotel Posada Carmina** (Cuna de Allende 7, tel. 415/152-8888, www.posadacarmina. com, US$125) seems to have been trapped in time. Spacious and sparely decorated rooms retain a lot of the mansion's original charms, with little luxury but plenty of character. The impossibly high, wood-beamed ceilings and thick white walls attest to the building's age. All the rooms in the old mansion are the same price, but their size, furnishings, and view can be quite different, so ask to see a few at check in. The best bedrooms overlook the *parroquia* from a small private balcony, though be aware that these rooms can also be noisy at night.

Villa Mirasol (Pila Seca 35, tel. 415/152-6685, www.villamirasolhotel.com, US$90–135) is a simple, well-located hotel. Carpeted guest rooms and suites are not particularly luxurious, but they are clean, modern, and comfortable, with large bathrooms and nice throw rugs. Some have small sitting areas while others have two double beds. There is cable TV and telephone in every room, wireless Internet service throughout the hotel, and nightly rates include breakfast. Upstairs, there is a small terrace for guests with a table and chairs.

US$150-250

The spacious terraced gardens at ◖ **Posada Corazón** (Aldama 9, tel. 415/152-0182, www. posadacorazon.com, US$145–165) are filled with distinguished trees and gurgling fountains. From the branches above, birds tweet merrily while friendly cats lounge lazily on the flagstone paths below. The inn itself—situated

© ARTURO MEADE

Beautiful and well-tended gardens hide behind the doorway of Posada Corazón, a cozy inn.

toward the back of the property—is a woody 1960s construction containing six comfortable and light-filled guest rooms. Decor is tastefully minimalist, with wood-beamed ceilings, white beds, and natural fiber carpets on the floor. There are no televisions, telephones, or radios in the rooms; the hotel is designed to feel like a retreat, and it does. Bathrooms are clean and beautiful, some with stone tubs, others with colorful tiles. The cost of a room includes a delicious morning breakfast, with a filling and largely organic menu. In fact, much of the produce is plucked directly from the posada's gardens. Just behind the town square on quiet Calle Aldama, Posada Corazón's location is perfectly central yet surprisingly peaceful.

Tucked behind an unassuming facade on the quietest block of Calle Recreo, **Susurro** (Recreo 78, tel. 415/152-1065, cell tel. 415/153-3129, U.S. tel. 310/943-7163, www.susurro.com.mx, US$155–185) is a small and incredibly charming bed-and-breakfast. The four guest rooms are lovingly decorated with Mexican crafts and textiles, yet comfortably equipped with big beds, fluffy comforters, and stone chimneys. Three of the four also have private patios with views of the surrounding city. Each private bathroom is equipped with ornate wood dressers, decorative tin-framed mirrors, and colorful tiled showers and tubs. The common areas are delightful and very well attended by the owner, Robert, and his adorable little pooch, Zeke. Downstairs, the gorgeous tiled kitchen adjoins a quaint dining area, where creative Mexican-style breakfasts are served each morning.

Adjoining the town square, the incredibly central **Hotel La Morada** (Correo 10, tel. 415/152-1647 or toll-free Mex. tel. 800/221-7432, www.lamoradahotel.com, US$150–200) has two types of rooms, suited to two entirely different types of people. Upstairs, the older part of the hotel contains 15 large bedrooms and suites in the colonial style, with vaulted ceilings, chimneys, Saltillo tile floors, and oversized wood furniture. The two-story Terraza Suite has a large private balcony overlooking Sollano and the *parroquia*—a piece

of paradise, all to yourself. Downstairs, the hotel's patio suites are clean and minimalist, with big white beds, abstract art on the walls, and modern bathrooms. The high-ceilinged one-story rooms are airier than the two-story rooms (which have a loft bed above the sitting area). No matter where you choose to stay, the hotel's location is smack-dab in the middle of everything. You'll enjoy an easy stroll to any destination in town and get used to the sound of church bells ringing through the night.

Set back from cobbled Calle Hospicio, **Casa Quetzal** (Hospicio 34, tel. 415/152-0501 or toll-free Mex. tel. 802/735-0833, www.casaquetzalhotel.com, US$125–275) is a favorite among both national and international tourists, with a range of funky guest rooms. Each room in this quirky colonial home has its own distinct character, some with Asian- or African-inspired decoration, others with private terraces and Jacuzzis. Browse the hotel's website to see all the options, or if the hotel isn't full, ask the friendly staff to show you around. On the whole, rooms are very comfortable and lovingly decorated, though the ubiquitous microwaves and minifridges feel a bit superfluous. The hotel's largest room, the Zen Suite, can comfortably accommodate up to four people, with two bedrooms, a large bath, and a kitchenette. Smaller rooms are cheerfully decorated and generally inexpensive, making them a good value in this price range.

Located in a beautifully restored colonial home, **Casa de los Olivos** (Correo 30, tel. 415/152-0309 or 415/154-9874, www.casadelosolivos.com, US$215–290) is a sweet five-room bed-and-breakfast that unites cushy comforts with the atmosphere of old San Miguel. Spacious and clean bedrooms open onto the shared courtyard, and each is equipped with a white canopy bed and fluffy pillows, terracotta tile floor, rustic wood furnishings, and a big bathroom with Jacuzzi tub. Despite modern comforts, the high-beamed ceilings, thick walls, and architectural details retain a distinctly Mexican aesthetic. Upstairs, the hotel's tiny bar serves hotel guests in the afternoon and evening. They can take their drinks out to the terrace and relax amid the historic domes and bell towers of San Miguel. Service is friendly and the location is ideal, just a block and a half from the town square.

Every bedroom at **(Casa Schuck** (Garita 3, tel. 415/142-6618, U.S. tel. 937/684-4092, www.casaschuck.com, US$200–275) is decorated with tremendous flair. Housed in a massive colonial-era mansion, the spacious guest rooms are decked out with jewel-colored walls, delightful crafts, stone chimneys, and colorful bedspreads. Second-floor bedrooms have large French windows that open onto the leafy trees of the central courtyard. Guests can relax in the home's various shared spaces, including a comfortable living area, a roof deck with views of the *parroquia,* and a garden patio. Morning breakfasts are included in the price and served in the beautiful blue dining room downstairs.

There may be no more peaceful place in San Miguel than the cascading gardens of the **Casa de Liza** (Bajada del Chorro 7, tel. 415/152-0352, U.S. tel. 816/984-3853, www. casaliza.com, US$150–450). Located along the lush Bajada del Chorro, Casa Liza's sloping grounds are filled with giant maguey, flowering fruit trees, winding stone walkways, and the happy motion of attending butterflies. Scattered across the property, each room at this unusual bed-and-breakfast feels like its own private cabin, with sloping wood-beamed ceilings and big comfortable beds. Some are more spacious than others, though each is individually decorated with Mexican crafts, original art, and unique furniture, some of which has been designed by surrealist artist and architect Pedro Friedeberg. Your best bet is to choose a room with a private patio, though all guests share the beautiful gardens, as well as the small outdoor Jacuzzi.

In the beautiful Atascadero neighborhood, **La Puertecita Boutique Hotel** (Santo Domingo 75, tel. 415/152-5011, www.lapuertecita.com, US$225–275) provides a nice alternative to staying in San Miguel de Allende's bustling downtown district. More than anything, the country setting is what makes this hotel unique, with beautiful gardens beside a lovely natural canyon. At night, you can see the stars and hear the crickets chiming. Large guest rooms have a distinctly Mexican decor, with colorful woven bedspreads and traditional *equipal* furniture. This hotel is one of the oldest boutique establishments in San Miguel, and the rooms reflect their age, though service and amenities are top-notch. Hotel guests can order spa service in their rooms, eat in the hotel restaurant, or relax in the hotel's gardens or common areas. There is also an on-site gym and parking.

Few hotels can boast the sheer history of **Antigua Villa Santa Monica** (Fray José Guadalupe Mojica 22, tel. 415/152-0451 or 415/152-0427, www.antiguavillasantamonica. com, US$230–270). Housed in an enchanting 17th-century mansion bordering the Parque Juárez, guest rooms at this beautiful hotel are entirely comfortable yet retain the original charms of the historic setting. Furnishings lean toward romantic, with white canopy beds, tile floors, and antique accessories. In the courtyard, the hotel's restaurant serves breakfast and lunch. Behind it, the lush gardens are filled with lime, jacaranda, and palm trees, well-tended lawns, and a very small but pretty swimming pool. Suites are more expensive than standard doubles but are incredibly spacious, with sitting areas and, in some cases, private terraces. Service is polite but, for this price, isn't as attentive as it could be.

OVER US$250

San Miguel de Allende's few luxury hotels are much more than a place to lay your head. Decorated with love and attention, thoughtfully attended, and incredibly comfortable, these places can become destinations themselves.

A sleek addition to San Miguel de Allende's slew of charming bed-and-breakfasts, **Dos Casas** (Quebrada 101, tel. 415/154-4073, www.doscasas.com.mx, US$295–450) is a contemporary six-room boutique hotel that doesn't sacrifice comfort for style. This upscale establishment occupies a colonial home on a busy street corner in the *centro histórico.* Behind its dark wood doors, the building's original architecture is complemented by carefully designed interiors: Clean lines and neutral colors define the bedrooms, where choice Mexican crafts and textiles make an elegant accompaniment to the modern atmosphere. To unwind, guests can order drinks in the first-floor wine bar or relax on the lovely roof deck with its pretty views of downtown San Miguel. Guest rooms have spacious bathrooms and flat-screen TVs; slippers, fluffy bathrobes, and L'Occitane en Provence toiletries add to the luxury.

On a small cobbled street just a few blocks from the town square, the boutique hotel **[€ Oasis** (Chiquitos 1A, tel. 415/154-9850, U.S. tel. 210/745-1457, www.oasissanmiguel. com, US$350–400) is, as the name suggests, a dreamy respite from real life. In this beautifully restored colonial home, rooms are lavish but tasteful, decorated with old-fashioned furniture, well-chosen antiques, Mexican craft, contemporary art, and beautiful old rugs. At the same time, they are fully equipped with modern conveniences, like flat-screen TVs and air-conditioning, ensuring a comfortable stay as much as a romantic one. Though the house itself is rather small, the four guest rooms are spacious and luxurious, decked out with high-thread-count sheets and all-natural toiletries. Service is as friendly and elegant as the hotel itself.

On the same tiny street as Oasis, **[€ Casa Misha** (Chiquitos 15, tel. 415/152-2921, www.casamisha.com, US$200–450) is a small seven-room hotel that drips with opulence. Here, every single room has been lavished with attention, from the guest suites to the library downstairs. The extravagant decor rings of the Old World, with gilded furniture, fine China, crystal chandeliers, and oil paintings. Rooms are all different yet every one is lavishly appointed with armoires and antiques, silky bedspreads, and four-poster beds, as well as gorgeous private bathrooms with ample space, big tubs, and French toiletries. There are several rooftop terraces with panoramic views of San Miguel de Allende and beautiful gardens throughout the central courtyard. The hotel is small yet fully

staffed, and service is incredibly hospitable, attentive, and friendly.

Mexico's president, Felipe Calderón, was the guest of honor at the official inauguration of **Rosewood San Miguel de Allende** (Nemesio Diez 11, tel. 415/152-9700, toll-free Mex. tel. 800/363-7373, toll-free U.S. tel. 888/767-3966, www.rosewoodsanmiguel. com, US$350–585) in early 2011. The town's newest and splashiest luxury accommodations, Rosewood San Miguel is a massive 67-room retreat, operated by the international hotelier, Rosewood Hotels and Resorts. Occupying a large swath of land between the Ancha de San Antonio and Parque Juárez, the grounds have been designed to match the city's colonial aesthetic, with stone arches, gurgling fountains, and saturated colors throughout the expansive grounds. The terraced pool is a particularly dreamy place to sip a drink under an umbrella or in a private cabana. Guest rooms are spacious and designed to be comfortable, dolled up with Italian bedsheets, gilt-framed mirrors, and Mexican rugs. Larger suites (US$545–1090) have private balconies and sitting areas, and upper-floor rooms boast some of the most breathtaking views in San Miguel. Even those who aren't staying at Rosewood can enjoy the panoramic vista from the hotel's Luna Rooftop Tapas Bar (daily from 4 P.M.).

A classic San Miguel establishment, **Casa de Sierra Nevada** (Hospicio 35, tel. 415/152-7040, U.S. tel. 800/701-1561, www.casadesierranevada.com, US$295–400) is a full-service luxury hotel, with 37 guest rooms located in the five different colonial mansions in San Miguel de Allende's *centro histórico*. With so many properties, rooms vary widely, though each is decorated with colonial-style headboards, overstuffed furniture, and terra-cotta floors. Comfort is key, with twice-daily housekeeping, fluffy bathrobes, and in-room spa services. Grounds are lovely and quiet in the hotel's Casa del Parque, located directly across from the *lavaderos públicos* on the Bajada del Chorro. The Recreo location has a small swimming pool, a sculpture garden, and deck chairs. If you have a preference, you can request the house you'd like to stay in when you make your reservation.

Every year, San Miguel becomes just a touch more slick and sophisticated. Ample proof is provided in the city's new luxury hotel, **Hotel Matilda** (Aldama 53, tel. 415/152-1015, toll-free Mex. tel. 855/628-4532, www.hotelmatilda.com, US$336–395 double, US$450–865 suites). In a town where crimson facades and crumbling fountains are the norm, Hotel Matilda is a shrine to clean geometric shapes, contemporary comforts, and subtle color schemes. Bedrooms are modern and spacious, comfortable as well as chic; overstuffed furniture and king-sized beds play nice accompaniment to modern art and cozy tan-and-chocolate colors. Private baths are comfortably minimalist, with marble tubs, big mirrors, square porcelain sinks, luxury toiletries, and stacks of fresh towels. Common areas are equally decked out and comfortable, including a small but appealing pool and deck chairs. The swanky lounge and restaurant downstairs has a contemporary, urban feeling you won't find in other parts of San Miguel.

EXTENDED STAY

Well priced and well located, **Tres Casitas** (Sollano 34, www.sanmiguelweeklyrentals.com, US$120–170 daily, US$595–735 per week) has three spacious, artsy-quirky apartments for rent on a daily or weekly basis. Each of these cozy living spaces is comfortably decorated and includes a small but fully equipped kitchen. The owner is an artist, and she has placed large paintings and ceramics throughout the little apartments. The central courtyard garden gives a cozy, private feel to the casitas, and also provides a relaxing home to some lazy felines.

For a longer visit to San Miguel, the small,

cheerfully decorated apartments at **Casa de Aparicio** (Aparicio 25, tel. 415/152-5524, U.S. tel. 856/559-0138, toll-free U.S. tel. 866/291-0218, www.casadeaparicio.com, US$450–850 monthly) are an excellent deal. Each is simply yet comfortably decorated, with sitting areas, outdoor spaces, and eat-in kitchenettes. On the edge of the *centro histórico,* the location is excellent.

VACATION RENTALS

For those planning to spend a week or two in San Miguel de Allende, renting a private home can be a nice way to visit the town and have a bit more space and independence than you would have at a hotel. From simple apartments to lavish mansions, there are literally hundreds of private homes available for short-term rental in San Miguel. Although a private home does not offer all the services of a hotel, many have cleaning and kitchen staff, gardens or outdoor spaces, and parking.

Bob Latta at **Casas Elegantes** (U.S. tel. 214/413-2131, www.casaselegantes.com) maintains a well-selected list of luxury rental properties in the center of San Miguel de Allende. The properties he represents range from a lovely modern house near Parque Juárez to lavish colonial mansions with swimming pools and expansive gardens. The Casas Elegantes staff will help arrange airport transfers and will even do a pre-arrival grocery run, at your request.

For every type of rental property, from simple apartments to huge haciendas, **Premier San Miguel** (tel. 415/154-9460, www.premiersanmiguel.com) can help you book a place to stay for short- or long-term excursions to San Miguel. The very friendly staff will answer your questions about rental properties, all of which are listed (along with pictures) on their website.

Food

Eating out is a big part of life in San Miguel de Allende. Throughout the town, there is a constant buzz about new restaurants opening up (or old ones closing down) and a spirited debate about the best bites in town. When it comes to identifying the tastiest tacos, the most elegant restaurant, or the most satisfying pizza, no one sees eye-to-eye. Fortunately, there is a little bit of something for everyone. Satisfying every taste and appetite, there are fruit stands, ice cream carts, traditional bakeries, casual eateries, charming bistros, and fine dining establishments peppered along the streets of the *centro histórico*.

QUICK BITES AND TACOS

San Miguel de Allende has many beautiful sit-down restaurants serving food from all over the world. However, some of the best and most authentic Mexican fare can be found in the little market stalls and taco stands across town. If you are new to Mexico, open-air taco joints can be tougher on the stomach than sit-down restaurants. That said, most of San Miguel de Allende's eateries—even the most casual—are hygienic and clean, and adventurous eaters will be well rewarded with memorable meals.

Early in the morning, **fresh juice stands** appear throughout the city, casually operating from the windows of local houses or in the doorway of a corner store. The most ubiquitous fresh juices are orange and carrot, though some also serve grapefruit, beet, and green juice with spinach and citrus.

Like juice, **tamales** are a ubiquitous breakfast meal. There are plenty of places to buy tamales throughout San Miguel; however, some of the very best are sold from a small table on the corner of Insurgentes and Pepe Llanos, right in front of the Oratorio San Felipe Neri (no tel., 7–11 A.M., US$1). There are always crowds of locals lining up to order savory tamales with *salsa verde, salsa roja,* cheese, or chile pepper. To accompany your *tamal,* try a steaming mug of *atole,* a sweet corn-based drink with

© ARTURO MEADE

Gorditas, warmed corn cakes stuffed with beans, prickly pear, or other fillings, are a traditional dish in the Bajío.

pre-Hispanic origins. Get there early; the stash can be depleted as early as 10:30 A.M.

With more than a hundred years in operation, **C La Colmena** (Relox 41, tel. 415/152-1422, 6 A.M.–2 P.M. and 4:30–9 P.M. Mon.–Sat., US$1) is a wonderful Mexican bakery, just off the main square. Every day, La Colmena's ovens turn out an astounding variety of traditional *pan de dulce* (sweet bread), as well as empanadas, cookies, cinnamon rolls, and whole-wheat breads. If you haven't tried Mexican sweet breads, *conchas* (a sweet roll topped with sugar) are a classic introduction; at La Colmena, *conchas* come fresh out of the oven every morning and are some of the best in Mexico. Known to many as the "blue door bakery," La Colmena is just a block from the central square, making it convenient place for a light breakfast or a snack. When buying bread, pick up a metal tray and a pair of tongs then pick out breads you want; the bevy of shop assistants will bag and total your purchase at the end. Those who love to linger may feel a bit rushed at this favorite local pit stop. It is always filled with a crowd of locals and residents, and (with a name that means The Beehive) a swarm of sugar-loving bees.

For a quick, cheap, and tasty meal, seek out **Los Burritacos** (Mesones 69-A, tel. 415/152-3222, 10 A.M.–6 P.M. Mon.–Sat., US$4), a tiny eatery just one block from the town square. This popular lunchtime spot serves little burritos made with fresh flour tortillas and filled with a range of Mexican *guisados* like *pipián* (green mole), *picadillo* (spiced ground beef), or potatoes. First, you pay for the number of burritos you want at the register. Next, you proceed to the steamy kitchen in back where you select your fillings. You can see the fresh tortillas being rolled and warmed as you order your food! Fresh fruit drinks round out the meal, which can be had for just a couple bucks. You can also do like many locals and get a package of their fresh tortillas to go.

Braised pork tacos, or carnitas, are one of Mexico's most popular dishes, usually eaten for breakfast or lunch. You can try some very tasty carnitas in downtown San Miguel at **Carnitas Apolo XI** (Mesones 42, tel. 415/154-6252, 8:30 A.M.–6 P.M. daily, US$4). If you order your tacos *surtida,* they will be prepared with mixed meat, including everything from snout to ear. If you order *maciza* instead, your tacos will be made with just pulled pork shoulder—not greasy, yet very flavorful. Apolo XI is good for a group; if two or more people are eating together, you can order a quarter or half kilo of carnitas to share, which they will serve with warm tortillas, salsa, and garnishes. There are casual tables on the roof of Apolo XI (which overlooks the *parroquia*!), but the place is pretty self-service. Order downstairs before you sit down, then grab a beer from the fridge.

Tortas are hot sandwiches served on a soft roll, and **Tortitlán** (Juárez 17, tel. 415/152-3376, 9 A.M.–11 P.M. daily, and Ancha de San Antonio 43, tel. 415/152-8931, 9 A.M.–7 P.M. Mon.–Fri., 10 A.M.–6 P.M. Sun., US$5) makes some of the best (and biggest) in town. The surprisingly extensive sandwich menu includes a chicken torta with cheese and poblano peppers, as well as a vegetarian sandwich with avocado and fresh cheese. Juice and a variety of *aguas frescas* are made at the moment you order. If you really want to overstuff yourself, accompany your torta with a side of French fries. Many people order their food for delivery, though you can also eat in. Both branches of this popular *tortería* are casual, though the Tortitlán on San Antonio is a bit nicer for a sit-down meal, with a small dining area where you can watch dozens of tortas being assembled at breakneck speed.

A very popular dish in the greater Bajío region, *barbacoa* is slow-cooked lamb, prepared over a wood fire in an earthen pit, which is then covered with maguey leaves. The result is soft, moist, and nicely flavored meat. Near the bus station, **El Pato** (Calzada de la Estación 35, 8 A.M.–3 P.M. Wed.–Sun., US$3) serves tasty *tacos de barbacoa,* as well as a strongly flavored *caldo* (lamb broth soup). You can also try the local rendition of *mixiotes* (steamed lamb in spicy salsa) and *montalayo* (lamb stomach), both of which are prepared differently in San Miguel de Allende than in other parts of Mexico. Located on a busy avenue, this little eatery is as loose and casual as they come, with plastic tables and a rudimentary kitchen where your tacos are assembled. Don't come expecting elegance, but you will get a good bite.

Gorditas (stuffed corn cakes) are a specialty of the Bajío region, and **El Comal de Doña Meche** (Insurgentes 62, tel. 415/152-0012, 9:30 A.M.–8 P.M. daily, US$3) serves a good (and filling) rendition of this cheap and popular meal. You can choose between a basic gordita with *requesón* (cheese) or *migajas* (pork drippings), then have it stuffed with one of many delicious fillings. The options are laid out in big clay pots at the eatery's informal kitchen, and usually include dishes like prickly pear and garbanzos, chicken with mushrooms, guacamole, poblano peppers, or scrambled egg in spicy salsa. You can also order quesadillas, flautas, chiles rellenos, and burritos to eat at

Doña Mecha's makeshift tables in the back of the restaurant. This inexpensive eatery can get very busy at lunchtime, when locals working downtown stop in for a bite.

After night falls, **taco trucks** appear throughout San Miguel de Allende, spreading their savory aroma for blocks and drawing a flock of diners like flies to honey. One of the best and most aromatic pit stops is on the corner of Mesones and Pepe Llanos (8 P.M.–midnight, US$3), just behind the Templo de San Francisco. Push through the crowds for *longaniza* (sausage), rib, or *pastor* tacos, which are served with double tortillas. If you get your tacos *con todo*, they will come with cilantro, grilled onion, and salsa. There are no stools (though some folks perch on the bumpers of automobiles parked nearby), so diners should be prepared to eat standing up, balancing a plate in one hand and eating with the other.

If you'd rather eat your tacos sitting down, try **La Fogata** (Salida a Celaya, 7 P.M.–3 A.M., US$4). This popular joint serves a wide variety of tasty tacos, like seasoned beef, sausage, rib, and the ever popular *al pastor,* as well as quesadillas, tostados, and stuffed baked potatoes. *Gringas*—a popular choice with an amusing name—are tacos that combine melted cheese and *pastor* meat in a flour tortilla. Early in the evening, full tables of American and Canadian expatriates are not uncommon at La Fogata. As it gets later, the crowd gets younger, as hungry revelers leave nightclubs to refuel on a cheap dinner out.

Although Dolores Hidalgo is famous for its *nieves* (ice cream), San Miguel's offerings are just as tasty. When the sweet tooth aches, there are **ice cream carts** all over town. One of the best and most popular is on the corner of Hernández Macías and Canal, just outside Bellas Artes. Here, a family of ice-cream vendors scoops heaping cones in exotic flavors like rice, rose petal, cheese, guava, mango, walnut, and peppermint. A single serving includes two flavors, favorable to the indecisive. You can order them in a cup, but the handmade sugar cones are almost as sweet and delicious as the ice cream that fills them.

MEXICAN

Located on the northwest corner of the town square, **Rincón Don Tomás** (Portal de Guadalupe 2, tel. 415/152-4119, 8:30 A.M.–10 P.M. Mon.–Sat., 8:30 A.M.–9 P.M. Sun., US$8) is a good place to kick off your visit to San Miguel de Allende, with a prime location and a tasty menu of traditional Mexican food. You can linger over a filling lunch while enjoying some excellent people-watching beneath the shaded arcades of the *plaza principal.* Don Tomás's tasty *sopa azteca* and squash blossom soup are popular ways to start a meal; follow them up with a Mexican specialty like *enmoladas,* chicken in yellow mole, or enchiladas in *chile pasilla,* a mild but flavorful dried chile. This restaurant is also a nice place to have breakfast, with some tasty egg dishes, good coffee, and an early-morning view of the *parroquia.*

A casual dinner spot favored by locals, **La Alborada** (Sollano 10, tel. 415/154-9982, 1–10:30 P.M. Mon.–Sat., US$5) specializes in traditional pozole, a hearty hominy soup that has been consumed in Mexico since the pre-Columbian era. Pozoles are popular fare throughout Mexico and the preparation varies by region. At La Alborada, they serve red pozole with chicken, pork, or beef (or all three!), accompanied by small plates of garnishes—typically, dried oregano, radishes, chopped onion, and dried chile pepper. When everything arrives at your table, you sprinkle the condiments over your soup to taste. In addition, La Alborada serves a variety of Mexican *antojitos,* like quesadillas, guacamole, tostadas, and enchiladas, as well as inexpensive beer and *aguas frescas.*

The perennially popular **Chocolate y Churros San Agustín** (San Francisco 21, tel. 415/154-9102, churros_sanagustin@hotmail.com, 8 A.M.–11 P.M. daily, US$8) is well known for its eponymous hot chocolate and fresh, crunchy *churros.* From morning until night, this bustling little eatery is filled with folks getting a serious sugar fix. In the spirit of pure excess, every hot chocolate includes an order of three sugarcoated

© ARTURO MEADE

Enchiladas are a popular dish in many of San Miguel's restaurants.

churros, made fresh on the premises and still warm when they arrive at your table. On the savory side, the restaurant is also a nice place for breakfast or lunch, with a tasty menu of egg dishes, spicy *chilaquiles,* sandwiches, and salads, plus espresso drinks, beer, wine, and spirits. During San Miguel's chilly winters, this café is a good destination for its warm and cozy (if quirky) atmosphere. It's owned by Argentine actress Margarita Gralia, and the walls of this lovely, high-ceilinged dining room are festooned with memorabilia from her screen career.

Just around the corner from San Agustín, **El Pegaso** (Corregidora 6, tel. 415/154-7611, elpegasomx@gmail.com, 8:30 A.M.–10 P.M. Thurs.–Tues., US$8) has a little something for everyone, with an eclectic menu that ranges from Caesar salads and Reuben sandwiches to traditional Mexican dishes like fish tacos, enchiladas, pork in mole sauce, and *chiles en nogada.* The cute, cozy dining room is decorated with miniatures and other crafts, with tall windows overlooking Calle Correo. In the

afternoon, you'll see plenty of local expatriates lingering over coffee.

The inexpensive and centrally located **Café de la Parroquia** (Jesús 11, tel. 415/152-3161, 8 A.M.–4 P.M. Tues.–Sat., 8 A.M.–2 P.M. Sun., US$6) is a favorite breakfast spot for locals and tourists alike. Set in a colonial courtyard surrounding a gurgling fountain, it is one of the most relaxing places to brunch alfresco while flipping through the latest edition of *Atención San Miguel.* While there is always a pleasant hum of diners during the morning hours, this popular café is packed on the weekends. The delicious morning menu includes a range of traditional Mexican dishes, like fried eggs in *mole negro,* huevos rancheros (fried eggs in tomato salsa), and chicken and cheese tamales in black bean sauce. With bottomless cups of coffee and pleasant courtyard seating, it's well worth the wait for Sunday brunch.

You need to make reservations at **Posada Corazón** (Aldama 9, tel. 415/152-0182, www.posadacorazon.com.mx, 8 A.M.–noon

Mon.–Fri., 8 A.M.–1 P.M. Sat.–Sun., US$11), but partaking of their lovely breakfast is worth a little advance planning. This small inn opens their kitchen to a limited number of daily visitors (as well as hotel guests), offering delicious breakfasts made with organic and local produce. The set-price menu includes juice or fruit, coffee or tea, and your choice from a substantial list of egg dishes, omelets, and pancakes. Every table is also treated to a basket of freshly baked bread, cookies, and jam. On the weekends, there is also a buffet of cheese and fruit, and, often, live music. One of the best parts of eating at Posada Corazón is having the opportunity to peek around the hotel's pretty gardens, which include a distinguished magnolia tree at the entrance.

San Miguel de Allende can spoil you with beautiful views, and **La Posadita** (Cuna de Allende 13, tel. 415/154-8862, noon–11 P.M. Thurs.–Tues., US$7) has one of the nicest views in town. From La Posadita's open-air rooftop dining room, you can have lunch beneath the spires of the *parroquia,* overlooking the sweeping river valley beyond San Miguel. The menu is diverse and appealing, with Mexican classics like guacamole and enchiladas, as well as more unusual plates like *mixiotes* (steamed meat in banana leaves) and *cochinita pibil* (spiced pulled pork). Food is generally good though not excessively seasoned (add some of their delicious salsas if you want some kick), and the kitchen can occasionally get backed up. The margaritas, including the tasty margaritas with tamarind, are the best choice on the cocktail menu.

With low prices, outdoor seating, and a casual atmosphere, **El Ten Ten Pie** (Cuna de Allende 21, tel. 415/152-7189, 9 A.M.–11 P.M. daily, US$5) is a laid-back place for a leisurely snack or a filling, inexpensive meal. Here, simple Mexican dishes like burritos or *sopes* (thick tortillas covered with beans, crumbled cheese, lettuce, and sour cream) are particularly tasty, especially when smothered with the restaurant's spicy red or green salsa. If you want to refuel in the afternoon, Ten Ten Pie is a good pick for a plate of guacamole or *queso fundido,* accompanied by an inexpensive

beer or lemonade. In addition to the menu, El Ten Ten Pie has a nice set-price lunch, which includes the soup of the day, a drink, and a choice of three daily entrées.

Ⅽ Tio Lucas Restaurant and Bar (Mesones 103, tel. 415/152-4996, noon–midnight daily, US$12) is a lively steakhouse right across the street from the historic Ángela Peralta theater. Starters and salads are good here, but Tío Lucas is best for enthusiastic carnivores. Try one of the Mexican cuts of beef, like *arrachera, puntas de filete,* or *norteña,* which are served with beans, rice, and guacamole. Cocktails are also a specialty, and the bar serves powerful margaritas with your choice of tequila. The atmosphere is among the best in town, with a nightly jazz band, constant crowds, and Mexican pottery and stamped metal decorations adorning the walls of the open-air dining room.

Down narrow Calle Loreto, an iron silhouette of a bull swings above the doorway of **Olé Olé** (Loreto 66, tel. 415/152-0896, 1–9 P.M. daily, US$12), a little restaurant that specializes in delicious chicken, shrimp, and steak fajitas. The dining room is decorated in wacky homage to the tradition of bullfighting (still rather popular in this part of Mexico), and the walls are covered in bullfight memorabilia, posters, and even a few stuffed bull heads! Other than fajitas, there are some tasty appetizers on the menu (mushrooms in garlic sauce and *queso fundido* are both popular), but they also bring a nice basket of chips and smoky salsa to the table when you sit down. Though thoroughly popular with San Miguel's expatriates, this little place still feels off the beaten path.

For a highly civilized taco experience, take a trip to **Tacos Don Felix** (Fray Juan de San Miguel 15, Col. San Rafael, tel. 415/152-5719, www.tacosdonfelix.com, 6 P.M.–midnight Fri.– Sat., 2–9:30 P.M. Sun., US$9). This weekends-only eatery started out as a small taco stand on the Avenida Independencia in 2007. Its tasty quesadillas with *huitlacoche* (corn fungus), flank steak tacos, shrimp tacos, and other tasty offerings quickly drew crowds, and Felix expanded the stand to include several tables (with tablecloths!) beneath a white tent. Today, the restaurant has moved into a big house just around the corner from the original location (use the handy map on Don Felix's website to find your way there) and offers a taco platter with their old standbys, plus a slew of larger plates like tortilla soup, enchiladas, cuts of meat, and grilled chicken. There is beer, wine, *aguas frescas,* and a full bar. While the atmosphere has changed, Felix's family still offers the great service—and the big smiles—that made this family-run establishment so popular.

Another inexpensive and tasty neighborhood joint, **El Rinconcito** (Refugio Norte 7, Col. San Antonio, tel. 415/154-4809, 1–9 P.M. Mon. and Wed.–Sat., 1–7 P.M. Sun., US$6) has garnered a loyal following with folks in the San Antonio area. This family-run eatery has three nice outdoor tables on a tiny patio, where you can watch the cooks whip up your food in the moment you order it. When the weather's chilly, they also have a few tables inside. Everything on the menu has a pleasing, homemade quality, from the grilled chicken salad to the guacamole. The giant vegetarian or shrimp quesadillas are particularly tasty, and you can wash it all down with a beer or fruit drink.

ITALIAN AND PIZZA

Right off the main plaza, the perennially popular **Mama Mia** (Umarán 8, tel. 415/152-2063, mamamia.com.mx, 8 A.M.–midnight Sun.–Thurs., 8 A.M.–3 A.M. Fri.–Sat., US$10) is a San Miguel de Allende institution. There are two bars, a gift shop, and a rooftop terrace inside Mama Mia's expansive Umarán location, as well as a large family-friendly restaurant in a pretty open-air courtyard. The bars draw big crowds at night, but the main restaurant is Mama Mia's flagship offering, consistently filled with local families and national tourists enjoying a lazy afternoon in the shade of magnolia trees. Food is decent Italian fare, like pastas, lasagna, and doughy, cheesy, homemade-style pizzas. Come in the morning for the restaurant's best culinary offering, a daily breakfast buffet with eggs in salsa, beans, chiles rellenos, *chilaquiles,* fresh quesadillas, menudo,

pozole, and other traditional Mexican dishes served in big clay pots. To make the mood especially pleasant, there is always live music in the restaurant during peak hours.

Located inside the picturesque garden of the Hotel Sautto, **Bacco** (Hernández Macías 59, tel. 415/154-5513, 1–10:30 P.M. Tues.–Sat., 1–6 P.M. Sun., US$12) is a lovely Italian restaurant serving fresh salads, well-prepared pasta dishes, and savory thin-crust pizza. Pastas are flavorful and served nicely al dente; however, pizzas are the specialty at this restaurant, baked in a huge stone oven and topped with fresh ingredients, like thinly sliced eggplant, fresh basil, or prosciutto. There is a full bar and cocktails, though the wine list could be more creative. During the warm spring and summer seasons, it is particularly pleasant to sit in Bacco's lush courtyard, an elegant colonial setting.

A cozy Italian restaurant with a long history in San Miguel, **La Grotta** (Cuadrante 5, tel. 415/152-4119, 1–10:30 P.M. Sun.–Thurs., 1 P.M.–midnight Fri.–Sat., US$9) specializes in crispy thin-crust pizzas and gooey, filling calzones. With a long list of toppings, you can order a pie exactly as you like it, whether that's topped with blue cheese and onion or pepperoni and bell pepper. Second-floor seating is a bit nicer than the dining room downstairs, especially if you can snag a window seat overlooking the street below. The good pizza and good prices have made this central restaurant a favorite with tourists, so during holiday weekends this little place is often filled to capacity.

The small dining room at **Socialitté** (Correo 47-A, tel. 415/154-4816, info@socialitte.com, noon–10 P.M. Sun.–Wed., noon–11 P.M. Thurs.–Sat. P.M., US$14) is a cozy place to snuggle up to a glass of wine and a plate of pasta. This little Italian restaurant makes everything in-house with high quality and often imported ingredients. The salad with Gorgonzola cheese and strawberries is a nice way to start the meal, as is the smoked salmon appetizer. Followed up with a plate of fish or pasta and accompanied by a big glass of red, Socialitté makes a satisfying dinner. In addition to the regular menu, there are always several daily specials, so be sure to ask what the chef is cooking. The owners of this restaurant own other restaurants in Mexico City and Playa del Carmen, so they run a tight ship. Food is fresh and service is exuberant.

A homey little restaurant in a quiet residential neighborhood, **Gombo's** (Tatanacho 2, Col. Guadalupe, tel. 415/152-8121, 1–10:30 P.M. daily, US$8) serves good, filling pizzas at reasonable prices. The pie with tomato, fresh basil, and anchovy is particularly flavorful, though you can also pick and choose your own ingredients. Located in an unassuming house on a tucked-away street, Gombo's interior was recently redecorated. Inside, the red walls, tin lamps, and a big wooden bar provide a surprisingly elegant atmosphere for a nice casual meal. If you don't want to trek out to the Guadalupe neighborhood, Gombo's will deliver pizzas anywhere in San Miguel.

Located on a busy street in the San Antonio neighborhood, the unapologetically casual **Juanita's Pizza** (Orizaba 19, tel. 415/154-5148, 1:30–10 P.M. Tues.–Sun., US$7) serves tasty and inexpensive pizzas, plus surprisingly good lasagna and pastas. This hole-in-the-wall joint is principally a delivery service, but it also has a few tables in their spare, open-air dining room upstairs. Pizzas are served with several types of accompanying hot sauce; Juanita's also serves beer and soft drinks. On Sundays, local families take their kids to Juanita's for an inexpensive meal.

The much beloved **((Ristorante da Andrea** (Hacienda Landeta, Carretera San Miguel-Dr. Mora, Km 2.5, tel. 415/120-3481, US$18) is many locals' top pick for the best restaurants in San Miguel de Allende. There are no printed menus at this Italian restaurant. When you sit down, waiters arrive to explain the day's menu and wine list. Starters, like octopus salad, are often particularly tasty, and the pastas and ravioli are the culinary highlight, all made fresh on the premises. Just as lovely as the food, the restaurant is located on the glorious ex-Hacienda Landeta, just east of San Miguel on the highway toward Los Rodríguez. Outdoor tables are shaded by umbrellas and offer a chance to soak up the beautiful surroundings. If you plan to go, make a reservation to ensure you'll get a seat on the patio.

INTERNATIONAL

The first fine dining restaurant to open in San Miguel de Allende, **((The Restaurant** (Sollano 16, tel. 415/154-7862, noon–4 P.M. and 6–10 P.M. Tues.–Sat., US$18) is one the nicest places to eat in town, housed in a beautifully restored colonial mansion with neoclassical and Moorish details. The courtyard seating plays perfect accompaniment to the seasonal, chef-driven menu, which incorporates both Asian and Mexican influences. For a town with generally uninspired wine lists, The Restaurant does well for itself, offering an excellent assortment of Mexican and Latin American glasses and bottles, as well as a full bar and specialty cocktails. On Thursday, The Restaurant hosts Hamburger Night, a popular destination for locals looking for a juicy cheeseburger and some good company.

In the early evenings, Café de la Parroquia re-opens as a charming French-inspired bistro called **La Brasserie** (Jesús 11, tel. 415/152-3161, 5–10 P.M. Tues.–Sun., US$7). This sweet little restaurant is popular with the local crowd for its good prices, fresh food, and charming atmosphere. With colorful oilcloth tables, French posters on the wall, and well-chosen crafts, La Brasserie is Mexico's version of a cool French bistro. The homey menu has a mix of crunchy pita sandwiches, pastas, and European style entrées, as well as a few Mexican dishes like enchiladas. The nightly special is often a good choice, which includes an entrée, salad, and dessert. The chocolate mousse is delicious.

Located in the courtyard of a beautiful 18th-century home, **((El Buen Café** (Jesús 36, toll-free Mex. tel. 888/407-3168, http://diezmohotelsanmiguel.com, 9 A.M.–4 P.M. Tues. and Thurs.–Sat., 10 A.M.–2 P.M. Sun., US$10) is a dreamy place to linger over breakfast or lunch. The restaurant makes everything in-house, from breads to jams, and the coffee is (as promised) *muy bueno.* On the menu, there is a selection of fresh sandwiches, salads, Mexican and international entrées, and homemade desserts, plus a range of daily specials using local ingredients. On Sunday, El Buen Café offers a brunch menu with some unusual specials, such as eggs benedict over corn cakes with chipotle hollandaise sauce—a surprisingly balanced blend of salty, sweet, spicy, soft, and crunchy. The café's seating is scattered throughout the courtyard gardens, where hummingbirds and butterflies flit between avocado and guava trees. The restaurant's owner—a cookbook author and cooking teacher—will sometimes take advantage of this bounty by making jams and sandwiches with fruit from the garden.

Cumpanio (Correo 29, tel. 415/152-2327, www.cumpanio.com, 8 A.M.–10 P.M. daily) is much more than a bakery, though the fine art of bread-making is at the heart of this establishment. Every morning, Cumpanio's busy ovens churn out fresh croissants, buttery pastries, baguettes, and crusty loaves. While you can stop in for a pastry and a cappuccino, you can also sit down for a savory meal in Cumpanio's sleek dining room. The restaurant maintains an extensive breakfast, lunch, and dinner menu, with dishes blending international and Mexican concepts. For lunch, try soup in a bread bowl. For dinner, order well-prepared dishes like mussels in wine sauce, accompanied by a cocktail or glass of red. Occupying the busy corner of Correo and Recreo, the atmosphere inside Cumpanio is upscale, modern, and comfortable, with warm lighting, benches, and blonde wood floors. You can peek into the kitchen from large windows on Recreo.

Sometimes, you need a taste of something familiar. For many American expatriates, that itch can be scratched at the tasty and inexpensive **Bagel Café** (Correo 24, Int. 2, tel. 415/154-6524, 8 A.M.–3 P.M. Mon.–Fri., 8 A.M.–2 P.M. Sat., US$4). In the restaurant's comfy dining room, you can sink your teeth into a big fluffy bagel with cream cheese and lox, or order up a full American breakfast, accompanied by juice

or a soy latte. In the afternoons, the Bagel Café also serves other nostalgia-inducing dishes, like club sandwiches and Texas-style chili. This central café has changed ownership a number of times but remains very popular with more than just the American population.

There are many tasty bites at ◖ **Café Rama** (Calle Nueva 7, tel. 415/154-9655, 8:30 A.M.–6 P.M. Tues.–Sat., US$10), a perfect place for a gourmet lunch in a low-key café setting. Located right behind the organic grocery Natura (you must walk through the store to get there), this little café's wicker chairs, wooden furniture, and chalkboard menus have a mellow hippie vibe. The diverse and appealing menu ranges from crunchy Asian-style salads to braised lamb shepherd's pie, complemented by a changing list of daily specials. The dessert menu is surprisingly creative and delicious, mixing flavors like goat-milk cheesecake and Earl Grey poached peaches. In addition to the daily lunch menu, Café Rama serves special set-price Friday dinners. For these limited-seating reservation-only soirees, the chef's imagination takes center stage, as he presents a series of dishes like radish and purslane salad followed by root-beer-braised short ribs. If you get there early, there are a few breakfast items on the menu, and the restaurant serves coffee, chai tea, delicious *aguas frescas,* and wine.

For warm and filling comfort food, head to **Hecho en Mexico** (Ancha de San Antonio 8, tel. 415/154-6383, noon–10 P.M. Sun.–Thurs., noon–11 P.M. Fri.–Sat., US$6). This inexpensive and casual restaurant serves big, tasty soups, salads, burgers, and sandwiches, as well as meat and seafood plates accompanied by indulgent side dishes like creamed spinach, cole slaw, and onion rings. Despite the name, cuisine is not strictly Mexican, though you will find guacamole and well prepared *arrachera* on the menu, plus tasty side dishes like grilled prickly pear and black beans. Cocktails, big desserts, and consistently satisfying food make this comfortable courtyard restaurant perennially popular with the local crowd.

With its rustic French decor, courtyard

seating, and flickering candlelight, **Chamonix** (Sollano 17, tel. 415/154-8386, 1–10 P.M. Tues.–Sat., US$12) is a perfect setting for a romantic date or a quiet dinner with friends. The changing continental menu might include dishes like tomato-basil soup, pasta with portobello mushrooms and camembert cheese, or roast chicken with sweet potato puree. Portions are generous and the food is well seasoned and tasty. Wines by the glass are limited, but the full list includes plenty of well-priced bottles; there is also a full bar and espresso. Service is attentive and highly professional, never lingering too long but never leaving you unattended.

For a fresh and healthy lunch, try **La Media Naranja** (Hidalgo 83, no tel., 8:30 A.M.– 4:30 P.M. Mon.–Sat.), a small café on the second story of a house on Hidalgo and Calzada de la Luz (look for the sign at the bottom of the staircase). If you need to nourish your inner hippie, this is a great place to enjoy a crunchy falafel sandwich and a big glass of carrot juice. There are also tasty soups and salads on the menu, many made with organic ingredients. The sunny second-floor dining room is simply decorated but entirely comfortable, and the service is friendly.

It is worth a trip to the Fábrica La Aurora to have a leisurely meal at **Food Factory La Aurora** (Local 1A, Fábrica La Aurora, Col. Aurora, tel. 415/152-3982, www.foodfactorylaaurora.com, noon–10 P.M. Mon.–Sat., US$12). The diverse and well-priced menu is mostly European, with dishes like Caprese salad, French onion soup, and seafood pasta, complemented by a few Asian-inspired dishes, like Vietnamese lettuce wraps and Thai pasta. It has a full bar, wines by the glass, and imported beers, as well as an extensive wine cellar with many more unusual bottles. Food Factory's indoor dining room is comfortable and elegant, though you can best enjoy the historic ambiance of La Aurora in the restaurant's patio seating, right below the sandstone arches of the factory's facade. Food Factory La Aurora is at the very end of the left hallway, just as you enter the factory. Service is welcoming and relaxed, never hurried.

For something hip, different, and undeniably fun, **Oko Noodle Bar** (Plaza Alhondiga, Local 7, tel. 415/110-3283, www.okonoodlebar.com, noon–11:30 P.M., US$5) serves inexpensive and tasty pan-Asian food, like Vietnamese spring rolls, noodle soups, and pad Thai. Cocktails are particularly exciting here—and surprisingly inexpensive. For a few bucks, you can plow into a wasabi martini or a cucumber fizz. The strip mall setting may feel a bit like Southern California, but once inside, the groovy Asian-inspired decor, great music, and hip young crowd help you forget about the parking lot outside.

An Argentine steakhouse, **Casa Payo** (Zacateros 26, tel. 415/152-7277, www.casa-payo.com, noon–11 P.M. daily, US$12) proudly specializes in big plates of charcoal-grilled meat. Depending on your appetite, you can order your steak small, medium, or large. No matter what the size, steaks come perfectly prepared. Filled empanadas and side dishes like creamed spinach add a bit of flour and crunch to the otherwise carnivorous menu. The restaurant's shaded porch is a pleasant place for a glass of wine and a steak. Often quiet, Casa Payo never feels as full as it could be, though the adjoining Manolo's Sports Bar can get quite lively during the NBA playoffs.

A giant mesquite-fired grill is the centerpiece of the casual country dining room at **La Burger** (Fraccionamiento el Cortijo s/n, Carretera San Miguel Allende-Dolores Hidalgo, Km 7.3, tel. 415/114-0073, 1–9 P.M. Wed.–Sun., US$14), located on the highway outside Atotonilco. Simple wood chairs and enameled metal tables surround this aromatic pyre, which feels worlds away from the bustle of downtown San Miguel. If you can take your eyes off the kitchen's near-constant activity, there are spacious views of the cactus-studded grasslands behind the restaurant. The namesake hamburgers are made of very finely ground beef and served rare on homemade buns with a side of shoestring potatoes. The restaurant also grills generous and juicy steaks, served on simple wood cutting boards. You need a car to get here, so the crowd is mostly local.

COFFEE SHOPS AND DESSERT

For top-notch baked goods in a mellow café atmosphere, **La Mesa Grande** (Zacateros 49, tel. 415/154-0838, lamesagrandesma@gmail.com, 10 A.M.–5 P.M. Mon.–Sat.) makes wonderful European-style breads fresh everyday, including the best and chewiest sourdough outside of San Francisco. Do like San Miguel's foodies and head to La Mesa Grande for sliced multigrain loaves, crusty baguettes, soft cinnamon rolls, and buttery croissants to go, or order a baked treat and an espresso drink to enjoy at the large communal table. Attracting a low-key local crowd, La Mesa Grande also serves a range of made-to-order sandwiches and pizzas during lunchtime, all at reasonable prices. Located in a small colonial home, the café's stone archways, wood furniture, and chalkboard menus make for a pleasantly romantic atmosphere.

For a cup of hot organic coffee and a sweet snack, stop by **La Ventana** (Diez de Sollano 11, tel. 415/154-7728, 8 A.M.–9 P.M. Mon.–Sat., 9 A.M.–3 P.M. Sun.). This popular coffee shop does most of its business from a small window that opens onto Calle Sollano. Sidle up to the open window, order an espresso to go, then take it around the corner to sip in the *jardín.* You can also go inside the café (enter through La Alborada restaurant) to have a seat or order roasted beans to take home.

Petit Four (Mesones 99-1, tel. 415/154-4010, elpetitfour.com.mx, 10 A.M.–6 P.M. Tues.–Sun., US$5) is the best place to satisfy your sweet tooth in San Miguel de Allende. This lovely French-style bakery's glass display case features a fresh, daily selection of perfectly prepared confections, like delicate vanilla-fig cake, tangy lemon meringue pie, chocolate-covered fruit, assorted truffles, decadent brownies, crisp biscotti, and individual fruit tarts. They also serve good coffee, as well as savory baguette sandwiches, croissants, and danishes. From the tiny dining room, a large glass window lets you peek into the goings-on in Petit Four's kitchen, where white-clad pastry chefs prepare delicate cakes and truffles right before your eyes.

Known locally as the Café de Juan, the eclectically decorated **Café Etc.** (Relox 37, no tel., 9 A.M.–4 P.M. Mon.–Sat., 9 A.M.–2 P.M., US$5) is a popular place for a meal or a coffee, often drawing a crowd of expatriates who've come to relax away the morning. Until midday, the kitchen prepares good Mexican-style breakfasts, like *chilaquiles* and huevos rancheros, while Juan himself mans the coffee bar. In the afternoon, this super casual café also sells a surprisingly luxe *comida corrida.* For those who need a caffeine fix, Juan's coffee is strong and inexpensive, and there is a good selection of black and herbal teas. Several plastic tables sit within a tiny courtyard, so you'll definitely overhear your neighbor's conversation in this cozy coffee shop, but that's part of the fun.

MARKETS AND SPECIALTY FOODS

The Bajío is a major agricultural region, producing a bounty of fruits and vegetables, local meats, and dairy. Here, farmers markets brim with an abundance of beautiful produce all year-round. In addition, the organic and local food movement has taken hold in San Miguel, and there are now numerous specialty shops selling handmade and local products, from organic milk to sourdough bread. San Miguel's discerning consumers have also created a large market for specialty products, like sushi rice and Greek olives. You can find everything you need for a fancy dinner party or healthy lunch in San Miguel's lovely food shops.

For a selection of organic teas, all-natural snacks, and even yoga mats and natural shampoos, head to **Pura Vida** (Pila Seca 9, 10 A.M.–7 P.M. Mon.–Fri., 10 A.M.–4 P.M. Sat.), a colorful little café and health food shop, associated with the holistic healing retreat, LifePath Center. Those looking for a healthy bite can choose from a daily selection of fresh soups, healthy salads, and veggie burgers, as well as delicious homemade sweets, like gluten-free coconut cookies and orange cake. Wash it all down with a fresh tropical juice or creative fruit smoothie. The store's friendly owners make all their food to go, but you can also order snacks

Habaneros are among the most spicy and flavorful chili peppers.

and smoothies to enjoy on one of the tranquil patios outside. For those who choose to eat in, there's wireless Internet for customers, in addition to a pleasant garden.

Behind the Iglesia de Nuestra Señora de la Salud and the Plaza Cívica, the **Mercado Ignacio Ramírez** (Calle Colegio, 8 A.M.–7 P.M. daily) is a small covered market selling an abundance of fresh fruits, vegetables, meat, chicken, and fresh flowers, as well as dry goods like chile peppers, rice, and beans. There is plenty of nice produce at this pretty urban market, and some of the vendors will offer samples to convince you of their fruit's quality. Behind the fruit and flower sellers, there are several food counters, where you can get a torta, a fresh juice, or a full meal for just a few dollars. Just behind the market (at the entrance to the Mercado de Artesanía), there are numerous more casual stands selling handmade tortillas, ranch cheese, roasted corn, steamed garbanzos, and prickly pear.

A small but well-stocked grocery store, the centrally located **Bonanza** (Mesones 43,

tel. 415/152-1260, 8 A.M.–8 P.M. Mon.–Sat., 8 A.M.–5 P.M. Sun.) is a great place to get all your kitchen basics. This popular little grocery sells range of dry goods, like rice, beans, pasta, nuts, raisins, bread, and crackers, as well as milk, yogurt, and cheeses. They also carry a selection of pricey luxury items, like jars of pesto, oyster sauce, dry sea vegetables, canned salmon, coconut milk, and tahini.

Lovely little **La Cava** (Zacateros 42A, tel. 415/152-3919, 10:30 A.M.–7 P.M. Mon.–Fri., 10:30 A.M.–4 P.M. Sat.) is San Miguel's oldest purveyor of fine imported and national cheeses, cold meats, gourmet sausages, and other specialty items, like olive oil, balsamic vinegar, olives, pastas, and bread. If you are in the mood for some nice Dutch gouda, go here. The owners take pride in their shop, and they will often offer a taste of what they've got in their fridges. If you are in town for the holidays, you can also order your Thanksgiving turkey at La Cava.

Vía Organica (Margarito Ledezma 2, tel. 415/152-8042, www.viaorganica.org,

8:30 A.M.–7 P.M. Mon.–Sat.) is a small organic supermarket that pleasantly reflects the sweet and earthy atmosphere of the town's nascent organic movement. The fruits and vegetables here are fresh and beautiful—lettuces and greens, in particular, are the nicest in town. In addition, the store stocks organic products like breakfast cereals and granola, nut butters, cooking oils, jams, ice cream, milk, cheese, hummus, rice milk, and spices. Prices are significantly higher than in the regular markets around San Miguel, but it all goes to a good cause. Behind the lovely storefront, Vía Organica is a nonprofit organization that runs an organic farm near the city and operates extensive outreach programs to local farmers. Vía Organic also runs a popular café in the store's entryway, which sells organic tapas, sandwiches, and salads, plus juice and coffee.

In downtown San Miguel, **La Buena Vida** (Plaza Golondrinas, Hernández Macías 72, Int. 14, tel. 415/152-2211, 8 A.M.–4 P.M. Mon.–Sat.) has been baking fresh artisan breads for decades. Located in a small plaza across the street from Bellas Artes (walk past the small café to find La Buena Vida's bakery's window on the right side), La Buena Vida's glass display case is always filled with a tempting variety of chocolate chip and peanut butter cookies, fluffy muffins, cinnamon rolls, pastries, and donuts. Behind the case, there is an assortment of whole-wheat loaves, multigrain rolls, and sourdough bread.

When you are in the mood for a treat, head to **Luna de Queso** (Salida a Celaya 51A, tel. 415/154-8122, maper2000@yahoo.com, 10 A.M.–8 P.M. Mon.–Fri., 10 A.M.–4 P.M. Sun.). This lovely deli has the largest selection of high quality, locally produced cheeses in town, many of which are made by the owner's mother. Here, you can find tangy French-style camembert and brie, soft goat cheese, fresh mozzarella, and aged chihuahua, plus sheep's milk yogurt, spreads, salamis, and cold cuts. In addition to the deli counter, Luna de Queso stocks all sorts of hard-to-find specialty items, like miso, couscous, teriyaki sauce, a wide variety of rices, and delicious marinated olives.

Just outside town on the highway to Querétaro, **Remo's** (Carretera San Miguel-Querétaro, Km 3, tel. 415/152-0453, 10 A.M.–5 P.M. daily) sells a homemade selection of Italian-style cheeses like mozzarella and provolone, as well as numerous locally produced soft cheeses, like camembert and brie. The shop's Italian owner also stocks well-priced imported parmigiano-reggiano and grana padano, Italian sausages and salamis, and a nice selection of imported pastas, sun-dried tomatoes, olives, and Italian wine and bubbly. The shop is a bit off the beaten track, but cheese lovers will make the trip.

A few blocks southeast of the central plaza, **Mercado San Juan de Dios** (between Calle San Rafael and Avenida Guadalupe, 8 A.M.–7 P.M. daily) is a large food market just east of the town square, which is more diverse and bustling than the smaller market downtown. At Juan de Dios, there are numerous large fruit and vegetable stands in the covered area, plus smaller vendors selling handmade tortillas, fresh cheese, and cactus paddles on folding tables. Its low prices and variety make this market very popular with locals. Crossing Calle San Rafael, the market continues down a covered pedestrian walkway, where you'll find assorted shoe stores and toy shops, as well as several fragrant and inexpensive flower stands. On Sunday mornings, there are always bustling families gathered around the food stalls in the market, which sell tortas, fruit juices, tamales, deep-fried quesadillas, *huaraches,* and many other types of greasy snacks. If you want tamales, go early; they usually run out by midday.

Information and Services

TOURIST INFORMATION

San Miguel's **tourist office** (Plaza Principal 10, tel. 415/152-0900, www.visitsanmiguel. travel) is on the main square. They will offer you an annotated map of the town. They can also arrange for a Spanish-speaking or bilingual tour of the city.

TRAVEL AGENTS

The only travel agent left standing, **Viajes Vertiz** (Hidalgo 1A, tel. 415/152-1856 or 415/152-1695, toll-free U.S. tel. 800/861-6423, www.viajesvertiz.com) can book plane tickets, cruises, travel packages, and tours, as well as transportation to and from the airports in León and Querétaro. Viajes Vertiz is also an American Express representative.

NEWSPAPERS AND PUBLICATIONS

The weekly periodical, *Atención San Miguel,* is required reading for anyone visiting San Miguel. Each week, *Atención* publishes a few news articles in Spanish and English about municipal events, as well as a slew of advertisements and promotional pieces about cultural happenings, art events, and upcoming speakers. The journalistic quality can be hit or miss, but there is no question that *Atención* is the number one source of information about events, happenings, music, art, or anything else going on San Miguel de Allende. Published principally for San Miguel's expatriate community, the classifieds are also a good place to turn if you are looking to rent a house or take an art class.

The Spanish-language newspaper *El Sol del Bajío* is published in Celaya and occasionally covers news and events in San Miguel de Allende. If you read in Spanish, it is the best place to get local news.

MAIL SERVICES

The Mexican **post office** is at Correo 16, on the corner of Correo and Corregidora. Inside, MexPost provides certified and expedited mail services through the regular postal system.

A mail services and shipping company, **Border Crossings** (Mesones 57, tel. 415/152-2497, 9 A.M.–6:30 P.M. Mon.–Fri., 10 A.M.–3 P.M. Sat.; Fábrica la Aurora, Local 2A-1, tel. 415/154-6858, 11 A.M.–5 P.M. Mon.–Fri., 10 A.M.–3 P.M. Sat.; www.bordercrossingsma.com) maintains a permanent mailing address in Laredo, Texas, which allows people in San Miguel de Allende to send and receive mail through the U.S. Postal Service. Monthly membership includes a personal mailbox at Border Crossings, free mail service to and from the United States (excluding the cost of postage), Internet access, and fax service. Nonmembers can also send and receive packages via Border Crossings' Texas address. In addition, Border Crossings offers shipping to the United States through UPS, DHL, and Mexican-operated Estafeta.

In business since the early 1990s, **La Conexión** (Aldama 3, tel. 415/152-1599, 9 A.M.–5 P.M. Mon.–Sat., 10 A.M.–2 P.M. Sun.; Plaza Real del Conde Local BA14, tel. 415/152-2312, 9 A.M.–5 P.M. Mon.–Fri.; Libramiento a Dolores Hidalgo 11, tel. 415/152-4223, 9 A.M.–5 P.M. Mon.–Fri.; www.laconexion.com.mx) offers daily mail service to and from a permanent address in the U.S. Members have a private mailbox in San Miguel de Allende, where they can receive regular mail, magazines, and newspaper subscriptions. La Conex also offers packing and shipping services, telephone and fax to the U.S., and wireless Internet in their office. They will also cash U.S. checks for members.

If you've bought more art or handicrafts than you can easily fit in your suitcase, **La Union** (Zacateros 37, tel. 415/152-5694, www. la-union.com.mx, 10 A.M.–6 P.M. Mon.–Sat.) provides packing and insured shipping services nationally and internationally through DHL, Estafeta, and FedEx, among others. Widely used by merchants in San Miguel, their service

San Miguel's main square is the focus of activity in town.

is excellent and prices for insured shipping are surprisingly reasonable. They also provide more inexpensive ground transportation to the U.S. and Canada.

MONEY

There are ATMs and teller service at **Banorte** (San Francisco 17, tel. 415/154-4760), plus currency exchange. **Banamex** (Canal 4, tel. 415/152-5423 or 415/154-8881) also has ATMs, tellers, and money exchange. They can also accept payments for telephone, electricity, and other services.

In most cases, the easiest and most efficient way to **change money** is to use ATM machines at Mexican banks, which are located throughout the *centro histórico.* If you do bring cash, you can change dollars to pesos at any bank in town (most will post their exchange rates in the window) or at one of several exchange houses around the central plaza.

When changing dollars to pesos, remember that Mexico has recently imposed much stricter controls on cash exchange. In any bank or exchange house in San Miguel de Allende, you will need to present a valid passport in order

to change money. Some exchange houses will also cap the amount of money you can change per day or per month.

In addition to changing American dollars, Canadian dollars, and euros, **Intercam** (Correo 15, San Francisco 4, and Plaza La Luciérnaga, Local 53, tel. 415/154-6707 or 415/120-4837, www.intercam.com.mx, 9 A.M.–5:45 P.M. Mon.–Fri., 9 A.M.–1:45 P.M. Sat.) will also change travelers checks. For clients in San Miguel de Allende, Intercam can also change American checks to pesos, though clients must register specifically with Intercam to use this service.

INTERNET ACCESS

In San Miguel de Allende, even 17th-century mansions are wired for Internet access. In most hotels, there is free wireless or a personal computer that guests can share. There are also plenty of places to hop on the web throughout town. If you brought your own computer, the **Casa del Café** (Hospicio 31) has free wireless Internet for customers, as well as good coffee, smoothies, juices, sandwiches, and pastries.

In addition to their shipping services, **Border**

VOLUNTEERING

Numerous nonprofit organizations and an active expatriate community make San Miguel de Allende an excellent place to get involved. Foreigners routinely volunteer for these organizations (or host benefits to support them); here's a short list of the many opportunities for big-hearted visitors and residents.

SOCIEDAD PROTECTORA DE ANIMALES

The Sociedad Protectora de Animales (SPA, Los Pinos 7, Col. Lindavista, tel. 415/152-6124, www.spasanmiguel.org, 11 A.M.-2 P.M. Mon.-Sat.) operates an animal shelter for strays as well as an animal clinic with low-cost veterinary care, sterilizations, and vaccinations. Most visibly, SPA has a very active animal adoption program, placing hundreds of stray dogs and cats in family homes each year. Walking through the town square, you often see SPA members showing off the newest dogs up for adoption.

SPA is always looking for animal-loving volunteers to help with fundraising, animal training, or simply socializing with resident dogs and cats. You can also help SPA by adopting a pet; the animals seeking homes are listed on the website.

CENTRO PARA LOS ADOLESCENTES DE SAN MIGUEL DE ALLENDE

CASA (Santa Julia 15, Col. Santa Julia, tel. 415/154-6060 or 415/154-6090, U.S. tel. 212/234-7940, www.casa.org.mx) is a multifaceted nonprofit organization that provides health services, social services, and health education to rural families. In 1994, CASA also opened a maternity hospital, where thousands of babies have been delivered. Two years later, this unique organization officially opened the first accredited School of Midwifery in Mexico, which has since trained midwives from dozens of Mexican states and foreign countries.

CASA operates a three-month long internship program for youth, as well as a professional volunteer program for doctors, nurses, midwives, and other medical professionals who would like to contribute to CASA's mission.

PATRONATO PRO NIÑOS

Patronato Pro Niños (Av. Reforma 75C, Fracc. Ignacio Ramírez, tel. 415/152-7290 or 415/152-7796, www.patronatproninos.org, 9 A.M.-4 P.M. Mon.-Fri.) is a nonprofit organization that provides free medical care to needy children in San Miguel de Allende and environs, in addition to free or very low cost dental care in their mobile Dental Van. They are currently developing a children's health center on land granted to them by the Mexican government. Patronato Pro Niños is always looks for volunteers who can go out into country towns and look for children in need of medical attention, as well as medical and business advisors. In addition, Patronato Pro Niños always needs doctors and dentists.

HOSPICE SAN MIGUEL

Hospice San Miguel (Manuel Rocha 35, Col. La

Crossings (Mesones 57, tel. 415/152-2497, 9 A.M.-6:30 P.M. Mon.-Fri., 10 A.M.-3 P.M. Sat., www.bordercrossingsma.com) offers Internet access in their downtown location via five in-office PCs, as well as black-and-white printing. There is a nameless **Internet café** (Hernández Macías 47, no tel., 10 A.M. to 9 P.M. daily) just below the Hotel Sautto. It has five PC computers connected to the Internet, a black-and-white printer, and a telephone booth for international calls.

LAUNDRY

Franco Tintorería (Ancha de San Antonio 15, tel. 415/154-4495 or 415/154-4495, 9 A.M.-7 P.M. Mon.-Fri, 9 A.M.-5 P.M. Sat.) offers inexpensive laundry and dry-cleaning service, with pickup and delivery to your home

Lejona, tel. 415/154-4287, www.hospicesma. org) provides skilled medical treatment to people with terminal illnesses and provides support and counseling to family members after the loss of a loved one. The hospice trains volunteers to support hospice patients and their families in a variety of areas, like fundraising, patient support, companion visits, and clerical work.

BIBLIOTECA DE SAN MIGUEL DE ALLENDE

The Biblioteca de San Miguel de Allende (Insurgentes 25, tel. 415/152-0293, www. bibliotecasma.com, 10 A.M.-7 P.M. Mon.-Fri., 10 A.M.-2 P.M. Sat.) is always looking for volunteers to help with their numerous education and literacy programs. Positions could range from a newsletter author to a children's art teacher to fundraising support.

JÓVENES ADELANTES

Jóvenes Adelantes (c/o La Conexión, Box 49A, Aldama 3, www.jovenesadelante.org) is a tutoring and college scholarship program for promising students at an economic disadvantage. The program seeks out exceptional rural high school students, who can receive up to five years of college scholarship money through the program. In addition, participating students are linked with mentors and tutors, and can participate in free English language classes. Volunteers can get involved with the nonprofit's activities through academic mentoring and academic tutoring, as a personal counselor.

or hotel. They will launder four kilos of clothes for about US$4.50.

Right in the center of town, **Tintorería Lavandería La Pila** (Jesús 25, tel. 415/152-5810, 8 A.M.–7 P.M. Mon.–Fri., 8 A.M.–3 P.M. Sat.) washes and dries your clothes for about US$5 for five kilos of laundry. They also have dry-cleaning service.

On the opposite side of the *centro,*

Lavandería Limpiecito (Quebrada 15, 10 A.M.–8 P.M. daily) offers ultra-friendly laundry services for less than a dollar per kilo.

MEDICAL AND EMERGENCY SERVICES

For all types of ailments, from stomach flu to altitude sickness, many expatriates turn to **Dra. Silvia Azcarate** (Codo 9A, tel. 415/152-1944), a general medicine doctor who speaks Spanish, English, and French. At Hospital de la Fe, **Dr. José Diez Sautto** (Libramiento a Dolores Hidalgo 43-2, Mesa del Malanquin, tel. 415/152-2233 or 415/152-2329) is an excellent generalist and surgeon.

At Clínica San Miguel, **Dr. Cesar Gil Hoyos** (Ancha de San Antonio 73, tel. 415/154-5111, http://clinica-sanmiguel.com) is a recommended doctor of Chinese medicine and acupuncture. There is also an English-speaking acupuncturist and well-recommended naturopathic doctor at **LifePath Center** (Pila Seca 11, tel. 415/154-8465).

In an **emergency,** you can reach the **Protección Civil** (Civil Protection Department, Bulevar de la Conspiración 130, Casco de Landeta) by dialing 066 or tel. 415/152-0911. The **Cruz Roja Mexicana** (Lib. José Manuel Zavala PPKBZON Las Brisas) emergency response, or Red Cross, can be reached at tel. 415/152-1616, 415/152-4229, or 415/152-4225.

The *bomberos* (fire department, Bulevar de la Conspiración 130, Casco de Landeta, tel. 415/152-2888 or 415/152-3699) is to the east of town. The general hospital, **Hospital General de San Miguel** (Primero de Mayo s/n, Fracc. Ignacio Ramírez) can be reached at tel. 415/120-4746 or 415/1200-4756. **Hospital de la Fe** (Lib. José Zavala PPKBZON 12) is a private hospital that also takes emergencies, and can be reached at tel. 415/152-2233, 415/152-2320, and 415/152-1229.

VETERINARY SERVICES

Dr. Ricardo López at **Animal Care** (Prol. Calzada de la Aurora 7, tel. 415/152-6977) is a friendly, experienced, and inexpensive veterinarian in the Aurora neighborhood. He will also make house calls. Dr. Kronish at **Animal Medical Center** (Salida a Celaya 67, tel. 415/185-8185, cell tel. 415/109-9957) also cares for pets, at the office to the south of the city center or at your home.

VISAS AND OFFICIALDOM

Thanks to the large American expatriate population, there is a **U.S. Consular Agency** (Plaza las Golondrinas, Hernández Macías 72, Int. 111 and 112, tel. 415/152-2357, 9 A.M.–1 P.M. Mon.–Thurs., consuladosma@gmail.com, clancyek@state.gov) in San Miguel de Allende. As a branch of the U.S. Embassy in Mexico City, the consulate can assist with lost or stolen passports, among other services.

To report a missing tourist card, apply for a resident visa, or perform any other immigration-related paperwork, go to the **Instituto Nacional de Migración** (Mexican Immigration Services, Calzada de la Estación, tel. 415/152-2542, 9 A.M.–1 P.M. Mon.–Fri.), just outside the center of town, almost to the railroad station. With so many foreigners in such a small town, Migración can get a bit backed up; plan ahead if you need to visit their offices.

Getting There

BY AIR

Getting to San Miguel from overseas can be a bit of a challenge. While well connected to other Mexican cities by highway, it is nonetheless a small town and relatively remote. If you are coming from outside of Mexico, the two airports closest to San Miguel de Allende are the Del Bajío International Airport (BJX) and Querétaro International Airport (QRO), though you can also fly to Mexico City.

Del Bajío International Airport

The most popular choice for visitors to San Miguel de Allende, the Del Bajío International Airport (BJX) has daily direct flights to and from Dallas/Fort Worth, Houston, and Los Angeles, as well as several flights to and from Mexico City and Monterrey. The airport is in Silao, Guanajuato, just outside the city of León, and about a 90-minute drive from San Miguel de Allende. From the airport, most people hire a shuttle or car service to drive them to San Miguel de Allende.

Querétaro International Airport

Querétaro International Airport (QRO) is northeast of the city of Querétaro, about a 90-minute drive from San Miguel de Allende. This airport is much newer, smaller, and less trafficked than its counterpart in León. Routes and rates change frequently, though there are direct flights from Houston, plus connecting service to other international destinations through Mexico City. As in León, it is necessary to schedule a shuttle pickup from Querétaro or to hire a taxi to take you to San Miguel.

Mexico City International Airport

The country's busiest airport is, unsurprisingly, Mexico City International Airport (MEX) in the capital. There are direct flights from Mexico City to more than 100 cities around the world. Flights to Mexico City can often be considerably more inexpensive than those to León or Querétaro, both much smaller airports.

From the airport in Mexico City, travelers must arrange for ground transportation to San Miguel de Allende, usually by bus or through one of San Miguel de Allende's transport companies. The trip from the capital to San Miguel is about four hours, depending on road conditions and the famous Mexico City traffic.

Shuttle Service

Many hotels and rental homes will help you arrange shuttle service from the airport in León or Querétaro to San Miguel de Allende. If you are making your own arrangements, the aptly named and highly professional **San Miguel Airport Shuttle** (Jesús 11, tel. 415/152-1999, U.S. tel. 202/609-9905, www.sanmigueltravelservices.com) offers door-to-door airport service to San Miguel from Mexico City, León, and Querétaro, and back again. They will make special arrangements for people traveling with pets. They offer private cars, as well as shared shuttles.

A popular choice with the local crowd, **Viajes San Miguel** (Sollano 4, tel. 415/152-2832 or 415/152-2934, www.viajessanmiguel.com) can provide a shared van or private car to both León and Querétaro, with a reservation. Viajes San Miguel will also provide assistance for travelers arriving in Mexico City. If you need to make last-minute arrangements, their emergency number is tel. 415/152-2537.

Turismo Ernie (Prol. Calzada de la Aurora 9, tel. 415/152-1350, cell tel. 415/105-1544, reservaciones@turismoernie.com) will also send a private car or Suburban to take you to and from the airports in León or Querétaro. The company can also provide transportation and friendly chauffeurs for day trips around San Miguel de Allende.

BY BUS

A network of comprehensive, comfortable, and reasonably priced bus lines connects all of Mexico. There is ample first- and second-class bus service between San Miguel de Allende and Mexico City, as well as direct service to all major cities in the Bajío and Guadalajara. Both first-class and second-class buses tend to be comfortable and air-conditioned, and all first-class buses have a bathroom. The major difference is that second-class buses tend to stop along the roadways to pick up and drop off passengers; therefore, travel on a second-class bus can be slower and more tiring, though also a bit cheaper.

A first-class bus company covering central to northern Mexico, **Primera Plus** (tel. 415/152-0084, toll-free Mex. tel. 800/375-7587, www.primeraplus.com.mx) offers direct service between the Terminal Central de Norte in Mexico City and the Central de Autobuses in San Miguel de Allende. Primera Plus also operates direct routes from San Miguel de Allende to Morelia, Guadalajara, Guanajuato, León, and Lagos de Moreno, with connecting service to more distant cities, like Puerto Vallarta and Manzanillo. Comfortable buses include bathrooms, snack packets, and reclining seats, plus televisions projecting noisy Hollywood movies—usually dubbed into Spanish.

If you are arriving on a flight to Mexico City International Airport, Primera Plus also offers direct service from both airport terminals to Querétaro's main bus station. From the bus station, you can hop a second-class bus for the remaining 80 kilometers (50 miles) to San Miguel de Allende. Alternatively, Querétaro's city taxis will drive you all the way to San Miguel de Allende from the bus terminal for about US$35. Before you go outside to grab a taxi, you must buy a ticket from the registered taxi stand inside the bus terminal and let them know you are going to San Miguel.

The poshest bus line in central Mexico, **ETN** (tel. 415/152-6407 or toll-free Mex. tel. 800/800-0386, www.etn.com.mx) also provides comfy first-class bus service between the capital and San Miguel de Allende, with five departures daily. These stylish coaches have reclining seats, bathrooms, snacks, and coffee service. ETN's routes are a bit more limited than Primera Plus, but the company also offers direct service to Guadalajara, León, Guanajuato, and Querétaro, with connecting service elsewhere. When planning your route, you will usually get more accurate information if you call the local telephone numbers, rather than the toll-free line.

For shorter trips or a more spontaneous agenda, it can be easiest to use second-class bus service, especially when traveling between San Miguel de Allende and Querétaro or San Miguel de Allende and Dolores Hidalgo. Second-class buses depart from San Miguel de Allende to Querétaro every 20–30 minutes until about 10 P.M., and vice versa. **Herradura de Plata** (tel. 415/152-0725) and **Servicios**

Coordinados Flecha Amarilla (tel. 415/152-0084, toll-free Mex. tel. 800/375-7587), the latter of which is run by the same company that operates Primera Plus, both offer second-class service to Querétaro and Dolores Hidalgo. No need to book ahead; it's easiest to simply arrive at the bus terminal and get on the next departing bus. The ticket sales loudly announce each departure.

BY CAR
From the United States
From the southernmost tip of Texas, San Miguel de Allende is just one (very long) day's drive from the U.S.-Mexico border. For decades, many Texan families drove down to Mexico's high plains to escape the summer heat in the Lone Star State. Unfortunately, driving to San Miguel de Allende from the United States has become less safe due to the widespread drug-related violence along Mexico's border. Even so, many people make the trip by car, without incident. If you plan to drive to San Miguel de Allende from the United States, use precaution by traveling during daylight hours and using toll roads, which tend to be in better condition and less dangerous than free highways.

Most drivers coming to San Miguel de Allende cross the border at the well-trafficked Laredo/Nuevo Laredo crossing or, alternatively, McAllen/Reynosa, two of the most southerly border crossings in Texas. From there, head south toward Monterrey then on toward Matehuala. From Matehuala, take the toll highway south toward San Luis Potosí, passing outside the city, and continuing on Highway 57 toward Querétaro. Turn off at the Dr. Mora/San Miguel de Allende exit (just past San Luis de la Paz), heading west until you arrive in San Miguel de Allende. The drive from the border should take about 10–12 hours, but getting lost in the outskirts of a major city can make the trip much longer. If you are going to do the drive, invest in a *Guia Roji* (www.guiaroji.com.mx), Mexico's most complete road map, and plot your route ahead of time.

From Mexico City
San Miguel de Allende is about 255 kilometers (160 miles) northwest of Mexico City. The drive takes 3–4 hours, on fairly easy and well-maintained highways. From Mexico City, exit the city via the Periférico Norte, and head north toward Tepotzotlán. After passing through the *caseta* (toll booth), continue on Highway 57 north toward Querétaro. Just past San Juan del Río (but before arriving in Querétaro), turn off at San Luis Potosí/San Miguel de Allende Via Corta. You will pass another toll booth and then cross Highway 57 again; continue straight on the overpass and follow the winding two-lane road another 30 minutes until you arrive in San Miguel de Allende.

If you miss the turn off for the Via Corta, you can continue straight on Highway 57 all the way to Querétaro. Once you pass the city, keep an eye out for the turnoff to San Miguel de Allende on the right-hand side. Cross the overpass, and follow the two-lane highway all the way to San Miguel de Allende.

Getting Around

If you come to San Miguel, you should be prepared to use your legs. This hilly little town is best for walking, though it will also give you quite a workout! When you're worn out, there are several other ways to get around.

BY CAR

With everything just a stone's throw away, it isn't necessary to have a car in San Miguel de Allende. However, a car can make it easier to visit the hot springs or the botanical gardens, or to eat at some of the nice restaurants outside the downtown area. Generally, drivers are courteous in San Miguel, even if streets feel a bit narrow for those used to suburbs and highways.

If you are itching for your own set of wheels, **San Miguel Rent-a-Car** (Codo 9, tel. 415/152-0198, www.sanmiguelrentalcar. com, 9 A.M.–3 P.M. and 5–7 P.M. Mon.–Fri., 9 A.M.–3 P.M. Sun.) rents compact cars, sedans, jeeps, and vans for a day or more. They also rent ATVs. All you need is a valid driver's license and a credit card. Prices are very reasonable.

The most difficult part about driving in San Miguel is finding a place to park downtown. Fortunately, there are several low-cost parking garages, if you get fed up with circling. There are covered spots at **Estacionamiento Hidalgo** (Hidalgo 57) between Callejón del Pueblito and Insurgentes, for about a dollar an hour. Around the corner on Insurgentes and Hidalgo, **Estacionamiento Insurgentes** is another large, covered lot that is close to everything.

BY TAXI

Taxicabs constantly circle San Miguel, providing the most convenient and inexpensive way to move around town. Anywhere within the town limits, a taxi ride costs about US$2. Longer trips to outlying neighborhoods, like the residential Los Frailes, will cost a buck or two more. Taxis will also take you out to the hot springs for around US$8, and, if you ask, most will be happy to return to pick you up at an appointed time. Taxis circulate through most of San Miguel, but if you are off the beaten track, you can also call **Radio Taxi** (Tesoro 10, tel. 415/152-4501) or **Sitio Allende** (Portal Guadalupe, tel. 415/152-0192) to pick you up.

BY ATV

Traffic in San Miguel is slow-moving and courteous, making it generally safe for smaller vehicles like ATVs to circulate along with automobiles. If you want to cruise around town on four wheels, **Bicentenario Todo Terreno** (Jesús 4, tel. 415/152-7342 or toll-free Mex. tel. 800/836-9758, www.bicentenariotodoterreno.com) will rent you an ATV by the hour, by the day, or by the week (they also run ATV sightseeing tours of the surrounding countryside with trained guides). Although their loud motors can make an unpleasant echo down San Miguel's narrow streets, ATVs are a popular way to move around the city center. They can also be a great way to get up to the botanical gardens or explore more outlying neighborhoods.

PUBLIC TRANSPORTATION

Inexpensive **city buses** crisscross the city of San Miguel, improbably turning around tight corners, barreling down narrow colonial streets, and filling the air with the sweet aroma of carbon monoxide. For less than 50 cents, the city buses will get you anywhere you need to go, though finding a direct route can be a bit of a challenge.

Generally speaking, it is much easier to find your way into the downtown district than to get out to a distant neighborhood. Buses head to the *centro histórico* from every corner of the city, and they will almost always have a sign in the front window that reads Centro.

Downtown, a major **bus stop** is located on

Insurgentes and Pepe Llanos, across the street from the Oratorio San Felipe Neri. Here, you can catch a bus to the Independencia, San Rafael, and San Antonio neighborhoods, among others. If you are going to the Tianguis Municipal, you can get a bus on Calle Colegio, to the east of the Plaza Cívica. Buses depart from the Mercado San Juan de Dios for La Cieneguita neighborhood. Most buses have their destination posted in the front window, and in many cases, the driver's assistant will shout out the bus's destination to the crowd at the bus stop. When in doubt, ask the driver where the bus is going.

Vicinity of San Miguel de Allende

ATOTONILCO

The small town of Atotonilco is 13 kilometers (eight miles) from downtown San Miguel de Allende, just off the highway to Dolores Hidalgo. Atotonilco is a small, sleepy, and dusty place, where little seems to have changed in the 400 years since its founding. Despite its wee size (there are fewer than 1,000 residents), Atotonilco has an important place in history and culture. Originally conceived as a religious retreat from San Miguel, it has attracted Catholic pilgrims for centuries. During the War of Independence, Atotonilco was the first place that Father Miguel Hidalgo rode with his cavalry after giving the historic call to war from the steps of the Dolores church. Hidalgo and his men borrowed a banner of La Virgen de Guadalupe from inside Atotonilco's Santuario de Jesús Nazareno, carrying it as a flag into San Miguel de Allende. Thereafter, a banner bearing the image of La Virgen de Guadalupe became a symbol of the independence movement.

Today, Atotonilco is a sleepy town that experiences just a small cultural overflow from San Miguel de Allende. In Atotonilco, there are always a few tourists wandering around, some resort hotels have opened in the nearby countryside, and a number of American and Canadian expatriates have bought homes here, preferring the rural setting to the bustle of San Miguel.

◖ Santuario de Jesús Nazareno de Atotonilco

The main attraction in the city is the magnificent Santuario de Jesús Nazareno de Atotonilco (Plaza Principal s/n, 8 a.m.–6 p.m. daily), one of the finest examples of baroque art and architecture in New Spain. Luis Felipe Neri de Alfaro, the same wealthy Catholic priest who oversaw the construction of the Iglesia de Nuestra Señora de la Salud, originally conceived of the shrine in Atotonilco as a religious sanctuary for the people of San Miguel. The majority of the church was constructed between 1740 and 1776, beginning with the facade, the main nave, and several adjoining chapels. After its construction, the artist Miguel Antonio Martínez de Pocasangre spent more than 30 years painting the walls and ceiling of the nave with detailed religious histories and personages. As you walk through the creaky entryway into the church, the visual stimulation from floor-to-ceiling murals is momentarily overwhelming. One could easily spend hours examining the many unusual figures and strange histories related on the sanctuary's walls.

In 2008, the United Nations named the Santuario de Atotonilco a World Heritage Site, together with San Miguel de Allende. Thereafter, the church underwent a massive restoration project. Today, it is easier to appreciate the incredible masterwork inside the church, as Martínez's frescos have been nicely restored. There are occasionally Spanish-speaking tour guides at the church's entryway who can help illuminate the fantastic meaning behind the elaborate frescoes (you can also hire a tour guide in San Miguel de Allende to accompany you to the site).

In addition to its historical and architectural

importance, the Santuario de Atotonilco is an important pilgrimage destination for Mexican Catholics throughout the region. In particular, many come to see and give thanks to the wooden figure of **El Señor de la Columna,** widely revered for its ability to perform miracles. Not far astray from its founder's intentions, the *santuario* also continues to serve as a religious retreat of the most austere variety, with dormers sleeping on cold stone floors and often subjecting themselves to corporal punishment. On some days, the plaza in front of the church is packed with pilgrims and vendors, some of which sell rough twine ropes for self-flagellation and real crowns of thorns. Other days, the town is as quiet as history, with nothing but the sound of wind whipping dust into the air.

Right next door to the Santuario de Atotonilco, there is a small **gift shop** (Plaza Principal s/n, no tel., 8:30 A.M.–6 P.M. Tues.–Sun.) operated by the nuns of Atotonilco, which sells religious souvenirs, rosaries, stuffed animals, and beaded jewelry, as well as a few small booklets (in English and Spanish) with information about the church. Within the shop, the nuns also run a small **café,** with an appealing row of cloth-covered wood tables and a simple menu of quesadillas, sandwiches, and instant coffee. The food here is nothing spectacular; for a better (and even more inexpensive) lunch, try one of the small stands right across the street, where they serve handmade gorditas and other quick bites for just a few dollars.

Hot Springs and Swimming

In the region surrounding the town of Atotonilco (about 13 kilometers/eight miles from downtown San Miguel), volcanic activity under the earth has produced copious natural, nonsulfurous hot springs. Many locals believe the water has healing properties, and after a dip you may agree. If you want to try the hot springs, there are a number of low-key places to enjoy this amazing natural resource. No

© ARTURO MEADE

an elaborate fresco in the Santuario de Jesús Nazareno de Atotonilco

matter where you choose to soak, don't forget to bring a towel! Besides cafés or small snack shops, there are very few services at most of these family-style swimming spots.

◖ LA GRUTA

La Gruta (Carretera San Miguel Allende-Dolores Hidalgo, Km 10, tel. 415/185-2162, www.lagrutaspa.com, 7 A.M.–6 P.M. daily, US$7) is probably the most popular bathing spot near San Miguel. On La Gruta's ample grounds, lush gardens surround two large outdoor pools, one tepid and the other quite warm. From the warmer pool, swim down a covered hallway to a domed cave that is filled with even warmer water, fed directly from the spring. (This is the *gruta,* or grotto, for which the spot is named.) After a dip, you can relax in the pretty gardens, which are shaded by fig trees and dotted with picnic tables and recliners. La Gruta's small café serves basic breakfasts and lunch—fruit, scrambled eggs, *chilaquiles,* quesadillas, guacamole, and the like—plus juice, soft drinks, beer, and margaritas. During the summer months, the pools are filled with splashing children and families; it's much quieter in the winter, when chilly air makes getting in and out of the warm water slightly torturous. For the most Zen experience, get there early in the morning, as the pools are just filling up with fresh water and few people have arrived.

ESCONDIDO PLACE

At Escondido Place (Carretera San Miguel Allende-Dolores Hidalgo, Km 10, tel. 415/185-2025 or 415/185-2202 8 A.M.–5:30 P.M. daily, www.escondidoplace.com, US$7), there are three covered thermal pools, each progressively warmer. Every morning, fresh water is pumped into the barrel-shaped caves that cover the pools, filling them with steam. There are also several outdoor pools, a small snack bar, and a picnic area with outdoor grills. The gardens are extensive, filled with towering trees and a lily-covered pond. Though the gardens are beautiful and the pools are warm, Escondido is less

popular with locals than La Gruta, so early-birds often have the place to themselves.

TABOADA

A popular hangout for locals and families, Taboada (Carretera San Miguel Allende-Dolores Hidalgo, Km 8, tel. 415/152-9250, www.hoteltaboada.com.mx, 9 A.M.–6 P.M. Wed.–Mon., US$7) has a tepid Olympic-sized swimming pool, which is fed by a natural spring. The slightly warm water makes Taboada's pool a nice place for laps during the cool winter months. If you come on a summer day, bring your Frisbee: Adjoining the pool is an expansive lawn, lined with enormous palm trees. It's a great place to spend the day. There is also a small snack bar at Taboada and a full bar, but you can bring a picnic lunch along to make a day of it. Like the other bathing spots, Taboada is busiest during summer vacations when big local families gather on the lawns. Just beyond the pool, Taboada also runs a large hotel.

XOTE

Close to Taboada, Xote (Carretera San Miguel Allende-Dolores Hidalgo, Km 5.5, tel. 415/155-8187, 9 A.M.–6 P.M. daily, US$8 adults, US$4 children) is more water park than relaxation center. This large, hilltop park caters to children and families; not only is there a large swimming pool at the park's summit, there are several high-speed water slides. If you arrive during the week, there are often just a few bathers (in the event that you are alone, the park staff will turn on the water slides so you can use them), though summer afternoons can become quite crowded. Children must be at least one meter (three feet) tall to use the slides. Once they are over 1.5 meters (4'10"), they must pay adult prices.

Accommodations and Food

Just a few minutes' drive from the sanctuary, **Nirvana Restaurant and Retreat** (Camino Antigua Estación FFCC 11, tel. 415/185-2194, noon–10 P.M. Wed.–Mon.) is a small hotel on a picturesque ranch in the Atotonilco countryside. To get there, turn down the dusty Camino Antigua Estación (the first major road after Atotonilco's east entrance) and continue for a few kilometers until you see signs for the ranch. For those who'd like to spend a day or two in the tranquility of the country, Nirvana has seven guest rooms, some of which are located in freestanding cottages. Decoration is different in each, with better effect in some than others. All rooms, however, have lovely views of the trees and gardens. Hotel guests can go horseback riding around the grounds, get spa treatments, or use the beautiful hotel pool, which is heated with natural thermal water. If you aren't staying overnight, you can still enjoy the atmosphere over a cocktail and a snack at their restaurant, which has particularly nice outdoor seating with lovely views of the gardens.

CAÑADA DE LA VIRGEN

To the southeast of San Miguel de Allende, there is a local archaeological site known as the Cañada de la Virgen (Carretera Guanajuato-San Miguel s/n, 9 A.M.–5 P.M. Tues.–Sat., US$2.50). Recently opened to the public, the ruins of this pre-Columbian city are believed to be the remnants of the Panteca people of the greater Toltec empire, who once lived along the flood plain of the Laja River. Occupied from around 540–1000 A.D., the site contains five groups of monuments, including a 15-meter pyramid-temple and a large sunken plaza. The structures of the main architectural grouping, known as the Casa de los Treces Cielos (House of the Thirteen Skies), were constructed to align with the sun's path. However, unlike in pre-Columbian cities such as Teotihuacan, Xochicalco, and Palenque, the sun rises in front of the main temple at the Cañada de la Virgen, rather than behind it. Archaeological study of the site is ongoing.

The Cañada de la Virgen is just over 24 kilometers (15 miles) from San Miguel de Allende. For visitors, there is a parking lot just off the highway to Guanajuato; from there, walk uphill just under a kilometer to the visitors center and archaeological site, operated by the Instituto Nacional de Antropología e Historia (INAH), Mexico's bureau of history and anthropology.

In addition to the archaeological site, the surrounding area, called the **Santuario Cañada de la Virgen** (offices at Orizaba 2, Col. San Antonio, San Miguel de Allende, tel. 415/154-8771 or 415/152-7044, www.canadadelavirgen.com), is a beautiful and expansive nature preserve, open to visitors for guided horseback rides, camping, and hiking, among other activities. Rugged and well preserved, the protected area is home to hundreds of native species of trees, shrubs, and cactus, and distinguished by a marvelous *cañada* (canyon) that cuts through the dry plain.

SAN MIGUEL EL VIEJO

Just past the train depot near the Presa Allende, the small settlement of San Miguel el Viejo sits at the same spot where Fray Juan de San Miguel originally founded the city of San Miguel de los Chichimecas. Today, it is a rural and dusty community, with few inhabitants. Though some expatriates have constructed homes here, the settlement remains largely off the beaten track. On the main road in town, the **Capilla de Casqueros** (Camino a San Miguel el Viejo s/n, hours vary) is a small 17th-century chapel with brick red walls and a simple stone facade. It is rarely open, but visitors can enjoy its exterior and plaza. As one of the oldest structures in the region, the chapel is wonderfully lopsided and worn by time.

While in San Miguel el Viejo, you can pick up some fresh greens at **Rancho La Trinidad** (Camino a San Miguel el Viejo 8, cell tel. 415/111-7894, 7 A.M.–3 P.M. Mon.–Fri., 7–11 A.M. Sat.). To reach San Miguel el Viejo, take the Calzada de la Estación past the train depot. Right after crossing the tracks, turn left down a small country road.

GUANAJUATO

As if plucked from the pages of a fairy tale, Guanajuato is unique and almost mythical in its beauty. From above the classical theaters and baroque churches crammed within the labyrinthine alleyways of the city center, haphazard stacks of sherbet-colored houses rise along the hillsides in perfect disorganization. Even higher above, rocky peaks rise over the valley floor, while the clear mountain sky complements the scene with its crystal blue canopy.

Guanajuato is a city to stroll in, to observe from courtyard cafés or from a shady bench in the Jardín de la Unión. The city is best explored on foot; it is a pleasure to get lost in the twisted maze of picturesque streets, where people walk uninhibited by traffic—in a pedestrian-friendly innovation, most roads in the *centro histórico* occupy a circuit of tunnels below the ground. Even without automobiles, the streets of Guanajuato are surprisingly busy, crowded with tourists and families, street musicians, candy sellers, and fruit stands. The atmosphere is decidedly bustling, bordering on hectic, during any of the city's large arts festivals or religious holidays.

Home to the prestigious Universidad de Guanajuato, the city is a place of students, intellectuals, and the arts. The university influences the local culture in many ways, most noticeably in its lively and youthful spirit. Visitors will enjoy all the perks of student life, like ample bookstores, cheap eats, and picturesque European-style cafés. For foreign exchange students and happy backpackers, Guanajuato is an appealing and inexpensive place to spend a few days (or a few months)

© ARTURO MEADE

HIGHLIGHTS

◖ Teatro Juárez: This majestic turn-of-the-20th-century theater is one of Guanajuato's principal performance venues. Even if you don't attend a concert or play, it is worth a peek inside the elaborately designed interior, which is open to the public throughout the week (page 113).

◖ Universidad de Guanajuato: Guanajuato's university campus dominates the city in more ways than one. Not only is its unusual white facade an iconic element in Guanajuato's quirky skyline, this large public school makes an enormous cultural contribution to the city (page 114).

◖ Mercado Hidalgo: Inaugurated on September 16, 1910, the unique municipal market was a gift to the city of Guanajuato at the 100th anniversary of the War of Independence. Inside, there are plenty of places to shop or grab a snack, and the atmosphere is one-of-a-kind (page 116).

◖ Alhóndiga de Granaditas: The fortress-like public granary was the site of one of the most famous and brutal battles in the early War of Independence. Today, it is a regional museum with an interesting collection of artifacts, old photographs, and didactic texts (page 117).

◖ Museo y Casa de Diego Rivera: The great Mexican muralist and painter, Diego Rivera, was born to a wealthy family in Guanajuato. Today, his childhood home has been converted to a nice museum showcasing some of the artist's early work, as well as work by his contemporaries and influences (page 119).

◖ El Pípila and the Funicular Panorámico: Take a ride on the funicular or wander up the ascending alleyways behind the Teatro Juárez to visit the monument to El Pípila, one of Mexico's great war heroes. The wide plaza surrounding this giant stone statue overlooks one of Guanajuato's most panoramic views (page 120).

◖ Templo de San Cayetano: There is no more-perfect reflection of the silver trade's enormous bounty than the elaborate Templo de San Cayetano in La Valenciana neighborhood. Commissioned by one of the owners of La Valenciana mine, this beautiful chapel is one of the most spectacular examples of baroque architecture in Mexico (page 123).

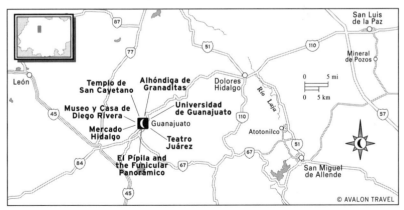

LOOK FOR ◖ TO FIND RECOMMENDED SIGHTS, ACTIVITIES, DINING, AND LODGING.

GUANAJUATO

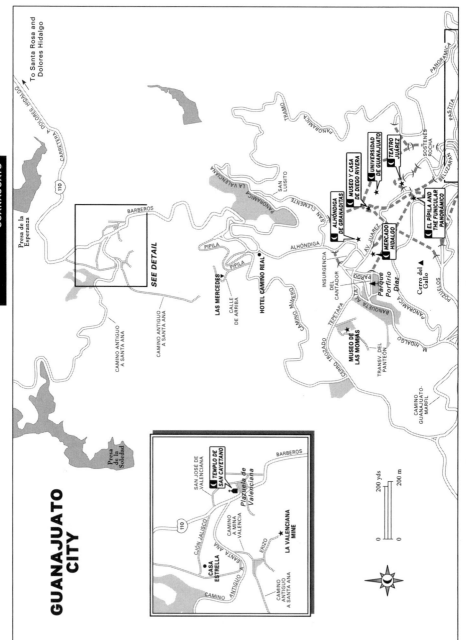

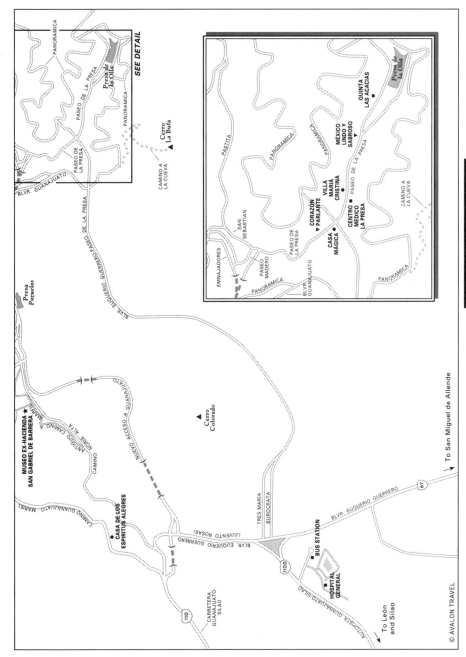

relaxing in coffee shops and meeting up with other travelers. Despite the youthful atmosphere, the city also offers a good measure of cultural sophistication. Visitors of every ilk will enjoy Guanajuato's unique architectural sights, urbane music and theater events at Teatro Juárez, and the smattering of international and gourmet restaurants.

Like the rest of the Bajío, Guanajuato is a town with a tremendous place in history. Once the home of the world's largest and most prolific silver mines, the city rose to prominence during the 17th century. It was among the first cities invaded by Miguel Hidalgo's army, and Guanajuato's Alhóndiga de Granaditas was the site of one of the most important battles in the War of Independence. Today, Guanajuato's historic structures and many museums bring the visitor close to the city's history, yet the vibe is never stuffy or old-fashioned. Here, contemporary art exhibitions take place in 17th-century cloisters, while medieval troubadours play songs for groups of Mexico City weekenders. The mix is appealing, unusual, refreshing, and unique. As visitors to this special city quickly learn, there is no place on earth quite like Guanajuato.

HISTORY

The settlement of Santa Fe and Real de Minas Guanajuato was established around 1548, when Spanish settlers discovered silver veins in the sierra around the city. Although Guanajuato is one of Mexico's quintessential silver cities, its initial contribution to the silver industry was much smaller than those of its neighbors to the north. Throughout the 16th and 17th centuries, the mines at Zacatecas were the most important to New Spain, while Guanajuato's mines faltered in productivity, hampered by lack of technology and periodic flash flooding. Guanajuato grew more slowly than other Bajío cities, and conditions in this mountain settlement were rough.

Guanajuato's silver production made a rapid improvement with the opening of La Cata mine in the 1720s. Around the same time, other local mines began using new technology to dig deeper into the earth and increase their output. As the mines began to produce more efficiently, Guanajuato began to prosper. A missionary delegation constructed a large San Diegan convent along the banks of the Guanajuato River. Churches and mansions cropped up around the city center, and shortly thereafter, the first Jesuit school was established (the precursor to the modern-day Universidad de Guanajuato). Water systems were built and the city's first dam, La Presa de la Olla, was constructed to curb destructive flooding downtown. The Spanish government officially recognized the city of Santa Fe and Real de Minas de Guanajuato in 1741; by then, there were almost 50,000 people living in the town.

Everything would change again in 1769, when Antonio de Obregón y Alcocer and Pedro Luciano de Otero discovered an incredibly rich silver vein at La Valenciana mine, north of downtown Guanajuato. This mine had been founded in the 16th century by Don Diego de Valenciana, who later abandoned it as unprofitable. The massive wealth from La Valenciana made Obregón a rich man and the city of Guanajuato a jewel on the crown of New Spain. With renewed vigor, mansions, churches, temples, and haciendas were built across town and the population continued to increase. When a great flood sank the San Diegan convent in 1780, the city had plenty of funds to replace the lost structure; the beautiful churrigueresque Templo de San Diego was built on the ruins of the previous cloister. Now a prosperous city, Guanajuato was named the capital of the province in 1790. By that time, Guanajuato was the world's single biggest silver city, annually producing between a fifth and a quarter of all New Spain's silver.

Wealth and stability were abruptly interrupted when the War of Independence broke out in the Bajío. As the seeds of independence were being sown in the nearby towns of San Miguel de Allende and Dolores Hidalgo, Guanajuato had come under the governance of Spanish intendente Juan Antonio Riaño y Bárcena. During his decade in power, Riaño

The Templo de San Diego was built in the 18th century.

The Mercado Hidalgo is one of several monuments in Guanajuato commissioned by Porfirio Díaz.

made many changes to the city's hierarchy and public infrastructure. A Spanish royalist, Riaño resisted Hidalgo's call for Guanajuato's surrender when the war broke out. The rebel army invaded Guanajuato on September 28, 1810, when the Alhóndiga de Granaditas, the public granary, would go down in history as one of the first important (and most bloody) battles in the War of Independence. At its conclusion, most of the wealthy criollo and Spanish families in Guanajuato had fled or were massacred.

While other Bajío cities went into decline after independence, Guanajuato's silver mines continued to produce throughout the 19th century. Following the war, the city was named the capital of the state of Guanajuato and it continued to retain an important position during the French rule of Mexico. During his iron-fisted rule at the end of the 19th century, president Porfirio Díaz commissioned several more monuments in Guanajuato, including the Teatro Juárez and Mercado Hidalgo. These two turn-of-the-century buildings added to the unusual mix of spectacular architecture in Guanajuato's city center.

In the late 1980s, Guanajuato began massive restoration projects on its many historic buildings. Today, the city's oldest chapels, civil buildings, and artwork have been magnificently restored, including the remarkable collections of 17th- and 18th-century oil paintings in many of Guanajuato's churches. Since 1988, the entire city center of Guanajuato, as well as its adjacent mines, has been a World Heritage designation from the United Nations. Today, Guanajuato is one of the most famous small towns in Mexico, widely visited by both national and international tourists.

PLANNING YOUR TIME

Guanajuato is one of Mexico's most popular destinations, welcoming national and international tourists, visiting artists, and exchange students throughout the year. Though well accustomed to the crowds, Guanajuato does not feel touristy, nor does the city particularly cater to its many visitors. There are a few free information booths in the town center,

GUANAJUATO

GUANAJUATO

trolley tours of the major sights, and plenty of friendly locals to give advice. However, visitors to Guanajuato should not expect to find a well-oiled tourist machine. In this low-key city, planning a worthwhile vacation is largely up to you.

Many people visit Guanajuato on a day trip from San Miguel de Allende or choose to spend a few days there in conjunction with a larger trip around the Bajío. Most of Guanajuato's interesting museums and architectural sights are located within a few blocks in *centro histórico*. Therefore, many day-trippers prefer to simply wander from plaza to plaza, stopping into museums or shops as they come stumble across them. If you want to make the most of a single day in Guanajuato, consider taking a guided tour of the city center or the outlying sights in La Valenciana.

Those planning to spend more than a day or two in Guanajuato don't need to plan their time too carefully. It is easy to see the major sights downtown in just a few days of exploring. In fact, you'll bump into most of them without even trying! Anyone staying a week or more should consider a jaunt outside the *centro histórico* to see the Templo de San Cayetano in La Valenciana, the sierra of Santa Rosa, or the Presa de la Olla neighborhood, among other worthwhile destinations. Those who enjoy a bit of natural scenery might consider a hike in the surrounding mountains or a day trip to another small town, like beautiful San Miguel de Allende or Dolores Hidalgo. On that note, Guanajuato can make an excellent home base for a longer trip to the Bajío, as it is affordable, authentic, and friendly. Many foreigners come here to study Spanish, while others simply practice their language skills during a longer sojourn in this inexpensive and interesting city.

No matter how long you stay, a good way to experience Guanajuato is through the many cultural offerings and performances (both formal and impromptu) throughout town. There are weekly concerts at the city's theaters, street performers, and the *callejonadas*, among other options for arts and entertainment. Check

the Universidad de Guanajuato's website to see what cultural events are going on around town or pass by the box office at the Teatro Juárez when you arrive. More informally, many of Guanajuato's bars and restaurants have live music, especially on the weekends. Look for announcements and fliers around town.

ORIENTATION

Guanajuato's unusual topography can be a challenge for newcomers. The urban city center is built along the walls of a canyon, dotted by public plazas and marbled with tiny pedestrian alleyways. It has no grid pattern to follow, no numbered streets, and few accurate maps. Alleys often zigzag in unexpected directions and can often become a serious cardiac workout as they make a steep ascent up the ravine. It may take a few hours—or even a few days—to get acquainted with the topsy-turvy street map. During the adjustment period, a sense of adventure is your greatest ally. Even as you find yourself lost in the tangle of small streets, there is always a sense of pleasant mystery about what lies around the next corner.

Unlike most Mexican cities, Guanajuato's downtown was not designed around a big central square or *zócalo*. However, the Jardín de la Unión is generally considered the city center, culturally if not geographically. Therefore, it can be easiest to start your tour of the city from there. From the Jardín de la Unión, several pedestrian streets run roughly from the northwest to the southeast across the downtown, making a few unexpected dips and turns. From the Teatro Juárez, follow Luis González Obregón northwest toward the Plaza de la Paz, where you will see the Basílica de Nuestra Señora de Guanajuato and the state government buildings. From there, take Juárez past the Plaza San Fernando and the Plaza de los Ángeles, until you arrive at the Mercado Hidalgo, just below the Alhóndiga. Heading southeast from Jardín de la Unión, Sopeña is a pedestrian street lined with shops and restaurants. One block to the east (just behind the Jardín de la Unión), Calle Cantarranas runs loosely parallel to Sopeña, though it is open to auto traffic.

© ARTURO MEADE

the Basílica de Nuestra Señora de Guanajuato, on Plaza de la Paz

Driving in Guanajuato is another challenge altogether. Throughout the city center, the former riverbed has been converted to an underground system of tunneled roads, marked with rather unspecific signage. Calle Belaunzarán is the only major thoroughfare that goes through the city center (it later becomes Calle Miguel Hidalgo, which runs underground). It is almost impossible to accurately map the routes through the tunnels, but don't lose your calm when driving through the *centro histórico.* Very few underground roads will lead you far from the downtown district before they come up for air. When in doubt, ask directions. In almost every case, it is easiest to park your car and walk when exploring the *centro histórico.* You don't get much of a view from underground anyway!

There are several restaurants, hotels, and sights outside the city center, specifically in the Marfil, San Javier, de la Presa, and Valenciana neighborhoods. These neighborhoods are easily accessible by taxi or bus. These outlying neighborhoods may not look very distant on a map, yet steep winding hills can make them quite a trek on foot! Plan to drive, take a taxi, or ride the bus. The exception is the neighborhood around the Presa de la Olla, which is a pleasant 30-minute walk from downtown.

Sights

Throughout the narrow streets and curving alleyways of Guanajuato's *centro histórico,* there is a veritable album of photo opportunities. Known for its interesting history, cultural scene, and incredible mix of architectural styles, the city boasts some of the finest 18th-century baroque architecture in the country, as well as a few lovely old structures dating back to the 17th century. Adding to the unique mix of architectural styles, the city also has some spectacular civil buildings from the 19th century, often characterized by neoclassical design. After its induction into the UNESCO World Heritage program in 1988, Guanajuato's churches, chapels, and civil buildings were beautifully restored, yet didn't lose the crumbling majesty of their age and history. In addition, there are many small but interesting museums, as well as several public galleries. When touring the city, it's worth a stop in one of the museums that catch your eye.

CENTRO HISTÓRICO

Guanajuato's charming city center is a compact mess of narrow streets and cobblestone plazas, crammed with old churches, theaters, and former mansions. While the elaborate churches and civic buildings are the city's most celebrated architectural sights, the entire downtown district is filled with colonial buildings that are historic and beautiful. As you walk, look up to see the crumbling facades, old stone

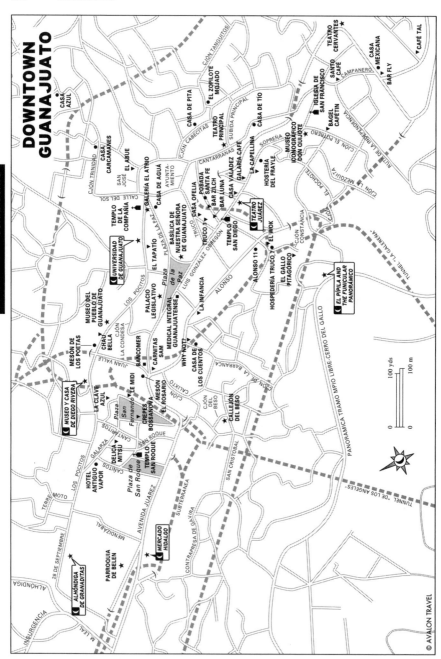

DOWNTOWN GUANAJUATO

CAFÉ TAL

TEATRO CERVANTES ★

CASA MEXICANA

CASA AZUL

BAR FLY

SANTO CAFÉ ●

IGLESIA DE SAN FRANCISCO ♦

CAMPANERO

CASA DE PITA ●

EL ZOPILOTE MOJADO ●

BAGEL CAFETÍN ●

CASA CARCAMANES

CJÓN TRINIDAD

CASA EL ABUE ●

TEATRO PRINCIPAL

CASA DE TÍO ●

MUSEO ICONOGRÁFICO DON QUIJOTE ■

SAN JOSÉ ●

CJÓN CABECITAS

CANTARRANAS

CAPELLINA

SOPREÑA

HOSTERÍA DEL FRAYLE ●

RUTE DE LA INGRESIOENESA

GALERÍA EL ATRIO ★

CALLE DEL SOL

AYUNTA- MIENTO

CASA DE AGUA

POSADA SANTA FE ●

CASA YALADEZ ●

GALERÍA CAFÉ

SUBIDA PRINCIPAL

EL POCHOTE

CJÓN LE MEZQUILA

■ UNIVERSIDAD DE GUANAJUATO

TEMPLO DE LA COMPAÑÍA

GALERÍA OFELIA

CASA OFELIA ●

BASÍLICA DE NUESTRA SEÑORA DE GUANAJUATO ★

BAR ZILCH ●

BAR LUNA ●

TRUCO 7 ●

TEMPLO SAN DIEGO

★ TEATRO JUÁREZ

● EL WOK

TUNNEL "LA GALERA"

EL TAPATÍO ●

PLAZA DE LA PAZ

Plaza de la Paz

LUIS GONZÁLEZ OBREGÓN

TRUCO

ALONSO 11 ●

EL GALLO PITAGÓRICO ●

CJÓN CONSTANCIA

MUSEO DEL PUEBLO DE GUANAJUATO ★

PALACIO LEGISLATIVO

MEDICAL INTEGRAL GUANAJUATENSE ■

LA INFANCIA ●

ALONSO

HOSPEDERÍA TRUCO ●

★ EL PÍPILA AND THE FUNICULAR PANORÁMICO

LOS POCITOS

CJÓN LA CONDESA

MESÓN DE LOS POETAS

CHAO BELLA ●

BANCOMER ●

CARNITAS SAM ●

WHY NOT? ●

CASA DE LOS CUENTOS ●

CJÓN DE LA BARRANCA

JUAN VALLE

■ MUSEO Y CASA DE DIEGO RIVERA

LA CLAVE AZUL ●

EL MIDI ●

CREPES BOSSANOVA ●

MESÓN EL ROSARIO ●

CJÓN CALIXTO

CJÓN DEL BESO

CALLEJÓN DEL BESO

SAN CRISTÓBAL

Plaza San Fernando

San Fernando

CANTARITOS

GALARZA

DELICA MITSU ●

SAN ROQUE

TEMPLO SAN ROQUE

Plaza de San Roque

AVENIDA JUÁREZ

SUBTERRÁNEA

LOS POCITOS

HOTEL ANTIGUO VAPOR

CANTOS

TERREMOTO

MENDIZÁBAL

28 DE SEPTIEMBRE

ALHÓNDIGA

INSURGENCIA

M LEAL

★ ALHÓNDIGA DE GRANADITAS ■

PARROQUIA DE BELÉN ★

■ MERCADO HIDALGO

CONTRAPRESA DE GAVIRA

PANORÁMICA TRAMO MPIO LIBRE-CERRO DEL GALLO

TUNNEL "DE LOS ANGELES"

0 100 yds
0 100 m

© AVALON TRAVEL

niches, and wrought-iron balconies of former mansions and government buildings. They are beautifully preserved and largely intact, so it is easy to imagine this city center as it was 200 years ago.

Jardín de la Unión

Built along the banks of a river, Guanajuato's winding downtown district is composed of small plazas linked by narrow streets. Of these many plazas, the Jardín de la Unión is the heart of the city. Once the atrium of a large San Diegan convent in the city center, it was converted to a public space during the post-independence Reformation of the early 19th century. Today, the Jardín de la Unión is the busiest plaza in Guanajuato, always buzzing with activity. From morning to night, its wrought-iron benches are packed with crowds of tourists and locals. By early afternoon, mariachis and *norteño* trios arrive to play live songs upon request. The party continues through the evening, as the garden's cafés fill with people dining alfresco. For any first-time visitors to Guanajuato, the Jardín de la Unión is a great place to put your finger on the pulse of downtown Guanajuato while relaxing in the shade of this clean and well-manicured garden.

【 Teatro Juárez

Teatro Juárez (Sopeña s/n, tel. 473/732-0183 or 473/732-2529, 9 A.M.–1:45 P.M. and 5–7:45 P.M. daily, US$2.50) is a sparkling jewel on the crown of Guanajuato's beautiful *centro histórico*. The building's opulent neoclassical facade is emblematic of the Porfiriato, the long 19th-century rule of President Porfirio Díaz, which ended with the Mexican Revolution of 1910. Designed by Antonio Rivas Mercado, Teatro Juárez was inaugurated in 1903 with a performance of Giuseppe Verde's *Aida*. Porfirio Díaz himself was in attendance at the opening event. After Díaz's presidency was toppled in the Revolution of 1910, the theater was leased for cinema and, eventually, fell into disrepair. Efforts to restore the building began in the 1950s, receiving an additional boost from the founding of the Festival Internacional Cervantino in 1973. Since then, Teatro Juárez has been a prominent performing arts venue,

GUANAJUATO

© JULIE DOHERTY MEADE

mariachis warming up in the gazebo of the Jardín de la Unión

PLACE OF FROGS

The name Guanajuato comes from the Pu-répecha language, generally believed to derive from the term *quanax-huato*, which means "place of the monstrous frogs" or "hill of frogs." It seems a strange nick-name for a semi-arid town in the crevice of the Cordillera de Guanajuato, and there are numerous theories about its origin. While some believe the name refers to the rock formations near the city center that resemble giant frogs, others contend that the frog refers to the god of wisdom in the Purépecha culture. Whatever the reason, the city has embraced its amphibious identity, mysterious though it is. In shops across town, frog souvenirs are popular merchandise, and a major thoroughfare is named Cantarranas (Singing Frogs). From the city's southwest entrance from León, you are welcomed to town by the Plaza de Ranas (Plaza of Frogs), where a host of sandstone frogs form an informal gateway to the city.

continually hosting high caliber theater, concerts, and dance performances. The Martha Graham dance company, Julián Carillo, and the Symphony Orchestra of Mexico are among the many famous acts that have graced the theater's main stage.

Towering over the Jardín de la Unión, Teatro Juárez has a striking neoclassical exterior, with twelve Doric columns supporting a cornice topped by a row of black stone muses. There is often a crowd of locals chatting on the staircase below the portico. Inside, the ceiling and floors of the main auditorium, the Gran Salón Auditorio, are spectacularly decorated with hand-cut wood-and-stucco relief, painted in a brilliant multicolor array of deep red, blue, and gold. Heavily influenced by Moorish design, the Gran Salón is elaborate and dazzling. From the Gran Salón, you can follow the creaky wooden staircases to the foyer upstairs, an art nouveau salon complemented by even more neoclassical marble sculptures. Even the bathrooms have gilded moldings.

Templo de San Diego

The Templo de San Diego (Jardín de la Unión s/n, tel. 473/732-2990, generally 8 A.M.–8 P.M. daily) was originally constructed as a part of the large Diegan convent that occupied the city center, including the current site of Teatro Juárez and the Jardín de la Unión. Of the entire complex, only this small temple is left standing today. One of the older buildings in Guanajuato, the Templo de San Diego's beautiful rococo exterior is replete with life-size saints surrounded by decorative hand-carved stone embellishments. Inside, the church has a lovely collection of large-format oil paintings from the viceroyalty through the 19th century. Two small temples adjoin the nave on either side of the neoclassical altar; the chapel to the south of the altar is smaller but has another impressive collection of 18th-century oil paintings depicting the life of San Pedro de Alcántra.

Since the days of its founding, the downtown district of Guanajuato was repeatedly flooded by the river that ran through the city center. After a devastating flood in the late 1700s, the entire city center was raised several meters, including the buildings of the San Diegan convent. On the temple's north side, a small staircase leads down to the **Museo Dieguino** (Jardín de la Unión, tel. 473/732-2990, museodieguino@yahoo.com. mx, 10 A.M.–6:30 P.M. Tues.–Sat., 10 A.M.–2:30 P.M. Sun., US$0.50), where the ruins of the original 17th-century temple have been excavated. The space is small but interesting, revealing the old crumbling walls and archways (now reinforced with wood supports) of the original cloister. Often, the museum exhibits contemporary art or photography within this historic space, adding a tasteful and interesting juxtaposition between the past and the present.

🔳 Universidad de Guanajuato

The Universidad de Guanajuato (University of Guanajuato, Lascuráin de Retana 5, tel. 473/732-0006, www.ugto.mx) is a large and prestigious public university, which has a major influence on the city of Guanajuato culturally and architecturally. The school's founding dates back to the early 18th century, when Jesuits founded the Colegio de la Santísima Trinidad in Guanajuato. This same school became a college in 1744. After the War of Independence, the school was designated a state college and the curriculum was reformed under the first state governor, Carlo Montes de Oca. In 1945, the college was elevated to the status of university, offering undergraduate, masters, and doctoral programs. Today, the Universidad de Guanajuato is one of Mexico's most prominent and well-respected institutions. There are around 30,000 students, and their jubilant and youthful attitude flavors the downtown district of Guanajuato.

The university is actually spread across several campuses in Guanajuato and other cities in the Bajío. However, the central campus is the school's most iconic structure, an unusual neoclassical building constructed in the 1940s. Soaring skyward above the narrow street of Lascuráin de Retana, the giant white facade dominates the cityscape to the east, peeking above the government buildings and chapels from the Plaza de la Paz below. Its long ascending stairway, cut of green sandstone, rises from the street below to auditoriums and classrooms above. If you don't mind a brisk workout, you can climb the many stairs for a nice view of the city.

Templo de la Compañía de Jesús

Also known as the **Oratorio San Felipe Neri**, the Templo de la Compañía de Jesús (Lascuráin de Retana s/n, tel. 473/733-9782, generally 8 A.M.–8 P.M. daily) is an exquisite pink sandstone church that was constructed 1747–1765 by Jesuit priests. Another boon of the silver trade, the large neoclassical cupola behind the main facade was added to the building during the 19th century, commissioned by the Jesuit brother of a mining magnate. Today, the church's lovely churrigueresque exterior and single bell tower are well preserved, yet enchantingly aged. After Guanajuato's inauguration into the World Heritage program in 1988, this church was the first structure to be totally restored.

Inside the church, the soaring nave is impressively high, with a vaulted dome where even pigeons drift comfortably from one sandstone perch to the next. Note the elaborately wrought sandstone columns that line the main corridor. Hand-carved altars line the walls, where there are several beautiful wood statues, a fine hand-painted pulpit, and a collection of 18th-century oil paintings, including some by master artist Miguel Cabrera.

Basílica de Nuestra Señora de Guanajuato

The striking yellow Basílica de Nuestra Señora de Guanajuato (Plaza de la Paz s/n, tel. 473/732-0314, www.basilicagto.com.mx, generally 8 A.M.–9 P.M. daily) was the city's first parish church. In 1957, the church was upgraded from *parroquia* (parish) to the elevated title of basilica. Built in the 1770s with funds from the mines, the building's brightly painted facade is largely original, though its churrigueresque bell tower was added in the 19th century. Each of the church's three entryways is surrounded by a lovely hand-carved sandstone facade.

In contrast to its bold exterior, the basilica's interior is a wash of delicate pastels, marble floors, and shiny crystal. The walls are painted with delicate frescos in pink, aqua, and white. The church's original baroque altarpieces were lost in the 19th century, and have since been replaced by a large neoclassical altar in the front and in the two side chapels. The centerpiece is the *Virgen de Guanajuato,* a carved wood sculpture of the Virgin Mary and son from the 16th or 17th century, displayed atop a baroque silver pedestal. When you go inside, be respectful of masses and people who have come to use the church. Even today, the church's congregation is very active.

Plaza de la Paz

Just below the *basílica,* the Plaza de la Paz is a lovely triangle-shaped esplanade, originally considered Guanajuato's main square until the establishment of the Jardín de la Unión in the early 19th century. In the center of the plaza, well-manicured gardens and metal benches surround the *Monumento de la Paz,* dedicated to the city by President Porfirio Díaz in 1903. (The original fountain that stood in the center of the Plaza de la Paz was relocated to the Plaza Baratillo to accommodate the new sculpture.) On the north side of Plaza de la Paz (just to the north of the basilica), the **Palacio Legislativo** is a noted neoclassical construction from the 19th century, which is now home to state government offices.

Mercado Hidalgo

One of the nicest examples of turn-of-the-20th-century architecture in Guanajuato is the beautiful Mercado Hidalgo (Juárez s/n, esq. Mendizábal, no tel., 8:30 A.M.–9 P.M. daily, hours vary by shop), inaugurated on September 16, 1910, by President Porfirio Díaz. It was a gift to the city in commemoration of the 100th anniversary of the Mexican War of Independence. Little did Díaz know that his own long presidency would come to a violent end just a few months later, with the outbreak of the Mexican Revolution of 1910.

Housed in an unusual structure that, according to local history, was originally designed as a train depot, this covered market houses a jumble of inexpensive shops, fruit stands, taco joints, and juice bars. The second floor is dedicated to crafts and souvenirs, though most vendors sell inexpensive trinkets like key chains and bottle openers, rather than high-quality artisan work. Nonetheless, it's worth a walk around the second-floor promenade to snap some photos of the market below.

Just across the street from the Mercado Hidalgo, the **Parroquia de Belen** (Av. Juárez s/n, tel. 473/732-2283, 7 A.M.–9 P.M. daily), also known as the Parroquia del Inmaculado Corazón de María, is a lovely parish church with a baroque facade. It was constructed by Bethlemite nuns in the 18th century. The original complex included a school, gardens, and a cemetery; today, only the church is left

standing. The spacious interior contains lovely mosaic walls and a nice collection of retablos and oil paintings.

Templo y Plaza de San Roque

An old and endearing 18th-century chapel, the Templo San Roque (Plaza de San Roque s/n, no tel., hours vary) overlooks a small plaza of the same name. Originally constructed in 1726 by father Don Juan José de Sopeño y Cevera, the building served as a *santa escuela* (Jesuit school) from 1746–1794. The pink sandstone exterior is enchanting in its simplicity; there are few embellishments here, just a simple stone entryway and three stone saints, embedded into a wall of thick-cut sandstone bricks. Inside the church, the crumbling frescos and incredibly weathered wood doors reflect the building's age and its many years of use. The series of paintings depicting the stations of the cross were painted in the 18th and 19th centuries by Lorenzo Romero. Restoration of the chapel is ongoing.

Right in front of the temple, the small Plaza de San Roque also has historical importance to the city of Guanajuato. Since the mid-20th century, the plaza has been the site of Guanajuato's famous *Entremeses Cervantinos. Entremeses,* the series of short comedies by Cervantes, are performed weekly in this square. Over the years, these performances became so popular that they eventually formed the cornerstone of Guanajuato's annual Festival Internacional Cervantino. On the south side of the church, there is a bronze statue of Enrique Ruela, the Universidad de Guanajuato professor who founded the tradition.

Jardín Reforma

Adjoining the Plaza de San Roque, Jardín Reforma is a peaceful public square, home to the architecture department at the Universidad de Guanajuato. The grounds were once a part of the Templo de Belen and were expropriated to make a public space in the mid-19th century. Quieter than neighboring Plaza San Fernando, this plaza is shaded by trees and filled with quiet spots to rest weary feet.

Callejón del Beso

There are only 70 centimeters separating one house from another on the teensy tiny Callejón del Beso (Alley of the Kiss). Located just above the Plaza de los Ángeles, this little alley is typical of those in Guanajuato, with a staircase cutting through a narrow passage between residences. However, the Callejón del Beso has become a bit of a tourist attraction, thanks to the local legend of two lovers who lived in houses on opposite sides of the alley. According to this Romeo and Juliet–style story, the young lovers were from different social classes and their families opposed the romance. Doña Ana was a rich young woman, while her lover, Don Carlos, was a poor miner. At night, they would lean over their adjoining balconies for evening kisses.

As characters in these legends often do, the lovers on the Callejón del Beso met a tragic end when Doña Ana's father discovered their affair and killed her young lover. Today, you can re-enact the lovers' secret romance by climbing up to one of the balconies and leaning over it for a photo opportunity; admission to the alley's balcony is free, but you will pass through a little gift shop on your way to the top. Many tourists simply choose to exchange a kiss on the staircase below, which supposedly brings good luck to your relationship—even though it didn't bring much luck to Doña Ana and Don Carlos!

◖ Alhóndiga de Granaditas

The public granary (Mendizábal 6, tel. 473/732-1111, 10 A.M.–5:45 P.M. Mon.–Sat., 10 A.M.–2:45 P.M. Sun., US$4) is an imposing stone structure with a particularly gruesome place in history. Originally commissioned by the Spanish governor of Guanajuato, Juan Antonio de Riaño y Bárcena, the building was completed in 1809. Its usefulness, however, was to be short-lived, as the Alhóndiga became one of the major battle sites early in the War of Independence in September 1810. After the battle, the Alhóndiga was cleared out and served as a military barracks and warehouse. During the 19th century, the Alhóndiga was the city jail for numerous decades. At last given a more dignified function, the building became a museum in 1949.

Designed in a spare neoclassical style, the

© JULIE DOHERTY MEADE

The Alhóndiga de Granaditas was the site of a major battle between royalists and rebels in Mexico's War of Independence.

GUANAJUATO

EL PÍPILA AND THE STORMING OF LA ALHÓNDIGA

Mexico's War of Independence began on the night of September 15, 1810, in the rural town of Dolores. Under the command of Miguel Hidalgo, the Mexican army rode through the Bajío, first taking San Miguel de Allende, followed by the city of Celaya. From Celaya, Hidalgo called for the capital city of Guanajuato to surrender. The city's royalist governors refused, and on September 28, 1810, Hidalgo's army of 20,000 rag-tag soldiers descended upon Guanajuato. As they marched through the city, the army released prisoners from the municipal jail, forcing them to join the fight. Miners from adjacent communities added to their ranks.

In anticipation of the army's arrival, the Spanish intendente, Juan Antonio Riaño y Bárcena, directed Guanajuato's wealthy criollo and Spanish families to take refuge in the Alhóndiga de Granaditas, the city's public granary. With its thick rock walls and towering height, La Alhóndiga's design is often compared to a fortress. Riaño believed that the wealthy families could shelter themselves from the invading army until reinforcements could be called from Mexico City. Indeed, La Alhóndiga was a difficult target for Hidalgo's ill-equipped army. With the Spanish royalists firing on the Hidalgo's soldiers from overhead, it was almost impenetrable. From a neighboring hillside, the rebel army launched a hailstorm of stones on the Spanish defenders, but the perimeter was well guarded. Riaño himself was killed early in the fighting.

It is here that Juan José María Martínez, also known as El Pípila, earned a place in history. An indigenous silver miner with a reputation for enormous strength, El Pípila tied a heavy stone to his back as a shield. Carrying a torch in one hand, he struggled beneath a shower of bullets to the base of La Alhóndiga. There, he set fire to the granary's wood doors. As they burned, the rebel army swarmed inside the granary and massacred the aristocratic families hidden within the thick sandstone walls. El Pípila has been forever immortalized for his incredible bravery.

The storming of La Alhóndiga is one of the most famous episodes in the history of the War of Independence, but it also tainted the rebel army with a reputation for brutality. Across Mexico, many Spanish and criollo families turned against the independence movement, hampering the cause. Even within the army, the massacre created a schism between Miguel Hidalgo and other prominent independence leaders. Ignacio Allende, himself a wealthy criollo with ties to other aristocratic families in the Bajío, renounced the violence at La Alhóndiga, distancing himself and Hidalgo.

A year after the storming of La Alhóndiga, the battle for independence was still raging, and Spanish forces took their revenge. In March of 1811, Allende, Hidalgo and other prominent insurgents were ambushed and arrested by royalist forces. A few months later, Ignacio Allende, Juan Aldama, and Mariano Jiménez were executed by firing squad in Chihuahua, followed by Miguel Hidalgo a few days later. Their bodies were decapitated and the heads of the insurgent leaders were paraded around the country as a warning to other conspirators. The heads were then carried to Guanajuato, where they were hung in cages from the four corners of La Alhóndiga on October 14, 1811. According to local history, the heads swung from the corners of the granary for more than a decade, until they were transported to the monument of the Ángel de Independencia in Mexico City. Today, there are plaques at La Alhóndiga bearing the names of the insurgent leaders posted next to the giant iron hooks that once held their heads.

Alhóndiga is a giant boxy building, which resembles a fortress from the outside. Inside the great rock walls, the granary is surprisingly lovely, with a spacious patio framed by heavy green sandstone columns. Adding to the charm, the walls of the building's staircases are painted with dramatic murals about the independence movement by a celebrated local artist, José Chávez Morado. On the northern side of the building, a stone staircase leads toward a large esplanade, which is used for public performances during the Cervantino festival.

Today, the Alhóndiga is a two-story museum, dedicated to regional culture and the history of Guanajuato. Upstairs, there are several rooms dedicated to pre-Hispanic art and culture, as well as several rooms with colonial artifacts and didactic texts. The lovely collection of pre-Hispanic stamps is one of the museum's highlights. From there, the visitor can follow the region's history from pre-Columbian cultures through the turn of the 20th century. There are 16th-century mining artifacts and reproductions of weapons and furniture from baroque Spain. In the final salon, a collection of vintage photographs shows Guanajuato as it was in the early 1900s.

◖ Museo y Casa de Diego Rivera

The famous early-20th-century artist Diego Rivera, was born in the city of Guanajuato. Today, his childhood home has been refashioned as a small museum, the Museo y Casa de Diego Rivera (Positos 47, tel. 473/732-1197, 10 A.M.–7 P.M. Tues.–Sat., 10 A.M.–3 P.M. Sun., US$1.50). Although the artist only lived in this house for the first few years of his life (relocating with his family to Mexico City), he is nonetheless one of Guanajuato's favorite sons.

On the first floor of the museum, the family's living quarters have been decorated with period furnishings, recreating the atmosphere typical to a wealthy family at the time of Rivera's birth. The three rather topsy-turvy floors above (the structure is sinking and slanted, which gives it a bit of a funhouse feeling) are filled with small, nicely designed galleries of Rivera's work, including some of his earliest oil paintings, drawings, watercolors, and lithographs. Several rooms display work from Rivera's contemporaries, many of whom were exploring the same themes in Mexican identity and culture. For fans of the artist, this museum is an essential stop, as it offers enormous insight into his artistic development. The museum also presents rotating exhibitions in a few gallery spaces, and there are often movies, artistic talks, and other cultural programs at the museum.

Museo Iconográfico del Quijote

Guanajuato is the proud bearer of the Cervantes tradition, and the figure of Don Quixote is a big part of the city's cultural identity. Statues of Cervantes's mythical hero are scattered throughout the city center, and the name Quixote is forever on the tip of your tongue, thanks to the dozens of namesake restaurants, hotels, and shops. If you cannot get enough Quixote, you can over-saturate yourself with his image at the fun Museo Iconográfico del Quijote (Manuel Doblado 1, tel. 473/732-6721, www.museoiconografico. guanajuato.gob.mx, 10 A.M.–6:30 P.M. Tues.–Sat., 10 A.M.–2 P.M. Sun., US$2). At this small but well-stocked museum, you can see hundreds of representations of Don Quixote and his sidekick, Sancho Panza, from highly abstract to highly figurative pieces in a variety of media. The predominantly Mexican collection includes numerous local artists, as well as some famous names, like Zacatecan artist Pedro Coronel. Taking advantage of its courtyard, the museum occasionally hosts cultural events, as well as weekly live music concerts.

In addition to the art collection, the building itself has a curious history. Built near the end of the 18th century, this historic home belonged to a series of wealthy criollo families from Guanajuato. In 1861, the celebrated governor of the state, Manuel Doblado, purchased the property. While Doblado lived there, Emperor Maximilian of Hapsburg was rumored to have spent several days in the building while he visited Guanajuato. The house continued to pass through ownership of notable Guanajuato families until it was fully restored to accommodate the museum in 1987.

Iglesia de San Francisco

Just beside the Quixote museum, the lovely Iglesia de San Francisco (San Francisco Church, Manuel Doblado 15, tel. 473/732-0377, generally 7 A.M.–8:30 P.M. daily) is a church and former convent, originally constructed in the 18th century by Franciscan friars as accompaniment to their school and orphanage. Situated along a pedestrian stretch of Manuel Doblado, this small church has a stunning pink sandstone churrigueresque entryway. Inside the church, there is a neoclassical altar and a nice collection of colonial era oil paintings, including a particularly nice piece from the 18th century, depicting San Francisco and Santa Clara.

El Pípila and the Funicular Panorámico

Above the city center, the giant rose statue of El Pípila towers over the ravine, presiding over a large public plaza with spectacular views of the city below. From just behind the Teatro Juárez, you can take a short but amusing ride up the hillside to the plaza in a glass-walled funicular (Constancia s/n, 8 A.M.–8:45 P.M. Mon.–Fri., 9 A.M.–8:45 P.M. Sat., 10 A.M.–8:45 P.M. Sun., US$2.50). Alternatively, you can follow the maze of alleys up to the top of the hill (if you are going to walk, one way to get there is via the alleyway of Constancia, just behind the Templo de San Diego and above the public parking lot; follow the signs from there). Once you get to the top, the attraction is the view of the city, which, from this vantage point, gives you a real sense of Guanajuato's unique urban landscape. The plaza offers a pleasant buzz of craft vendors, some snack shacks, and lots of other tourists snapping the ultimate Guanajuato photo.

WEST OF THE *CENTRO*

The Marfil neighborhood to the west of the city center was once a small village, quite separate from downtown Guanajuato. Originally set up as a protective settlement to guard the nearby mines, it eventually became the center of Guanajuato's metal refineries during the colonial era. Some of these refineries were later converted to haciendas, some of which are now museums and restaurants. Though it's a bit of walk, it only takes about 10 minutes in a taxi to get to Marfil from the *centro histórico,* or you can take a bus from the Juárez tunnel (look for the buses marked Marfil).

Ex-Hacienda San Gabriel de Barrera

The Ex-Hacienda San Gabriel de Barrera (Carretera Guanajuato-Marfil, Km 2.5, Col. Marfil, tel. 473/732-0619, 8:30 A.M.–4 P.M. daily, US$1.75) is a green and pleasing respite from downtown Guanajuato's inexhaustible bustle. Located in the Marfil neighborhood, the extensive grounds of this former hacienda were originally designed as a metal refinery. It was among numerous refineries owned and operated by a wealthy businessman, Gabriel de la Barrera, in the 17th century. With several acres of space, the hacienda's crumbling courtyards are home to a series of beautifully designed and well-tended gardens. Wander through the neat English garden with its tall shady trees and a Mexican garden featuring a lovely collection of cactus. You can linger beside gurgling fountains on one of the many crumbling stone benches or have a drink at the small coffee shop near the hacienda's entrance. Unfortunately, the hacienda is right next to the highway into Guanajuato, so you never fully lose touch with the 21st century.

Admission to the hacienda also includes entrance to the museum, located within the complex's former living quarters. Here, family rooms have been redecorated with period furniture, which displays the strong Spanish influence popular with wealthy families during the colonial era. Huge chandeliers, old rugs, and massive wood furnishings provide a glimpse into upper-class life during the 17th century. There is also a small but impressive chapel inside the home, with a gilded Spanish altarpiece from the 15th century. This incredibly old and beautiful retablo was likely imported from Spain; it is one of the few antiques of this age in Mexico. Since 1975, this hacienda and its grounds have been owned by the state of Guanajuato. To get to the Ex-Hacienda San Gabriel de Barrera, you can hail a taxi from the *centro histórico* or take a bus marked Marfil from the tunnel of Hidalgo (beneath Av. Juárez), getting off at the Hotel Misión de Guanajuato (the hacienda is just below the hotel).

Museo de las Momias

The famous Museo de las Momias (Mummy Museum, Explanada del Panteón Municipal s/n, tel. 473/732-0639, www.momiasdeguanajuato.gob.mx, 9 A.M.–6 P.M. daily, US$4) is one of Guanajuato's most unusual yet well-known sights. This museum's backstory begins in the early 19th century, when several mummified corpses were dug up in the Santa Paula cemetery. The mummification occurred naturally due to the unusual mineral content in the soil, which preserved the corpses in a state of horrific recognizability. Thereafter, more corpses were dug up, with similar results. This curiosity has now become the concept behind a macabre museum, where the bodies of more than 100 disinterred and mummified corpses are on display for visitors behind glass cases.

It's not recommended for the squeamish; there are children and babies among the mummified bodies.

NORTH OF THE *CENTRO*

Departing the city center to the north, the state highway that leads to the village of Santa Rosa ascends a beautiful, curving route into the sierra. Just before departing the city of Guanajuato, La Valenciana is a beautiful neighborhood that has held one of the most important roles in the history of the city's development. Here, on the rocky bluffs, the mining industry continues to play a big role in Guanajuato's economy and identity.

La Valenciana Mine

A silver vein larger than any other in Mexico

EL SANTO VS. THE MUMMIES OF GUANAJUATO

With so many other things to recommend a trip to the city, it's a bit curious that Guanajuato's mummy museum has become such a vitally important part of the town's public image. Perhaps Guanajuato's tourists have a deep-seated predilection for macabre spectacles, or perhaps there is something universally intriguing about a museum dedicated to disinterred corpses. Whatever the reason behind their popularity, the mummies of Guanajuato have become almost as famous as the Alhóndiga de Granaditas.

In 1972, Guanajuato's mummies were immortalized in the Mexican film *Las Momias de Guanajuato* (The Mummies of Guanajuato). This campy semi-action flick stars wrestling hero El Blue Demon, who is called upon to save the city of Guanajuato from the attack of a mobile band of mummies who had made a pact with the devil. As the mummies wreak havoc downtown, El Blue Demon and his companion, Mil Máscaras, must protect the city from these bald and oddly slow-moving villains (a wildly adored wrestling hero, El Santo, also makes a cameo toward the end of the film). In the final sequence, a gang of masked wrestlers attacks

a legion of strong but stiff-jointed mummies (dressed in suits!) in Guanajuato's municipal graveyard.

In addition to the gripping storyline, *Las Momias de Guanajuato* depicts the city of Guanajuato in amusing detail. As the movie begins, a group of tourists visit Guanajuato's Mummy Museum, where they are told the story of the evil mummies. Later, a key scene includes the Estudiantina troubadours playing for a band of tourists on the stairs of the university. Thanks to the film's popularity, *Las Momias de Guanajuato* was followed by several other mummy movies, including a lower-budget flick the following year, *El Castillo de las Momias de Guanajuato*. This film stars the wrestlers Superzan, Blue Angel, and Tinieblas, and was shot in Guatemala, not Guanajuato.

Though not a classic of Mexican cinema, this film is emblematic of Mexico's popular *Lucha Libre* movies of the 1950s, 1960s, and 1970s. Studios no longer make these flicks, but films starring El Blue Demon, and especially El Santo, continue to garner a loyal cult following for their comic-book-style story lines, theatrical violence, and hammy acting.

SILVER CITIES

In the early years of New Spain, Franciscan friars and Spanish settlers made slow inroads into the vast territories north of Mexico City, hoping to find precious metals among the craggy mountains and Christian converts among the nomadic tribes of the region. In 1546, their dreams were realized. In an uncharacteristically peaceful encounter, the indigenous Zacateco people led a small band of Spanish and Indian explorers to a large silver vein near present-day Zacatecas. At that time, this desolate semi-arid territory presented many perils for the Spanish settlers. However, the desire for silver wealth was far more powerful than their fears of violent natives and isolation. By 1550, Zacatecas had a fully functioning and productive mining industry, the origins of the great wealth that would transform New Spain.

After the discovery of silver in Zacatecas, there was a race to find more precious metals within the Sierra Madre. The Spanish found considerable silver veins near Guanajuato, San Luis Potosí, Real de Catorce, and Mineral de Pozos, among others. These cities began as little more than makeshift mining settlements along the banks of the nearest river, but they quickly attracted a large population of migrants, who came to work in the mines or in related industry.

As the mines began to flourish, opulence quickly followed. In the silver cities, mine owners and merchants built lavish mansions for their families. Silver wealth also brought the colonies new trading power with Spain, and they imported altarpieces, statues, fabrics, food, and jewels from the Old World to Mexico. To thank the divine for their worldly successes, owners of the mines contributed large funds for churches and convents, as well as civic buildings. During the 17th century, the remote city of Zacatecas became Mexico's third largest settlement, replete with baroque sandstone cathedrals and an impressive city center. In Guanajuato, Catholic altars were drenched with gold from the mines.

Trade flourished and highways were built across the Bajío region. In the beginning, these roads were difficult, dangerous, and subject to attack from indigenous raiders. Therefore, the Spanish established protective ports along the route. Though not silver cities themselves, San Miguel de Allende, Querétaro, and León became important protective towns, benefitting from the great wealth and industry of the silver trade. Here, wealthy criollo (or Spanish Mexican) families used the spoils of their family's industries to build elaborate churches and haciendas. As the Bajío's silver industry expanded during the 18th century, the cities began to grow in both industry and population. Querétaro and San Miguel de Allende were major producers of wool and textiles, while León became known for its leather goods. Ranchers brought cattle to graze on the Bajío's grasslands, and new cities like Celaya were founded as agricultural capitals of the New World.

The mining industry had a pretty face, but the reality for most mine workers was incredibly grim. Most mines employed poorly paid migrants and, though prohibited by law, enslaved Indians. In the early years, most mines were built entirely by hand, with explosives introduced in the 17th century. There was little ventilation in the shafts below; miners often died early deaths from inhaling the fine crystal dust that filled the air from their hammering. In addition, the labor was extremely tough. In those days, there was no electricity to power the mines or even, in most cases, mining carts. Therefore, heavy loads of rock and ore were pulled from the depths through a combination of human strength and donkey.

After the protracted War of Independence, the silver bonanza finally began to decline, though mines continue to play an important role in the local economy in several Mexican cities. After independence, the massive mine at La Valenciana continued to produce fruitfully for another two centuries, halting production in 2005. Thanks to its continuing riches, Guanajuato remained a prominent city, while other towns like San Miguel de Allende and Mineral de Pozos went into decline.

GUANAJUATO

view of the Templo de San Cayetano from La Valenciana mine

was discovered at La Valenciana in 1769. In the early years, the mine's owners did not have the funds they needed to properly exploit their bounty; to compensate, they introduced an unusual labor system, which granted mine workers a small share of the profits instead of a regular salary. Workers, however, had to provide their own materials. The new system worked well, and the mine produced prolifically for centuries. Once it reached peak production, La Valenciana was New Spain's largest silver producer, as well as an important source of other minerals, like gold, quartz, and amethyst.

While other mining centers went into steep decline after the War of Independence, La Valenciana continued to yield rock, metal, and mineral until the modern day. The entire mine was under the direction of a workers cooperative until the mid-2000s, when it was bought by a Canadian company and finally closed to production (however, subsidiary mines continue to be worked and developed). Despite its important place in history, the Valenciana mine is, unfortunately, usually closed to the public. However, the mine occasionally opens for tours during important tourist seasons like the Cervantino festival (at the cost of around US$3.50 per person). If you arrive at the mine, you may be able to find someone to show you around the complex, which is an interesting mix of old and new. Surrounded by the original seven-pointed stone walls, a miner's temple still stands at the mine's entryway, while heavy machinery has been left behind, gathering dust. If you have no problem with vertigo, you can stand over the principal mineshaft, dubiously referred to as the *tiro de sangre* (shaft of blood), which measures more than 500 meters in depth.

🄲 Templo de San Cayetano

Antonio de Obregón, the Spanish co-owner of La Valenciana silver mine, became incredibly wealthy during his lifetime. To thank God for his great fortune, he constructed the spectacular Templo de San Cayetano (Plazuela de la Valenciana, Carretera Guanajuato-Dolores Hidalgo, tel. 473/732-3596, generally 6:30 A.M.–6 P.M. Tues.–Sun.). Built between 1765 and 1788, this mountaintop temple is one of the greatest examples of Mexican baroque architecture in the country, presiding over the city of Guanajuato and drawing daily busloads of tourists.

The church's highly elaborate sandstone facade is lavishly carved with saints, angels, and decorative adornment. Inside, the church is a direct testament to the riches of the adjoining mines, a splendor of hand-carved wood altarpieces washed in gold leaf. Wonderful multicolored wood saints are embedded within the many niches, all beautifully restored. Also note the delicately carved and painted wood pulpit.

Obregón's former estate is across the street from the temple and is the subject of many tales of wealth and splendor. Among other legends, it is said that when his daughter married in the Templo de San Cayetano, the count presented her with a rug of silver and gold coins, which led from her doorstep to the church. Today, Obregón's home is known as the Casa del Conde (Obregón was later titled the *conde,* or count, of La Valenciana), with a fine dining restaurant inside.

SIGHTSEEING AND CULTURAL TOURS

The official state tourist office, the **Oficina de Convenciones y Visitantes** (Plaza de la Paz 14, tel. 473/732-0369, 10 A.M.–5 P.M. Mon–Sat. www.vamosaguanajuato.com), offers guided walking tours of the downtown district three times daily, covering major sights in the city center. It also offers two daily tours to outlying sites, including the mummy museum, the Templo de San Cayetano in La Valencia, and El Pípila. Both tours cost about US$8 including the cost of the guide; the second includes the cost of transportation, though not museum entry fees. In addition, there is one evening tour to El Cristo Rey del Cubilete, a giant monument to Christ located on a hillside just outside Guanajuato. This tour departs around 5:30 P.M.

Directly across the street, **Transportes Turísticos de Guanajuato** (Bajos de la Basílica 2, tel. 473/732-2134, 9 A.M.–9 P.M. daily) offers guided tours of the *centro histórico* in a motorized trolley bus, at the cost of about US$5 per person. These tours can be great for those who are easily winded, though you'll certainly miss the charm of ambling on foot along Guanajuato's high-altitude alleys. Keep in mind that weekend traffic can make the experience more frustrating. Like the tourist office, Transportes Turísticos also offers a three-hour tour of outlying sights (including the mummy museum and El Pípila), which runs about US$8 per person.

Arts and Entertainment

In this city of the Cervantes tradition, there is a citywide passion for the arts, cinema, and performance, with frequent events in the city's churches, theaters, or public plazas. The university is a major cultural influence, hosting concerts, art exhibitions, and festivals throughout the year. There are also numerous municipal events and holidays, which often draw crowds from throughout the city and beyond. There is music in the streets and the bustling city center is constantly flooded with people and events.

NIGHTLIFE

Guanajuato is a bustling, noisy, and occasionally rowdy city, filled with students, backpackers, and tourists looking to have a good time. In the evening, there is always a crowd pushing through the Jardín de la Unión, while groups of friends chat on the steps of Teatro Juárez. In sidewalk cafés, musicians mill through the crowd as bars and cantinas turn up the volume on their sound systems. While life can be more subdued during the week, Guanajuato feels like a citywide party on the weekends. Throughout the *centro histórico,* bars, cafés, and nightclubs cater to a late-night crowd. Most don't start pumping until after midnight, and some stay open until the break of dawn. Even if you don't indulge, you may hear the pumping beats of *reggaeton* from your hotel room!

In the Jardín de la Unión, **Bar Tradicional Luna** (Jardín de la Unión 10, tel. 473/734-1864, 10 A.M.–2 A.M. daily) is a wonderful place to tip back a tequila. As the name indicates, Luna is a traditional cantina—often full, noisy, and packed with tourists and locals enjoying a view of the plaza and a friendly Mexican atmosphere. On the weekends, it can be difficult to snag a seat on the patio. At any hour, traditional Mexican tunes play loudly on the jukebox, as mariachis and trios gather around tables offering their services for a live song (on a Saturday night, they'll find plenty of takers among the tipsy crowds). During the day, polite waiters serve drinks along with complimentary *botanas* (appetizers), like shrimp soup or pork skin tostadas. There's a fine list of tequila.

The ideally located **El Galería Café** (Sopeña 10, tel. 473/732-2566, 8 A.M.–11 P.M. daily) is a lovely place for a drink, a snack, or a coffee. While the café itself is on Calle Sopeña, the attraction is the outdoor seating just beside the stairs of the Teatro Juárez. In the evenings, this little bar is a great place to sip a glass of wine while staring up at the beautifully illuminated columns that run along the theater's facade. Service is friendly and prices are reasonable, so there is always a crowd of tourists and locals sitting at the little enameled tables under big cloth umbrellas. It closes early, so head here around dusk.

Just across the street from the university, **El Tapatío** (Lascuráin de Retana 20, tel. 473/732-3291 or 473/732-4159, 9 A.M.–10 P.M. daily) is a small bar and restaurant with a laid-back student-friendly atmosphere. Throughout the day, there are inexpensive breakfasts and *comida corrida* in the dining room downstairs. However, the second floor of this colonial building is also a nice place for a leisurely evening drink, with big windows overlooking the university's famous staircase. The traditional Mexican atmosphere makes El Tapatío particularly appealing, as strains of traditional *ranchera* music pour over the sound system, complemented by the high wood-beamed ceilings and small iron chandeliers of a colonial home. Drinks are inexpensive and the crowd is generally young.

One of the owners of the much beloved (but now defunct) bohemian hangout Bar Ocho has opened another drinking establishment in Guanajuato, called **Zilch Bar** (Jardín de la Unión 4 Altos, zilch.gto@gmail.com, 7 P.M.–3 A.M. daily). Located in the Jardín de la Unión above the restaurant La Oreja de Van Gogh, Zilch is a stylish joint that presents an ongoing roster of live jazz, reggae, and rock bands, as well as open mike nights. To complement the live music, they also have frequent drink specials, from discount pitchers to two-for-one cocktails. It is popular with the local crowd, as well as those passing through, and a good place to enjoy an evening out.

Hippies and hipsters reign over the scene at **Why Not?** (Alonso 34 Altos, tel. 473/732-9759, 8 P.M.–2 A.M. daily), a big bar on the second story of an old colonial building. From the street below, a funky painted staircase leads upstairs, decorated with scraps and skater-style decor. From the bar, there are a few balcony tables overlooking the street below. At Why Not?, the clientele is unmistakably laid-back; pumping *reggaeton,* piercings, and dreadlocks are the norm. The lively crowd and inexpensive drinks draw merry crowds on Friday and Saturday nights. Even though it is on a main drag and attracts plenty of tourists, this place has a great, low-key, locals-only vibe.

You can dance until the break of dawn at **La Dama de las Camelias** (Sopeña 32, tel. 473/732-7587, 8 P.M.–4 A.M. daily). This second-floor dance hall has a fun, artsy, and upbeat Latin vibe, attracting students, visitors, and residents of all ages. The huge bar overlooks Calle Sopeña and the walls are painted with festive murals. Things get going early in the evening, and after midnight it's standing room only. Open later than many bars in Guanajuato (most close around 2 A.M.), the place really gets hopping in the wee hours when other drinking establishments shut their doors. Sometimes there are live salsa or Latin bands.

If you're up for a loud and social night out, the perennially popular **Bar Fly** (Sostenes

Rocha 30, 8 P.M.–2 A.M. Mon.–Sat., 8 P.M.– midnight Sun.) is the place to bump to reggae, whoop it up, and share cheap drinks with cheek-to-jowl crowds of students and expatriates. Known to many as El Fly, this bar is one of Guanajuato's most popular (and youthful) watering holes. The owners profess an anarchist affiliation, which is reflected in the bohemian decor. The young waitstaff and bartenders take part in the nightly fun, where foreign exchange students mingle with Guanajuato youth. There are often special events and live music.

LIVE MUSIC AND THEATER

Guanajuato is a theatrical town, deep in the throes of a love affair with Cervantes and surprisingly inclined toward medieval-style pageantry. On the esplanade below Teatro Juárez or in the Plaza de los Ángeles, clowns, magicians, and other amateur performers delight an informal audience with impromptu performances in the open air. In the Jardín de la Unión, live musicians roam the plaza, looking for someone to commission a tune. Throughout the year, there are numerous theatrical, musical, and film events produced by the university or the city government, among other organizations, as well as a summer arts festival and organ concert.

For first-time visitors to the city, **calle-joneadas** are the quintessential Guanajuato experience. Led by the Estudiantina, a group of Medieval-style troubadours dressed in capes and pantaloons, *callejoneadas* are walking minstrel shows that traverse the city every evening. These large student bands play guitars and mandolins as they jubilantly stroll through town, singing in unison. Behind them, an informal band of tourists and revelers follows, often passing flasks of wine or spirits between them. For new visitors to the city, these evening jaunts can provide a sort of nocturnal tour of Guanajuato, as the Estudiantina often stops at the Callejón del Beso, the Plaza de San Roque, and other famous locales. *Callejoneadas* usually begin around 8 P.M., departing from the Jardín de la Unión or Mercado Hidalgo, though you can also join them on their way around town. You do not need to buy tickets in advance; just join in the fun when the Estudiantina arrives at the square.

Under the directorship of the Universidad de Guanajuato, the **Teatro Principal** (Hidalgo s/n, esq. Cantarranas, tel. 473/732-1523 or

© ARTURO MEADE

A comedian entertains a crowd on the steps of Teatro Juárez.

473/732-1073, www.ugto.mx) presents a changing program of dance, live music, film, and theater throughout the year, including performances by the university's Ballet Folklórico (traditional Mexican dance). It is also a venue for major artists during the Cervantino festival in October, as well as the annual **Expresión en Corto** short film festival, co-hosted by San Miguel de Allende and Guanajuato. The first of Guanajuato's city theaters, the original building was constructed in 1788 but destroyed by fire; it was rebuilt in 1955.

The beautiful **Teatro Juárez** (Sopeña s/n, tel. 473/732-0183 or 473/732-2521, box office hours 10 A.M.–8 P.M. daily) has been Guanajuato's most important performance venue since its inauguration more than a century ago. Here, you can see theater, opera, symphonies, and more. During the Festival Internacional Cervantino, many big names take the stage, though there are ongoing events throughout the year. The box office is in a small window on the theater's southeast side, and it handles sales for all Cervantino events.

A boxy stone theater overlooking the Plaza Allende, the **Teatro Cervantes** (Plaza Allende s/n, tel. 473/732-1169 or 473/732-0289, cultura@redes.int.com) is a small venue that sporadically opens for concerts, films, dance, and opera throughout the year. Like other city theaters, it is a major venue during the Cervantino festival—not suprising given the theater's name. Run by the State Cultural Institute, the theater is also used occasionally for government functions or talks. It was inaugurated in 1979.

ART

The beautiful old building that houses the **Museo del Pueblo de Guanajuato** (Positos 7, tel. 473/732-2990, 10 A.M.–7 P.M. Tues.–Sat., 10 A.M.–3 P.M. Sun., US$1) contains three stories of small galleries exhibiting the museum's permanent collection, as well as rotating exhibitions by Mexican and international artists. Downstairs, the Sala Teresa Pomar has a nice collection of traditional Mexican miniatures, including ceramics, masks, *alebrijes,*

and corn-husk dolls. Upstairs, the museum's permanent collection is on display; it includes some 18th- and 19th-century oil paintings from the region. There is one gallery downstairs plus two large galleries upstairs that are dedicated entirely to temporary art exhibitions. These shows usually feature Mexican artists and often address interesting and well-thought-out themes. Depending on when you visit, you may see work by young artists or great Mexican masters.

At the Museo del Pueblo, the lovely building itself is part of the attraction, housed in the former mansion of the wealthy Sardeneta family. Of particular note, there is a small 18th-century baroque chapel within the building, which was later decorated by Guanajuato's beloved artist José Chávez Morado. Here, Chávez Morado depicts the cruelty of the Spanish rule over New Spain and the dehumanizing mining industry.

The Universidad de Guanajuato has several well-managed gallery spaces, overseen by the university art department. These galleries feature rotating exhibitions with a focus on contemporary art, and they are free and open to the public. Located just beside the university's famous sandstone staircase, the small but beautiful **Sala Tomas Chávez Morado** (Lascuráin de Retana 5, 10 A.M.–2 P.M. and 3–6 P.M. daily, free) is named after one of Guanajuato's most famous muralists and painters. This small space shows rotating contemporary art exhibitions, often by local artists. The gallery itself is unusual, with an arched entryway leading into a cave-like salon with thick stone walls and a bilevel exhibition space—a surprising backdrop for the experimental pieces that the gallery exhibits. Sometimes, the entire space is dedicated to a single piece of work.

Located just inside the Puerta del Antiguo Colegio Jesuita (the door to the old Jesuit school) on the main university campus, **Galería Polivante** (Lascuráin de Retana 5, 10 A.M.–2 P.M. and 3–6 P.M. daily, free) is a large modern exhibition space. With high ceilings, clean white walls, and exposed piping, the gallery feels incredibly contemporary, as do the artists who show there. With two large rooms, plus several smaller spaces ideal for installation, this gallery can accommodate large-format pieces and extensive collective exhibitions. Recently, the gallery exhibited a high-profile contemporary show of work from the Fundación/Colección Jumex, widely considered to be Mexico's most important contemporary art collection.

Just a block from the main university campus, **Galería El Atrio** (Plazuela de la Compañía s/n, 10 A.M.–2 P.M. and 3–6 P.M. daily, free) is an unusual art gallery, fitted into a long and thin salon that runs along the base of the Templo de la Compañía de Jesús. Since there isn't enough room to really step back from the work, this gallery tends to show smaller-format pieces, ranging from painting to photography. The gallery has a rotating schedule of exhibitions, showing contemporary work by local artists in group or individual exhibition. You can get more information about any of the galleries or upcoming exhibitions at the university's **Departamento de Artes Visuales** (Visual Arts Department, Mesón de San Antonio, Alonso 12, tel. 473/735-3700, ext. 2731).

FESTIVALS AND EVENTS

In the party-loving town of Guanajuato, there are constant cultural events, religious festivals, and live music in the *centro histórico*. If you choose to visit Guanajuato during a well-known festival or holiday, you will likely see an increase in national tourism, fewer hotel rooms, and a lot of activity. Of particular note, the Cervantino festival in October is a huge event, during which the city is very full and rather expensive. You can get more information about Guanajuato's cultural events at the Dirección Municipal de Cultura de Guanajuato (Av. 5 de Mayo 1, tel. 473/732-7491 or 473/734-0136).

Semana Santa

Generally considered the most important religious holiday of the year, Semana Santa (Holy Week) is colorfully celebrated in the city of Guanajuato. The festivities begin with the beautiful celebrations in honor of Viernes de

Dolores, observed on the sixth Friday of Lent. For this popular festival, the Jardín de la Unión is a locus of activity, filled with people and decorated with *papel picado* and lavish bouquets of flowers. Politicians and local government officials weave through the crowds, handing out flowers and ice cream to passersby. It is also traditional for young men to give flowers to young women in love or friendship and then walk together through the Jardín de la Unión. Throughout the city's homes, offices, businesses, mines, markets, and plazas, small altars are built in the Virgin's honor, traditionally decorated with Easter candles, chamomile, dill, gold-painted oranges, wheat, and flowers, as well as an image of the Virgin. Visitors to the altars are given *aguas de fruta,* usually limeade. In the Valenciana neighborhood, the mines also host large celebrations and are often open to the public.

A week later, the city expresses a more solemn portrait on **Viernes Santo** (Good Friday), generally considered the most important day of Holy Week. At midday, the Passion of the Christ is reenacted in the city center with townspeople playing the roles of Romans and Hebrews. In the evening, the Procesión de Silencio (Silent Procession) commemorates Christ's suffering and death in a moving parade, during which hundreds of mourners march in chilling silence through the twisting alleys of downtown Guanajuato. The procession continues for hours, often concluding late into the night.

Easter Sunday itself, usually called **Domingo de Gloria,** is a quieter day in Guanajuato, when most families spend time together and possibly attend mass. If you plan to visit during Holy Week, book your hotel reservations in advance. Most of Mexico's schools and businesses take their spring break during Semana Santa so there is a lot of national tourism, especially in popular destinations like Guanajuato.

Expresión en Corto

Along with San Miguel de Allende, Guanajuato hosts the annual Expresión en Corto short film festival (Fábrica La Aurora, Local 5-B, tel.

415/152-7264, www.expresionencorto.com) during the final week of July. During a long weekend of near-constant screenings, hundreds of films (which were selected from thousands of entries worldwide) are shown, with genres ranging from horror to documentary. Films are screened in the Teatro Principal and other traditional venues, as well as in more unusual locations like the subterranean streets and the municipal graveyard. Screenings are free and open to the public, and most are subtitled in both English and Spanish.

Apertura de la Presa de la Olla and the Fiestas de San Juan

The Presa de la Olla, a small reservoir to the east of the city center, was originally built in the 18th century to help prevent the frequent flooding that plagued Guanajuato's city center. Today, the reservoir is surrounded by a lovely colonial neighborhood, flanked on its west side by the Florencio Antillón Park. The reservoir can be a relaxing place to visit for an afternoon stroll, and it is also the site of an annual festival, the Apertura de la Presa (Opening of the Dam). The festival is believed to date back to the mid-18th century, when locals gathered together to drain and clean the river to prevent backups and flooding. Though originally organized for utilitarian purposes, the cleaning and opening of the dam has also become a merry municipal party.

Today, the ritual cleaning continues on the first Monday of July, with the city's mayor arriving to command the opening of the dam's floodgates at 1 P.M. The rushing water creates a rather pleasant breeze through the neighborhood. Thereafter, the party continues with swimming competitions and a big local party in Florencio Antillón Park. There are dozens of food stands and live music from the state band. The festival is generally associated with St. John the Baptist, whose feast day is June 24 and whose association with water is reflected in the opening of the dam.

Festival de Verano

A bonanza of music, art, dance, and other cultural events, the Festival de Verano is a month-long arts festival, sponsored and organized by the Universidad de Guanajuato. During the entire month of August, professional and student groups perform throughout the city's churches and theaters, as well as the town squares and plazas. The festival invites such varied acts as traditional Mexican bands, baroque ensembles, choirs, or children's theater; many performances are held in public spaces. In addition to performances, the festival coordinates educational workshops and lectures. Though less crowded than the Cervantino festival, it is still a wonderful time to visit Guanajuato and enjoy some of the city's excellent performance venues.

Of particular note, Guanajuato's churches contain some of Mexico's most beautiful and historic organs. Every year, these organs are put to good use at the annual **Festival Internacional de Órgano Antiguo de Guanajuato Guillermo Pinto Reyes** (International Antique Organ Festival), a subset of the summer arts festival. For this unique event, artists from across Mexico are invited to perform in the city's chapels and churches. Events are free and open to the public.

Día de la Independencia

The capital of a state known for its large role in the independence movement (not to mention, the site of one of the most famous battles in the War of Independence), Guanajuato is a fitting place to spend the *fiestas patrias,* the patriotic festivals commemorating the anniversary of Mexico's independence from Spain. Like most Mexican cities, Guanajuato gets dressed up in patriotic attire during the month of September, decked out with tri-color flags, lights, and banners that read, *¡Viva México!* At 11 P.M. on September 15, the town's mayor holds a brief ceremony in the Palacio Municipal (in the Plaza de la Paz), calling out *"¡Viva México!"* to the crowd. Fireworks and general merriment follow. The big thing to do, however, is hit the bars and party until dawn.

In the nearby municipality of Santa Rosa (just 16 kilometers/10 miles northeast of the city center), there is an elaborate reenactment of the taking of La Alhóndiga performed annually on September 16. The reenactment has been staged every year since 1864 (though it was suspended for several years during the Mexican Revolution). The pageant begins with parade, which departs from La Cruz Grande beside the highway. As the crowd swells, "Spaniards" and "rebels" reenact seven battles along the roadway, accompanied by cannons and fighting. In the final scene, El Pípila takes the Alhóndiga. While the reenactment is fictional, the ensuing parties are very real.

If you didn't get your fix of independence events, on September 28 the city of Guanajuato celebrates the first major battle of the War of Independence, the **Día de la Toma de la Alhóndiga** (Anniversary of the Taking of the Alhóndiga) with a municipal parade.

Festival Internacional Cervantino

Guanajuato's most famous and well attended event is the month-long Festival Internacional Cervantino (tel. 55/5615-9417 or 55/5615-9403, www.festivalcervantino.gob.mx) held every autumn, from mid-October to early November. Overseen by the National Council for Arts and Culture, the festival's emphasis is the performing arts, with dance, theater, opera, and music events held throughout the city's theaters, churches, and plazas. Every year, many well-known ensembles, soloists, and performers are invited to Guanajuato to perform. The immense annual program includes tons of daily performances in a wide range of styles, from jazz to *cumbia* to traditional dance to classical music. In addition to the impressive roster of formal concerts, there are also many free events held in civic plazas and in the square adjoining the Alhóndiga. Although Mexican artists are well represented in the program, the event is distinctly international, with several foreign countries elected as honorary guests each year. Several Mexican states are also specially invited, with each setting up a special showroom dedicated to that state's crafts, food, and culture.

Part of the festival's great attraction is the crowds of artists and revelers that come to

© JULIE DOHERTY MEADE

Teatro Cervantes is a major venue for music, dance, and theater during the city's Festival Internacional Cervantino.

Guanajuato to participate in the Cervantino events. During the festivities, the streets are constantly filled, restaurants and cafés are hopping, and amateurs take advantage of the crowds to show off their talents (expect plenty of young street musicians, clowns, or living statues performing in coffee shops and open spaces). In addition, there are often special events and visual arts exhibitions in the city's museums, galleries, and shops, as well as special shows in the university's art galleries.

Tickets for Cervantino events can be purchased through Ticketmaster or directly from the box office at Teatro Juárez. Students and teachers with a valid ID can get half price off tickets to all events, as do residents of the city of Guanajuato.

QUIXOTIC GUANAJUATO

Guanajuato is veritably smitten with the great Spanish author Miguel de Cervantes. The image of his fanciful hero, Don Quixote, is sprinkled throughout the city center in bronze and stone, and nearly every block has another bookstore, hotel, or shop named after the legendary knight. Most notably, the annual **Festival Internacional Cervantino** draws enormous crowds, and Guanajuato has been declared the Cervantes capital of the New World.

Widely considered one of the greatest writers in the Spanish language, Miguel de Cervantes Saavedra was an early 17th-century novelist, playwright, and poet from Madrid. His greatest work is the novel *The Ingenious Hidalgo Don Quixote of La Mancha*, usually referred to as just *Don Quixote*. In this world-famous story, the novel's namesake hero fancies himself a chivalrous knight, heading off on imaginary adventures with his sidekick, Sancho Panza. According to some literary historians, Don Quixote is the first prototype for the modern novel, widely read and translated throughout the world. In addition to his magnum opus, Cervantes wrote numerous full-length plays and several *entremeses,* shorter comedies or farces.

When *Don Quixote* was published, Guanajuato was little more than a mining outpost of New Spain, far from the world and society described by Cervantes. Not surprisingly, the city's connection to the Spanish bard is much more recent. In the 1950s, two university professors, Enrique Ruelas and Armando Olivares Carrillo, founded a theater group at the University of Guanajuato. Every week, the group performed Cervantes's *entremeses* in the Plaza de San Roque. After 20 years of performing, the project attracted the attention of Mexico's president, Luis Echeverría. With the president's support, the city began to plan the first international arts festival, which would invite performers, artists, and musicians to Mexico from throughout the world.

On October 12, 1972, the very first Festival Internacional Cervantino was inaugurated in Guanajuato, funded by the government and directed by the famous Mexican actress Dolores del Río. Since then, the festival has invited artists to perform from across Mexico and the world. Special invitees in the past have included classical composer Philip Glass, Mexican rockers Café Tacuba, and alternative British group Radiohead. Visiting Guanajuato during the Cervantino festival can be extremely exciting, especially for those who love music, dance, and theater. It is also a great time to visit for those who love a party. The town fills to capacity during this month-long event, bustling with visiting artists and connoisseurs, as well as plenty of tourists on day trips from León, Celaya, or other cities in the region. It's the modern mother lode for Guanajuato's tourist-driven industries; hotels, shops, and restaurants make a lot of money during the festival, often raising their prices considerably to do so. Budget and midrange hotels can cost two or even three times the price during the month-long event, even if they aren't filled to capacity. Book ahead to find something reasonable. You can also consider staying in San Miguel de Allende, just an hour's drive away.

Shopping

Although Guanajuato is not a shopping destination like San Miguel de Allende, the town offers plenty of places to pick up a nice gift or do some casual browsing. In the *centro histórico*, several traditional crafts shops sell clothing and ceramics, and several famous artisans work in the city. There are lots of little shops where you can pick up a trinket, a souvenir, or a piece of inexpensive jewelry, plus plenty of bookshops for the literary-minded.

TRADITIONAL CRAFTS

Next door to the Museo Iconográfico del Quijote, **La Casa del Quijote** (Sopeña 17, tel. 473/732-8226, www.lacasadelquijote.com, 11 A.M.–9 P.M. daily) is a large craft and jewelry shop located in a beautiful old building. The huge and airy showrooms are not particularly complemented by the sleek electronic music playing on the sound system, but they are well stocked with textiles and pottery from across Mexico. In addition to some nice ceramic work by artisans from the state of Guanajuato, the store has a large supply of Mata Ortiz pottery from Chihuahua, as well as Oaxacan textiles. There is also a wide selection of jewelry design in silver, showcased in the shop's two large front rooms.

For regional craftwork, **Rincón Artesanal** (Alonso 15A, tel. 473/734-1435, 10 A.M.–8 P.M. daily) exclusively sells the distinctive pottery produced in the small city of Tarandacuao, Guanajuato. Unlike the majolica-style pottery that is most commonly sold in the Bajío region, this hand-wheeled ceramic is painstakingly painted with delicate geometric patterns, applied in a high-temperature glaze. Rincón Artesanal presents work from several Tarandacuao artists, each producing a slightly different version of this traditional craft with a different palette of colors. Small espresso cups and saucers are sweetly sophisticated and sold by the set, while the large ceramic platters are impressively detailed. With decades in business, the store's senior owners will be happy to tell you about the work.

A famous Guanajuato ceramics artist, Javier Hernández Capelo, has opened the store **Capelo** (Positos 69, tel. 473/732-0612, www.capeloart.com, 10 A.M.–3 P.M. and 5–8 P.M. Mon.–Sat.) in the center of town. Here, you'll find plates, platter, pitchers, urns, mugs, and plenty of other creative flatware hand-painted with flowers, fruits, animals, and other traditional designs. There is something to fit a variety of tastes; some designs are very lively and colorful while others are more subdued and detailed. All of Capelo's hand-wheeled ceramics are fired at high temperatures, making them durable and lead-free. Capelo is also a painter, though the store does not stock paintings (for those who are interested, they do have a catalog). While the store has plenty of products, Capelo still maintains a studio in La Valenciana (Cerro de la Cruz s/n, Col. La Valenciana, tel. 473/732-8964), which welcomes visitors during the week or by appointment.

If you are interested in Mexico's ceramic traditions, it is worth a visit to the studio of **Gorky Gonzalez** (Ex Huerta de Montenegro s/n, Col. Pastita, tel. 473/731-0389, www.gorkypottery.com). With decades at work, Gonzalez is an internationally recognized, award-winning creator of talavera-style pottery in traditional Mexican designs. From decorative platters and vases to candlesticks and figurines, everything is beautifully crafted and colorfully hand-painted. Although the studio is usually open in the mornings, call or drop a line before you go out there; you can take a taxi from the *centro histórico*.

CLOTHING AND JEWELRY

Just a block from the Alhóndiga de Granaditas, **Corazón de Plata** (Positos 20, tel. 473/734-2266, guanajuato_corazondeplata@hotmail.com, 10 A.M.–7 P.M. daily) sells handmade silver jewelry with lighthearted, Mexican-inspired designs. Here, you'll find necklaces and earrings made of ornamental hearts, birds, and flowers, some further embellished with colored gems or stones. The jeweler herself usually tends the shop, which is small and simple, but well laid-out with glass display cases for each of the different lines.

A small storefront on Sopeña, **La Florecita** (Sopeña 13 bis, tel. 473/732-2069, 9 A.M.–2:30 P.M. and 4–8 P.M. Mon.–Sat., 9 A.M.–2:30 P.M. and 4–6 P.M. Sun.) sells textiles and clothing from nine Mexican states, as well as a small selection of woven textiles from other Latin American countries, like Bolivia and Guatemala. Here, you'll find well-priced wool bedspreads, embroidered manta blouses, hand-woven table runners, and cute knit hats. Prices are reasonable and the store's owner is knowledgeable about the products and their origins.

SWEETS

Sweets are produced throughout the Bajío region, and *dulces típicos* are for sale at the stands inside the **Mercado Hidalgo,** as well as in a number of wonderful old sweets shops in the city. The delightfully sugary **La Catrina** (Sopeña 74, tel. 473/732-6089, 9 A.M.–9 P.M. daily) is a massive Mexican sweets shop, right across the street from Teatro Juárez. Within this shiny two-story shop, there are some wonderful and unusual candies, like fig and walnut paste, shredded coconut bars, and *palenquetas* (honey-covered discs of nuts, pumpkin seeds, or amaranth). Regional treats include *cajeta* (caramelized goat milk candy), which is largely produced in nearby Celaya, as well as *xoconostle* jam, made from the fruit of a sour prickly pear that is popular in the region. The store's employees will be happy to give you a basket to collect your goodies, as well as free samples of some of the more unusual candies.

BOOKSTORES

The lovely **Viejo Zaguan** (Positos 64, tel. 473/732-3971, www.viejozaguan.com, 10:30 A.M.–3 P.M. and 5–8 P.M. Mon.–Sat., 11 A.M.–3 P.M. Sun.) sells literature in Spanish,

© JULIE DOHERTY MEADE

Inside the Mercado Hidalgo, you'll find sweets for sale, as well as fruit and vegetable stands, crafts, and tons of little eateries.

QUESO DE TUNA AND OTHER SWEETS

The Bajío region has a serious sweet tooth. *Dulces típicos* (traditional sweets) are produced in various Bajío cities and consumed by the populace with appetite and pleasure. In the city of Guanajuato, there are wonderful sweets stands in the market and numerous traditional sweets shops boasting enormous selections and unique regional candies.

Among the most popular flavors in Mexico, *cajeta* (slowly simmered caramelized goat milk) is produced in the Bajío region and popular throughout Mexico. Originally invented in the famous candy-producing city of Celaya, *cajeta* is sold in jars as a caramel syrup or is incorporated into sweets. A popular treat is *cajeta* spread between two *obleas*, thin wafers made with the same process as the communion wafers served in Catholic churches, yet not blessed by a priest. Chewy milk caramels *(dulce de leches)* are also produced in the Bajío region and can be bought by the piece.

The Bajío is a big producer of *ate*, concentrated fruit pastes, which are often served with cheese. Quince, guava, and mango are among the most popular flavors for *ate*,

though these delicious pastes can be made of many different fruits. Crystallized fruits and cactus are also popular desserts, commonly made from orange, fig, or lime stuffed with shredded coconut. In the desert environment, confectioners also make use of the abundance of cactus and succulents. You can find crystallized *biznaga* (barrel cactus) and *xoconostle* (sour prickly pear fruit) in many shops and sweet stands.

For the adventurous, the strongly flavored *queso de tuna* (or prickly pear cheese) is one of the more unusual sweets of the semi-desert. While it's difficult to get your hands on some, it is more widely available in the city of Guanajuato than in other Bajío cities, usually for sale in the shops and stands surrounding the Mercado Hidalgo. This thick and heavy sweet is made from ground prickly pear fruit mixed with unrefined sugar, which is slowly cooked until it forms a thick, dark paste. The paste is then cooled in giant molds and cut into blocks. The resulting sweet is unusually dense and chewy, with a rich and concentrated flavor quite unlike anything else.

art books, postcards, magazines, and a small selection of CDs. They also carry a wonderful series of hardcover books and magazines by *Artes de Mexico*, each volume focused on a different theme in Mexican architecture, art, and craft. Behind the bookstore, there is a small café where you can soak up the pleasant literary atmosphere over a cup of coffee. The shop occasionally hosts art exhibitions, and there is also a nice collection of artisan crafts, like baskets, metalwork, and jewelry. Just steps from the university, this artsy little place caters to the intellectual crowd.

Friendly **Donkey Jote** (Positos 30, tel. 473/734-0455, 10:30 A.M.–5 P.M. Mon.–Sat.) is a neat little bookstore with great selection of reasonably priced new and used books in English. The emphasis is on literature, though there are also books on history and culture. The selection is always changing as the owner

heads up to the United States to bring new merchandise to the store. Those looking for a piece of literary fiction to occupy their vacation will certainly find something among the good selection here. Guanajuato's English-speaking expatriates, as well as many travelers, pick up their pleasure reading at this literary nook.

There is a branch of the **Librería de Porrúa Hermanos y Compañía** (Alonso 12, tel. 473/732-2153, www.porrua.com.mx, 10 A.M.–8 P.M. Mon.–Fri., 10 A.M.–2 P.M. Sat.) in downtown Guanajuato, which sells a range of books in Spanish published by the Mexican press of the same name. Many are educational texts and reference books for university students, but you will also find books on spirituality, poetry, and literature in Spanish. The editions are rather minimally designed functional texts, but there are some great titles for those who read (or are learning to read) in Spanish.

Sports and Recreation

HIKING, BIKING, AND HORSEBACK RIDING

There are lots of little paths leading into the craggy peaks around Guanajuato, some of which are well-maintained and easily accessible. A quick taxi ride from the *centro histórico* will take you to a trailhead leading to the **Cerro de la Bufa,** a tall, craggy peak just above the Presa de la Olla. Where the road ends, a trail begins. It is a steep ascent, and it takes about 1.5–2 hours to climb to the top. (You'll make it back in about half the time.) On the way up, you may pass local livestock grazing, as well as a few small villages. Once there, the view is panoramic, with a distant vista of the valley beyond the city of Guanajuato. The beautiful views and the accessibility of this trail make it one of the most popular day hikes around the city.

If you'd like to take a guided hike or explore regions farther off the beaten path, **Cacomixtle** (Calle Burócrata 4, Col. Marfil,

tel. 473/733-1244, cell tel. 473/738-5246, www.cacomixtle.com) offers ecotours in the countryside around Guanajuato. Hiking and bird-watching trips often head to the craggy peaks of Sierra de Santa Rosa; though just outside the city, this small mountain range offers a chance to visit a largely untouched wilderness and small rural communities. The company also runs off-road biking tours (some several days long) to Atotonilco, San Miguel de Allende, the Huasteca, and beyond. Tours generally run US$50–60 per person for a day trip, including transportation and gear, though overnight trips cost more. Cacomixtle can also organize horseback riding tours to the city's mines or along the old Camino Real.

YOGA AND MARTIAL ARTS

Just off the Plaza de San Roque, **Dojo Tao** (Jardín Reforma 25, tel. 473/119-2294, dojotaogto@hotmail.com) offers Hatha yoga classes, karate, kung fu, belly dancing, and

© JULIE DOHERTY MEADE

The trails leading to the top of the Cerro de la Bufa are nice for a day hike.

You can find yoga, martial arts, and other recreational activities at Dojo Tao.

Tibetan massage, among other workshops. The door of the studio opens onto the pretty Jardín Reforma. Write or stop by the center to see what's coming up; though they don't maintain regular office hours, the class schedules are posted on the door.

Casa Solaris (Calle del Sol 15, tel. 473/734-0880) also hosts twice-weekly yoga classes, meditation sessions, reiki and tai chi workshops, and kung fu classes for kids. This small space across from the Templo de la Compañía de Jesús is only open during class times, so swing by to see the class schedule posted on the door.

SPAS

The luxury boutique hotel **Villa María Cristina** (Paseo de la Presa 76, tel. 473/731-2182 or toll-free Mex. tel. 800/702-7007, www.villamaria-cristina.net, 9 A.M.–5 P.M. daily) operates a lovely little spa on the first floor of hotel in the dreamy neighborhood near the Presa de la Olla, one of the municipal reservoirs. The spa facilities include a dry sauna, Swiss showers, a gym, and a Jacuzzi, and are open to all hotel guests. The spa is also open to the public for a daily rate of about US$150, which includes a massage and facial treatments, tea and snacks, and access to all spa facilities for up to six hours. The space is one of the nicer ones in the Bajío.

Language and Education

For many foreigners, Guanajuato an ideal place to spend several weeks on the cheap, hanging out with other travelers, sipping coffee in inexpensive eateries, studying Spanish, or reveling in rowdy nightlife. Fortunately, there are plenty of excellent language schools in this little town, plus plenty of educational opportunities throughout the year. Even if you don't sign up for a formal language program, check out the university's art and cultural offerings, which often include lectures and workshops open to the public.

SPANISH LANGUAGE

Guanajuato is a popular and inexpensive place to study Spanish. There are plenty of good language schools and, for the total immersion experience, English is less widely spoken in Guanajuato than it is in neighboring San Miguel de Allende. Foreign students can take Spanish classes at the **Universidad de Guanajuato** (Departamento de Lenguas, Universidad de Guanajuato, Calzada de Guadalupe s/n, tel. 473/732-0006 ext. 8031, www.idiomas.ugto.mx, 9 A.M.–3 P.M. Mon.–Fri.) for a full semester or in one-month increments. The university offers intensive Spanish-language programs for beginning, intermediate, and advanced students, as well as curriculum in Mexican history, Mexican literature, and reading in Spanish. Students may augment their language study with courses in art history or dance, among other subjects, as well as optional seminars or field trips. The university does not have dormitories; however, it will help students arrange for a home-stay with a local family. College credit can usually be obtained for the semester-long program.

The affordable **Escuela Mexicana** (Potrero 12, tel. 473/732-5005 or 473/732-7393, www.escuelamexicana.com) is located in a cheerful colonial building in Guanajuato's *centro histórico*. This school's highly flexible and diverse Spanish programs let you tailor coursework to your personal interests or needs. Depending on your level and availability, students can enroll in group classes in grammar, conversation, and culture, or sign up for private instruction. This school donates a percentage of its proceeds to charitable causes in the region. Depending on your desires, Escuela Mexicana will help students to arrange a homestay with a local family, or students can rent private rooms on the campus for a very reasonable price.

One of Guanajuato's oldest and most popular language schools, Academia Falcon, closed its doors a few years ago. However, some of the teachers from this well-loved program formed a new institution, the **Escuela Falcon** (Callejón de Gallitos 6, tel. 473/732-6531, www.escuelafalcon.com). Thanks to low enrollment and reasonable tuition cost, you'll get plenty of bang for your buck at this serious school. In addition to Spanish language, students have the opportunity to take classes on Mexican art and culture, dance, history, and politics.

Classes are capped at five students at the **Colegio de Lenguas Adelita** (Callejón Agua Fuerte 56, tel. 473/732-0826, www.la-adelita.org), which gives each student a chance for real one-on-one interaction with their teachers. Be prepared to participate, though! Both private classes and group classes are incredibly well priced, with further discounts for students who choose to study for a full trimester. Classes start every Monday and are appropriate for a variety of levels (the school provides an entry exam to determine what level Spanish you should take). In addition to grammar and conversation, students can sign up for history and culture classes or professional programs in legal or medical Spanish.

GUANAJUATO

© ARTURO MEADE

Foreign exchange students and Mexican undergraduates enjoy a relaxing atmosphere at the cafés near the Universidad de Guanajuato.

Accommodations

Guanajuato is a big national and international tourist destination, drawing crowds of visitors year-round. While winter is technically the high season in Mexico, Guanajuato's tourist season is a bit more inconsistent. In fact, hotel rates tend to fluctuate on a fairly regular basis in Guanajuato, depending on demand. The city's many cultural events, especially the annual Festival Internacional Cervantino, draw large crowds. Most hotels double or even triple their rates during October, even if they aren't at capacity. With the exception of the Cervantino festival, Semana Santa, and the Christmas holidays, hotels rarely fill up. Usually, it is possible to snag a room on short notice. However, to spare yourself trekking around steep alleyways, it's best to have a hotel destination in mind before you arrive.

Perhaps because demand is high and fairly continuous, very few of Guanajuato's hotels offer really great value. Many of the hotels in the *centro histórico* are unapologetically basic, offering little more than a spring bed and a small bathroom—not even a poster on the wall. Nicer hotels may add a bit of charm, but most tend to be fairly pared down. In Guanajuato, you will pay extra for a nice location, but you are likely to spend most of your time in the streets, not in your accommodations.

UNDER US$50

Guanajuato is a backpacker's paradise, with dozens of ultra-cheap youth hostels peppered throughout the city center. For solo travelers, Guanajuato's hostels can also be a great place to make friends in the city, while friends traveling together can rent cheap private rooms with shared baths. Those looking for the quintessential hostel experience will find a happy home at **La Casa del Tío** (Cantarranas 47, tel. 473/733-9728, www.hostellacasadeltio.com, US$11 dorms, US$25–45 double). This popular hostel is in a funky red-and-white stucco house, right in the center of downtown. Shared dorms have large windows, lots of light, and cost just US$11 per night. All guests also have access to the hostel's laundry facilities, computer and Internet, and a nice roof deck. Private rooms are a little pricier per person, depending on if you have a shared or private bathroom, but they are still among the cheapest accommodations in town.

The laid-back and quirky **Casa de Pita** (Callejón Cabecita 26, tel. 473/732-1532, http://casadepita.com, US$40) is a great find in the budget category. Tucked into into an enchanting alleyway behind the Plaza Mexiamora and only a few blocks from the Jardín de la Unión, the location could not be better. Larger rooms have cute little kitchenettes that can be used to whip up a snack, and most are eclectically decorated with tiles and lamps. While these aren't luxury accommodations, the rooms

The quietest hotels are located in alleyways and small plazas, where there is less traffic and nightlife.

There is a slew of inexpensive youth hostels in central Guanajuato, many with rather charming locations.

are comfortable and the style is fun and colorful. Pita herself is a friendly host, who enjoys chatting with her guests over breakfast. Rooms vary but are all roughly the same cost; larger rooms with kitchens do not include breakfast in the price while small rooms do.

Clean and well located, the **Casa Mexicana** (Sóstenes Rocha 28, tel. 473/732-7393, www.casamexicanaweb.com, US$36–50) offers comfortable, sufficiently spacious, and very well-priced accommodations for one, two, or three travelers. Organized around a central walkway, rooms are decorated with brightly colored wood furniture and, in some cases, funky paint jobs. All have windows and plenty of natural light. Each room is different and some feel a bit like a kid's bedroom, so ask to see a few when you check in. If you are willing to share a bathroom, the rates can drop as low as US$28 for a double. There is an adjoining café and language school, operated by the same owners as the hotel.

US$50-100

It is a steep walk up a narrow alley, but the aerobic workout is just another benefit of staying at the friendly, family-run █ **La Casa Azul Hotel** (Carcamanes 57, tel. 473/731-2288, www.lacasaazul.com.mx, US$55). Perched high above the Plaza Baratillo, this six-room inn feels like staying in the home of your *abuela,* with the quirky details and comfort to match. The rooms vary in size and decor, but each is full of creaky old wooden furniture, crooked lamps, and thick Mexican bedspreads. Comfortably appointed, all rooms are equipped with a private bath and cable television, and some have sitting areas. There is a beautiful terrace on the roof; from here, you can enjoy the views you earned after the walk up the hill. In the basement, the hotel also has a small, windowless cantina, only accessible by ladder—atmospheric and cool, though a touch claustrophobic, too! It's owned by a Guanajuato family, and service here is friendly and personable.

A plain but serviceable option in the very center of town, **Hotel Mesón del Rosario** (Av. Juárez 31, tel. 473/732-3284, www.hotelmesondelrosario.com.mx, US$55) is a good home base for exploring Guanajuato. Although located on busy Avenida Juárez, rooms are set back from the noise and bustle, surrounding a pleasant central walkway. Rooms are rather unembellished though tidy, with cold tile floors and small double beds topped with woven bedspreads and wooden headboards. Some rooms are a bit more atmospheric than others; if it isn't a busy holiday weekend, press the staff to show you additional options if you aren't satisfied with their first offer.

The central alleyway location is what most recommends **La Casa de los Cuentos** (Barranca 8, tel. 473/732-2033 or 477/327-4440, info@casacuentos.com, US$60), a little posada that maintains 13 small guest rooms, each with an even smaller private bath. Decor is minimal, but functional, with a few cute details to counteract the otherwise sterile feeling. Two upstairs guest rooms have windows overlooking the alley; the others have interior windows that stare into the hotel's hallways. Downstairs, there is a large and somewhat spare communal kitchen where guests can cook or convene for a chat. There is free wireless Internet throughout the building. While not the most adorable accommodations in town, they are serviceable and central, and the hosts are friendly.

((El Zopilote Mojado (Plaza Mexiamora 51, tel. 473/732-5311, www.elzopilotemojado.com, US$60) is a cute and tidy hotel, located in two small houses on the pretty Plaza Mexiamora. Above a nice coffee shop of the same name, this doubles-only establishment has just three pretty guest rooms in the main building, plus several more rooms in another building on the same plaza. The guest rooms are decorated with cheerful Mexican-style furnishings and comfortably outfitted with fans, electric blankets, closets, clock radios, bathrobes, and plenty of lighting. Some also have small balconies or terraces. At night, guests let themselves in via coded lock on the door. Management can feel a bit absent on Sundays when the café is closed, but this hotel is one of the nicer establishments in its price range. For those who like a little more space, El Zopilote also rents small apartments with kitchenettes.

Hospedería del Truco 7 (Constancia 15, tel. 473/732-6513, www.hospederiadeltruco7.com, US$60) is owned by the same folks that own the popular Truco 7 restaurant behind the Jardín de la Unión. The guesthouse, however, is not at Truco 7, as the name implies. In fact, this seven-room posada is perched on a hillside just behind the Teatro Juárez and the Templo de San Diego. Rooms are simple and cozy, with comfortable Mexican-style furniture, oversized headboards, and cotton bedspreads. Every room has a small tiled bath with hand-painted sinks and showers, low wood-beamed ceilings, and TV. The nicest rooms in the front of the house have small balconies that open onto the alley below, offering a wonderful view of downtown Guanajuato. There's not much by way of sitting areas or shared facilities, but all of Guanajuato is at your doorstep. Just across the street from the Normal

School, the friendly **Casa Mágica** (Paseo de la Presa 79A, tel. 473/731-2301, www.casamagicahotel.com, US$72) is a simple and clean hotel, not far from the Presa de la Olla reservoir. Rooms are clean and cozy, with big beds and cotton bedspreads, safes, and satellite television. Adjoining private bathrooms are small but cute, with hand-painted ceramic sinks and showers. Most rooms have interior windows overlooking the hotel's sunny central atrium. Service is incredibly friendly and laid-back, and there is parking if you need it.

Hosteria del Frayle (Sopeña 3, tel. 473/732-1179 or 473/732-5738, www.hosteriadelfrayle.com, US$64–96) is a hotel with a lot of history. This creaky 17th-century structure was once the city's official mint, where metals from the mines were printed to coins. For the opportunity to sleep in a historic atmosphere, few places in Guanajuato boast such history. The hotel's 37 guest rooms are all different. Some are more spacious and lighter than others, but most are carpeted, worn, and rather dark. Furnishings are rather quirky, but some rooms have nice antique pieces, in addition to oversized wood headboards and dusty glass light fixtures. It is worthwhile to ask to see the available options before settling in for the night. Service is friendly and the location—right off the pedestrian street, Sopeña, and a stone's throw from Teatro Juárez—is ideal.

US$100-150

The centrally located **Hotel Antiguo Vapor** (Galarza 5, tel. 473/732-3211, www.hotel-vapor.com, US$135) is perched on a hill just above the city center, overlooking the Mercado Hidalgo and the monument to El Pípila. Rooms are small and simple, but clean and tastefully decorated with a Mexican flair. Each has warm tile floors and cheerful Mexican bedspreads, a television, wireless Internet, and a nice private bath with hand-painted tiles and showers. The best rooms are on the south side, with wee balconies and beautiful views overlooking the ravine below. The location is ideal—close to everything, yet just a bit removed from the noisy nightlife of downtown.

A popular hotel close to the Diego Rivera museum, **El Mesón de los Poetas** (Positos 35, tel. 473/732-0705 or 473/732-6657, www.mesondelospoetas.com, US$112) has more than 30 comfortable guest rooms in a restored 18th-century home. From the street, a pretty tiled atrium leads you to the bedrooms upstairs. Arranged around the hotel's maze-like central hallways, rooms are nothing fancy but have comfortable beds, televisions, and private bathrooms with showers. The two largest suites have views overlooking the facing hillside; the rest have interior windows, overlooking the indoor hallways. Rooms upstairs often have more natural light, but some require you to walk up several stories (and there is no elevator), so choose accordingly. The dining room downstairs is a highlight, adjoined by an old stone retaining wall and fountain; breakfast is included in the price and served downstairs every morning.

Part of a small Mexican-owned chain of luxury hotels, the **Camino Real Guanajuato** (Alhóndiga 100, Col. San Javier, tel. 473/102-1500 or toll-free Mex. tel. 800/901-2300, www.caminoreal.com/guanajuato, US$120) is a comfortable place to stay, just above the city center in the San Javier neighborhood. It inhabits the site of a former hacienda, and the entryway and lobby maintain much of the majesty of the original structure by blending new construction with the old. Crumbling rock walls and beautiful gardens give a pleasant colonial touch to the lobby and dining areas. Situated toward the back of the property, the 100-plus guest rooms are very small but clean, and decorated in a plain, modern style. Catering to business travelers in addition to tourists, Camino Real offers some services and amenities you won't find in other Guanajuato establishments, such as room service, minibars, satellite TV, air-conditioning, and high-end toiletries. Service is friendly, and the hotel includes an excellent breakfast buffet in the nightly price. The grounds are pretty and well kept, with big lawns, a pool, and an old stone fountains, and there is on-site parking.

Right across the street from the Templo de la Compañía de Jesús, **Casa de Agua** (Plazuela de la Compañía 4, tel. 473/734-1974 or 473/731-2257, US$120) is in a three-story 17th-century home. The charming blue exterior belies the rather sleek interior renovation; while the atrium and staircase retain a colonial style, the rooms have been thoroughly refurbished with a modern look. Though lacking a bit of colonial charm, bedrooms are generally spacious and clean, with minimal furnishings, white tile floors, and white bedspreads. The most atmospheric rooms have French doors that open onto a beautiful view of the pink sandstone facade of the Templo de la Compañía de Jesús, though the busy street below can certainly add rather unpleasant traffic noise to the otherwise spectacular view. Windowless bathrooms have large Jacuzzi tubs and showers. At high season rates, this hotel can feel a bit overpriced, though the cost can drop significantly during the low season. Service is a bit cold, but a generous breakfast is included in the price.

An old hotel on the Jardín de la Unión, **Posada Santa Fe** (Jardín de la Union 12, tel. 473/732-0084, www.posada-santafe.com, US$140) will put you smack-dab in the middle of it all. The lobby of this old colonial mansion is absolutely beautiful, with hand-painted tiles on the walls, big chandeliers, and carpeted hallways. Rooms are decidedly less fancy and have an old-fashioned feeling, with carpets, high ceilings, old bedspreads, and creaky furniture. Best for the romantically inclined, this hotel isn't necessarily the most modern in the city, but it does give you the opportunity to sleep in one of the oldest buildings in town. Some rooms are much nicer and brighter than others, while others are quieter. Service can be a little lackluster, but the hotel's restaurant is a relaxing place to have breakfast. Parking is included in the price.

A charming bed-and-breakfast in the Marfil neighborhood, **Casa de los Espíritus Alegres** (La Ex-Hacienda La Trinidad 1, Col. Marfil, tel. 473/733-1013, www.casa-spirit.com, US$145–165) is located within the crumbling stone walls of a former hacienda.

GUANAJUATO

There are five guest rooms and three suites, which open onto the central atrium. Each room is decorated individually with enormous flair and plenty of interesting folk art. Some rooms have a distinctly Mexican feeling with tin lamps and ceramics, while others are decorated with a more eclectic mix of crafts and colors (the Raj Mahal suite is decked out with artifacts and textiles from Rajasthan, India). While the decor varies, comfort is key. Here, every room is equipped with a fireplace, comfy beds with lots of pillows, big bathroom (most with tubs), and a private terrace. In the garden, the funky Rajastani tent is the main common space; there is an honor bar for guests. All rooms include the price of a full breakfast on the patio.

US$150-250

On the lovely Paseo de la Presa, just a few blocks from the reservoir, **Quinta Las Acacias** (Paseo de la Presa 168, tel. 473/731-1517, toll-free U.S. tel. 888/497-5129, www.quintalasacacias.com.mx, US$185–205) has a creaky Old World feeling. Located in a converted 19th-century mansion, the common areas and restaurant feel like an old-fashioned parlor, with crystal chandeliers, heavy curtains, and floral wallpaper. In the bedrooms, furnishings are designed in an antique style, complementing the mansion's high ceilings and old wooden floors. Everything looks aged and full of character, yet doesn't feel worn or shabby. In fact, there are plenty of comforts in each guest room, including safes, televisions, and bathrobes. Rooms in the front of the house have windows overlooking a leafy park, which is a particularly nice way to greet the day. For those who want something a bit more New World, there are also eight Mexican-themed suites located in the back part of the house.

Located on a small street in the quiet La Valenciana neighborhood, the beautiful views from **C Casa Estrella** (Callejón Jalisco 10, Col. Valenciana, tel. 473/732-1784, U.S. tel. 562/430-0647, toll-free U.S. tel. 866/983-8844, www.mexicaninns.com, US$240–315)

put the city at your feet. This lovely six-room inn is one of the nicest places to stay in Guanajuato, with comfortable and beautifully decorated guest rooms. Decor is elegantly Mexican, with terra-cotta tile floors, hand-woven rugs, and hand-painted tile bathrooms. Each room has different amenities, from fireplaces or private terraces to big whirlpool bathtubs and sitting areas. Fortunately, every single room has plenty of natural light and beautiful views from ample windows. The Valenciana suite has a small private balcony with city views and a hot tub. Rates can drop during the low season but always include a full breakfast.

OVER US$250

Guanajuato's most luxurious establishment is the **C Villa María Cristina** (Paseo de la Presa 76, tel. 473/731-2182 or toll-free Mex. tel. 800/702-7007, www.villamariacristina.net, US$290–390). In this lovely renovated mansion, 13 guest rooms sparkle with brass and marble, and are arranged around tiled terraces, overlooking the green point of the Cerro de la Bufa. Rooms have high ceilings and French furniture, and they are decked out with every luxury, like heaters in the bathrooms, French toiletries, iPod docks, and Dutch-made sound systems. The hotel's gorgeous restaurant has its own small wine cellar, and guests can order drinks on any of the hotel's terraces or at the Jacuzzi. Guests can also use spa facilities, including the sauna and Swiss showers. Service is impeccably attentive.

A new boutique hotel run by a León-based hotelier, **Alonso 10** (Alonso 10, tel. 473/732-7657, restalonso_10@yahoo.com.mx, US$350) brings a bit of chic to the *centro histórico*. The hotel's modern brown-and-white color scheme and a contemporary minimalist decor make a distinct contrast to the old colonial home in which the hotel is located. Every room in this small hotel has the same nightly rate, though each is different (ask to see what's available when you check in or ask for your preference beforehand). Some have interior windows, opening into the hotel's atrium, while others have windows opening onto the street. Perhaps the nicest are the rooms with private terraces overlooking Calle Alonso and the many cupolas of the city. Every room is equipped with down comforters, flat-screen televisions, safe deposit boxes, and spacious bathrooms with glass-walled showers. Downstairs, there is a restaurant and wine bar.

Food

There are tons of tourist-friendly restaurants in Guanajuato, filling the Plaza San Fernando, the Jardín de la Unión, and other picturesque locales. These eateries can be a great pick for a cold beer, a plate of guacamole, and an amazing atmosphere (not a bad combination, by any standard). Generally speaking, however, the most visible restaurants may not be the best place for a satisfying or authentic Mexican meal in Guanajuato. Catering to a transient tourist crowd, service can be slow and the food unmemorable.

That said, Guanajuato is a fun city to go out for a bite to eat or to linger over a cappuccino in a pretty tree-lined courtyard. It has a plethora of inexpensive and casual eateries, which cater to the city's many students and tourists. For cheap eats, there are tons of options around the university. In addition, most restaurants offer a daily *comida corrida,* an inexpensive three-course meal, usually comprising soup, a rice dish, a main plate, and, sometimes, a small dessert. Though not renowned for their cuisine, Guanajuato's restaurants have steadily become more diverse and high quality. Mexican food is the most prevalent, though there is also a smattering of Italian, pizza, and Asian-inspired joints downtown.

QUICK BITES AND TACOS

Throughout Guanajuato, there are casual **food stands** on almost every corner, many selling

There are little cafés and eateries in many of Guanajuato's plazas.

© JULIE DOHERTY MEADE

GUANAJUATO

gorditas (stuffed and griddled corn cakes), tamales, sweets, fruit, potato chips, snacks, and juices. For a quick meal, you'll find the most variety on the first floor of the Mercado Hidalgo, where there are a host of tacos, tortas, gorditas, seafood and shrimp cocktail, fruit juices, cakes, and sweets at a variety of informal food stands. Carnitas (braised pork) are a specialty here, and you can order them as individual tacos or in a torta, served sandwich-style between a white roll. Outside the left entrance of the market, the Mercado de Gavira offers a collection of very casual eateries, most serving cheap Mexican dishes and *comidas corridas.*

For a quick snack or a light breakfast, Mexican bakeries offer a tasty and inexpensive option. Traditional Mexican breads are generally lightly sweetened, meant to be accompanied by hot chocolate or coffee. In Guanajuato, you can buy traditional sweetbreads and rolls at **La Infancia** (Alonso 22, tel. 473/732-9922, 7 A.M.–10 P.M. daily, US$1). This old-style bakery has stacks of pastries, bread, and cookies in the windows, as well as a daily spread of tempting multicolored meringues, incredibly sweet yet tasty. Here, you pick up a metal tray and a pair of tongs and then choose your breads from the selection on display. At the counter, they'll put everything in a paper bag and tell you how much you owe. Breads usually cost US$0.50–1 per piece.

Right in the center of town, the very casual **Carnitas Sam** (Av. Juárez 6, tel. 473/732-0355, 9 A.M. 6 P.M. daily) specializes in carnitas (slow-cooked braised pork), a traditional dish popular throughout Mexico. At Carnitas Sam, you can order savory carnitas chopped up and served in a warm corn tortilla (tacos) or served on a soft roll as a torta. Dip into Sam's big vats of spicy salsa to douse your meal in some tasty heat. Though carnitas are Sam's specialty, they also serve quesadillas and *tacos dorados* (deep-fried tacos). Just behind the carnitas counter, there are several wooden tables and benches where you can enjoy your tacos.

For a super cheap lunch, locals flock to **El Wok** (Constancia 9, no tel., 2–9 P.M. Mon.–Sat., US$4). This hole-in-the-wall Asian-fusion joint makes quick and filling fried rice and noodle dishes, served to go in folded white cartons. You choose between noodles or rice and then pick four vegetables from the list, which includes bamboo shoots, broccoli, sprouts, peanuts, and peppers. Next, you pick a protein, like chicken or tofu, and finally, a sauce, which range from teriyaki to chipotle. There is always a youthful crowd crowded around the restaurant's entryway, where the restaurant has placed a few mismatched couches and stools for diners.

MEXICAN

An atmospheric restaurant on the Jardín de la Unión, **Casa Valadez** (Jardín de la Unión 3, tel. 473/732-0311, www.casavaladez.com, 8 A.M.–11 P.M. daily, US$7) gets double points for style. This big family eatery is always packed with tourists and families, dining alfresco or lounging indoors in one of the restaurant's big booths. Located on the east end of the Jardín de la Unión, Casa Valadez's old-fashioned dining room is decorated with gray-and-gold columns, brass chandeliers, and patterned wallpaper. Bathrooms are particularly fancy. The menu covers a full spectrum, including soups, salads, burgers, sandwiches, enchiladas, and meat dishes; plates run from economical to pricey. For those familiar with the famous Mexican chain, Sanborns, this restaurant has a similar approach, traditional and tasty. Everything is served with a generous hand and smothered in cheese and salsa.

On a small alley just a block from the Jardín de la Unión, **Truco 7** (Truco 7, tel. 473/732-8374, www.hospederiadeltruco7.com, 8:30 A.M.–11 P.M. daily, US$6) is a very popular and inexpensive café that serves a range of tasty Mexican staples, as well as a daily *comida corrida,* a three-course set-price lunch (though standard menu items tend to be tastier). This casual restaurant has the cozy and convivial atmosphere of a cool college hangout, with exposed brick walls, comfy wood furniture, low lamps, and eclectic art on the walls. The restaurant is open from early in the morning until late at night, and the menu is filled with

Mexican dishes, like enchiladas, good *sopa azteca,* sopes (thick corn tortillas topped with beans and chicken), and several mole dishes, as well as breakfasts. Espresso drinks and desserts are also good here.

Right next door to Truco 7, **Casa Ofelia** (Truco 11, tel. 473/731-2639, 9 A.M.–11 P.M. daily, US$6) serves inexpensive Mexican food in a cheerful setting. From big morning breakfasts of scrambled eggs, omelets, or *chilaquiles* (all accompanied by refried beans and tortillas) to classic dinners like pozole and enchiladas, plates are very generously served and prepared with a homemade touch. Service is attentive and affable, and the clientele tends to reinforce the friendly atmosphere, drawing big groups of families and young backpackers on vacation. Tasty (and sweet!) *café de olla* is served all day, and there are also *aguas frescas,* hot chocolate, beer, and margaritas. Right in the middle of the *centro histórico,* Ofelia is a convenient place for an inexpensive meal.

Toward the back of the Jardín de la Unión, **La Bohemia** (Jardín de la Unión 4, tel. 473/732-9772, 8:30 A.M.–11 P.M. daily, US$5) is a surprisingly inexpensive place for a casual meal, despite its prime location in the central square. This small, traditional eatery serves range of typical Mexican breakfasts, like *huevos a la mexicana* (eggs scrambled with chile pepper, tomato, and onion) and an inexpensive *comida corrida,* which usually includes soup, rice, a main plate, and a drink for a set price. With small tables, the atmosphere is functional rather than fancy, though large doorways open onto the jovial bustle of the Jardín de la Unión. Food is tasty, though simple, and service is friendly and attentive. Easy on the wallet and with plenty to recommend it, La Bohemia is popular with both locals and visitors.

A nice place to eat among a mellow local crowd, **El Abue** (San José 14, Plaza Baratillo, tel. 473/732-6242, www.elabue.com, 8 A.M.–10:30 P.M. Tues.–Sun., US$7) is a tasty, low-key restaurant with a predominantly Mexican menu. Here, you can dine on well-prepared plates like enchiladas and *sopa azteca,* or more elaborate regional dishes like *chiles en nogada*

and *cochinita pibil.* The menu is rounded out with some Italian pastas, salads, and hamburgers. Bread and pastas are made fresh on the premises and have a nice homemade taste. There is also a daily *comida corrida*—a fixed price menu that is a bit more luxurious than what you'll find at other downtown establishments—served from the early afternoon to the early evening. The atmosphere is ultra cozy, with wooden booths and benches fitted into a tiny dining room. Cute chalkboard menus list the wines for sale by glass and bottle, which are offered at great prices and with an emphasis on Latin American and Mexican brands. There are also tasty *aguas frescas* made from tamarind or hibiscus, among other choices, and a full coffee bar.

It is well worth a trip to the San Javier neighborhood to dine at the lovely family-run restaurant ◖ **Las Mercedes Banquetes y Restaurante** (Calle de Arriba 6, Col. San Javier, tel. 473/732-7375 or 473/733-9059, lasmercedesrestaurante@gmail.com, 2–10 P.M. Tues.–Sat., 2–6 P.M. Sun. US$15). Presenting heirloom Mexican recipes with a modern touch, Las Mercedes manages to blend traditional flavors with creative flair, surprising yet eminently palatable. From starters like cream of cilantro soup to entrées like chicken in pistachio mole, it is tempting to try everything on the menu. Whatever you choose, you'll receive flavorful, unique, and perfectly prepared food. In accompaniment, the restaurant offers a small selection of Mexican wines by the glass, and there are margaritas, spirits, and beer. Located in the bottom floor of a family home, the cozy dining room has the feel of an elegant dinner party at a friend's home. Service is tasteful and pleasant, and the proprietor makes a point of visiting every table. Despite its off-the-beaten track location, this restaurant has gotten enough buzz to attract a nightly seating of tourists and locals. Make a reservation and come with an appetite.

Away from the bustle of the *centro histórico,* **Mexico Lindo y Sabroso** (Paseo de la Presa 154, tel. 473/731-0529, 9 A.M.–11 P.M. daily, US$7) is a nice place to linger over an afternoon meal. The airy dining room has a pleasingly Mexican atmosphere, with red-lacquer furniture, crafts on the walls, and *ranchera* music overhead. In front, the lovely covered patio overlooks the Paseo de la Presa, with big comfortable seats and large tables. Service is attentive, and the wait staff adds to the Mexican atmosphere with spiffy tri-color bow-ties and white collared shirts. The extensive menu is entirely Mexican, offering a range of inexpensive and generously served dishes like enchiladas, *enmoladas,* and *sopa azteca,* as well as some more unusual yet tasty Yucatec dishes, like *papadzules* and *cochinita pibil.* Everything tastes freshly prepared and is nicely seasoned; chips and salsa at the table make a nice start.

In a tiny alley at the very back of the Plaza San Fernando, **La Clave Azul** (2a de Cantaritos 31, tel. 473/732-1561, laclaveazul99@hotmail.com, 1:30–11 P.M. Mon.–Thurs., 1:30 P.M.–midnight Sat.–Sun., US$6) is a lovely old cantina. Like most classic cantinas, La Clave Azul serves a small plate of food, or *botana,* along with each drink you order. However, the food at La Clave Azul has become so well known that it has almost become better known as restaurant than as a bar, despite the tavern-like atmosphere of the building's exposed rock walls and dim lighting. Although the menu changes daily, the *lechón* (suckling pig) is one of the cantina's specialties. To get here, walk to the very back of the Plaza San Fernando. Just behind the Café Bossanova, a teensy alleyway ascends from the plaza; La Clave Azul is just a few yards beyond the mouth of the alley.

INTERNATIONAL

From the Jardín de la Unión, you can see the royal blue facade of **El Gallo Pitagorico** (Constancia 10, tel. 473/732-9489, 2–11 P.M. daily) peeking over the top of the Teatro Juárez. You will have to walk up quite a few stairs (more than 100!) to get to this creaky Italian joint, and the view from the windows is worth the climb, overlooking the backside of the Templo de San Diego, Teatro Juárez, and the sweeping cityscape beyond. The extensive menu is standard Italian fare, with appetizers

like fried calamari and minestrone soup, and a nice selection of pasta and lasagna. When you order, they bring you a basket of bread and pesto sauce to the table. There is beer and a limited wine list. Food is standard Italian and portions are generous, but the view makes this restaurant a lovely place to watch the sun go down over a glass of white wine.

There are many restaurants around the beautiful Plaza San Fernando, all of which will provide you with a romantic setting, excellent people-watching, and a leafy ceiling of trees. When it comes to lunch, **€ Le Midi** (Plaza San Fernando 41, cell tel. 473/108-0892, 10 A.M.–10 P.M., Mon.–Sat., US$6) is one of the best bites around. This little French-owned eatery is as casual as they come with no table service during the day. Here, you serve yourself from a changing buffet of healthy salads, quiches, couscous, and pasta; your plate is then weighed and charged by kilo. To accompany your meal, grab a fresh baguette and order a creative *agua fresca,* like cucumber and peppermint, or a glass of wine. This little café is best in the early afternoon when the buffet is available but hasn't been excessively picked through. At night, there is regular table service with a more limited menu. Tasty desserts, very low prices, and plenty of vegetarian options make this little café a popular lunch spot with locals, as well as the smattering of French expatriates.

Right next door to Le Midi in the Plaza San Fernando, **Bossanova Cafe** (Plaza San Fernando 24, tel. 473/732-5674, 10 A.M.–11 P.M. daily, US$5) is a laid-back eatery, specializing in crepes and coffee. The simple menu includes savory crepes with eggplant, mushrooms, or other fillings, plus sweet crepes with fillings like *cajeta* or chocolate. Accompany your meal with an espresso or a glass of wine and then enjoy the afternoon in the plaza. The wait staff is unrushed and the vibe is mellow. With several umbrella-shaded tables in the heart of the Plaza San Fernando, this restaurant's biggest attraction is the atmosphere.

€ Delica Mitsu (Callejón de Cantaritos 37, tel. 473/732-3881, noon–9 P.M. Mon.–Sat., US$6) is a little Japanese deli tucked into the wall of a tiny pedestrian alleyway. For surprisingly low prices, you can order a lovely plate of sushi rolls or teriyaki chicken with sides from the deli case, or choose a made-to-order bento box with three, four, or five selections from the deli (get there early if you want salads; the food runs out around 4 P.M.). While the lineup changes daily, Delica Mitsu always offers wonderful salads and noodle dishes, as well as more unusual dishes like cabbage cakes and teriyaki potatoes. There is also delicious miso soup, tempura, Japanese green teas, Japanese beers, and sake. You can sit at one of the three creaky tables just outside the deli or order your food to go. To find this little gem, look for the sign in the northwest corner of the Plaza San Fernando; right behind it, head up the little alleyway. You'll hear the strains of jazz music before you see the restaurant's three little tables.

When in the mood for casual Italian fare, **Chau Bella** (Positos 25, tel. 473/732-6764, 2–10 P.M. daily, US$8) is a nice place for a late lunch or dinner. The best choices on the extensive menu are the made-to-order thin-crust pizzas. Salads are big, fresh, and crunchy, and mildly seasoned pasta dishes are accompanied by a tasty basket of fresh bread. The airy dining room fills two large rooms in a colonial mansion and is attended by a friendly and attentive wait staff. There's nothing particularly Italian about the decor, but the space is light and comfortable, with tall ceilings and windows opening onto Calle Positos. Just a block from the university, this little Italian restaurant caters to the older university crowd, who come for dignified discussion, a glass of red, and grub.

Just around the corner from Teatro Juárez, **La Capellina** (Sopeña 3, tel. 473/732-7224, www.lacapellina.com, 1:30–11 P.M. Mon.–Wed., 1:30 P.M.–midnight Thurs.–Sat., 1:30–7 P.M. Sun., US$10) has an elegant atmosphere, with three umbrella-shaded sidewalk tables and a spacious, romantically lit, modern dining room. The menu at this fusion restaurant really runs the gamut, from steak and tacos to crispy salads and sushi grade tuna. However, the restaurant's pastas and thin-crust pizzas are the most popular dishes on the menu, and probably the best among them. You'll often see a sophisticated crowd sipping big glasses of wine and overlooking busy Calle Sopeña. While the elegant atmosphere really lends itself to a glass of nice wine or a cocktail, the wine list doesn't play a robust role in the restaurant's offerings. On the weekends, there are often live musicians playing jazz, Latin rhythms, or classical guitar.

COFFEE SHOPS

Guanajuato is a coffee shop kind of place. There is never a shortage of local and foreign students looking for an inexpensive place to check their email, finish homework, or simply hang out with friends over a *cappuccino frío*.

With outdoor seating on a tiny footbridge over the Calle Campanero, **Santo Café** (Puente de Campanero, Campanero 4, santocafe@hotmail.com, 10 A.M.–midnight Mon.–Sat., noon–midnight Sun.) might have the city's most romantic location. Walking past, it seems there is always a small crowd relaxing away the afternoon in a ray of golden sunlight. There is also wireless Internet. They sell beer, wines, and coffees, as well as sandwiches, *flautas*, and salads. The food is good, and the setting makes it all the better.

Open from early in the morning until late at night, **Café Tal** (Sostenes Rocha, 7 A.M.–midnight Mon.–Sat., 8 A.M.–midnight Sun., US$1) is the type of place that takes coffee seriously. Here, all beans are dark roasted in-house and expertly brewed to be strong and full-bodied. Indoors, the shaky granite tables are continuously populated with smoking ashtrays and hipsters on laptops, while waiters in black T-shirts serve brew and breads. There is a little table at the entryway with thermoses of strong self-serve drip coffee, which you can take to go.

Just beside the Iglesia de San Francisco and at the mouth of yet another winding alleyway, the casual **Bagel Cafetín** (Callejón de Potrero 2, tel. 473/733-9733, www.bagelcafetin.com, 8:30 A.M.–10 P.M. Mon.–Sat., US$3) has a big list of fresh bagel sandwiches, plus coffee

© JULIE DOHERTY MEADE

Santo Café has picturesque patio seating on a tiny pedestrian footbridge.

drinks, smoothies, and tea. It is a great place to check your email over a freshly prepared yet inexpensive breakfast, or to hang out during a lazy afternoon. You can take advantage of their wireless Internet inside the small café or sit at one of the small outdoor tables among expatriates, tourists, and local youth.

Café Carcamanes (Plazuela Carcamanes 10, tel. 473/732-5172, 8 A.M.–11 P.M. daily, US$2) exudes the relaxing and bohemian atmosphere that every Guanajuato traveler craves. Situated at the crest of a small plaza behind a sprawling magnolia tree, this small wooden coffee shop and adjoining patio are just the place to relax away the afternoon in the company of other laid-back expatriates or locals. The friendly owners will serve you coffee

and sweets, as well as other snacks and breakfast items, like baguettes and sweets. There is, of course, wireless Internet. The same owners also manage a laid-back and funky youth hostel upstairs.

On the Paseo de la Presa, **Corazón Parlante** (Paseo de la Presa 52A, tel. 472/731-2305, www.corazonparlante.com.mx, 9 A.M.–10 P.M. Mon.–Sat., US$4) is a large café with big selections of loose leaf teas, herbal infusions, coffee drinks, and smoothies, as well as baguette sandwiches and huge cakes. There is plenty of space to find your own nook for reading, writing, or typing on a laptop; you can sit indoors in the airy café or outside on the big shaded patio. The café also sells silver jewelry handcrafted by local artists.

Information and Services

TOURIST INFORMATION

The **Oficina de Convenciones y Visitantes** (Tourist Office, Plaza de la Paz 14, tel. 473/732-0369, www.ocvguanajuato.com, 10 A.M.–5 P.M. Mon.–Sat.) will provide you with a map of Guanajuato's *centro histórico,* which points out the city's most important sights. They also offer daily walking tours of the city center, as well as package tours of the city's more distant sights. In the doorway, there is a collection of publicity materials for local restaurants, hotels, and attractions, and there is usually a list of ongoing events in the city posted on their bulletin board. During busy times, the office is open for tour reservations as late as midnight.

TRAVEL AGENTS

Close to the Jardín de la Unión, **Viajes Frausto Guanajuato** (Luis González Obregón 10, tel. 473/732-3580 or 473/732-0115, vjs-fraustoguanajuato@prodigy.net, 9 A.M.–2 P.M. Mon.–Sat.) can book airline tickets and tours. Pleasingly, they can also book first-class bus tickets with ETN or Primera Plus, saving you a long trip out to the bus station.

MEDIA

The daily Spanish-language newspaper *El Correo* (Apartado Postal 32, tel. 473/733-1253, http://correo-gto.com.mx) is published in Guanajuato. *El Correo* covers regional, national, and international news, with sections dedicated to the cities of León, Irapuato, Salamanca, and Guanajuato. There is a weekly cultural supplement on Saturdays. It is the best place to read up on what's going on in Guanajuato; all text is in Spanish.

The eclectic university radio station, **Radio Universidad** (www.radiouniversidad.ugto.mx), will keep Spanish-speaking listeners up to date with the city's news and cultural events. They also broadcast an excellent international news program from the Latin American correspondent of Radio Francía Internacional each morning at 9 A.M. Even if you don't speak Spanish, it can still be great fun to tune into the music programs on this arts-and-letters radio station. Depending on the DJ, you will hear a rather eclectic range of music, from jazz to classical to The Beatles. You can tune in at 970 AM or 100 FM in Guanajuato. From San Miguel de Allende, Radio Universidad is at 91.3 FM.

MAIL SERVICES

The *oficina de correos* (post office, Ayuntamiento 25, tel. 473/732-0385, 8:30 A.M.–4:30 P.M. Mon.–Fri., 9 A.M.–noon Sat.) is at the corner of Ayuntamiento and San José, just across the street from the Templo de la Compañía de Jesús.

For speedier delivery, **Red Pack** (Sóstenes Rocha 18, tel. 473/732-4949, www.redpack.com.mx) provides insured and expedited international shipping, as well as national packaging and shipping services.

MONEY

Right between the Jardín de la Unión and the Plaza de la Paz, **Banorte** (Luis González Obregón 1, tel. 473/732-2568, 9 A.M.–5 P.M. Mon.–Fri.) has a bank branch with tellers, currency exchange, and two ATMs, all located in a lovely historical building. There is also a 24-hour Banamex ATM at Plaza de la Paz 20 (sharing the same plaza as the Medica Integral Guanajuatense).

INTERNET ACCESS

In this town of university students, writers, romantics, and backpackers, there is no shortage of Internet service. Most coffee shops, hotels, and hostels have free wireless for their patrons; even some restaurants expect you to log on while chowing down. If you didn't bring your laptop, **Technet Internet** (San José 24, 10 A.M.–midnight daily) has several

Internet-connected PCs, black-and-white printing, and incredibly long hours. They are right behind the Jardín de la Unión in the Plaza Baratillo. Near the Alhóndiga, **Centro de Impresión y Copiado El Barreto** (Galarza 90, tel. 473/731-1284, 8 A.M.–10 P.M. Mon.–Fri., 10 A.M.–11 P.M. Sat.–Sun.) has several PCs with Internet connection, as well as black-and-white and color printers, scanning equipment, and even offset printing services.

MEDICAL AND EMERGENCY SERVICES

Right in the city center, **Medica Integral Guanajuatense** (Plaza de la Paz 20, tel. 473/732-2233 or 473/732-2305) has doctors that specialize in gynecology, pediatrics, internal medicine, dermatology, and surgery, among other fields. They also offer 24-hour pharmacy service and emergency care.

The well-regarded **Centro Medico La Presa** (Paseo de la Presa 85, tel. 473/731-1135, 473/731-2908, or 473/731-2909, www.centromedicolapresa.com.mx) is a full-service medical clinic with general medicine doctors, specialists, and surgeons. In the case of emergency, there are doctors in the clinic 24 hours. The government-run **Hospital General** (Carretera a Silao, Km 6, tel. 473/733-1573 or 473/733-1576) is outside the city center on the toll highway toward Silao. It also receives emergencies.

In the city center, **Farmacias Santa Fe** (Plaza de la Paz 52, tel. 473/732-0170, 9 A.M.–10 P.M. daily) sells prescription drugs and toiletries.

For police and other emergencies, dial 066 from any ground line to reach the city emergency services. For medical emergencies, the **Cruz Roja** (Red Cross, Av. Juárez 131, tel. 473/732-0487) offers emergency response and ambulances. The *bomberos* (fire department, Pozuelos s/n, Conjunto Pozuelos, tel. 473/732-3357) will respond to fire 24 hours a day.

VISAS AND OFFICIALDOM

The closest **United States Consular Agency** (Plaza las Golondrinas, Hernández Macías 72, Int. 111 and 112, tel. 415/152-2357, consuladosma@gmail.com, clancyek@state.gov, 9 A.M.–1 P.M. Mon.–Thurs.) is in San Miguel de Allende. As a branch of the U.S. Embassy in Mexico City, the consulate can replace lost or expired passports, among other services (though it may take a bit longer through the consulate than if you go directly to the embassy). There is often a wait for services, so arrive early or call ahead to see if you can schedule an appointment. For most other countries, including Australia, Canada, and the United Kingdom, the closest consular agency is in the capital.

San Miguel de Allende is also home to the regional delegation of the **Instituto Nacional de Migración** (INM, Mexican Immigration Service, Calzada de la Estación FFCC, tel. 415/152-2542, 9 A.M.–1 P.M. Mon.–Fri.). You can visit INM to extend your tourist card, apply for a resident visa, or report a missing tourist card. If you arrive from Guanajuato by bus, the immigration offices are just a short walk or taxi from the station, on the Calzada de la Estación behind the Bodega Aurreras. You will pass the office on your way into town.

Getting There

BY AIR
Del Bajío International Airport

Guanajuato is about 40 kilometers (25 miles) from the Del Bajío International Airport (BJX, Carretera Silao-León, Km 5.5, Col. Nuevo México, Silao, tel. 472/748-2120), on the highway to León, just beyond the auto plants in Silao. From BJX, there are daily direct flights to and from Dallas, Houston, and Los Angeles, as well as several flights to and from Mexico City and Monterrey.

From the airport, you can take a registered taxi to Guanajuato for about US$30. The drive to downtown takes about 30 minutes. There are taxis available at the airport to meet arriving flights, even late at night. Buy a ticket for your taxi at the ticket booth inside the airport terminal and then meet the cabs curbside. Alternatively, you can rent a car at the airport and drive it to Guanajuato; there are several rental car companies with offices in the airport, most open from early morning to late night.

Mexico City International Airport

It can be more inexpensive and, in some cases, more convenient for international visitors to fly to Mexico City International Airport (MEX) in the capital. From the airport in Mexico City, travelers must arrange for ground transportation to Guanajuato, usually by bus. Direct buses leave from the Mexico City Terminal de Norte for Guanajuato several times a day. The trip from Mexico City to Guanajuato takes about four hours, though many buses stop in Irapuato en route, adding an additional half hour to the trip. Travelers should also prepare for heavy traffic leaving the capital, which can affect travel time.

BY BUS

Guanajuato's **Central de Autobuses** (Carretera de cuota Guanajuato-Silao, Km 7) is about eight kilometers (five miles) outside the city center on the highway toward Silao.

Once you arrive at the terminal, you can take a city bus downtown for about US$0.50; they are marked Centro in the front windshield and depart from right in front of the station every 15 minutes or so. Buses often stop in the underground tunnels below the *centro histórico*, so if you have never been to Guanajuato before, ask the driver to notify you when to get off. For quicker service, you can take a city taxi from the bus station to the *centro histórico* for about US$3.

From Mexico City, San Miguel de Allende, and other points in the Bajío, there is ample first-class bus service to and from Guanajuato, as well as connecting service to cities all over the country. **Primera Plus** (Carretera de cuota Guanajuato-Silao, Km 7, Central de Autobuses, toll-free Mex. tel. 800/375-7587, www.primeraplus.com.mx) operates more than a dozen direct first-class buses between the Terminal Central de Norte in Mexico City and the Central de Autobuses in Guanajuato every day. Primera Plus also operates direct routes to and from San Miguel de Allende, León, and Celaya, as well as connecting service to Puerto Vallarta and the airport in Guadalajara.

Buses are comfortable, air-conditioned, and equipped with bathrooms; Primera Plus even provides its clients with a small snack and soft drink for the ride. During big events like the Cervantino festival or nationwide holidays like Semana Santa, Primera Plus will often extend its daily service to include two or three extra departures.

Another swanky first-class bus line serving central and northern Mexico, **ETN** (Carretera de cuota Guanajuato-Silao, Km 7, Central de Autobuses, tel. 473/733-1579 or 473/733-0289, toll-free Mex. tel. 800/800-0386, www.etn.com.mx) has 10 first-class buses between Mexico City and Guanajuato each day. As on Primera Plus, you'll get bathrooms, snacks, and a movie, though ETN's seats are even bigger and more comfortable (though a bit costlier). ETN also offers service from Guanajuato to Guadalajara, San Miguel de Allende, and León, with connecting service to the beach or to other major cities.

Another alternative for intercity travel is **Group Estrella Blanca** (Carretera Guanajuato-Silao, Km 6, Central de Autobuses Guanajuato, tel. 473/733-1344 or toll-free Mex. tel. 800/507-5500, www.estrellablanca. com.mx), which offers first-class bus service to Guanajuato from the capital and other parts of the Bajío on their luxury line Futura Plus and their first-class line Futura. It also offers second-class bus service on its economy line, Estrella Blanca, which services most towns and cities in the Bajío and central Mexico.

For local travel, **Servicios Coordinados Flecha Amarilla** (Carretera a Silao, Km 8, tel. 477/710-0001 or toll-free Mex. tel. 800/375-7587) offers second-class buses service to the town of Dolores Hidalgo, departing every 20 minutes from about 7 A.M. until about 10 P.M. You don't need to book your ticket ahead of time; just arrive at the station and buy a ticket for the next departing bus. Alternatively, buses to Dolores pass through the city center and depart via La Valenciana neighborhood. You can save time by catching the bus from there. Look for the sign in the window indicating the bus's destination in Santa Rosa or Dolores Hidalgo.

Getting Around

The easiest and most efficient way to get around Guanajuato's city center is on foot. In fact, many of Guanajuato's sights and restaurants cannot be accessed any other way, since roads run underground in many parts of the *centro*. However, if you are planning to spend some time outside the downtown district, you may need to arrange other transportation.

BY CAR

If you plan to do some driving while in Guanajuato, the easiest place to rent a car is at the airport. There, you will find desks for several major car rental companies. **Hertz** (León-Bajío International Airport, Carretera Silao-León, Km 5.5, tel. 999/911-8040, www. hertz.com, 5:30 A.M.–11:30 P.M. daily) rents compact cars, regular-sized sedans, SUVs, and minivans at low daily rates. **Alamo Rent A Car** (León-Bajío International Airport, Carretera Silao-León, Km 5.5, tel. 472/748-2069, 6 A.M.–midnight daily) also rents cars and vans by the day and by the week, directly from the airport.

As many residents or visitors can tell you, having a car can be a bit of a nuisance in Guanajuato, as many streets in the *centro*

histórico are reserved for pedestrian traffic or are too small to allow automobiles. For those who come with wheels, it is best to look for parking on the street or in a lot while you explore the city center. You can park along the underground tunnels (look for signs that indicate where parking is permitted); however, there is also an inexpensive multilevel public parking lot, **Estacionamiento El Patrocinio** (Padre Hidalgo s/n, tel. 473/735-3300, ext. 3210), along the major tunnel, Hidalgo, just below the Jardín Reforma. There is also a public bathroom on the first floor of the lot.

While a car is generally a nuisance in central Guanajuato, it can be helpful to have wheels if you are staying in a hotel outside of the city center, or if you'd like to explore small towns or hiking opportunities in the surrounding country. Like walking, driving in Guanajuato can be a bit of a diverting challenge. Maps tend to be confusing, thanks to the bilevel structure of the city. However, there are road signs at every fork and turn. In most cases, if you follow these signs, you will eventually get to your destination (though probably not without a few wrong turns!). The most important thing is to keep an eye out for one-way signs before making a

GUANAJUATO

© ARTURO MEADE

In downtown Guanajuato, most auto traffic passes through a system of underground tunnels.

turn—not all streets are open to two-way traffic—and to be careful of the many pedestrians and frequently stopping buses.

BY TAXI

There are inexpensive taxis circling throughout Guanajuato's downtown district, as well as around the bus station. Most charge a flat rate for service anywhere in the downtown area, usually about US$2.50. For service to neighborhoods outside the *centro histórico,* like La Valenciana or the bus station, the rate may go up to US$3 or US$4. You can also call a taxi from **Grupo Alianza Radio Taxi** (Callejón de Griteria 13, Col. Gavilanes, tel. 473/732-6649) within the city of Guanajuato. They have 24-hour service.

While cabs are inexpensive, they aren't omnipresent. Remember, many of Guanajuato's alleys and plazas are not accessible by taxi. Most cabs will get you as close to your destination as they can, but door-to-door service isn't always possible.

PUBLIC TRANSPORTATION

Inexpensive **city buses** can take you to all of Guanajuato's major neighborhoods from the city center. Most buses run from morning until night, roughly 7 A.M.–10 P.M. Bus routes are not numbered; however, each bus lists its destination in the windshield. While the system may seem a bit disorganized, it is actually fairly simple to master. There are very few major thoroughfares in Guanajuato's city center, and likewise few bus routes.

Buses to the Marfil neighborhood depart from bus stops in the *centro histórico* via the largest underground thoroughfare, Hidalgo, and run into the Marfil neighborhood via the Marfil–Guanajuato Camino Real. You can catch the city bus up toward La Valenciana neighborhood on Avenida Juárez, right near the Alhóndiga, which then travels northward via the Guanajuato–Dolores Hidalgo highway. When in doubt, ask the driver where the bus is going.

Vicinity of Guanajuato

SANTA ROSA

In the green and surprisingly alpine sierra just beyond the city of Guanajuato, the tiny town of Santa Rosa de Lima is a picturesque pit stop on the highway toward Dolores Hidalgo. At an elevation of more than 2,400 meters (8,000 feet), this rural municipality is crisp and mountainous, with pine trees and cool winds. Though Santa Rosa's homes are scattered throughout the hillsides, there is just one main street in town, largely unpaved. There, you will see the lovely old parish church with its sandstone entryway. Though just a 15-minute drive from Guanajuato's city center, Santa Rosa can feel miles away from the surrounding Bajío.

Tin-glazed majolica-style ceramics have been produced in Puebla and Guanajuato since the early colonial era. The ceramics tradition has continued in the small town of Santa Rosa, and today, the large workshop of **Mayólica Santa Rosa** (Carretera Guanajuato-Dolores Hidalgo s/n, tel. 473/739-0572, 8 A.M.–5 P.M. Mon.–Fri.) produces some wonderful and highly detailed hand-painted urns, flower pots, flatware, and tiles. At this large factory store, you can see artisans at work and ceramics in various stages of development, from unworked clay to unfired vessels to ceramics in the process of being painted.

For *dulces típicos* (traditional sweets) and handmade liquors, stop in at **Conservas Santa Rosa** (Camino Real s/n, Santa Rosa de Lima, www.ccg.org.mx/santaeng.htm). Associated with the Cuerpos de Conservación Guanajuato (Conservation Bodies of Guanajuato), this women's cooperative produces all-natural sweets using local fruit and products. Jams are the specialty, though they also sell pickled chile peppers, *ates* (fruit paste), and *xoconostle* (sour prickly pear) in syrup, all of which make excellent little gifts. Everything here has a wonderful homemade feeling, including the packaging.

If you make the trek up to Santa Rosa, there are a few casual places to grab a bite to eat. The most visible is the large **Restaurante de la Sierra** (Camino Real s/n, Santa Rosa de Lima, Km 14, tel. 473/102-5036, 8:30 A.M.–8 P.M. daily), just off the main highway. From the arched window of this enormous dining hall, there is a beautiful view of the green Sierra de Santa Rosa below. This place is popular with local families on the weekends, though it seems unlikely to see the restaurant fill to capacity. Food is standard Mexican fare, with well-served dishes like *queso fundido,* enchiladas, and cuts of meat accompanied by rice and beans. You can accompany your meal with mezcal produced right in Santa Rosa.

CRISTO REY DEL CUBILETE

Just beyond the city of Guanajuato, there is a towering 2,700-meter (8,860-foot) peak, topped with a giant statue, the Cristo de la Montaña. This 23-meter (75-foot), 80-ton monument to Christ was built in the 1940s (the previous sculpture of Christ on this mountaintop was destroyed following the Mexican Revolution). It is reputed to be the largest bronze statue of Christ in the world. Technically located in the municipality Silao, the site is visited frequently by pilgrims, and it is especially crowded on November 21, the day of Cristo Rey. The monument is also a popular destination for tourists to the Bajío, who visit this hilltop for its gorgeous panoramic views of the countryside. Many say that this statue is located at the exact geographical center of Mexico, though the town of Tequisquiapan in Querétaro state also lays claim to that distinction.

Visitors can take a bus from Guanajuato's city center to the Cristo Rey del Cubilete, though it is easiest to book your place in a tour group from the tourist office downtown. The bus will take you up a winding road that wraps around the rock face.

THE BAJÍO

The wide cactus-studded plains of the Bajío seem to call out for adventure. Even today, their empty expanses are just as fitting to a horse and rider as a car and driver. Fortunately for travelers, those who venture off the beaten track will be duly rewarded. The sinewy highways of the northern Bajío will lead you to historical sights, sweeping views, and charming small towns. To the south, the state of Querétaro is a largely agricultural and industrial region, carpeted with cornfields and dotted with pueblos. Here, the romance of ghost towns, cattle ranches, and agave plantations still flavors the modern era, even as industry and tourism bring changes to the landscape.

The Bajío is important to the country both economically and culturally. Situated in the geographic center of Mexico, the Bajío is a physical and social bridge between the north and south, and an important contributor to Mexico's economy since the colonial era. The land of the Bajío has always been known for its fertility, and during the 16th and 17th centuries, Spanish settlers set up extensive farms and ranches in the region. As the mining industry grew, the Bajío grew with it, and towns along the silver route began to produce wood, leather, and other products to feed the massive demands of the silver trade. Today, the Bajío's farms and ranches produce meat, greens, and dairy, while the bustling cities of León and Querétaro are home to major corporations and big business.

Most people visit the Bajío when they plan a vacation to San Miguel de Allende or Guanajuato, the two major tourist attractions

© ARTURO MEADE

HIGHLIGHTS

◖ Plaza de Armas: A beautiful 18th-century plaza surrounded by colonial mansions, the Plaza de Armas is the historic heart of Querétaro and the perfect place to begin a walking tour of the city (page 165).

◖ Museo de Arte de Querétaro: Housed in a former Augustinian convent, Querétaro's fine art museum is an architectural jewel. In addition to its historic importance, the space hosts interesting exhibitions throughout the year (page 167).

◖ Templo y Ex-Convento de Santa Rosa de Viterbo: A unique former convent and temple, Santa Rosa de Viterbo stands out among Querétaro's many impressive colonial-era constructions (page 167).

◖ Plaza Miguel Hidalgo: The mellow main plaza in Tequisquiapan is drenched in laid-back country charm, ringed by tall trees and Mexican restaurants, and crowned with a lovely pink parish church (page 180).

◖ Peña de Bernal: One of the world's largest monoliths, the Peña de Bernal towers over the tiny town of the same name, lending a natural majesty to this pretty colonial settlement. You can climb the shoulder of its rocky peak or simply enjoy a view of the monolith from a restaurant in downtown Bernal (page 187).

◖ Parroquia de Nuestra Señora de los Dolores: The parish of Dolores Hidalgo may be the most famous church in all of Mexico. From the steps of this baroque beauty, Father Miguel Hidalgo heralded the beginning of the Mexican War of Independence (page 193).

◖ Cinco Señores Mine: One of several abandoned mining camps in Mineral de Pozos, this expansive ruin hints at the opulence and wealth of the 19th-century mining settlements (page 202).

◖ SAPICA: León is one of the world's largest shoe manufacturers. For discount prices on every style of footwear imaginable, the city's biannual SAPICA festival is a true shoe-lover's paradise (page 207).

LOOK FOR ◖ TO FIND RECOMMENDED SIGHTS, ACTIVITIES, DINING, AND LODGING.

in the region. Often, these destinations are so absorbing that they leave little time to explore the surrounding countryside. However, if time permits, venturing outside these cities will give you a greater context for your travels. Echoes of San Miguel's quieter past can be found in the charming little ghost town of Pozos, while the monolith at Bernal is a natural highlight of the countryside. Querétaro is a particular attraction in the region, a large yet low-key city with a friendly population, little tourism, and a grand historic center. In recent decades, the population of Querétaro has increased rapidly, as beleaguered *chilangos* flee Mexico City for the more tranquil and friendly lifestyle in this medium-sized metropolis. Here, you can see some of the finest examples of Mexican baroque architecture in the country, while also enjoying cosmopolitan bars and restaurants typical of a bigger city.

HISTORY

Sedentary pre-Hispanic cultures settled in the Bajío around A.D. 300–650. Today, there are ruins of these civilizations scattered throughout the states of Guanajuato and Querétaro; to date, the majority have not been studied or opened to tourism. After A.D. 650, the cultures of the Bajío began to decline or move elsewhere. When the Spanish arrived in the New World, the Bajío was a transition zone between the Aztec empire that dominated Mesoamerica and the nomadic tribes of El Gran Chichimeca in the north. Most Bajío residents were nomads, though there were also a few sedentary settlements scattered throughout the plains.

Not long after the fall of Tenochtitlan, Spanish conquest of the Bajío began, mainly centered around the modern cities of San Juan del Río, Huimilpan, and Querétaro. After silver was discovered in the northern territories, the settlers were eager to expand their settlements. The Spanish government handed out land grants to ranchers and farmers, who found that the Bajío's wide plains and fertile soil provided an excellent environment for agriculture. As silver production increased in the north, the Bajío began to prosper. To accommodate the

silver trade, roads were built throughout the Bajío, and the related industry, agriculture, and artisan work in the Bajío's cities contributed to one of the most robust economies in the New World. During the 17th and 18th centuries, the Bajío had a higher population density than almost anywhere else in the New World and even most of Europe.

Historically, the Bajío has always been an influential region, particularly the well-located city of Querétaro, which was the setting for many of Mexico's most important historical events. Of particular note, the Mexican independence movement began in the cities of the Bajío, where rich and powerful landowners plotted their liberty from the Spanish crown in the cities of San Miguel de Allende, Querétaro, and Dolores Hidalgo. Earlier than planned, Spanish governors in Querétaro discovered the conspiracy, and in a rush to avoid capture, Miguel Hidalgo declared war on the Spanish from the small city of Dolores on September 16, 1810. Today, the Bajío's prominent role in the independence movement has earned it the moniker "The Cradle of Independence."

After the end of the War of Independence, the stately cities of the Bajío were largely destroyed and the silver trade began to wither. The city of Querétaro remained prominent, despite the regional decline, as strong industries and proximity to Mexico City helped the city retain its importance. It was twice declared the capital of the Mexican republic during times of political unrest; the modern Mexican constitution was signed and ratified there.

Today, the Bajío is a politically and culturally influential part of Mexico, as well as a major tourist destination. It is a stronghold for the conservative political party, the PAN, and the first PAN president, Vicente Fox, was the former governor of the state of Guanajuato. Over the past two decades, UNESCO has inducted Querétaro, Guanajuato, and San Miguel de Allende into its World Heritage program. In 2010, the entire Camino Real de Tierra Adentro (Royal Inland Route)—the colonial-era silver route—was inducted into the World Heritage program, along with its adjoining cities.

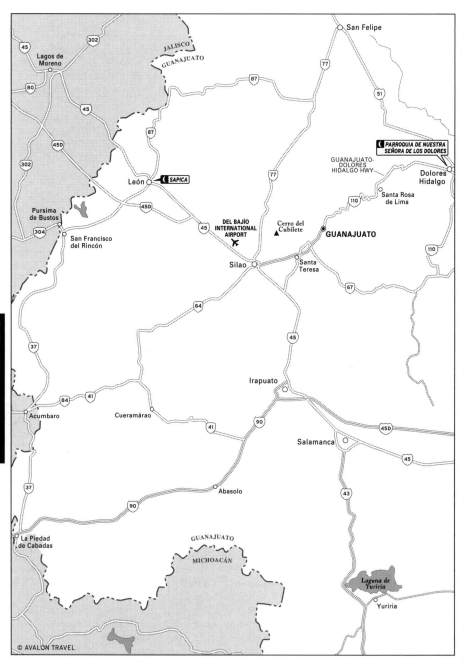

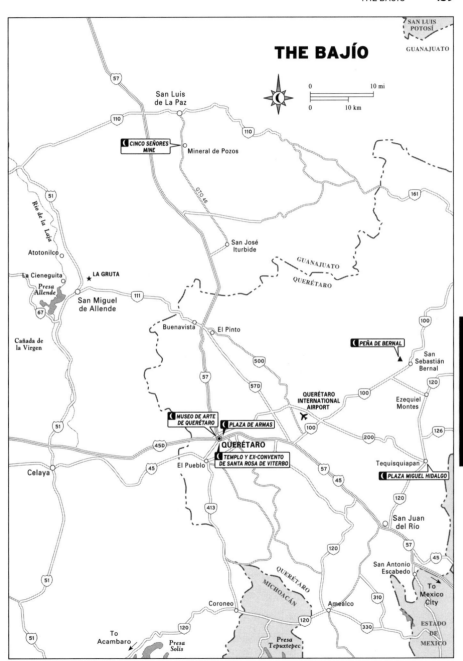

THE BAJÍO

PLANNING YOUR TIME

When visiting San Miguel de Allende or Guanajuato, it is easy to make day trips to sights around the Bajío or to plan an overnight stay in a small town in the countryside. If you have time in your itinerary, getting to know the greater region can be interesting and rewarding. At the same time, keep your travel expectations in check. The Bajío is expansive and largely connected by small two-lane highways. Travel isn't arduous but it can be time-consuming. If you will be in San Miguel de Allende or Guanajuato for a week or less, one excursion outside of town will probably be sufficient. If you are visiting the Bajío as part of a larger trip to Mexico, it is worth stopping through several of the region's interesting sights and cities, in addition to San Miguel and Guanajuato.

The small towns of Mineral de Pozos, Tequisquiapan, and Bernal all support a burgeoning tourist industry, with a few nice places to sleep and eat in town. Though they aren't chock-full of sights and activities, Mexican pueblos can be relaxing places to spend time or enjoy a peaceful evening or weekend. With those cities as exceptions, it is generally better to visit the Bajío's towns during the day but spend the night in San Miguel de Allende or Guanajuato. Both San Miguel and Guanajuato offer more restaurants and inns to accommodate guests, as well as more services, like banks, currency exchange, and tour operators.

Mass transportation and buses to the countryside can be a bit inefficient, though there are routes connecting every city in the Bajío. The larger the city, the easier it is to visit via bus. If you want to see a lot of the countryside, consider renting a car and driving to some small towns. Roads are generally in good condition, and there are often nice views along the way. Alternatively, many tour groups will provide transportation to sights near San Miguel and Guanajuato.

ORIENTATION

The name Bajío refers to the high plains in the central Mexican states of Guanajuato and Querétaro, as well as small sections of the states of Jalisco and Michoacán (geographically part of the same plain). Though *bajío* technically means "lowlands," the region is actually in the high plains of central Mexico, about 1,800 meters (6,000 feet) above sea level. The Sierra de Guanajuato in the north and the Sierra Gorda to the east border the Bajío.

The largely agricultural and ranching region of the southern Bajío is dominated by the state of Querétaro and its capital city of the same name. A major industrial center, as well as gateway to Mexico City from the north, the city of Querétaro has become increasingly more populous in recent years. It is propitiously located along Highway 57, which runs from Mexico City to the United States. Beyond the city, there are a few charming towns in the surrounding countryside, which can make for a nice day trip to the country. Recently, the state has begun to promote its burgeoning organic food and wine culture, and there are several ranches and wineries open to visits from the public. Tourism, though not historically a strong industry in this state, has been slowly and steadily increasing, as more visitors learn about Querétaro's lovely colonial cities and fertile countryside.

Near San Miguel de Allende, the semi-desert plains are dotted with small towns, corn fields, cactus, and winding highways. Of particular interest, the former mining town of Mineral de Pozos is a wonderful day trip, transporting its visitors to an older era among the desert chaparral. To the north of San Miguel, the little town of Dolores Hidalgo is the best place in the region to buy inexpensive talavera-style pottery and tiles. It is also a historically important destination, as it is the place where Mexico's independence movement officially began.

Heading north past Guanajuato, the Bajío begins to change. In cities like León, the prevalence of cowboy boots and oversized belt buckles tells you that you are heading toward Mexico's northern deserts. It's a largely industrial area, and there is a major auto manufacturing industry in Silao, just outside Guanajuato, as well as a massive shoe and leather industry in the large city of León. Not the most picturesque part of Mexico, León is nonetheless a destination for shopping, especially for those looking for bargain prices on shoes and leather goods.

Querétaro City

The large capital city of Santiago de Querétaro—generally referred to as just Querétaro—has played an important role in the history of Mexico, from pre-Hispanic times to the modern era. Among the oldest and most historic in the country, Querétaro's *centro histórico* was named a World Heritage Site in 1996. Largely unchanged since the 16th and 17th centuries, Querétaro's *centro histórico* is considered one of the finest surviving examples of architecture and city planning during the Spanish viceroyalty.

Querétaro and its neighbor, San Juan del Río, have grown rapidly in the past few decades, becoming a major industrial center close to Mexico City. Today, industrial and residential neighborhoods surround Querétaro's colonial downtown, and the city is home to such major international companies as Siemens, Hitachi, Procter and Gamble, and Pilgrim's Pride. Passing through the city on the highway, it is easy to imagine that there are nothing but chugging big-rigs and massive factories from one end of Querétaro to the other, but it's quite the contrary; Querétaro's stately *centro histórico* is quiet, clean, and pedestrian-friendly, boasting a host of handsome churches and museums, wonderful restaurants, and an easygoing Mexican atmosphere.

Thanks to its propitious location, Querétaro has received quite a bit of overflow from Mexico City, with thousands of capital residents

THE BAJÍO

© ARTURO MEADE

one of the many bustling pedestrian streets in downtown Querétaro

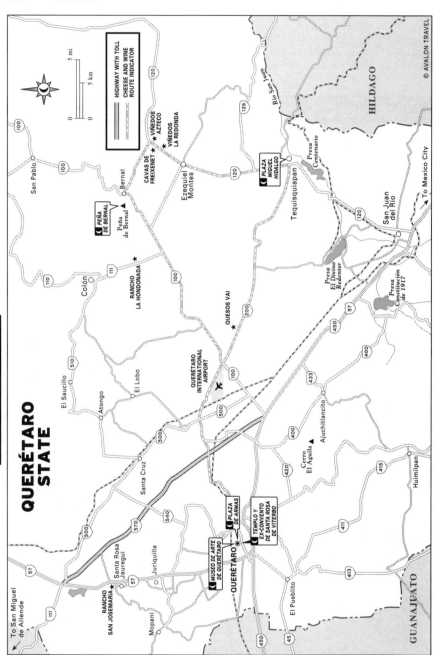

© AVALON TRAVEL

QUERÉTARO STATE

choosing to relocate to the relative peace and safety of this medium-sized city. As a result, Querétaro's culture has become increasingly cosmopolitan, as new residents open cool bars, creative restaurants, and contemporary galleries in town. Youth culture is also prominent, with a major university in the city center, plus many smaller colleges about town. For nightlife, there are rowdy pubs and classic cantinas throughout the *centro histórico*.

Despite its impressive architecture, proximity to the capital, agreeable climate, and important place in history, Querétaro has remained relatively undiscovered by tourists. The result is a surprisingly cosmopolitan and largely authentic city, where restaurants, museums, and other attractions are pleasingly aimed at a local crowd, rather than visitors. The city's busy cinema and art events are well attended by *querétenses* (Querétaro locals), and there is always a bustle of families and friends wandering through the public plazas downtown. At the same time, the local government has taken steps to improve the city's reputation as a tourist destination, to good effect. There are ample guided tours and visitor services, the tourist office is outgoing and helpful, and there are plenty of well-marked and interesting sights throughout the city center. All in all, Querétaro is a wonderful place to visit, either for a day, a weekend, or an extended trip.

HISTORY

The Spanish were eager to settle lands in northern Mexico but met with fierce resistance from the indigenous populations. In 1531, a battle broke out between the local inhabitants of the Querétaro region and Spanish forces led by Hernán Pérez Bocanegra y Córdoba. According to local history, the battle was interrupted when a miraculous image of Saint James appeared in the sky over the hill of Sangremal, awing the local people into submission to the Spanish and causing instant, widespread conversion to the Catholic church. (According to some theories, a solar eclipse took place during the battle.) The new city of Santiago de Querétaro was founded on the hilltop, with Santiago (the

Spanish name for Saint James) honoring the miraculous circumstances of the city's founding. Even after the legendary Spanish victory, there continued to be intermittent clashes between Querétaro's old and new inhabitants.

Shortly after the region's conquest, Franciscans and other evangelicals arrived in Querétaro. Like San Miguel de Allende, Querétaro was a strategic town on the silver route, and it grew prominent and wealthy during the 17th and 18th centuries. The wealth from the silver mines and Querétaro's industries helped to fund numerous religious and municipal projects about town, from the city's magnificent baroque churches to the impressive 1,200-meter aqueduct that provided water to the city center. Querétaro was first recognized as a city by the Spanish crown in 1656.

Like other cities in the Bajío, Querétaro played a role in the Mexican War of Independence, and was home to several prominent independence conspirators. Of particular note, the wife of the town's mayor, Josefa Ortiz de Domínguez, sent a crucial warning to Ignacio Allende and Miguel Hidalgo when the plot against the crown had been uncovered by royalist officials in Querétaro. Today, she is celebrated throughout Querétaro for her role in the early independence movement, though she was unrecognized during her lifetime. After the War of Independence ended and Mexico gained its freedom from Spain, Querétaro was officially named a state in the new republic and the city of Querétaro was declared state capital. When the United States invaded Mexico City in 1827, Querétaro became the temporary capital of the country. In an infamous moment in history, President Santa Anna signed the 1827 Treaty of Guadalupe Hidalgo in Querétaro, which ceded half of Mexico's territory to the United States.

During the beginning of the 20th century, Mexico was again wrought with upheaval when the Mexican Revolution began. Querétaro was not the site of major battles, but, like the rest of the country, the city suffered the effects of political unrest. In post-revolutionary upheaval, Querétaro was renamed the capital of Mexico

THE BAJÍO

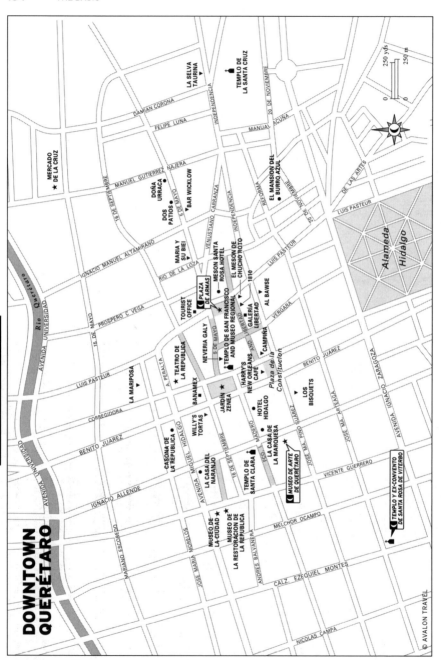

DOWNTOWN QUERÉTARO

Río Querétaro

AVENIDA UNIVERSIDAD

MERCADO DE LA CRUZ ★

LA SELVA TAURINA ▼

TEMPLO DE LA SANTA CRUZ ✝

20 DE NOVIEMBRE

250 yds
0
250 m
0

MANUAL ACUNA

DE LAS ARTES

EL MANSION DEL BURRO AZUL ●

LUIS PASTEUR

Alameda Hidalgo

DAMIAN CORONA

FELIPE LUNA

INDEPENDENCIA

REFORMA

20 DE NOVIEMBRE

MANUEL GUTIERREZ NAJERA

DOÑA URRACA ●

BAR WICKLOW ●

DOS PATOS ●

5 DE MAYO

IGNACIO MANUEL ALTAMIRANO

18 DE SEPTIEMBRE

RIO DE LA LOZA

MARIA Y SU BIEI ▼

VENUSTIANO CARRANZA

INDEPENDENCIA

MESON SANTA ROSA HOTEL ●

EL MESON DE CHUCHO ROTO ●

1810

LUIS PASTEUR

PROSPERO C. VEGA

15 DE MAYO

PLAZA DE ARMAS

TOURIST OFFICE

AL BAWSE

VERGARA

GALERIA LIBERTAD

TEMPLO DE SAN FRANCISCO AND MUSEO REGIONAL ✝

NEVERIA GALY ▼

LIBERTAD

CAMPIRA ▼

LUIS PASTEUR

LA MARIPOSA ▼

A. PERALTA

TEATRO DE LA REPUBLICA ★

5 DE MAYO

HARRY'S NEW ORLEANS CAFÉ ●

Plaza de la Constitución

BENITO JUAREZ

CORREGIDORA

BANAMEX ●

JARDIN ZENEA ★

LOS BISQUETS ▼

BENITO JUAREZ

CASA DE LA REPUBLICA ●

WILLY'S TORTAS ▼

HOTEL HIDALGO ●

MADERO

JOSE MA. PINO JUAREZ

JOSE MA. ARTEAGA

AVENIDA IGNACIO ZARAGOZA

IGNACIO ALLENDE

AVENIDA MIGUEL HIDALGO

16 DE SEPTIEMBRE

LA CASA DEL NARANJO ●

TEMPLO DE SANTA CLARA ✝

LA CASA DE LA MARQUESA ●

MUSEO DE ARTE DE QUERÉTARO

VICENTE GUERRERO

JOSE MARIA MORELOS

MARIANO ESCOBEDO

AVENIDA UNIVERSIDAD

MUSEO DE LA CIUDAD ★

MUSEO DE LA RESTAURACION DE LA REPUBLICA ★

ANDRES BALVANERA

MELCHOR OCAMPO

TEMPLO Y EX-CONVENTO DE SANTA ROSA DE VITERBO ✝

CALZ. EZEQUIEL MONTES

NICOLAS CAMPA

© AVALON TRAVEL

LA CORREGIDORA: HEROINE OF THE INDEPENDENCE

A celebrated heroine of the War of Independence, Josefa Ortiz de Domínguez, or "La Corregidora," is a favorite daughter in the city of Querétaro. One of the few women known to have participated in the early independence movement, she was vital to the success of the conspirators who sought Mexico's sovereignty from New Spain.

Josefa Ortiz was born to a wealthy family in Valladolid (today, Morelia) in the state of Michoacán. She married Miguel Domínguez, who was later appointed *corregidor* (magistrate) of Querétaro – the city's top government administrator. High government posts were almost always held by Spanish-born officials. However, Domínguez was criollo (born in the New World but of Spanish descent). As the wife of the *corregidor*, Josefa Ortiz was known as the *corregidora*. Domínguez and Ortiz had 14 children together.

According to her biographers, Josefa Ortiz was a critic of the rigid class system in New Spain. Despite her Spanish heritage, Ortiz sympathized with the mestizo and indigenous people of Mexico, who lived in poverty and benefited little from the great wealth of the colonies.

When Napoleon invaded Spain in 1808, frustrated criollo elite in the Bajío region began to make plans for independence from the Spanish crown. Both Miguel Domínguez and Josefa Ortiz were privy to the private meetings held in Ignacio Allende's home in San Miguel, and they supported the movement from Querétaro.

Originally, the independence conspirators had planned to launch their attack against the government in December of 1810. However, royalist governors uncovered the conspiracy plot in September. As they conducted a search of the town, Ortiz was locked in her home. Knowing the plan was in danger of failure, Ortiz managed to send warning to co-conspirator Ignacio Perez, who in turn sent word to San Miguel de Allende. The revolution began the following night, when Miguel Hidalgo gathered the Mexican army in Dolores Hidalgo. Both Domínguez and Ortiz were imprisoned, though they were eventually cleared of charges. Though she died in obscurity, today Ortiz is remembered for the ingenuity that saved the independence movement.

THE BAJÍO

in 1917, and the Mexican constitution (which is still in use today) was signed and ratified there.

SIGHTS

When the city of Querétaro was founded in the 16th century, distinct indigenous and Spanish neighborhoods were constructed side by side. While the Spanish town was laid out in a neat grid pattern, the indigenous neighborhood was planned in the native style, with narrow and sinuous streets winding along the hillside. Today, Querétaro's central district retains the original street plans from these two neighboring districts. In the eastern end of the *centro histórico,* wide avenues and large esplanades are flanked by Mexican baroque churches and mansions. On the western end (near the hill of Sangremal), the streets are more winding and circuitous, with small alleyways and low colonial homes.

Though it is a big city, most of Querétaro's interesting sights are located in the *centro histórico,* within easy walking distance of one another. In a well-planned day, tourists can see most of this city's most beautiful buildings and museums, though two days will give you more time to really explore and enjoy this cosmopolitan metropolis.

◖ Plaza de Armas

The Plaza de Armas is a good place to begin your tour of Querétaro. This picturesque 18th-century plaza was constructed in the Spanish style, with arcades and mansions surrounding a neat public square and a stately stone fountain.

THE BAJÍO

© ARTURO MEADE

The Plaza de Armas is a beautiful and well-maintained 18th-century plaza in the center of Querétaro.

Pick up a map at the tourist office (beside the plaza), then plan your day on a public bench beneath perfectly manicured trees and hanging flower pots. On Sundays, the Plaza de Armas is a nice place for people-watching or to enjoy a drink in one of the many cafés or eateries along the square.

On the north side of the square, the historic **Casa del Corregimiento** is an 18th-century mansion and the current home of the state government offices. Once the home of Querétaro's mayor *(corregidor)*, this aristocratic house was written into history during the War of Independence. Here, Josefa Ortiz de Domínguez alerted the revolutionary hero Ignacio Pérez that the independence conspiracy had been discovered by the Spanish. Today, you can walk into the covered courtyard of the Casa de Corregimiento, where there is a statue of Ortiz de Domínguez in the foyer.

Jardín Zenea

If you follow one of several pedestrian pathways *(andadores)* west from the Plaza de Armas, you will reach the lovely Jardín Zenea, occupying a full city block between Calles Corregidora and Juárez in the *centro histórico*. Named after a former Querétaro governor, Benito Santos Zenea, this lovely garden is one of the most popular gathering points in town. Often, there are performances in the round kiosk in the middle of the plaza.

Just across the street (on the corner of Corregidora and 16 de Septiembre), the **Plaza de la Corregidora** is a smaller public square surrounding a monument to Josefa Ortiz de Domínguez. There are many little coffee shops and restaurants lining the plaza, which can be a pleasant place to relax and watch the crowds.

Museo Regional and the Templo de San Francisco

Standing above the Jardín Zenea, the Templo de San Francisco (Corregidora s/n, tel. 442/212-0477, 7 A.M.–10 A.M. and 2:30–9 P.M. Mon., 7 A.M.–9 P.M. Tues.–Sun.) is one of Querétaro's oldest and loveliest buildings. Construction on this church and adjoining

© ARTURO MEADE

The Jardín Zenea is a popular gathering place, bordered by the Templo de San Francisco.

Franciscan convent began as early as the 1540s, though the temple wasn't completed until the middle of the following century. The church's original baroque sandstone entryway is adorned with life-size saints, which stand in relief against the construction's tall, rust-colored facade. Formerly Querétaro's cathedral, the church is still in use today.

The beautiful former monastery that adjoins the church is now home to the Museo Regional (Regional Museum of Querétaro, Corregidora Sur 3, tel. 442/212-2031, 10 A.M.–5 P.M. Tues.–Sun., US$3.25). The 11 rooms in this historic space each display artifacts from Querétaro city and state, including a nice collection of ceramics and sculpture from the region's pre-Hispanic cultures. As you progress through the museum, exhibits address each era in Querétaro's history, with rooms dedicated to the viceroyalty or colonial era (including personal affects of the famous Josefa Ortiz de Domínguez), the Reformation, the American invasion, the 19th century, and the Mexican Revolution. Texts are in Spanish.

◖ Museo de Arte de Querétaro

The spectacular fine-art Museo de Arte de Querétaro (Allende 14 Sur, tel. 442/212-2357 or 442/212-3523, www.museodeartequeretaro. com, 10 A.M.–6 P.M. Wed.–Sun., US$3, Wed. free) is housed within a former Augustinian monastery, built between 1731 and 1745. It's among Querétaro's most impressive buildings, and the monastery's baroque courtyard is filled with elaborately carved sandstone archways, replete with astonishing stone gargoyles and carefully carved adornments. Around the courtyard, exhibition spaces extend from a series of long porticoes with arched ceilings and carefully restored frescos. If you want to take pictures of the building, you must pay an extra fee at the ticket booth (exhibitions are off-limits to cameras).

Besides the spectacular setting, the museum often shows some interesting artwork, with a well-planned schedule of rotating exhibitions, as well as a nice permanent collection. Often on view in the large exhibition halls downstairs, the museum's permanent collection includes religious paintings from Querétaro from the 17th and 18th centuries. However, the museum's newest director has made great efforts to plan original exhibitions by contemporary artists from the Bajío region, as well as prominent exhibitions by important Mexican masters. As a result, there is a pleasing mix of work in the museum's large galleries.

◖ Templo y Ex-Convento de Santa Rosa de Viterbo

The magnificent temple of Santa Rosa de Viterbo (General Arteaga esq. Ezequiel Montes tel. 442/214-1691, generally 9 A.M.–6 P.M. daily) is one of the finest baroque structures in the city. This former convent and its adjoining church were originally designed and built by architect Ignacio Mariano de las Casas in 1754. Quite distinct from other baroque churches in Mexico, Santa Rosa de Viterbo distinguishes itself with an ornately designed exterior, replete with massive flying buttresses, carved stonework, delicate frescos, and garish gargoyles. It stands over a small stone fountain in Plazuela

Templo y Ex-Convento de Santa Rosa de Viterbo

Mariano de las Casa, and the overall effect is impressive. Inside, the church is equally spectacular. In the main nave, there are six gold-drenched churrigueresque altars from the 18th century, as well as a collection of important colonial-era paintings and retablos. Be sure to note the carved confessional and baroque organ above the nave. The former cloister surrounds a lovely interior courtyard, with arched arcades showing a Moorish influence. Well worth a visit, Santa Rosa de Viterbo is one of the most original structures in the region.

Templo de Santa Clara

The beautiful Templo de Santa Clara (Francisco I. Madero 42, tel. 442/212-1777, generally 9 A.M.–6 P.M. daily) is a convent and temple originally commissioned by Diego de Tapia, the son of one of Querétaro's wealthy founders. Begun in 1606, this chapel and its adjoining convent were considered one of the most beautiful architectural achievements in the country during the colonial era. Today, just the chapel and a small annex remain; large

parts of the church and convent were destroyed during the Reformation. Nonetheless, Santa Clara is still recognized among the country's finest baroque buildings, particularly noted for its elaborate interiors. Step inside to marvel at the beautifully carved baroque altars, washed in gold leaf and accompanied by painted saints. Few churches rival Santa Clara, filled with the unique handwork of master craftsmen.

In the lovely plaza outside the Templo de Santa Clara, be sure to note the neoclassical **Fuente de Neptuno** (Neptune Fountain), right on the corner of Madero and Allende. Originally constructed in 1797, the fountain's pink sandstone arch frames a statue of the Roman god, Neptune. One of the city's most noted landmarks, this opulent fountain was originally built as a part of the Convent of San Antonio, which was located in what is today the Jardín de la Corregidora. When the government decided to build a monument to the independence movement in 1908, the entire fountain was picked up and moved to its current location.

Museo de la Restauración de la República

During the post-independence turmoil of the mid-19th century, the French monarchy took control of Mexico with the backing of the French government and a group of prominent monarchists in Mexico. Led by Benito Juárez, Mexico's liberals resisted French rule, eventually forcing the monarchy into its final stronghold in the city of Querétaro. Emperor Maximilian I of Hapsburg spent his last days in a Querétaro jail; he, along with other monarchist leaders, was executed by firing squad at the Cerro de las Campanas in Querétaro.

The Museo de la Restauración de la República (Museum of the Restoration of the Republic, Guerrero 21-23 Nte., tel. 442/224-3004 or 442/224-3005, museoqro@prodigy.net.mx, 9 A.M.–5 P.M. Tues.–Fri., 10 A.M.–5 P.M. Sat.–Sun., free) is dedicated to this unusual era in Querétaro's history. A museum most fit for history buffs, this small but beautiful space exhibits documents, maps, and artifacts from 19th century Querétaro. Most of the collection chronicles the history of the French rule through photos, texts, and mockups, though there are also some nice 19th-century costumes and antique weapons. The six small rooms were once a part of 18th-century Capuchin convent, and the space itself is just as interesting as its contents. It was in this very building that Emperor Maximilian spent the last night before his execution.

Templo y Ex-Monasterio de la Santa Cruz

On the west end of the *centro histórico,* the hill of Sangremal was the historic site of the Spanish victory over the Otomí people, which resulted in the conquest and founding of Querétaro. Today, Templo de la Santa Cruz (Ejército Republicano, esq. Felipe Luna, 9 A.M.–2 P.M. and 4–6 P.M. Tues.–Sat., 9 A.M.–4 P.M. Sun., free) stands at this important locale. This church and its adjoining monastery were originally built by Franciscan friars, who arrived in Querétaro shortly after the Spanish victory in the 16th century. Here, the monastery's school trained many other missionaries to carry on the Franciscan tradition throughout the New World, and its alumni traveled as far south as Guatemala.

Today, visitors can wander through the former monastery's quarters, including the original kitchen and dining room, as well as the cells where Emperor Maximilian was imprisoned in the 19th century. Inside the main nave of the church, a large sandstone cross hangs above the altar, meant to replicate the miraculous cross that appeared above the battle for Querétaro's conquest.

Querétaro Aqueduct

Cutting east 1,200 meters from the *centro histórico,* Querétaro's spectacular 74-column aqueduct was built between 1726 and 1735 by the Marquis de la Villa del Villar del Águila. At its highest point, the aqueduct soars 23 meters above ground. It is an astonishing architectural achievement that still lends incredible character and majesty to downtown Querétaro and its surrounding neighborhoods. You can get the best view of it from just a block or two behind the Templo de la Santa Cruz. From here, the hill of Sangremal makes a dramatic drop, with the aqueduct stretching across the valley below.

Mercado de la Cruz

Querétaro's large covered market, Mercado de la Cruz (Manuel Gutiérrez Nájera s/n, 8 A.M.–9 P.M. daily, hours vary by shop) is a wonderful place to shop for fresh produce, fish, meat, flowers, and crafts. It is also a great place to get a bite to eat, with a wide array of food stalls and fruit stands throughout the interior. It opened on September 28, 1979.

Mercado de la Cruz is a bustling urban market, typical to many large Mexican cities, though more picturesque (and photogenic) than many. Visitors can shop or simply take in the sights, wandering past fresh whole fish chilling on ice, neatly stacked towers of vegetables, big cauldrons of menudo, and overflowing

© ARTURO MEADE

A vendor at Mercado de la Cruz sells squash flowers, *huitlacoche* (corn fungus), limes, and green tomatoes.

THE BAJÍO

flower stands. On the weekends, the market spills into the back parking lot.

ARTS AND ENTERTAINMENT

Querétaro's population becomes larger and more cultured every year. With the support of the local and state government, Querétaro has developed a lively art scene. Throughout Querétaro, music, cinema, theater, and visual art events are frequent and well attended.

Nightlife

As a big university town, this lively city has great bars and cantinas. A wonderful old cantina near the Convento de la Santa Cruz, **La Selva Taurina** (Independencia 159, tel. 442/248-3733, 11:30 A.M.–3 A.M. Mon.–Sat., US$3–5 per drink/course) is an excellent place to quench your thirst and fill your stomach. During the day, food is served cantina style: With each drink, they bring you a small plate of food. The meal usually starts with a *caldo* (broth soup), followed by dishes like pork in green sauce, prickly

La Selva Taurina is a traditional cantina and a shrine to bullfighting.

pear tacos, or chorizo. You don't get to pick the dish, but the quality is across-the-board excellent. A shrine to bullfights, the walls are decorated with the heads of unfortunate bulls and festooned with vintage photos. At night, the place is hopping with a crowd of mixed ages, attended by easygoing bartenders.

Though their flagship restaurant is in downtown San Miguel de Allende, the Querétaro branch of **Harry's New Orleans Café** (Juárez Sur 7, Plaza Constitución, tel. 442/214-2620, www.harrysneworleanscafe.com, noon–1 A.M. Mon.–Thurs., noon–2 A.M. Fri., 10 A.M.–2 A.M. Sat., 10 A.M.–midnight Sun.) is just as popular as the original. Located in the picturesque Plaza de la Constitución, Harry's is geared toward a young adult crowd. The nicest part of drinking or dining at Harry's is enjoying the ample patio seating overlooking the plaza. Order up a cocktail with a broad choice of liquors and a fish sandwich, jambalaya, or a plate of fried calamari to enjoy the evening. Seafood is fresh and well prepared, as are the drinks. This place is very popular with locals and the outdoor bar seats are often full on the weekends. Sometimes the music and atmosphere can be a bit too loud for casual conversation; come in the mood for a party.

The youthful **Bar Wicklow** (5 de Mayo 66, tel. 442/212-0947, www.wicklow.com.mx, 5 P.M.–2 A.M. Tues.–Sun.) is a vast, student-friendly Irish pub, dolled up with walls painted kelly green, a big wood bar, and a pool table for customers. In addition to the selection of Mexican beers (including XX on tap), the pub also maintains an impressive selection of artesian and imported brands like Samuel Adams, Lowenbrau, Carlsburg, and Guinness. There is also a bar menu with snacks and pizzas. On the weekends, this place is popular with Querétaro youth, slurping up cheap brews and swaying to loud music. Often, the bar brings live musicians for the weekend crowd.

Visual and Performing Arts

The wonderful **Museo de la Ciudad Santiago de Querétaro** (Guerrero 27 Nte., tel. 442/224-3756 or 442/212-3855, http://

© ARTURO MEADE

Musicians often play around the Plaza de Armas.

museodelaciudadqro.org, US$0.50) has an extraordinary commitment to emerging artists and contemporary art. Located in the Capuchin convent that houses the Museo de la Restauración de la República, the museum's old and crumbling space plays perfect accompaniment to a largely youthful and experimental set of rotating exhibitions, many by local artists. The director seeks contemporary proposals for the museum's numerous gallery spaces, and video art and installation pieces are not uncommon. In addition to art, there is a cinema series and numerous workshops held on-site. The museum's well maintained website will keep you up-to-date on upcoming events.

Among the largest of Querétaro's many public exhibition spaces, **Galería Libertad** (Andador Libertad 56, tel. 442/214-2358, 9 A.M.–8 P.M. daily, free) is a massive two-story gallery with three large exhibition spaces. Since 1984, this space has been showing rotating exhibitions of fine art by *querétenses* and other local artists. The gallery is just steps from the Plaza de Armas on the pedestrian street, Libertad.

The historic **Teatro de la República** (Juárez 22 Nte., tel. 442/212-0339) was built in 1845 and was the very first place that the Mexican national anthem was played. Today, it continues to function as one of Querétaro's most prominent performance spaces. It is the home of Querétaro's philharmonic, as well as a venue for high-profile concerts, government functions, dance events, and plays. Its neoclassical, semicircular interior has terraced balconies and plushy red seats, creating a rather sophisticated backdrop for any performance.

SHOPPING

For jewelry, T-shirts, and other knickknacks, there are dozens of **craft stands** along the Andador Libertad in the city center. These informal vendors fill the tiny walkway from Thursday to Monday of each week (taking Tuesday and Wednesday off). Here, you can find every manner of inexpensive craft, from beaded necklaces and woven scarves to embroidered manta shirts and silver earrings. There are also numerous **traditional craft shops** along the same pedestrian alleyway, though most don't specialize in high-quality collectibles.

For a very nice selection of traditional crafts, seek out **Quinto Real** (Reforma 80, tel. 442/212-8601, www.quintoreal.com.mx, 10 A.M.–2 P.M. and 3–7 P.M. Mon.–Sat.). This lovely little crafts shop is set in the living areas of a colonial-era home, a cozy showroom for the store's nice collection of arts and crafts. Here, you'll find a little bit of everything, including tin ornaments, textiles and table runners, wood masks, and handmade jewelry, as well as a large selection of glassware. Merchandise is artfully designed and displayed, making it easy to imagine one of these colorful accents in your own home.

Anyone with a sweet tooth will enjoy **Dulzura Mexicana** (Juárez Nte. 69, tel. 442/312-1873, 10 A.M.–8 P.M. Mon., 10 A.M.–10 P.M. Tues.–Sun.), a small but super-stocked

THE BAJÍO

traditional candy shop across the street from the Teatro de la República. Here you'll find all the most popular goodies, like *ate* (fruit paste), *jamoncillo* (flavored milk-fudge), and crystallized fruit, as well as more unusual sweets like *queso de tuna* and *gomitas de guanábana* (tropical fruit gumdrops). The staff is very friendly and can explain the difference (in Spanish) between different types of sweets, as well as provide samples of some items. Pile your pickings into a wicker basket, then get ready for a sugar high.

ACCOMMODATIONS

Querétaro offers a nice range of accommodations in every price range. There are numerous executive hotels catering to business travelers, and, due to the constant visitors, most of Mexico's largest hotel chains have locations in Querétaro. Even smaller boutique hotels often cater to the business traveler, and usually boast very friendly and knowledgeable service. For the best experience, tourists should stay in Querétaro's city center.

Under US$50

Located on a narrow street between the Iglesia de Santa Clara and the Jardín Zenea, the simple and friendly **Hotel Hidalgo** (Madero 11, tel. 442/212-0081 or 442/212-3673, www.hotelhidalgo.com.mx, US$38–45) is a great deal in the historic center of the city. The hotel's guest rooms are on the second story of a colonial mansion, with doors opening onto a pretty central courtyard and restaurant. The colonial exterior suggests a posh accommodation, but once inside, bedrooms are as simple as they come. Each has one double or two single beds in a small, carpeted space, as well as televisions and bottled water. Bathrooms are basic and smell vaguely of cleaning products, but the price is low, the rooms are quiet, and the hotel is perfectly located in the center of the city. Hotel staff is very friendly and knowledgeable, making Hotel Hidalgo a great pick in the budget range.

US$50-100

On a quiet street in the north city center, the low-key, funky, and very friendly **La Mansión del Burro Azul** (Altamirano 35, tel. 442/224-2410 or 442/148-7156, www.mansiondelburroazul.com, US$56–67) is a great find, just a bit off the beaten track. The rooms at this small hotel are jumbled and quirky, with mismatched wood furnishings, crooked iron chandeliers, big king-sized beds, and colorful bathrooms. In the casual central courtyard, guests can hang out on the chaise lounges and deck chairs, or make use of the basic communal kitchen. There is also a small but peaceful massage room where guests and nonguests can order massage and spa services. Prices include continental breakfast.

(La Casa del Naranjo (Hidalgo 21, tel. 442/212-7606 or toll-free Mex. tel. 800/832-8660, www.lacasadelnaranjo.com, US$80–120) is a small but stylish family-run hotel in the center of Querétaro. There are only six guest rooms in this little inn, each of which is decorated in a tastefully rustic style, with exposed rock walls and soft fluffy bedspreads. All rooms have flat-screen televisions, bathrobes and slippers, and pretty bathrooms with onyx accessories and shower massagers. Upstairs bedrooms are more luxurious, with sofas and sitting areas or canopy beds, some opening onto the roof garden. However, even the smallest room downstairs (which is rather small) gets points for its well-designed atmosphere. There is a small bar downstairs, and guests can also relax on the hotel's roof deck, which has a Jacuzzi, chaise lounges, and pretty views of the city. The hotel also offers spa services.

Hostería Dos Patios (5 de Mayo 109, tel. 442/212-2030 or 442/214-3894, toll-free Mex. tel. 800/831-5790, www.hosteriadospatios.com, US$88–105) is a quiet and comfortable hotel in a large colonial mansion in the eastern downtown district. Despite the colonial building, the hotel's 20 rooms are rather modern in their comforts, with plush beds and cotton bedspreads, televisions, big armoires, and clean bathrooms. Most rooms also have small couches or love-seats where you can read or watch TV. The nicest accommodations are those surrounding the back garden, which are set back off the street and feel both quiet and private. The hotel caters to both tourists and business travelers, and there is an efficient 24-hour desk staff that can answer your questions about the city.

US$100-150

Ideally located on the western arcade of the beautiful Plaza de Armas, the **Mesón Santa Rosa Hotel** (Luis Pasteur 17, tel. 442/227-0600 or toll-free Mex. tel. 800/017-7372, www.hotelmesonsantarosa.com, US$120–167) occupies a stately 17th-century mansion. Best for the romantic traveler, this hotel shows its age (it's been in operation for almost 20 years) in the quirky details, dark carpet, and painted wood decor. Though some of the accommodations are a bit dark and cavernous, all rooms are spacious, unique, and equipped with a huge bed and television. Large private baths each boast a bathtub, which are hidden behind wood-paneled doors. There is a small blue-tiled pool in the back courtyard and a restaurant in the entryway, which is covered in hanging vines. The friendly and attentive service makes the experience particularly pleasant.

US$150-250

Querétaro's most famous hotel is the **Casa de la Marquesa** (Madero 41, tel. 442/212-0092 or toll-free Mex. tel. 800/401-7100, www.lacasadelamarquesa.com, US$180–350), an opulent colonial-era mansion on Calle Madero. This beautiful building is one of Querétaro's most prized; in fact, it is often listed among the city's most notable tourist attractions, even though the building is privately owned (for that reason, the hotel often keeps the lobby closed to the public). The interior of the hotel retains many of the Old World charms you'd hope to find in a historical building: tiled walls, Moorish archways, and tons of antique furniture. Guest rooms are actually divided between the main house, or Casa de Marquesa, and a neighboring structure, the Casa Azul. Rooms in the main house are the nicest, with more light than the

back rooms; however, the room quality can vary in both buildings. Ask to see your options on check-in. The atmosphere is elegant, but the indifferent service doesn't bring the same charm to the experience.

Casona de la República (Hidalgo 4, tel. 442/251-8500 or toll-free Mex. tel. 800/227-6627, www.casonadelarepublica. com, US$185–256) is a boutique hotel in a nicely restored 19th-century mansion. The 15 suites are arranged around a lovely art nouveau patio in front or the quieter patios in back. When it comes to decor, you can pick your poison: The hotel has chosen a different design theme for each room, ranging from art deco to Italian Renaissance. You can see all the options on the hotel's website, or you may ask to see a few options when you arrive. No matter what the decor you choose, each room is comfortably outfitted with big beds, down comforters, and flat-screen TVs. Some of the bigger rooms have a second-story loft with a private Jacuzzi or television; however, standard bedrooms may be a bit prettier since you can really appreciate their high ceilings and gracious architecture without the addition of the loft. (In a slightly gratuitous touch, all master suites have both in-room Jacuzzis and saunas.) Bathrooms are clean and well laid-out, though they don't match up to the opulence of the rooms themselves. The hotel also offers spa services and a 24-hour concierge, as well as a "pillow menu" for guests who are picky about down versus cotton.

Light, modern, and incredibly friendly, **Doña Urraca Hotel and Spa** (5 de Mayo 117, tel. 442/238-5400 or toll-free Mex. tel. 800/021-7116, http://donaurraca.com, US$200) is a relaxing place to spend a few days in Querétaro's *centro histórico*. Built within the remains of a colonial mansion, the hotel's architecture blends old and new; stone archways from the site's original structure are nicely incorporated into the hotel's clean and modern design. Inside the guest rooms, decor is minimalist and comfortable, with big fluffy beds, leather sofas, and spacious baths. White was the decorator's color of choice, complemented by wicker and leather

THE BAJÍO

details, which gives the whole place a rather earthy feeling. All 24 suites overlook the central pool and lawn, cascading with plants and flowers; upstairs, the rooms also have private balconies. There is an airy bar and restaurant inside the hotel, which serves haute Mexican cuisine in an casual atmosphere. The hotel's spa services include shiatsu massage, reflexology, and facials, and can be arranged in-room. Service is excellent.

FOOD
Quick Bites and Tacos

For a quick but tasty bite, there are dozens of mouthwatering taco stands and casual eateries in the extensive **Mercado de la Cruz** (Manuel Gutiérrez Nájera s/n, 8 A.M.–9 P.M. daily, hours vary by shop). A rule of thumb in any market is to follow the crowds: popular food stalls tend to be the tastiest.

For a sure thing, try the delicious (and award-winning!) **Barbacoa Lucia** (Mercado de la Cruz, Local 98, 8 A.M.–2 P.M. daily, US$1–3), which serves flavorful *barbacoa* (lamb steamed in an earthen pit) tacos and fragrant broth soup. Order a few tacos and do like the locals by adding cilantro, chopped onions, and salsa to the meat. The small metal stools that surround this informal stand are almost always filled, but turnover is quick, so you'll likely snag a seat as you wait for your tacos to be prepared.

Tamales are a classic Mexican breakfast or dinner food, traditionally accompanied by *atole,* a sweet corn-based drink. In Querétaro, there are numerous small storefronts specializing in tamales and *atole* along Arteaga, a few blocks east of Santa Rosa de Viterbo. Most are open, as is traditional, in the early morning and late night. Try **Super Tamales y Atoles de Querétaro** (Arteaga 41 Pte., tel. 442/212-4298 or 442/212-7816, 7–11 A.M. and 6–11 P.M., US$2), where you can order delicious tamales stuffed with chicken, cheese, red salsa, green salsa, chile peppers, or pork. In addition to traditional tamales steamed in cornhusk, Super Tamales prepares Oaxacan-style tamales, which are steamed in banana leaves

and generally denser and moister. Whether you go in the morning or in the evening, get there before closing as many of the options sell out.

While there are only a few flavors on the menu, all the ice cream at friendly **Nevería Galy** (Andador 5 de Mayo 8, noon–9 P.M. daily, US$1–2) is made with all-natural ingredients, a fact they proudly display on many jovial posters tacked along the shop's walls. The delicious and icy lime *nieve* is the perfect salve to a hot afternoon. Take it to go or enjoy your ice cream at a Formica table inside the authentically retro shop. They also serve ice cream with a shot of wine on top, an unusual yet popular option.

With more than 30 years in operation, **Willy's Tortas** (16 de Septiembre Pte. 2, tel. 442/212-7354, www.tortaswillys.110mb.com, 8 A.M.–10:30 P.M. daily, US$2) can make you a quick and filling meal for just a few bucks. Sidle up to an orange bar stool at this corner snack shop and order a torta with your choice of filling. They have a wide range of options, like yellow cheese, sausage, egg, avocado, and ham. For a real food bomb, try the meaty *torta al pastor,* which is stuffed with seasoned and chile-rubbed pork, complemented by a few slices of avocado and tomato. With good food at inexpensive prices, Willy's is always busy, morning to night.

Just across the street from the Plaza Constitución, the bustling little eatery **Campiña** (Corregidora Sur 15A, tel. 442/214-1403, 8 A.M.–11 P.M. daily, US$5) pays serious homage to hand-ground Oaxacan chocolate and mezcal, preparing a dazzling variety of unique beverages and snacks. The chocolate-based drink menu is incredibly extensive, and every beverage can be served hot, cold, or as a frappe. There are some fabulous combinations on the menu, like spicy chile, clove, cinnamon, and dark chocolate mixed into a frothy, water-based drink. Accompany your beverage with cornbread (more like a sweet pound cake than the Southern quick bread from the United States), churros, or enchiladas in a chocolate and mole sauce, or order one of the many Oaxacan dishes on the menu. In the open kitchen, you can see the cooks blending salsas and toasting *tlayudas* (large Oaxacan tortillas stuffed with beans and cheese). In addition to the chocolate, this little restaurant offers a range of wonderful Oaxacan mezcales, which (no surprise here) can also be served in hot chocolate. The atmosphere can be hectic (especially on the weekends), with wait staff running between the tiny tables in a somewhat cramped space. It's worth the noise and buzz for the unique flavors and sugar high afterward.

Mexican

The enchantingly preserved and perennially popular ◖ **La Mariposa** (Ángela Peralta 7, tel. 442/212-1166, 8 A.M.–9:30 P.M. daily, US$4) is a casual and inexpensive place to enjoy a Mexican breakfast or lunch in a genuinely retro atmosphere. You can have a seat in the bustling dining room, a throwback to 1950s Mexico with tan vinyl chairs, Formica tabletops, and delicate wallpaper covered in roses. The vintage espresso machine is still in use and aglow with pink neon lights, from which milky coffees are served by a no-nonsense and efficient waitstaff. A nice place to eat, La Mariposa offers a simple and traditional menu containing many Mexican classics like tamales, pozole (hominy soup), and egg dishes, as well as coffee, tea, and *atole*. Their signature dish is *enchiladas queretanas* (Querétaro-style enchiladas), which are a take on the traditional *enchiladas mineras* served throughout the Bajío region. La Mariposa's traditional Mexican bakery is popular with Querétaro locals, who often order bags of sweet breads to go.

Another Querétaro classic, ◖ **Cafetería Bisquets** (Pino Suárez 7, tel. 442/214-1481, 7:30 A.M.–11 P.M., US$4) is always bustling with a local crowd. Savory *chilaquiles* with a fried egg or spicy *huevos a la cazuela* (eggs and salsa cooked in a clay pot) are two of the many delicious options on the breakfast menu. *Café con leche* (coffee with milk) is served in the traditional style; wait staff brings hot pitchers of milk and strong coffee to the table and you indicate how much you'd like of each

served in your mug. In the afternoons, *enchiladas verdes* and *enchiladas queretanas* are two solid choices, though there is also a daily *comida corrida*, which is cheap and filling. The atmosphere could not be more casual, with a small courtyard dining room as well as a larger dining room overlooking the street below. Service is efficient and professional, if not particularly verbose.

There is nothing nicer than watching the crowd mill through the Plaza de Armas while relaxing in one of the restaurants along the picturesque plaza. A classic choice for visitors to the city, **El Mesón de Chucho Roto** (Pasteur 16, Plaza de Armas, tel. 442/183-1243, 8 A.M.–11 P.M. Sun.–Thurs., 8 A.M.–midnight Fri.–Sat., US$10) serves classic Mexican food in a pleasant garden setting. With a gated patio beneath the trees of the Plaza de Armas, this restaurant is a perfect place for leisurely meal and excellent people-watching. On Sundays, El Mesón de Chucho Roto often draws a crowd of chic locals; expect to share the dining room with ladies in heels and sunglasses or men in sport coats and shiny watches. Start the meal with a *sopa azteca* or tacos with prickly pear and shrimp, or choose from a wide selection of big meat dishes, enchiladas, and other regional specialties.

Right next door, the restaurant **1810** (Andador Libertad 62, Plaza de Armas, tel. 442/214-3324, 8 A.M.–midnight Mon.–Sat., 8 A.M.–10 P.M. Sun.) offers a very similar menu and atmosphere, though it is perhaps a touch more casual than Chucho Roto. Street performers often gather in front of these two restaurants on the weekends, adding a bit more color to the scenery.

A few blocks from the Plaza de Armas, ◖ **Maria y Su Bici** (5 de Mayo, 11 A.M.–6 P.M. Mon., 8 A.M.–11 P.M. Wed.–Sat., 1–6 P.M. Sun., US$3–8) serves delicious, Oaxacan-inspired dishes in a colorful and casual setting. Here, you can sample well-made renditions of Oaxacan regional cuisine, including stuffed *chile pasilla*, quesadillas with yellow mole, and crunchy *tlayudas* made with or without meat. In addition to beer and wine, the restaurant offers a lovely selection of Oaxacan mezcal as well as various mezcal cocktails, which are served in a gourd and garnished with salt and chile powder. The dining room is small and cute, with Oaxacan decor, murals, and painted wood furniture. Service is unhurried, so come in the mood to relax. The dining room is small so there can be a wait for a seat on the weekends.

International

For something different, try **Al Bawse** (Independencia 74, tel. 442/403-4320, 2–10 P.M. Wed.–Mon., US$10), a chef-driven Lebanese restaurant in the north city center. Best for those who love to share, the menu includes lots of tasty small plates, like hummus, falafel, spiced meatballs, fattoush salad, and tabbouleh. If your appetite allows, you can follow up appetizers with a selection of main plates, including rice dishes, gyros, and marinated meats. For dessert, the restaurant's lovely selection of Middle Eastern sweets is well complemented by a strong Turkish coffee, served in a tiny pitcher. To accommodate the restaurant, the pretty foyer of a colonial home has been converted to a small dining room, with a touches of elegance like crisp cloth napkins and tables set with wine glasses. The pretty atmosphere completes the experience.

INFORMATION AND SERVICES

Querétaro is a clean, efficient, and well-organized city, with plenty of services to assist the short-term visitor. The municipal and state governments have made a strong effort to promote tourism in the city, providing plenty of free information, websites, and publications to help you plan a visit to town.

Tourist Information

The **Secretaría de Turismo de Estado de Querétaro** (State Tourism Office, Pasteur 4 Nte., tel. 442/238-5067 or toll-free Mex. tel. 888/811-6130, www.queretaro.travel, 9 A.M.–8 P.M. daily) will set you up with clear, annotated maps of the city center (in Spanish),

as well as maps of the surrounding attractions in Querétaro state. Staff is helpful and more than willing to answer questions about the city or state.

Tour Operators

There are numerous tour operators in the city of Querétaro, who can offer cultural tours of the city as well as guided tours and transportation to the countryside.

Descubre Turismo Alternativo (tel. 442/212-4565, www.descubremex.com) offers guided tours of Querétaro's city center, visiting the Santa Cruz ex-convent, the Teatro de la República, and other important sights. City tours cost around US$12 per person for two hours, though it can be more economical if you reserve a tour for a group. They can arrange for an English-speaking guide, for a slightly higher cost. If you enjoy your time with these guides, you might consider booking one of their longer tours to the Querétaro countryside or the Sierra Gorda.

Several tour operators offer motorized trolley rides *(tranvía turística)* around the city center, as well as trips to more outlying sights. If you want to pack in as much Querétaro as you can, trolley tours are probably the easiest and most efficient way to cover a lot of ground. The professional folks at **Paloma's Tours** (Corregidora s/n, tel. 442/190-6001) offer guided trolley rides around the city departing every hour on the hour 11 A.M.–7 P.M. Monday–Friday. On the weekends, tours run every 30 minutes 11 A.M.–7:30 P.M. Paloma's offers both one-hour tours of the *centro histórico* for about US$5 for adults (US$4.50 seniors and children) and two-hour tours for about US$10 adults (US$9 seniors and children). These tours depart from the Museo Regional on the street Corregidora, just across the street from the Plaza Constitución. No need to reserve a spot; just show up and climb on board.

Newspapers and Publications

An excellent guide for Querétaro's visitors, the free monthly booklet *Asomarte* (www. asomarte.com) lists cultural and arts events throughout the city of Querétaro. It is an excellent place to get a bead on the city's best happenings, as well as restaurant and hotel reviews (everything is published in Spanish), plus a handy map of the city center. *Asomarte* is distributed for free throughout the city. Look for a copies at the front desk of museums or hotels.

There are several local periodicals published in Querétaro, including the Spanish-language newspaper *Diario de Querétaro* (www.oem. com.mx/diariodequeretaro), which covers local and international news as well as arts and culture in town. Every week, the *Diario* publishes weekend itineraries for art and activities in and around the state of Querétaro, as well as a section dedicated to Mexican tourism and travel. The newspaper *El Corregidor* (www.elcorregidor.com.mx) also covers local, state, and international news, though its cultural offerings are more limited than those of *Diario*.

Money

There are large national banks throughout the city center in Querétaro, all equipped with ATM machines. Most bank branches can also exchange currency, including Mexican-owned **Banorte** (Corregidora 158 Nte., tel. 442/212-2767 or 442/212-1345, 9 A.M.–5 P.M. Mon.–Fri., 9 A.M.–2 P.M. Sat.) and **Banamex** (Av. 16 de Septiembre esq. Corregidora, tel. 442/211-9005, 9 A.M.–6 P.M. Mon.–Fri., 9 A.M.–4 P.M. Sat.), both in the *centro histórico*.

Internet Access

There are plenty of Internet cafés throughout the *centro histórico* in Querétaro, most filled with college students and teenagers (for more peace and quiet, it is best to visit them in the morning when school is in session). There are more than a dozen Internet-connected PCs at **El C@fe** (Paseo Niños Heroes 8, tel. 442/216-2967, info@michaser.com.mx, 8 A.M.–10 P.M. Mon.–Fri.), near the university, as well as laser printers. You can use the machines for about a dollar an hour. **Mundo Virtual** (Hidalgo 87A, tel. 442/212-7439, mv_qro@hotmail.com, 10 A.M.–9 P.M. daily) is downtown and also costs about a dollar per hour.

Medical and Emergency Services

The **Hospital General de Querétaro** (Av. 5 de Febrero 101, Col. Virreyes, tel. 442/216-0039 or 442/216-0664) will treat emergencies. A well-recommended private hospital, **Hospital Ángeles de Querétaro** (Bernardino del Razo 21, Col. Ensueño, tel. 442/215-5901), also takes emergencies, in addition to offering a full staff of doctors available by appointment.

Dial 066 from any ground line in Querétaro to reach the emergency response services. You can reach Querétaro's fire department *(bomberos)* directly (tel. 442/212-0627 or 442/212-3939). The Protección Civil police department (tel. 442/227-1600 or toll-free Mex. tel. 800/400-4700) will respond to emergencies.

Visas and Officialdom

The regional delegation of the **Instituto Nacional de Migración** (Calle Francisco Peñuñuri 15, Fracc. San José Inn, tel. 442/214-2712 or 442/214-1538, 9 A.M.–1 P.M. Mon.–Fri.) is in the *centro histórico*. They can extend tourist cards, process resident paperwork, and assist with lost or stolen visas. There is also an immigration office at the Querétaro airport, but this branch is only equipped to provide exit and entry permits.

GETTING THERE AND AROUND

Centrally located Querétaro is a big city and a business hub, with plenty of options for transportation to and from the city.

By Air

Transportation to Querétaro has become even more convenient with the opening of international and national flights to **Querétaro International Airport** (QRO, Carretera Estatal 200, Querétaro–Tequisquiapan 22500, tel. 442/192-5500, www.aiq.com.mx), about 32 kilometers (20 miles) outside the city center. Currently, Continental Airlines (tel. 442/314-2021 or toll-free Mex. tel. 800/900-5000) and Aeroméxico (tel. 442/215-5989 or toll-free Mex. tel. 800/021-4000) offer service to this small airport. There are daily flights to and from various locations in the United States and Mexico. Once on the ground, there is both taxi and shared shuttle service from the airport to the city center; most will drop off anywhere in town for a flat rate. The airport's taxi dispatch can be reached at tel. 442/148-6272.

Depending on where they are coming from, visitors to Querétaro may find an easier route or more inexpensive flight into Mexico through **Mexico City International Airport** (MEX), in the capital. In bus or car, the drive from Mexico City to Querétaro takes about three hours (depending on traffic leaving the city, which can be tremendous on the weekends or during road construction projects). From the airport, Primera Plus offers direct bus service from both terminals directly to the bus station in Querétaro.

By Bus

There are dozens of daily buses between Mexico City and Querétaro, as well as dozens more buses linking Querétaro to other cities in the Bajío, Guadalajara, Puerto Vallarta, and beyond. There are four major bus stations in the capital; generally, buses depart Mexico City's Terminal Norte for Querétaro. **Primera Plus** (Prol. Luis Vega y Monroy 800, Central de Autobuses, tel. 442/211-4001 or toll-free Mex. tel. 800/375-7587, primeraplus.com.mx) is one of the biggest bus lines serving Querétaro, with buses between Mexico City and Querétaro departing every 30 minutes between 6 A.M. and midnight daily. During peak hours, buses leave for Querétaro from Mexico City every 15 minutes. Primera Plus also offers direct service between both airport terminals in Mexico City and Querétaro's main bus station, departing every hour 6:30 A.M.–midnight.

Between San Miguel de Allende and Querétaro, **Herradura de Plata** (Prol. Luis Vega y Monroy 800, Central de Autobuses, Exhacienda de Carretas, tel. 442/290-0245, www.hdp.com.mx) and **Servicios Coordinados Flecha Amarilla** (Prol. Luis Vega y Monroy 800, Central de Autobuses, tel. 442/211-4001 or toll-free Mex. tel. 800/375-7587) both offer second-class service to and from Querétaro,

with buses running every 20 minutes or so 6 A.M.–10 P.M. You do not need to book ahead; just buy a ticket at the bus station.

Querétaro's Central de Autobuses (Central Bus Station, Prol. Luis Vega y Monroy 800, tel. 442/229-0181) is near the south end of the city, just off Highway 57. A taxi ride to the downtown district takes about 15 minutes from the bus station and costs about US$3.

By Car

Querétaro is on Highway 57, a major and well-marked federal thoroughfare that runs from Mexico City to the north via San Luis Potosí. From Mexico City, take the Periférico Norte to exit the city, following the signs toward Tepotzotlán. After passing through the toll booth, continue straight on Highway 57. The drive takes 2–3 hours. Once you arrive in the city, exit at Constituyentes and follow the signs downtown.

From San Miguel de Allende, the drive to Querétaro takes about 45 minutes. Follow the Salida a Querétaro southwest out of the city, continuing through the traffic circle and onto the two-lane highway (Mexico 111) for about 40 kilometers (25 miles). After passing through the small town of Buenavista, exit left on Highway 57. Continue south on Highway 57 for about 40 kilometers (25 miles), exiting either via the Boulevard Bernardo Quintana (a large avenue that runs through Querétaro and includes many popular chain stores, like Costco and Home Depot) or Constituyentes, an avenue just before the bus terminal, which leads downtown.

Like driving anywhere, driving in Querétaro can be challenging for those who don't know the city well. In addition, heavy traffic can be a problem during peak hours, since many of Querétaro's residents drive to and from their jobs. Fortunately, Querétaro is much easier to navigate than many other large Mexican cities, with decent signage and generally courteous drivers. For reference, Pasteur and Corregidora are two major avenues that lead to the city center.

If you plan to spend time outside of Querétaro's historic downtown or you would like to explore the surrounding countryside, **renting a car** can be a convenient and fairly inexpensive option. Most of Querétaro's car rental companies operate out of the international airport, though several also have offices in downtown Querétaro. **Hertz** (Carretera Estatal 200, Querétaro, 6 A.M.–9:30 P.M. daily; Bulevar Bernardo Quintana Arrioja 227, 8 A.M.–8 P.M. Mon.–Sat.) has locations at Querétaro International Airport and downtown. Hertz offers low daily rates for cars, SUVs, and minivans.

If you are arriving in Querétaro via bus, an inexpensive rental car company, **EHL Rentacar** (Terminal de Autobuses, Prol. Luis Vega y Monroy 800, Local 120, tel. 442/229-0219; Calle Brasil 39, Col. Lomas de Querétaro, tel. 442/242-5141; http://ehlrentacar.mx) has offices in the main bus terminal, as well as near the Plaza de Toros. You only need a credit card and a driver's license to get a set of wheels, but do book ahead to avoid delays. All cars have automatic transmissions and air-conditioning.

By Taxi

Within the downtown district, it is easy to get everywhere on foot. However, Querétaro is a large and urban city, with 800,000 inhabitants and sprawling residential neighborhoods. Most residents travel by car; public transportation is rather limited. As a visitor, either renting a vehicle or taking taxis is usually the easiest solution when heading outside the downtown district.

Cheap and reliable taxis circle throughout Querétaro. Fares start as low as US$2 within the city center and generally run about US$3 from the bus station to downtown. You can also call **Radio Taxi Los Arcos** (Andador 6 1916, Lomas de Casa Blanca, tel. 442/222-8293) or **Radio Taxi Querétaro** (Marqués de la Laguna 159, Lomas del Marqués, tel. 442/245-6505) if you need a lift.

VICINITY OF QUERÉTARO

You can get a glimpse of Querétaro's pre-Hispanic past at the ruin and archaeological site of **El Cerrito** (Calle de la Pirámide s/n, Corregidora, 9 A.M.–2:30 P.M. Tues.–Sun.), in the municipality of Corregidora in the Querétaro metropolitan area. The main attraction is the large pyramid of El Pueblito, a tall, terraced structure that was originally built by the Toltec people. Though a bit smaller than the massive pyramids at Teotihuacan or Cholula, this pyramid is nonetheless of impressive proportions.

After the Toltec abandoned the site, other tribes, including the Chichimeca, intermittently inhabited the same spot. When the Spanish arrived, they rechristened the region the sanctuary of the Virgen del Pueblito. In 1995, INAH began to excavate the ruin, opening it to the public. During the spring equinox, massive crowds arrive at the pyramid at El Cerrito to celebrate the special energy and change of seasons.

The site is in the municipality of **Corregidora,** about 10 kilometers (six miles) south of the city. It takes about 20 minutes to get to El Cerrito from downtown Querétaro. To get there, take the highway toward Celaya, then exit about eight kilometers (five miles) outside of Querétaro in the municipality of Corregidora or, as it is also known, El Pueblito. From there, take the Calle de la Pirámide or Don Bosco, following signs to the site.

THE BAJÍO

Tequisquiapan

A warm little town in the heart of Querétaro's fertile plains, Tequisquiapan is often considered the center of the state's wine and cheese region. Founded in 1551, Tequisquiapan has a lovely colonial atmosphere, with narrow streets and stucco houses lining the city center. It is also propitiously located above copious natural springs, some boasting thermal water. As a result, Tequis (as it is called) is greener than many Bajío locales, with large trees shading the city sidewalks and plenty of swimming pools at local hotels. This small city doesn't offer much by way of sights, per se, though its pretty downtown and country ambiance can be a relaxing place for a respite. It is an easy and pleasant day trip from San Miguel de Allende or Querétaro, as well as a nice place to stay the night after driving around the countryside.

On the weekends, Tequisquiapan gets a significant influx of tourism, mostly day-trippers from Querétaro and weekenders from Mexico City. It can actually feel somewhat bustling during a Sunday on the square, where families stroll between shops or rest on a bench with ice cream. Those who prefer utter peace and quiet may choose to visit Tequisquiapan during the week; however, many restaurants and shops may be closed or have reduced hours Monday–Wednesday.

SIGHTS
◖ Plaza Miguel Hidalgo

Plaza Miguel Hidalgo is Tequisquiapan's central square and the locus of activity in town. The colonial buildings that surround the plaza are filled with shops and restaurants. Presiding over the square, the lovely **Templo Santa María de la Asunción** began construction during the 16th century, though it wasn't finished until the end of the 19th century. This church

Tequisquiapan's laid-back central square and the delicate Templo Santa María de la Asunción

© ARTURO MEADE

THE BAJÍO

isn't an opulent baroque spectacle, like you'd find in Guanajuato or Querétaro; however, its delicately painted pink facade and large pink cupola have a stately, ladylike appeal. At the front of the church, the stone entryway surrounds a pretty, stained-glass window. Santa María de la Asunción is Tequisquiapan's patron saint, and her feast day, August 15, is merrily celebrated in the town square.

Parque La Pila

A sprawling park in the city center, Parque La Pila (Av. Ezequiel Montes, 7 A.M.–7 P.M. daily) is filled with large and stately cypress and ash trees, as well as expansive lawns. On Sundays, it is a popular place for locals to relax in the shade.

Geographical Center of Mexico

The town of Tequisquiapan in Querétaro state and the monument to El Cristo Rey del Cubilete in Guanajuato State both duly claim the honor of being Mexico's exact geographical center. It's unclear who really holds the title. However, in 1916, President Venustiano Carranza inaugurated a modernist monument in Tequisquiapan, at the spot that marks the center of the country. The monument is just a block from the Plaza Miguel Hidalgo on Centenario and 5 de Mayo.

FESTIVALS AND EVENTS

A friendly little town with a constant stream of day-tripping tourists, Tequisquiapan is always dreaming up new events and festivals to attract a little crowd. If you are going to be in the area, you can check out the website for the **state tourist bureau** (www.queretaro.travel) for information about events in Tequis.

One of the longest-running and most well-known festivals in Tequisquiapan, the **Feria de Vinos y Quesos** (Food and Wine Festival) is held every summer during the last week of May. This fun, weeklong event includes wine and cheese tasting, food-related speakers, and various live music and dance shows held in the Plaza Miguel Hidalgo and the Parque La Pila. Invited guests and food producers come to the festival from throughout the Mexican republic. It's a great weekend for food lovers and a great time to beat the May heat in Tequisquiapan, so book your hotel ahead.

SPORTS AND RECREATION

Tequisquiapan is a great place to take advantage of the countryside, either on foot, on horseback, or with a wine glass in hand. If you want to get back in the saddle, you can easily find horses for hire during the weekends in Tequisquiapan. There are usually a few tied to a tree in the town's entryway; you can stop and ask the hourly rate for a ride. For a more organized affair, the **Casa del Caballo** (Francisco Márquez 54, Barrio de la Magdalena, tel. 414/219-5648, US$12/ one hour, US$30/three hours) will take small groups out to the country with their team of trained horses and cowboys.

Tequisquiapan is a popular place to take a hot-air balloon ride, which affords incredible views of the valley surrounding Querétaro. **Globos Aerostáticos en México** (tel. 427/129-0421 or 427/129-0422, www.vuelaenglobo.com) will arrange an overnight trip to Tequisquiapan, including a night's accommodation in La Casona Tequis (or the hotel of your choice) and a break-of-dawn balloon ride the following morning. Prices depend on the hotel you choose, but hover around US$150 per person.

ACCOMMODATIONS

Tequisquiapan has been a popular weekend getaway for families from Mexico City and Querétaro since the mid-century. As a result, a lot of Tequis accommodations feel a bit like a blast from the past, where kids gather in courtyard pools and hotel rooms are equipped with worn floral bedspreads and giant TVs. However, most hotels have pools and spas (and even croquet or tennis courts), even if facilities are a bit outdated. As long as you don't expect full luxury, you won't be disappointed in Tequis, where warm weather, natural waters, and the laid-back country attitude make it a nice place to spend the evening.

THE BAJÍO

Accommodations at **Cabañas Quinta Patricia** (Nautha 7, Fracc. Nautha, tel. 414/273-0358, www.tequisquiapan.com.mx/qp, US$60 double, US$92 cabaña) are spread across a sprawling property, which includes ample lawns and a cold-water swimming pool. An old family-style resort, it has several billiard tables in the common rooms and even a small croquet field for guests. Quinta Patricia has double rooms, as well as private cabins equipped with kitchenettes and chimneys. This little resort isn't exactly luxurious, but it has the rustic charm of a country getaway. Some of the cabins can accommodate large groups of up to 10 people.

In classic Tequis style, **Hotel Hacienda Las Delicias** (5 De Mayo 1, Col. Centro, tel. 414/273-0017 or 414/273-0180, www.hotel-haciendalasdelicias.com, US$120–160) is a peaceful, family-friendly establishment with a big pool in the center of the property. The hotel's 28 guest rooms are divided into two types: colonial and modern, with the nightly rate for colonial rooms a touch more than the modern rooms. Walkways surround a sunny courtyard lawn and pool, with tables and umbrellas for relaxing, leafy trees, and palms. You can order something to eat at the hotel's restaurant and enjoy it in the garden, though the hotel's location (just a block from the central plaza) makes it easy to hit the town for eats. Rooms are nice but nothing special, with clean tile floors, large beds, and colorful bedspreads.

For Las-Vegas-meets-Rome in the Mexican countryside, check out **Villa Florencia** (Nautha 6, tel. 414/273-3029, www.villaflorencia.com.mx, US$145–175). Arriving at this palatial establishment, visitors are greeted in a giant glass atrium topped with a golden dome. The main grounds hold a cold-water pool, carefully manicured shrubbery, and well-tended lawns, all designed to look and feel like an Italian villa. The hotel's bar and restaurant are decked out with painted angels, mirrors, and neoclassical statues, overlooking the gardens and their spraying fountains. Guest rooms here are spacious and comfy (and a little less over-the-top in terms of decor), with shiny stone floors, fluffy king-sized beds, and spacious bathrooms The overall effect is a bit campy, but this hotel distinguishes itself with very friendly service and ample amenities. Prices vary here and can be lower during the weekdays.

FOOD

Despite being the center of the wine and cheese region, food in Tequisquiapan is pretty standard stuff. Around the Plaza Hidalgo, there are numerous casual restaurants serving standard Mexican fare in a casual setting. One of these restaurants is **Rincón Mexicano** (Independencia 5, 2nd floor, tel. 414/273-4678, noon–8 P.M. Mon.–Fri., 9 A.M.–11 P.M. Sat.–Sun., US$8), located on the second floor of a colonial home overlooking Plaza Hidalgo. Here, you can order generous plates of *chilaquiles, caldo tlalpeño,* enchiladas, and other Mexican specialties. The restaurant has a full bar, beer, and wine, so it's also a nice place to have a drink and a plate of guacamole. Food isn't particularly memorable, but Rincón

© ARTURO MEADE

There are dozens of cafés and restaurants ringing Tequisquiapan's central square.

Mexicano's patio dining room is a great place to dine in the shade while enjoying a view of the central square.

Tequisquiapan's most popular eatery is **La Charamusca** (Ezequiel Montes 1, tel. 414/273-0781, 8 A.M.–11 P.M. daily, US$5). During the weekends, this large cafeteria and bakery is filled with tourists filling up on an inexpensive lunch or snack. The spacious dining hall is more functional than charming, with doors that open onto Plaza Hidalgo. Specializing in Mexican food, La Charamusca serves enchiladas, *chilaquiles,* and other Mexican dishes, as well as a tasty selection of *pan de dulce* and coffee. There is a take-out only bakery in the back of the restaurant, which is flocked by crowds of bread-lovers on the weekends.

Just off the main plaza on a small pedestrian street, **La Charcutería** (Andador Juárez 5, Plaza Santa Rosa, tel. 414/273-2210, 1–11 P.M. Wed.–Sun., US$6) is a new addition to Querétaro's bars and restaurants, offering a menu and atmosphere that complement the city's location in a developing wine region. Here, you can order regional cheeses and homemade pâté, quiches, baguette sandwiches, and other Continental-inspired small plates. They also have a selection of meats and pastas on the menu, as well as a wine list including local names. Inside the restaurant, there are small wooden tables in a cozy setting. If the weather is sunny, it is nicer to sit outside, where you can dine alfresco with a view of the square.

If you spend the evening in Tequisquiapan, drop by the casual wine shop and bar **Todos a Beber** (Manuel Mateus 2, tel. 414/273-6420, www.todosabeber.com, 3–10 P.M. Wed.–Thurs., 1 P.M.–1 A.M. Fri.–Sat., 1–6 P.M. Sun.). There are more than 400 well-priced bottles of wine from various regions. Customers simply buy the bottle they'd like to sip and then take it home or drink it at one of the small wooden tables inside. If you choose to drink at the bar, Todos a Beber charges a small corkage fee (about US$3.50), which includes glassware and table service. In the evenings, there is a small menu of tapas, plus live music on Saturday nights. The atmosphere here is extremely

casual, and the owners often sit among the crowd at one of the bar's tall tables.

Just across the plaza, **Freixenet World's Wine Bar** (Andador 20 de Noviembre s/n, tel. 414/273-3995, 2–10 P.M. Tues.–Thurs. and Sun., 4 P.M.–2 A.M. Fri.–Sat.) is run by the sparkling wine producer Cavas Freixenet. Here, you can order bottles and half-bottles of Freixenet's tasty sparkling wine, as well as glasses of champagne and mimosas. The decor is tasteful, with many blonde wood tables and chairs arranged around a spacious modern dining room. World's Wine Bar is busy on the weekend evenings; come during the afternoon or during the week and you may be one of only a few people there.

INFORMATION AND SERVICES

Though small, Tequisquiapan is a friendly town and well equipped to receive its many weekly visitors. Tequisquiapan's helpful tourist office, **Dirección de Turismo de Tequisquiapan** (Independencia 1, tel. 414/273-0295, turismo@tequis.info, 9 A.M.–7 P.M. Sun.–Fri., 9 A.M.–9 P.M. Sat.), is right on the main plaza. The friendly Spanish-speaking representatives can answer questions and provide you with an annotated map and booklet about the town, as well as maps of the Querétaro countryside. Although they do not provide walking tours of the city, the tourist office can recommend several tour operators that do.

In the central square, there is a **Bancomer** branch (Independencia 5, 8:30 A.M.–4 P.M. Mon.–Fri.) with ATMs open 24 hours, located just next to the tourist office and the restaurant Rincón Mexicano. There is also a **Banamex** branch (Niños Heroes 40, tel. 414/273-0808, 9 A.M.–4 P.M. Mon.–Sat.) with ATMs right behind the central plaza, near the monument to the geographic center of Mexico.

GETTING THERE AND AROUND

There are daily buses between Querétaro and Tequisquiapan, but the easiest and most popular way to get there is by car. From the city of Querétaro, it is an easy 45-minute drive to Tequis. From San Miguel de Allende, you can get to Tequisquiapan in about twice that time.

By Bus
Although the majority of Tequisquiapan tourists drive into town, you can also catch a bus from Querétaro's bus station to Tequisquiapan with **Transportes Queretanos Flecha Azul** (Plaza Capuchinas 105, Plazas del Sol, tel. 442/229-0102, www.flecha-azul.com.mx). From Mexico City, the bus line **ETN** (Central de Autobuses Tequisquiapan, Carretera San Juan del Río-Xilitla s/n, tel. 414/273-3797 or 414/273-3623, toll-free Mex. tel. 800/800-

0368, tequis@etn.com.mx) offers numerous daily buses between the Terminal Norte in the capital and the bus station in Tequisquiapan. The trip takes about three hours.

By Car
The most direct way to get to Tequisquiapan is to take Highway 57 México-Querétaro (south from Querétaro or San Miguel and north from Mexico City). Exit at the signs for the Sierra Gorda and take Highway 120 north until you reach Tequisquiapan. If you are feeling more adventurous, pick up a map from the tourist office and take Highway 200 from Querétaro to Tequisquiapan, traveling past the Querétaro airport along smaller highways.

Wine and Cheese Route

The Bajío has a long history as an agricultural center; today, it is building on that tradition with a new emphasis on artisan and locally produced foods. In a nice day trip from the city of Querétaro or San Miguel de Allende, visitors can take a tour of the region's ranches and wineries, stopping to rest or eat in the small towns of Tequisquiapan or Bernal. You must pass through some industrial towns on your way, but the overall landscapes are lovely and interesting.

If you are thinking about visiting Querétaro's countryside, stop by the state tourist office in the city, **Secretaría de Turismo de Estado de Querétaro** (Pasteur 4 Nte., tel. 442/238-5067 or toll-free Mex. tel. 888/811-6130, www.queretaro.travel, 9 A.M.–8 P.M. daily). The tourist office can provide you with an annotated map of the region, which includes the ranches and wineries open to the public, as well as the small towns of Tequisquiapan and Bernal.

WINERIES
Wine arrived in Mexico along with the Spanish; it has been produced throughout the country since the colonial era. Though Mexico has not been traditionally recognized as a

wine-producing region, things have begun to change. Today, Baja California's hearty wines have become more internationally renowned, while vineyards in the states of Aguascalientes and Chihuahua also produce some excellent vintages. In the Bajío, grape growing and wine producing are nascent industries, yet appear poised for expansion. Today, there are a few wineries in the region, worth a visit when driving through the state of Querétaro.

Though it's surrounded by rather unappealing ranch land, you really get an authentic wine country feeling once inside **Viñedos La Redonda** (Carretera San Juan del Río, Km 33.5, Ezequiel Montes, tel. 441/277-1444, www.laredonda.com.mx, 10 A.M.–5 P.M. daily). From off the industrial highway near the town of Ezequiel Montes, you suddenly find yourself surrounded by the gentle green leaves of grapevines. La Redonda operates a small country store at the front of the property, where you can buy bottles of the wines as well as other local products. However, the real action takes place toward the back of the property. Follow the small road to the country-style barn to find a lovely patio, a small Italian restaurant, and a bar where you can sample small glasses of La

© ARTURO MEADE

The grounds at Viñedos La Redonda have a pleasant wine-country feeling.

Redonda's wines for about US$1.50. Many of the wines are young, but robust and tasty. For Mexican bottles, they can also be rather inexpensive. During the weekends, there are ongoing free tours of the vineyard noon–4 P.M., plus tours at 1 P.M. during the week. The entire place can be rented for special events.

A well-known producer of sparkling wine, **Cavas de Freixenet** (Carretera San Juan del Río-Cadereyta, Km 40.5, Ezequiel Montes, Querétaro, tel. 441/277-0147, www.freixenetmexico.com.mx) has a long history in Querétaro, predating most of the state's other vineyards. The massive cellars draw hordes of tourists every week, where there are tours of the facilities, frequent weekend festivals, and a big tasting room (no free tastings, though). There are interesting tours of the wine cellars every day at 12:30 P.M., 1 P.M., and 3 P.M. during the week, and tours every hour 11 A.M.–5 P.M. Saturday and Sunday). Freixenet also offers a more intensive tour through the biweekly program called "A Day in the Cellar," as well as numerous annual events, like the Paella Festival

in the spring. On the weekends, the scene can be rather overwhelming, as huge groups of local families descend upon the Freixenet complex to slurp up champagne. There are plenty of tables around the central courtyard where visitors can consume their bottle of bubbly; you can also order wine by the glass at the Freixenet store.

The Freixenet cellars are on the highway between Tequisquiapan and Cadereyta, just past the town of Ezequiel Montes. After you exit Ezequiel Montes, Cavas de Freixenet is about five minutes down the road on the right-hand side. There aren't many vines around the Freixenet offices and cellars as you'd see at La Redonda, though you will enjoy some bubbly.

Just down the road from Freixenet, **Los Azteca Hacienda Mexicana** (Carretera San Juan del Río-Cadereyta, Km 40, Ezequiel Montes, Querétaro, tel. 441/277-2978, www.losazteca.com, 9 A.M.–6 P.M. daily) is an 18th-century hacienda and ranch open to the public. Visitors can tour the property, which includes a small chapel, stables, and vineyards. Tours cost about US$4 per person and include a chance to visit the wine cellars. More central Mexico than Napa Valley, Los Azteca doesn't have the classic wine region atmosphere—but that's OK! The old hacienda makes a nice backdrop for wine drinking and the place is great for families. It is also a popular spot for Querétaro locals on the weekend.

CHEESE PRODUCERS

What goes better with wine than cheese? The state of Querétaro has brought this eternal pairing to central Mexico. When driving through Querétaro's countryside, you can stop in at one of many small cheese factories around the state, where you sample the local products and, in some cases, take a tour of the ranch. On Sundays, the highways can get quite busy, as Querétaro families do a turn around the countryside with their kids.

On the highway to Tequisquiapan from the city of Querétaro, **Quesos VAI** (Carretera Querétaro-Tequisquiapan, Km 30, Municipio de Colón, tel. 442/190-7618, http://quesos-vai.com, 8 A.M.–6 P.M. daily) is one of the most well-known cheese factories in the state of Querétaro. Though originally founded by a Spanish cheese-maker, VAI is a local Mexican-owned business today. All their cheese is produced by the hundreds of sheep and cows on VAI's Querétaro ranch. Their wonderful roadside food shop sells VAI-produced products, including provolone- and manchego-style cheeses, as well as other artisan and local products, like homemade *cajeta,* jams, and honey, as well as wines by La Redonda.

Fun for families (though a bit hokey for adults), tours of the cheese-making process and the ranch are offered. They cost about US$2 and last an hour or so, including samples of assorted VAI cheeses. The best part of the tour is getting to visit the ranch's live animals, including a large bovine who is particularly fond of visitors. If so inclined, you can buy a bottle of wine and a piece of cheese from VAI's small and nicely stocked shop, then sit amid the sheep and chickens while you eat it.

© ARTURO MEADE

A flock of sheep enjoy the sunshine at Quesos VAI.

Querétaro's certified organic dairy brand, Flor de Alfalfa, is produced at **Rancho la Hondonada** (Carretera Ajuchitlán-Colón, Km 9.2, tel. 419/292-0204 or toll-free Mex. tel. 800/288-2662, www.saberysabor.com.mx), just a bit off the beaten track. Visitors must take the highway toward Bernal and then turn off again on the highway toward Ajuchitlán to reach this extensive ranch. Once there, you'll definitely feel you're out in the country. This green ranch is home to dozens of organically raised cows and chickens, as well as the company's cheese factory. There are tours of the ranch facilities at 10 A.M. and noon on Saturday and 11 A.M. and 1 P.M. on Sunday, or any other day by appointment. Tours will take you to the duck pond, the pasture, and the museum of cheese, toward the back of the property. At the Flor de Alfalfa store, you can pick up the company's aged and fresh cheese, as well as other dairy products. The thick yogurt is especially tasty.

Rancho San Josemaría (Carretera Querétaro-San Luis Potosí, Km 22.5,

Santa Rosa de Jáuregui, tel. 442/130-2161, www.quesosdeoveja.com) produces a line of artisan sheep's milk cheeses. The friendly proprietors attend visitors and give guided tours of their pretty ranch by appointment. Walk among a flock of adorable brown and white sheep and learn about the cheese-making process. All tours end with a cheese tasting; the ranch produces manchego-style and other aged cheeses. To get to Rancho San Josemaría, exit the Querétaro–San Luis Potosí Highway 57 toward Santa Rosa Jáuregui.

The wine, cheese, and local food industry in Querétaro is beginning to blossom. In addition to the ranches listed above, several more farms are open to the public. Drop into the **tourist office** in Querétaro, where they can give you a map of the tourist-friendly ranches and other regional highlights.

San Sebastián Bernal

The tiny town of San Sebastián Bernal (usually referred to as just Bernal) is a lovely colonial town. Founded in 1642, Bernal was recently inducted into Mexico's Pueblos Mágicos program, designed to recognize special or historic cities across the country. Bernal is indeed a magic place, with a small and charming city center boasting impressive views of a towering monolith. It can be a wonderful place to stop for lunch or to spend a quiet evening.

SIGHTS
◖ Peña de Bernal

The Peña de Bernal is one of the world's largest monoliths, rising above the semi-arid plains of Querétaro state with natural majesty and power. On clear days, you can see the rock's pointed crown for miles. Many believe the *peña* (rock) has healing energy, and it is a popular pilgrimage site during the spring equinox. However, it is a stunning sight to behold at any time of year.

The monolith is Bernal's most famous and unmistakable sight. Measuring over 335 meters, the Peña de Bernal is one of the tallest and largest rocks in the world. According to the Querétaro tourist office, only the Rock of Gibraltar and Rio de Janeiro's Sugar Loaf are taller. On the weekends, the *peña* is illuminated by floodlights, so you can enjoy its dramatic face under a canopy of stars.

For those who'd like to feel Bernal's healing energy for themselves, there is a trail leading to a shoulder of the monolith, which takes about an hour or two to hike. (Several tour companies will guide you to the monolith's shoulder, but you can easily make the journey on your own.) Once at the top of the trail, you can sit on a sloping ledge of the *peña* and gaze over the valley below. The views are beautiful and

The Peña de Bernal is one of the world's largest monoliths.

© ARTURO MEADE

THE BAJÍO

sweeping. Professional climbers are permitted to scale the tip of the monolith to its peak, though they must advise the municipal offices in the city center before setting up the climb.

If you'd like to climb the monolith in the company of a trained guide, contact **La Peña Tours** (Independencia 4, Bernal, Ezequiel Montes, tel. 441/296-7398, cell tel. 442/101-4821, www.lapeniatours.com). They can arrange for individual or group tours to the top of the rock, as well as rock climbing and rappelling adventures.

Parroquia de San Sebastián

Constructed 1700–1725, Bernal's pretty parish church, the Parroquia de San Sebastián (Plaza Principal s/n, 9 A.M.–7 P.M. daily), stands right in the center of the town square. Although the church does not represent any dominant architectural style, it has a small neoclassical facade, set against its striking yellow walls and bold brick-red trim. The work of indigenous architects is visible in the bell tower.

The Parroquia de San Sebastián stands in Bernal's charming central plaza.

El Castillo

Of the many lovely buildings that surround Bernal's main square, El Castillo (The Castle) is clearly the most unusual. This 17th-century structure was built in typical Spanish colonial style, with an arched arcade and painted facade. At the top of the tower, there is a German-made clock, added along with the bell tower in commemoration of the new century. The lovely red-and-white stucco finish makes El Castillo stand out. Today, it houses Bernal's municipal offices.

Capilla de las Ánimas

At the foot of the monolith, the Capilla de las Ánimas is a small country chapel with yellow stucco walls and brick-red trim. According to local legend, a local merchant took refuge from thieves in the spot where the chapel now stands. He prayed to the souls in purgatory to keep him safe. In appreciation, he began the construction of a church at the site. Built in the 18th century, the church boasts a little but lovely domed ceiling and the three original church bells, hanging over the entryway. The country setting makes this church particularly appealing.

Sightseeing and Cultural Tours

A tour company based in the city of Querétaro, **Querétaro Lindo** (Plaza Zimapán 72, Plazas del Sol 2da. Sección, tel. 442/213-8287, 442/341-8659, or 442/341-8661, www.queretarolindo.com) specializes in cultural tours of the city; however, they also offer tours from the city to Bernal, including transportation and a guide. If you'd like to visit Bernal without all the hassle of renting a car and consulting maps, Querétaro Lindo will cover the logistics.

La Peña Tours (Independencia 4, Bernal, Ezequiel Montes, tel. 441/296-7398, cell tel. 442/101-4821, www.lapeniatours.com) can arrange for a day trip around the wine and cheese region or cultural tours of Bernal. A tour of the sights in Bernal lasts about an hour and costs about US$6 per person, while a tour of the country takes about three hours and costs about US$15.

THE BAJÍO

© ARTURO MEADE

El Castillo is one of the more unusual structures in Bernal's central square.

FESTIVALS AND EVENTS

At the Peña de Bernal, the **spring equinox,** or March 21, is considered a very powerful day to visit the monolith. The event is celebrated annually with pre-Hispanic rituals in town and massive groups of pilgrims heading the top of the rock, most dressed in white. In the evening, the monolith is lit up and fireworks fill the sky. For those who'd like to experience the healing energy of Bernal, the equinox is an exciting time to visit. At the same time, the town of Bernal is incredibly crowded and bustling during the event, so book your hotel ahead of time or plan to stay in nearby Querétaro or Tequisquiapan.

At the beginning of May, the **Fiesta de la Santa Cruz** (Day of the Holy Cross) is another nice event in the town of Bernal. In commemoration, Bernal locals head to the top of the monolith, where they install a Christian cross, also recognized by indigenous cultures as an *árbol de la vida* (tree of life).

SHOPPING

There are many small **souvenir shops** around Bernal's central plaza, most catering to Querétaro families who have come to Bernal on a day trip. These little stores generally carry a mix of *artesanías,* trinkets, and clothing, some offering a nicer selection than others. In terms of traditional crafts, wool is considered a specialty in Bernal, so many people like to shop for ponchos, sweaters, and other wool products in town.

A small storefront with a nice selection of crafts, **Pisos y Rebubrimientos de Barro Colonial** (Iturbide 1, tel. 441/296-4146, generally noon–3 P.M. Mon.–Fri., 10 A.M.–6 P.M. Sat.–Sun.) has some lovely wool ponchos, as well as hand-stitched wool stuffed animals. They also carry shawls and textile tablecloths from the artisans of Aguascalientes. The store's owners do most of their business on the weekends, though you may find them open for a few hours during the week.

ACCOMMODATIONS

Comfortable and well located, **Casa Tsaya Hotel** (Ignacio Zaragoza 6, tel. 441/296-4041, www.casatsaya.com, US$52) is an inexpensive guesthouse right in the center of Bernal's downtown. Located in a lovely colonial mansion with a terra-cotta and ceramic tile facade, this hotel's 14 guest rooms are small and not particularly luxurious, though each boasts a television and private bath. Rooms surrounding the courtyard and restaurant may be a bit noisier during the weekends, so choose a room in the back promenade. From here, you can see the Peña de Bernal from the outdoor hallways. Service is incredibly friendly and the location could not be better, just steps away from Bernal's main plaza.

If you are planning a romantic getaway to the country or a family trip to La Peña de Bernal, **C Casa Mateo** (5 de Mayo s/n, esq. Colón, tel. 441/296-4472, www.hotel-casamateo.com.mx, US$105–120) is a well-designed boutique hotel in the very center of Bernal. Guest rooms are comfortable and tastefully furnished, equipped with ceramic floors, fireplaces, down comforters, and modern bathrooms. Though each room is slightly different from the next, decor is pleasingly minimalist throughout the hotel; family-style rooms have a loft bed for the kids. In the center of the hotel, there are nice views of the *peña* rising above a small swimming pool and lawn. Just a block from the main plaza, this hotel is right in the middle of town but feels secluded and private. Service is friendly and attentive.

FOOD

El Mezquite (5 de Mayo s/n, tel. 441/296-4146, 9 a.m.–6:30 p.m. Sat.–Sun.) is the most popular restaurant in Bernal, and it is easy to see why. This open-air patio has the best view in town, overlooking the *peña*. Despite the million-dollar view, El Mezquite is a casual, inexpensive, and family-oriented restaurant, where big groups of weekenders convene for a leisurely afternoon meal. On the patio dining room, plastic tables are covered with colorful oilcloths and shaded by the large tree that is the restaurant's namesake. The menu is standard Mexican fare, with meat, beans, and rice dominating the menu. Food is tasty enough and the view is unbeatable. To get to this convivial spot, look for a small colonial plaza on 5 de Mayo, just off the main square. The restaurant is in the patio behind the gift shops (there are signs at the entryway).

Just inside the Casa Tsaya Hotel, the surprisingly chic **C Arrayán** (Ignacio Zaragoza 6, tel. 441/296-4041, 1–9 p.m.Mon.–Tues. and Thurs., 1–11 p.m. Sat.–Sun., US$12) serves creative Mexican-inspired dishes, combining traditional ingredients with contemporary preparations. The menu includes appealing plates like shrimp in vanilla and turkey with hibiscus sauce, which are exotic yet tasty. An assortment of pastas and salads round out the menu, and there are a few options that lean more toward traditional than experimental, such as *arrachera* with beans and guacamole. A particular delight of dining here is the drink menu, which includes numerous Mexican-made small-batch beers, mezcal, tequila, and Mexican wines. The street-side dining room is clean and modern, with contemporary art on the walls. If you'd like a more traditional setting, the restaurant has a second dining room in the hotel's colonial courtyard.

Just next door to Arrayán, **Piave** (Ignacio Zaragoza 13, tel. 441/296-4008, 1–10 p.m. Fri.–Sun., US$8) is an Italian joint in a crumbling 18th-century building. The atmosphere is decidedly cozy, with wooden tables and window seats overlooking the Plaza Baratillo and its old stone fountain. A basket of fresh bread comes to the table as soon as you sit down. The appealing menu offers Italian specialties like lasagna, ravioli, meat, and risotto, as well as tasty wood-fired pizzas. Here, the Italian owner brings a traditional flair to the food, which you can wash down with a nice glass of red.

INFORMATION AND SERVICES

Technically a part of the municipality of Ezequiel Montes, Bernal is a small town—even smaller than its neighbor, Tequisquiapan. Although Bernal is well accustomed to tourism, there are few services here. The tourist office is actually located in the industrial city of Ezequiel Montes (the municipality to which Bernal pertains). To make things all the more complicated, many shops and restaurants are closed during the week (Bernal's tourism is principally weekenders). The upshot of visiting Bernal from Monday through Friday is that you will enjoy the tranquility of a sleepy country town.

Money

There are no banks in Bernal; however, there is one ATM in the city's central plaza. If you need to visit a bank or change money, the closest banks are in downtown Ezequiel Montes. Right on the main highway passing through Ezequiel Montes, there is a Banamex branch (Av. Constituyentes 114-A, tel. 441/277-1279, 9 A.M.–4 P.M. Mon.–Fri.), with ATMs, currency exchange, and other services.

Emergency Services

You can reach Bernal's police department at tel. 441/277-0019 or 441/277-0707.

GETTING THERE AND AROUND

There are no taxis in Bernal, nor is there extensive bus service around the city. Fortunately, it is very easy to get around this small city on foot. To get to Bernal from Querétaro, take Highway 57 Mexico–Querétaro and exit at the signs for Sierra Gorda. From there, take State Highway 100 for about 40 kilometers (25 miles) until you reach Bernal.

If you are coming from Tequisquiapan, follow the highway toward Cadereyta, passing through the industrial town of Ezequiel Montes. Continue on the highway past Cavas de Freixenet until you reach a fork in the road; signs indicate that Bernal is to the left, or east, along a small two-lane highway. You will be able to see the monolith as you approach the town.

THE BAJÍO

Dolores Hidalgo

The small city of Dolores Hidalgo is about 32 kilometers (20 miles) northeast of San Miguel de Allende and about 48 kilometers (30 miles) southeast of Guanajuato. The city is well known for its lovely ceramic artisan work, as well as for its important role during the Mexican War of Independence. There are a number of small but interesting sights in the city's downtown district, as well as good shopping for pottery and hand-painted ceramic tiles. If rather less spectacular than its neighbors, San Miguel de Allende and Guanajuato, Dolores has nonetheless won some loyal fans with its low-key and traditionally Mexican atmosphere.

Most of the activity in Dolores Hidalgo is concentrated in the few blocks around the city center. The exceptions are the ceramics workshops along the highways near town, which also draw their share of visitors. If you come to Dolores by bus, the terminal is conveniently located just a few blocks from the city's central square. From there, almost everything is accessible on foot.

HISTORY

An early settlement in the Bajío region, the town of Cocomacán (today, Dolores Hidalgo) was founded in the 1540s. Cocomacán, meaning "place where they hunt herons" in Otomí, was part of a large ranch, Hacienda de la Erre, which originally fell under the jurisdiction of San Miguel El Grande. In 1710, La Erre was incorporated into the new parish of Nuestra Señora de los Dolores (Our Lady of Sorrows). The first stone was laid for Dolores's parish church on February 2, 1712.

A small agricultural outpost in the state of Guanajuato, Dolores would not be well known if it weren't for its native son, Miguel Hidalgo, and his role in the Mexican War of

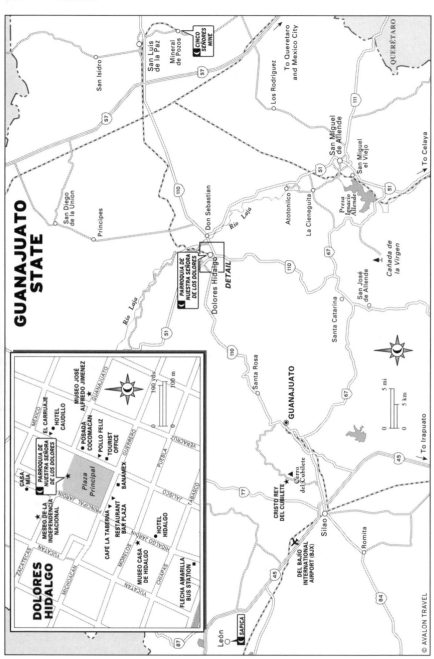

GUANAJUATO STATE

QUERÉTARO

CINCO SEÑORES MINE

San Isidro

San Luis de la Paz

Mineral de Pozos

57

To Queretaro and Mexico City

Los Rodriguez

111

San Miguel de Allende

57

San Diego de la Unión

Principes

110

Don Sebastian

Río Laja

51

PARROQUIA DE NUESTRA SEÑORA DE LOS DOLORES

Dolores Hidalgo

DETAIL

San Miguel el Viejo

51

To Celaya

Atotonilco

La Cieneguita

Presa Ignacio Allende

67

San José de Allende

Cañada de la Virgen

Santa Catarina

110

110

Río Laja

51

Santa Rosa

GUANAJUATO

67

5 mi

0   5

5 km
0   5

León

87

SAPICA

45

DEL BAJÍO INTERNATIONAL AIRPORT (BJX)

Silao

Romita

84

To Irapuato

45

CRISTO REY DEL CUBILETE

Cerro del Cubilete

77

© AVALON TRAVEL

DOLORES HIDALGO

ZACATECAS

YUCATAN

MICHOACAN

MORELOS

MEXICO

CASA MÍA

PARROQUIA DE NUESTRA SEÑORA DE LOS DOLORES

MUSEO DE LA INDEPENDENCIA NACIONAL

PRINCIPAL

JARDIN

Plaza Principal

EL CARRUAJE

HOTEL CAUDILLO

MUSEO JOSÉ ALFREDO JIMENEZ

GUANAJUATO

POSADA COCOMACÁN

POLLO FELIZ

TOURIST OFFICE

BANAMEX

VERACRUZ

PUEBLA

GUERRERO

CAFÉ LA TABERNA

RESTAURANT BAR PLAZA

HOTEL HIDALGO

HIDALGO   JARDIN

JALISCO

TABASCO

MUSEO CASA DE HIDALGO

YUCATAN

CHIAPAS

FLECHA AMARILLA BUS STATION

100 yds
100 m

Independence. The parish priest of Dolores, Miguel Hidalgo was an early conspirator against the Spanish rule. He attended the famous meetings in Querétaro and San Miguel de Allende, hosted by wealthy criollo families who wished to free Mexico from the tightening grip of the Spanish crown. Hidalgo was an important element to the conspiracy, as he was extremely popular with the large mestizo and indigenous population that lived in and around Dolores.

In 1810, Spanish royalists uncovered the criollo plot against the crown. To avoid arrest, the Mexican conspirators quickly jumped to action, and Miguel Hidalgo was named general of the Mexican army. Though he was only a parish priest with no formal experience in war, Hidalgo oversaw an army that included numerous high-ranking Queen's Dragoon Army officers, like Ignacio Allende. To rally soldiers to the cause, Hidalgo arrived on the steps of Dolores parish on September 16, 1810, where he issued his famous cry, *"¡Viva México!"* From there, he rode with his cavalry to San Miguel de Allende, which became the first town to fall (though peacefully) in the independence movement. Thereafter, the War of Independence was arduous and protracted. Hidalgo himself was captured and executed in July 1811. The Mexican army finally took the city of Dolores on September 10, 1811, almost a full year after Hidalgo issued the call to arms.

After the war ended, the city was renamed Dolores Hidalgo on May 21, 1824. Regarded as the birthplace of an independent Mexico, Dolores Hidalgo continues to be an important site in the country's history. Many of Mexico's important leaders have passed through here during their tenure, and each Mexican president comes to celebrate at least one independence day in town. The *grito* (the nickname for the annual reenactment of Hidalgo's cry on Día de la Independencia of each year, delivered by the town's mayor) in Dolores always draws big crowds.

SIGHTS
Plaza Principal

Like many cities, the downtown district in Dolores Hidalgo is organized around a *plaza principal* (central square). The plaza is at the heart of the city's busiest commercial zone, and it is a popular spot with local families. In the very center of the plaza, there is a bronze statue of the famous pastor, Miguel Hidalgo, originally commissioned by President Benito Juárez. On the west side, the plaza is bordered by the **Casa de Visitas** (Plaza Principal 25), an 18th-century mansion. During the War of Independence, Dolores's Spanish governor and his wife were held in the Casa de Visitas as prisoners of the rebel army.

◖ Parroquia de Nuestra Señora de los Dolores

One of the most famous churches in all of Mexico, the Parroquia de Nuestra Señora de los Dolores (Parish of Our Lady of Sorrows, Plaza Principal s/n, generally 8 a.m.–8 p.m. daily) is the jewel of Dolores Hidalgo's central

From the steps of Dolores Hidalgo's parish, Father Miguel Hidalgo raised his famous cry, "¡Viva México!"

square. This impressive sandstone church has an elaborate churrigueresque facade, topped by two soaring bell towers. Inside, wood floors and rows of creaky wood pews stand before a neoclassical altar. In the left transept, there is an ornate, hand-carved baroque altar washed in gold leaf. Even more impressive is the walnut altar to the right, which has been carefully carved in wood but left without gold leaf or paint. Not only is the untreated wood especially beautiful, it really illustrates the incredible craftsmanship behind many of Mexico's baroque altarpieces. On your way out, note the large organ in the balcony over the entryway.

Museo Casa de Hidalgo

Just a block from the central square, the Museo Casa de Hidalgo (Calle Morelos 1, tel. 418/182-0171, www.inah.gob.mx, 10 A.M.–5:45 P.M. Tues.–Sat., 9 A.M.–4:45 P.M. Sun., US$2.50), also known as the Casa de Diezmo, is the former home of Mexico's most famous pastor, Miguel Hidalgo. This large colonial building has been outfitted with period furnishings and didactic texts about the life of the parish priest. The kitchen is particularly interesting. There is also a small collection of artifacts from the War of Independence, including an antique banner with the image of the Virgen de Guadalupe—Father Hidalgo's improvised flag for the Mexican army. Don't bother paying the extra camera fee; most of the scenery is behind glass.

Museo de la Independencia Nacional

The sprawling Museo de la Independencia Nacional (National Independence Museum, Zacatecas 6, tel. 418/182-0193, ext. 150, 9 A.M.–5 P.M. Mon.–Sat., 9 A.M.–3 P.M. Sun., US$1) is in the city's former jailhouse. From this very building, Miguel Hidalgo freed the city's prisoners before issuing his famous *grito,* or call for independence, from the steps of the parish church. Today, the former jail is filled with dioramas and colorful oil paintings depicting scenes from the War of Independence, accompanied by long didactic texts, principally

in Spanish. There are also a few artifacts from the era, including old coins and weapons used in the rebellion, as well as facsimiles of famous documents signed by Miguel Hidalgo. This spacious and rather unusual museum drags on a bit too long, though it's not an unworthy pit stop if you are in town.

Museo José Alfredo Jiménez

The great *ranchera* singer and songwriter José Alfredo Jiménez was born to a middle-class family in Dolores Hidalgo. Located in the composer's childhood home, the charming Museo José Alfredo Jiménez (Guanajuato 13, tel. 418/154-4070, www.museojosealfredojimenez.com, 10 A.M.–5 P.M. Tues.–Sun., US$3) offers a nostalgic look into the life of the legend. Through photographs, quotes, and artifacts, the museum chronicles the life of this gentleman singer, showing his humble beginnings as a musician in Mexico City and highlighting his notable influence on traditional *ranchera* music. Alfredo's old family house provides a

altar honoring José Alfredo Jiménez, the great Mexican songwriter

THE BAJÍO

JOSÉ ALFREDO JIMÉNEZ

José Alfredo Jiménez was born in 1926 to a middle-class family in the small town of Dolores Hidalgo. With no formal training as a musician – or even the ability to play an instrument – Jiménez became one the most prolific and beloved songwriters in Mexican history.

Jiménez began composing songs during childhood in Dolores. After the death of his father, his family relocated to Mexico City. As a young man, he wrote and performed throughout the capital, singing on the radio with the group Los Rebeldes in 1948. He rose to prominence with the breakthrough hit "Yo" two years later. Thereafter, he continued to pen one hit song after another. As his fame grew, he appeared in cinema, radio, and television, frequently traveling overseas to perform.

Jiménez wrote music principally within the traditional Mexican genre *ranchera*, and his melodic songs recall a romantic Mexico of cantinas, tequila, serenades, small towns, and country life. Jiménez wrote hundreds of songs during his lifetime, which were interpreted by some of the biggest names in Mexican music, such as Pedro Infante, Lola Beltran, Javier Solís, and Lucha Villa. Jiménez himself also performed his own songs, often dressed in a *charro* suit and serape. Visitors to the Bajío may be particularly interested in Jiménez's wonderful tribute to his home state, the song "Caminos de Guanajuato." In this lovely and well-known ballad, Jiménez immortalizes the Bajío cities of León, Salamanca, and Santa Rosa, as well as his beloved home town of Dolores Hidalgo.

Like many of Mexico's Golden Age stars, Jiménez died at an early age, succumbing to hepatitis at the age of 47. Today, José Alfredo Jiménez's body is buried in the cemetery of Dolores Hidalgo, his grave lovingly adorned with a giant concrete sombrero and tiled serape. The city recently inaugurated a new annual festival in the songwriter's honor, which includes music and art events, as well as lectures.

THE BAJÍO

nice backdrop to the singer's life story. In the back, the family's original blue-and-white tiled kitchen is still intact. Just beside the kitchen, the museum operates a small café where you can soak up the ambiance with a coffee and snack. For fans of this celebrated composer, the Museo José Alfredo Jiménez is a must-see; however, even those who aren't familiar with Jiménez's music may still get a charge out of the exhibits about his life, as well as artifacts like his beautiful old *charro* suits with silver buttons, old letters and telegrams, and photographs from the 1950s Golden Era of Mexican cinema.

Tomb of José Alfredo Jiménez

José Alfredo Jiménez's original tombstone was just a simple granite block decorated with a quote from one of his most famous songs, "Caminos de Guanajuato." It read, *La vida no vale nada* ("Life is worth nothing"). Today, the simple headstone that once marked his resting place has been replaced by a giant concrete sombrero and serape, decorated with multicolor ceramic tiles from Dolores. Visitors can walk inside the serape to leave flowers at the grave of the singer. Beloved throughout the country, José Alfredo's unique tomb receives its fair share of visitors each year.

SHOPPING

Talavera, a type of hand-painted ceramic work, has been produced in several Mexican states since the 16th century. After the conquest, the Spanish introduced tin glazing to indigenous artisans, who were already skilled potters. The result was a new and wholly Mexican craft tradition, based on both New World and Old World craft. While the state of Puebla is home to the oldest talavera workshops in Mexico, the town of Dolores began its line of ceramics a bit later, under the direction of famous pastor Miguel Hidalgo. Generally speaking, the painting on Dolores's ceramics is freer and less detailed than the work produced in Puebla. As a result, it usually is far less expensive as well. While not as painstakingly created, the saturated colors and whimsical designs from Dolores can be incredibly sophisticated and charming. Today, Dolores is a major exporter of ceramic tile and craft throughout the world.

For many tourists, the main reason to visit Dolores is to shop for low-cost and high quality talavera ceramics. It is especially useful to visit if you plan to buy in bulk; for instance, if you are looking for a complete dinner set or tiles for the bathroom, you'll find unbeatable deals here. There are inexpensive factory stores throughout Dolores Hidalgo; although many produce the same products (principally flatware, flowerpots, and tiles), they each have their own creative flair. Check out a few different shops to find your favorite. Most will gladly help with shipping overseas.

Stocking a selection of anything and everything that can be created in ceramic, **JMB** (Puebla 60, tel. 418/182-0749, www.dtalavera.com, 10 A.M.–6 P.M. daily) is a huge ceramics shop near the city center. Don't be fooled by the small storefront; this cavernous factory store contains room after room with hand-painted ceramic goods. The staff will turn on the lights to each showroom as you make your way down the narrow hallways. Anything you've ever dreamed of owning in brightly colored talavera can be found here, including hand-painted flower pots, liquid soap dispensers, light-switch adornments, platters, side plates, demitasses, toothbrush holders, segmented salsa dishes, and more. There is also a pretty line of lead-free products.

Just across the street from JMB, **Azulejos y Loza Talavera Vázquez** (Puebla 56 and 58, tel. 418/182-2914 or 418/182-0630, www.vazquezpottery.com, 9:30 A.M.–7 P.M. daily) is easily recognizable, thanks to its blue-and-white tile facade. Inside, this spacious factory store stocks an extensive selection of beautifully painted ceramic work. You'll find lots of oversized products, like large ceramic urns and flower pots, as well as decorative wall pieces and tile sets. Vázquez also stocks a really lovely selection of delicately painted platters, dishes, and other housewares. The quality of the work is high and prices are excellent.

Right on the *plaza principal,* **La Casa de las Artesanías** (Plaza Principal 6, tel. 418/182-2266, 9:30 A.M.–7 P.M. daily) feels a bit like a craft clearing house, with everything from coffee mugs and T-shirts to hand-woven tablecloths and bags. Among the wildly diverse crafts, there is a beautiful selection of talavera pottery, sold in sets or individual pieces, as well as tiles. The store also stocks a very nice selection of blown-glass cups, wine glasses, and pitchers from Tonalá, Jalisco, some of which are very artful yet inexpensive.

On the highway between San Miguel de Allende and Dolores Hidalgo, several large factory stores offer a wonderful range of talavera. Among the most popular, **Arte San Gabriel** (Carretera Dolores-San Miguel, Km 14, tel. 418/185-5037) has been in business since 1973. This vast store sells a large selection of flatware and dinner sets, as well as larger pieces, like urns, flower pots, and statues. They are also a major ceramics exporter.

ACCOMMODATIONS

Most people don't choose to spend a night in Dolores Hidalgo, and because the town is so close to the numerous hotels in San Miguel de Allende and Guanajuato, they really don't need to. However, those who'd like to spend the evening in Dolores can choose between plenty of inexpensive options in the downtown district. Luxury hasn't quite hit Dolores Hidalgo yet, but many Dolores hotels are a good bargain for the price, clean, and well attended.

Dolores Hidalgo's reputation as an inexpensive city to visit is amply confirmed at **Casa Mia** (San Luis Potosí 9B, tel. 418/182-2560, www.hotelcasamia.com.mx, US$26). Just around the corner from the central square, rooms at this friendly inn are cozily decorated with printed bedspreads, curtained windows, and terra-cotta tile floors, and equipped with a small private bath decorated with ceramic tile. Decor is cute and comfortable enough to make this hotel feel like a serious bargain. Rooms upstairs surrounding the hotel's back patio are the nicest, getting more natural light than those downstairs. All rooms include television.

Near the parish, **Hotel Caudillo** (Querétaro 8, tel. 418/182-0198 or toll-free Mex. tel. 800/836-1166, www.hotelcaudillo.com.mx, US$36) has more than 30 small bedrooms surrounding a central atrium in the back section of the building. While not particularly spacious or bright, accommodations are cozy, with cotton bedspreads, wood headboards, and wall-mounted televisions. Each has a nice bathroom with (what else?) hand-painted majolica tiles. In a more unusual decorative embellishment, the bedrooms' ceilings are also decorated with round ceramic tiles. Downstairs, there is a sit-down restaurant, decorated with *papel picado* and serving Mexican fare, as well as a daily *comida corrida*. There is parking on the premises for hotel guests.

Right on the main plaza, **Posada Cocomacan** (Plaza Principal 4, tel. 418/182-6086 or 418/182-6087, www.posadacocomacan.com.mx, US$45) is one of Dolores's larger hotels. Bedrooms are decidedly small and simple—even a bit stuffy. However, staying right on a town's main square is a pleasure that doesn't usually come at such a reasonable price. Most rooms surround a central courtyard and restaurant; the nicest are on the second floor and have windows that overlook the Dolores parish. There is a restaurant in the lobby, which caters to the hotel's largely national clientele, as well as to tourists passing through Dolores.

Forget colonial at **Hotel Hidalgo** (Hidalgo 15, tel. 418/182-0477 or 418/182-2683, www.hotelposadahidalgo.com, US$40), a modern establishment right between the bus station and the town square. There are 28 simple rooms in this tidy inn, each equipped with television, telephones, wireless Internet, and private bath. There is also a gym on-site. Though lacking a bit of character, this hotel is clean and efficient; it is a good value for its price.

FOOD

Quick and tasty snack food abounds in Dolores Hidalgo's central plaza. Around the square, there are numerous informal carts selling sliced fruit, roasted corn, and, most famously, delicious *nieves* (ice cream). In fact, Dolores has made a bit of a reputation for itself with its diverse selection of *nieves* in flavors that range from exotic (guanabana) to downright bizarre (shrimp). Gregarious ice cream vendors will allow you to sample a few flavors, if you are curious about the taste of seafood ice cream. Great for the indecisive, cones or cups can come with two (or three) flavors. It's a cheap and delicious sugar rush.

For a more formal meal, there are several places to eat around Dolores's central plaza. Popular with locals, **Restaurant Bar Plaza** (Plaza Principal 17B, tel. 418/182-0259, cell tel. 418/181-0417, angelgg33@hotmail.com, 8 A.M.–10 P.M. daily, US$10) is a nice place to relax over a leisurely lunch. On the south side of the central plaza, this restaurant's big open windows give you a nice view of the action in the center of town. Grilled meats and creamy pastas dominate the menu, and there is a full bar. The food and service can feel a bit old-fashioned in this long-time Dolores establishment.

One of the most atmospheric choices on the square, **El Carruaje** (Querétaro 8, tel. 418/182-0474, 8 A.M.–10 P.M. daily, US$8) caters to the tourist crowd with a range of inexpensive Mexican dishes, plus pastas, brochettes, and salads. Just inside the Hotel Caudillo, the dining room is decked out in swaying *papel picado* and colorful tablecloths. During busy tourist weekends, the restaurant may augment its menu with a buffet, and sometimes there is live music. There is a full bar and beer.

Occupying a vast second floor space in the main plaza, **Café La Taberna** (Plaza Principal 18, tel. 418/182-0055, noon–midnight daily) is an inexpensive coffee shop and popular youth hangout. Look for the sign hanging over the staircase to find this casual joint. Here, the young staff serves up inexpensive coffee, teas, milkshakes, and sugary *cappuccino frío,* as well

AVOCADO ICE CREAM

A country famous for its warm and sunny weather, Mexico has also perfected the art of creating delicious cold sweets. *Raspados* (shaved ice), ice cream, and popsicles are all popular throughout the country. First-time visitors to Mexico should try a cup or cone of *nieve*, a refreshing and icier version of ice cream, sold in plazas, markets, and on street corners.

In literal translation, the word *nieve* means snow. Most resembling ice milk or sorbet, *nieve* is not as creamy as ice cream, though some flavors are made with milk while others are water-based. Throughout Mexico, *nieves* are still a cottage industry, made by hand with family recipes and scooped on street corners from metal containers lodged in ice. These highly flavorful ices are almost always made with fresh ingredients (you may even find pieces of fruit in your cone) in a range of flavors, from vanilla and walnut to mango and peppermint.

Though *nieve* is popular (and delicious) throughout the Bajío, Dolores Hidalgo has developed particular culture with regards to creating and scooping flavors. In Dolores, massive *nieve* vendors occupy the four corners of the main plaza, each offering an extensive menus of flavors. Of course, you can find classics, likes chocolate or vanilla; however, Dolores vendors head toward wacky, with ice cream flavors like shrimp, tequila, cheese, beer, pork rind, and avocado. You can ask to sample a flavor before taking the plunge or you can take your chances; most flavors, even the most bizarre, are surprisingly sweet and appealing.

Just as fun for the foreign palate, Dolores *nieves* always include more unusual tropical fruits like tuna (prickly pear), guayaba (guava), zapote (sapodilla), guanabana (soursop), and other delicious exotics. If you really want to taste a range of sweets, keep an eye out: Dolores has hosted several ice cream festivals and flavor competitions in the past.

as inexpensive snacks, like nachos and sandwiches. The place gets pretty crowded after school is out; Dolores teens gather here to talk and do homework at the collection of wobbly tables in back. On the weekends, the café occasionally hosts live music performances. You can check the fliers outside the doorway to see what's coming up.

A chain of restaurants originally founded in Sinaloa, **Pollo Feliz** (Plaza Principal 8B, tel. 418/182-4219 or 418/182-2352, 10:30 A.M.–6:30 P.M., US$5) is popular throughout Mexico and with good reason. Their savory spit-roasted chicken is inexpensive and filling, and each bird comes served with salsa and corn tortillas. In addition to poultry, Pollo Feliz serves giant quesadillas with thick hand-rolled tortillas, a good alternative for vegetarians. Although this joint lacks the atmosphere you might find at other establishments around the town square, it is a great place to get a quick and inexpensive lunch.

Near the entrance to Dolores from San Miguel along the busy Avenida Norte, famously tasty **◖ Carnitas Vincente** (Av. Norte 65, tel. 418/182-7017, www.carnitasvicente.com.mx, 8 A.M.–4 P.M. daily) is an inexpensive and casual place for a filling *almuerzo*. Specializing in carnitas, this excellent little eatery serves delicious braised pork, either by the kilo or wrapped in individual tacos. Their *maciza* is richly flavored yet not greasy, well complemented by the *pico de gallo* salsa laid out on the tables. Carnitas Vincente also serves deep fried tacos, quesadillas, and soft drinks. You can order your food to go or eat in; there is casual seating at plastic-clothed tables in an unspectacular courtyard dining room, with table service.

INFORMATION AND SERVICES

Dolores Hidalgo's friendly **Oficina de Turismo** (Tourist Office, Plaza Principal 11, tel. 418/182-1164, www.doloreshidalgo.gob.mx, 10 A.M.–5 P.M. Mon.–Fri.) is on the second floor of a colonial house in the *plaza principal.* They can provide a sightseeing map of the downtown district, as well as tips on what to see and do in Dolores.

There are several **banks and ATMs** in Dolores Hidalgo's main plaza. There is a **Banamex** (Plaza Principal 15, tel. 418/182-1816, 9 A.M.–4 P.M. Mon.–Sat.) branch on the plaza's south side, as well as a 24-hour ATM on the west side of the square. There is also a **Banorte** (Guerrero s/n, esq. Jalisco, tel. 418/182-0938 or 418/182-2938, 9 A.M.–5 P.M. Mon.–Fri., 9 A.M.–2 P.M. Sat.) just off the plaza.

In a medical emergency, you can call the **Cruz Roja** (Red Cross, Calzada de los Héroes 179, tel. 418/182-0000) day or night. **Seguridad Pública** (México 2, tel. 418/182-0021) is also available to respond to emergencies.

GETTING THERE AND AROUND
By Bus
Operated by Flecha Amarilla, second-class buses depart for Dolores Hidalgo from the main bus terminal in San Miguel de Allende every 30 minutes. The ride takes 30–45 minutes. Flecha Amarilla also operates second-class buses every 20 minutes between Guanajuato and Dolores Hidalgo. If you are traveling to Dolores from Guanajuato, you can pick up the bus at the terminal or on the highway passing through La Valenciana. There is no first-class bus service between Dolores Hidalgo and San Miguel de Allende or Guanajuato.

By Car
The drive to Dolores Hidalgo from San Miguel de Allende is fairly quick and easy. A benefit to driving is that you can stop in some of the ceramics factory stores on the way to town. To get to Dolores, take Highway 110 from San Miguel about 48 kilometers (30 miles), then follow the Centro signs for Dolores Hidalgo's downtown. After passing through Dolores, you can continue on Highway 110 to Guanajuato. From here, the highway becomes incredibly scenic, climbing into the Sierra de Guanajuato and passing through the small town of Santa Rosa.

By Taxi
Though most of Dolores's attractions are easy to access on foot, there are inexpensive taxis throughout Dolores Hidalgo's city center. You can also call Super Taxi Linea Dorada (tel. 418/182-7978) to pick you up.

THE BAJÍO

Mineral de Pozos

It seems that time swept right past Mineral de Pozos, a chilly half-abandoned city perched on a sloping hillside in the high desert chaparral. A place of whispers and legends, this crumbling little pueblo was a prosperous city during the 19th century, home to an estimated 70,000 people and several prolific mineral mines. Slowly, the town's resources were depleted, the mines flooded, and the population dwindled. Without industry or stewards, Pozos was left to the elements.

Today, Pozos exudes the eerie, half-ruined romance of a ghost town, filled with crumbling adobe walls and muddy roads where tiny cactus grow freely in the rocky nooks and crannies. It is surprisingly beautiful, with some fascinating ruins from the former mining camps just outside the city's small but charming *centro*. A wonderful place to visit, the town has made a modest resurgence over the past few decades. It's not far from the tourist capital of San Miguel de Allende; travelers have begun to take notice of this unusual destination, and the romance of a desert ghost town has inevitably convinced some artists and expatriates to settle down there permanently. Around downtown Pozos, there is now a small selection of restaurants, hotels, and shops, some with a rather sophisticated feeling. In fact, many speculate that Pozos will become the next San Miguel de Allende (Pozos residents think otherwise, though). Whatever the future holds for Pozos,

MUSIC IN THE AIR

Little is known about pre-Columbian music and dance traditions, though anthropologists know that performance, music, and poetry were a part of many indigenous cultures in Meso-america. Archaeologists have identified a few instruments from the pre-Columbian era, such as clay whistles and animal skin drums. These artifacts give a small window into the musical traditions in Mexico and have sparked an interest in further study.

Studies suggest that most pre-Hispanic musical instruments used percussion or wind to make sound. Clay whistles and clay flutes with tonal holes appear to have been common in Mexico, as well as flutes fashioned from reeds or wood. Evidence of whistles and flutes exists in central Mexico and the Huasteca coast near Veracruz. There is also evidence of a wide array of drums and other percussive instruments. A tortoise shell or hollow gourd floated in water also produces a lovely tonal sound when struck with the end of a stick.

In Mineral de Pozos, among other Mexican cities, there is a growing interest in recreating and playing pre-Hispanic instruments. Many of these instruments are recreated in Pozos at artisan workshops, using a combination of materials like wood, water, bones, clay, and stone. In addition to copying pre-Hispanic design, many of Pozos's artisans have invented new instruments based on the same materials and percussive principals.

Every few years, Pozos hosts the **Fiesta de la Toltequidad,** a festival dedicated to the study and celebration of pre-Columbian music and dance. Neither well publicized nor commercial, the festival and instrument workshops struggle for support, despite the dedication of the town's artisans and the inherent interest in the topic.

---

it is a wonderful place to spend a day, offering the perfect blend of off-the-beaten-track charm and contemporary panache.

While Pozos is definitely one of the most interesting places to visit near San Miguel de Allende, visitors should keep in mind that it is a very small town and a relatively quiet place. During the weekdays, most shops and galleries are shuttered, and the town's few sights, though fascinating, are also limited. If you plan to spend more than a day in Pozos, bring a book, a camera, or some other peaceful form of self-entertainment. While the tranquility in Pozos is undeniably inspiring, the town isn't as tourist-ready as San Miguel. Romantic self-starters will be happiest here.

HISTORY

The Spanish arrived in Pozos in the mid-16th century, as they expanded their settlements northward to accommodate the new silver industry in Zacatecas. Located near the Camino Real de Tierra Adentro silver route, the first settlement in Pozos was established as a protective fort for merchants traveling by donkey train to the capital. Not long after the settlement was founded, Jesuit missionaries arrived and discovered that the indigenous people of the region had been mining minerals from a large open pit. With this discovery, the Jesuits immediately began metal extraction in the same pit mine, which is known today as Santa Brígida. When the Jesuits were expelled from Mexico in 1767, the mining industry in Pozos ceased.

Toward the end of the 19th century, the mines in Pozos were reopened under new direction. Metal deposits were discovered near the city's western edge, and the industry began to boom. By the end of the century, there were more than 300 active mines in Pozos. The president of Mexico renamed the city after himself, christening it Ciudad Porfirio Díaz. The ruins of this era can be witnessed just outside Pozos, in the mining camps and ex-hacienda Cinco Señores.

When the Mexican Revolution broke out in 1910, mining operations in Pozos abruptly ceased. Though their closure was meant to be temporary, the mines flooded and the global price of silver dropped significantly, making it impossible for them to reopen when the revolution ended. The final mine closed in 1927. Without income from the silver industry to support its population, Pozos was quickly abandoned. By the mid-20th century, only a couple hundred residents remained in town.

For many years, Pozos was a ghost town, supporting a teeny population in crumbling old buildings. Still, its beauty and historical significance remained intact. In 1982, the president of Mexico named Pozos a National Historic Monument Zone. Today, it has a modest population of several thousand residents and a burgeoning tourist industry.

SIGHTS

For a taste of Old Mexico, the entire city of Pozos is a sight in itself. Here, the windswept dirt roads are lined with crumbling adobe houses, stray dogs mill through the sleepy central plaza, and the desert landscape is stark and beautiful. The mines themselves, both sorrowful and majestic, are one of the most interesting places to visit in the Bajío.

Plaza Principal

It is easy to imagine tumbleweeds rolling through the dusty *plaza principal* in Pozos, a shady gathering place in the center of town. Catering to very opposite needs, this lovely little square is equipped with a cantina on one corner and a church on the other. The **Iglesia San Pedro** and its massive dome preside over the square, while a little string of galleries and hotels occupy the east side. On the weekends, there are many more tourists in town and vendors arrive in the square to sell sweetbreads, roasted corn, *aguas frescas,* and other small snacks. Look for the unusual bright pink beverage *pulque de tuna* (a fermented prickly pear beverage) during the late summer or early fall.

Templo del Nuestro Señor de los Trabajos

Just east of the main plaza, a large church stands on the hillside. Most notable for its

THE BAJÍO

© ARTURO MEADE

The Iglesia San Pedro in downtown Pozos peeks above a quiet street.

giant half dome, this temple appears to be a ruin. In fact, it is simply unfinished. The wealthy patron of this church was struck by the ruin of the silver trade and never completed construction.

Santa Brígida Mine

The former mining camps in Pozos, now magnificent and mysterious ruins, are one of the most interesting sights in the Bajío. It is also a good exercise for the imagination, as you wonder about the maze of unmarked structures, half-reclaimed by the desert wilderness. Out in Pozos, there are no informational placards posted at historic sights, no tourist office to feed your need for information, and no books or brochures published about the city's great silver boom and bust. Hired guides can offer a deeper perspective, but the history is incomplete.

Just outside the city center, Santa Brígida was the very first mine in Pozos. Unique to the region, Santa Brígida was actually mined by indigenous people before it came under Spanish control. As you approach the mine, you can see three large smokestacks that were the mine's smelting ovens. If you've come without a guide, park near the large red-and-white building, which was the mine's former management offices (it isn't open to the public). From there, you can easily wander into the mining camp.

Santa Brígida was a pit mine, so it doesn't have a traditional mine shaft. Instead, a large crevice runs through the earth, bordered on the north side by the beautiful arched ovens used for mercury amalgamation, which extracts metals from the rock. The rubble surrounding the mines still gleams with mineral-rich rocks. Without a guide, you should watch your step everywhere around Pozos, though especially here. The mouth of the mine is unmarked and gravelly, plunging deep into the earth. In addition to the mine, there are several deep wells around the mining camp, with no signs to indicate their existence. Keep a close eye on dogs and children!

To reach the Santa Brígida Mine, follow the highway through town north toward San Luis de la Paz and, just as the pavement begins, take a right on a large dirt road. It is unmarked. At the first major fork, go left (or north) toward the mine. After a kilometer or so, you will see the smokestacks in the distance. Unfortunately, there is no signage for Santa Brígida; however, you can get detailed instructions from the locals in town.

◖ Cinco Señores Mine

Though the city was long home to a mining industry, Pozos reached its height during the Porfiriato era of the late 19th century. The incredible ex-hacienda Cinco Señores offers a fascinating glimpse into the splendor of Pozos's former wealth and prestige. This expansive mining camp and its associated buildings covered a complete hillside on the southwest of the city; today, you can wander among roofless buildings, crumbling porticos from 19th-century offices, huge stone tubs filled with moss-rich water, and the dark mouths of numerous abandoned mine shafts. Within the site, there are several of the wells, or *pozos*, for which the city is famous. They are marked with barbed wire and, if you dare to lean over the edge, are dizzyingly deep and cavernous. Likewise, there are several mine shafts littered throughout the property. Use care when walking near the edge of these, as the ground can be uneven and some shafts are only minimally marked.

Just as spectacular as the ruins, the hills around the ex-hacienda afford a lovely view of the surrounding valley and a rather stunning collection of wild plants, cactus, and succulents, which are often occupied by birds, butterflies, and other insects.

To reach Cinco Señores, head west up Manuel Doblado from the main square. Continue one block past the Plaza Zaragosa (only about three large blocks from the square) and then veer left on a dirt road. You will pass a shop, Venado Azul. Continue along the dirt road for a few kilometers, passing tiny homes and agave farms, until you see the mining camps on the hillside. There is no admission, though often there are local

© ARTURO MEADE

From the ruins of the Cinco Señores mining camp, there are lovely views of the desert below.

people in front of the site selling rocks and minerals from Pozos.

El Panteón

El Panteón, a municipal cemetery, offers a mournful glimpse into the city's former opulence. It's beside the highway just outside the city's south entrance, and you can visit this interesting graveyard and wander among the tombstones of Pozos residents. You'll find large headstones and mausoleums built by the city's wealthy residents.

SHOPPING

Pozos is a surprisingly sophisticated little ghost town, with a smattering of nice galleries, shops, and restaurants. Art lovers will be happy to find several contemporary art spaces in town, as well as occasional city Art Walks. On the northeast corner of the central plaza, the lovely **Galería 6** (Aldama 6, Plaza Principal, tel. 442/205-0811, galeria6@mac. com, 11 A.M.–5 P.M. Wed.–Sun.) hosts rotating exhibitions of contemporary Mexican

and international artists who are living and working from the Bajío region. The exhibition spaces are light-filled, airy, and white, beautifully showcasing the photography, sculpture, and painting that the gallery's curators have chosen. Despite the contemporary slant to the art, the building itself is enchantingly colonial, with flagstone tiles, pretty gardens, and some cats and dogs that seem to wander freely around the space. It is worth a visit inside just to soak up the incredible atmosphere.

Just next door to Galería 6, **Arte y Diseño de Pozos** (Juárez 4B, Plaza Principal, tel. 442/293-0293 or 442/293-0284, www.artey-disenodepozos.com, generally 10 A.M.–6 P.M. Thurs.–Sun.) is a lovely little boutique that sells original clothing, accessories, and jewelry. Fitting for a town known for its minerals, most of the shop's oversized rings, necklaces, and bracelets are made of silver and stone. The work is creative and prices tend to be rather reasonable for the handmade accessories on sale. The space also exhibits colorful work by local artists from Pozos and San Miguel de Allende; look out for one of their opening events or stop by during one of the infrequent but entertaining Pozos Art Walks.

If you would like your home to resemble the gorgeous guest rooms in Hotel Casa Mexicana, arrange a visit to **Emporio Pozos** (Jardín Principal 2, tel. 442/293-0014, hours vary, open to hotel guests) Here, you can peruse a lovely collection of Mexican-made handicrafts, including furniture, ceramics, glassware, and textiles, as well as a smattering of craftwork from other cultures. Located in the lobby of the Hotel Casa Mexicana, this little shop's high ceilings and colonial environment perfectly complement the products on sale. The hotel's owner also manages a collection of fine art, which includes Picasso etchings as well as work by Mexican masters like Rufino Tamayo.

On the other end of the square, artist Daniel Rueffert's colorful landscapes can be seen in a posh gallery setting at **Galería La Fama** (Hidalgo 1, cell tel. 415/149-1230 or 415/109-2452, U.S. tel. 505/216-5221). Rueffert has been living in Mexico for several decades, and he is also the owner of a restaurant, Los Famosos de Pozos, just down the street. There are both small- and large-format oil paintings, many depicting the town of Pozos itself in saturated color. All are nicely framed and presented.

Pozos is internationally recognized for its numerous high-quality workshops producing pre-Hispanic musical instruments; **Venado Azul** (Centenario s/n, tel. 468/117-0387, azulvenado@hotmail.com, 8 A.M.–5 P.M. daily) is home to some of the most prominent artisans in town. On the dusty dirt road out to the ex-hacienda Cinco Señores, the beautifully painted exterior of Venado Azul stands out against the rows of brown adobe. Inside, there are various patios within this large store and workshop, each filled with cactus, knick-knacks, crafts, and animal bones. Peruse the interesting store and its large collection of unique musical instruments. The selection of hand-carved wooden drums is particularly nice. Venado Azul is also a major contributor and

venue in the annual pre-Hispanic music conference in Pozos, La Festival de la Toltequidad. This conference was founded in 1987 and takes place every summer.

Overlooking the Plaza Zaragosa, **Camino de Piedra** (Leandro Valle 13, Plaza Zaragoza, tel. 442/293-0123, generally 10 A.M.–5 P.M. Fri.–Sun.) is owned by a family of artisans who create a line of instruments based on pre-Hispanic designs. In the front room, Camino de Piedra sells a small and inexpensive selection of local crafts, including copper jewelry, whistles, and pottery. However, the real treasure hides in the adjoining room, where the family keeps their collection of handmade pre-Hispanic instruments. If you ask, they may give you a demonstration of the turtle-shell drums, whistles, percussive gourds, conch shells, and sweet-sounding flutes.

ACCOMMODATIONS

Close to San Miguel de Allende and Querétaro, Pozos has become a modestly popular place to visit. Spending a night in Pozos can be relaxing—and even a bit otherworldly. Far from the city lights, you can only hear the sound of a distant barking in the evenings. There are just a few hotels in town, but they are all rather lovely and appropriate for a romantic night in the high desert.

Right on the main square, ◖ **Hotel Casa Mexicana** (Jardín Principal 2, 442 293-0014, http://casamexicanahotel.com, US$78–90) is precisely the type of place you'd like to rest your head during a romantic weekend in Pozos. The very first guesthouse in town, this establishment has a distinctly Mexican ambiance; rooms with clay floors, vaulted ceilings, and white washed walls surround a sunny courtyard. Each has been lovingly decorated with special details, like antique furniture, old chandeliers, original artwork, and traditional crafts. Loft beds and sitting areas in the larger suites can be nice for reading and relaxing when you've finished visiting the limited attractions in surrounding Pozos.

Just next door to Hotel Casa Mexicana on the main square, **El Secreto de Pozos** (Jardín Principal 6, tel. 442/293-0200, www.

elsecretomexico.com, US$68–85) is a small pension with three clean and comfortable rooms. Each is comfortably decorated with traditional Mexican furnishings, a small wood-burning chimney, hand-woven rugs, and cute private baths. The thick white walls and creaking wooden doorways give this place an unmistakably romantic charm. Though just on the square, rooms feel tucked away and entirely private; their windows overlook a small communal garden.

Although the **Posada de la Minas** (Manuel Doblado 1, tel. 442/293-0213, www.posadadelasminas.com, US$78–120) is the largest establishment in Pozos, there are only eight rooms in this attractive boutique hotel. Located in a restored 19th-century mansion, the guest rooms are comfortable and nicely decorated with a Mexican flair. The atmosphere is perfect for Pozos, with cute tiled bathrooms with bathtubs, oversized wooden furniture, and hand-woven comforters on the beds. Since the hotel is situated on a small hill a block above the city center, some rooms have nice views of Pozos; the largest has a small balcony and chairs. The nightly price includes a full breakfast in the hotel's restaurant or served in your room.

FOOD

The largest establishment in town, **[** **Posada de las Minas** (Manuel Doblado 1, tel. 442/293-0213, www.posadadelasminas.com, 8:30 A.M.–10 P.M. daily) is a beautiful colonial-style hotel with a wildly pleasant courtyard restaurant. Mexican specialties like guacamole, enchiladas, and stuffed peppers are the best dishes here, though they serve a range of sandwiches, burgers, fish, and pastas. The mixed appetizer plate is a nice way to start a meal with a group. There is beer, wine, and a full bar, which includes a varied list of inexpensive tequilas. The service is attentive, if a bit slow, and the atmosphere is casually luxurious, with dining tables set around a sunny, flower-filled courtyard. Thanks to the restaurant's great prices and friendly, family-style atmosphere, it is always busy on the weekends with local tourists and families. In addition, the restaurant often hosts special events on Valentine's Day, New Year's, or other holidays, which include special menus and live music.

Just off the main square, the casual eatery **Los Famosos de Pozos** (Hidalgo 10B, tel. 442/293-0112, noon–8 P.M. daily) is a nice and inexpensive option downtown. Follow the stairs from the street to a spacious dining room with wood furniture, a big wood bar, and windows overlooking the city. Food is a mix of Mexican and American staples, from burgers to enchiladas, as well as desserts and coffee. Service can feel rather relaxed, so don't come in a rush.

INFORMATION AND SERVICES

On the weekends, Mineral de Pozos has a nice buzz, when a handful of tour groups and families arrive from Querétaro or San Miguel de Allende. Although the atmosphere can feel rather posh for a ghost town, Pozos offers very little to the visitor in terms of services. There are no banks or ATMs in town, so you must bring cash with you (a few places will also take credit cards). It has no tourist office, no local publications, and no taxis. Sometimes, even phone service and electricity can be unexpectedly cut off, so be prepared for anything when visiting Pozos.

GETTING THERE AND AROUND

The best way to get to Mineral de Pozos is in a car. Although there is occasional bus service to and from the town, you will not be able to visit the town's fascinating mines without a set of wheels. Driving to Pozos from San Miguel de Allende or Querétaro is rather easy; it takes about 45 minutes to an hour from either city. From Mexico City, Pozos is about four hours north.

To get to Pozos from San Miguel de Allende, follow the Salida a Querétaro out of the city. Arriving at the traffic circle, head east, following the signs toward Doctor Mora and Los Rodríguez. Follow this two-lane highway

THE BAJÍO

through Los Rodríguez (watch out for speed bumps!), crossing over Highway 57 on an overpass. About eight kilometers (five miles) from the highway, you will reach an intersection indicating the turnoff for Pozos and San Luis de la Paz; turn north toward these cities. About 16 kilometers (10 miles) down the road, the highway turns to dirt and you have arrived in Pozos.

From Querétaro or Mexico City, take Highway 57 north toward San Luis Potosí. About 80 kilometers (50 miles) north of Querétaro exit toward Doctor Mora and head east. About eight kilometers (five miles) later, you will reach an intersection; turn north toward San Luis de la Paz and travel about 16 kilometers (10 miles) to reach Pozos.

León

Once a small 16th-century ranching town, modern León is now a big and industrial city. Its strong economy leans heavily on manufacturing; it is best known for its leather products, including the mass production of shoes, belts, bags, and leather accessories for some of the most famous apparel lines in the world. Although there are a few sights in downtown León, most tourists visit this city for its great shopping. Here, you'll find top-of-the-line shoes and leather products at very low prices.

SIGHTS

With booming industry in manufacturing and ranching, León has been the victim of rapid growth and urban sprawl. Today, big avenues, factories, multi-room cinemas, and chain restaurants surround the city's historic downtown district, which has been almost completely swallowed up by the growth. Nonetheless, León is one of the oldest cities in the region, and there are a few historic sights worth visiting if you are in town.

Plaza de los Mártires

León's attractive central plaza is flanked by arcaded colonial buildings and filled with well-tended dome-shaped trees. There is a small pedestrian district surrounding the square, which can be a nice place to have a coffee alfresco or rest on a bench during a warm afternoon. The city's cathedral adjoins the plaza, as does the **Palacio Municipal,** an impressive

neoclassical structure that was once a military barracks but is now home to the city's government offices.

Catedral Basílica de León

Located in the central plaza, the Cathedral Basílica (Alvaro Obregón s/n, esq. Hidalgo, tel. 477/716-1038, 10 A.M.–2 P.M. and 5–7 P.M. Mon.–Sat., 10 A.M.–2 P.M. Sun.) was originally commissioned by Jesuit missionaries in 1746. Shortly thereafter, King Charles of Spain expelled Jesuits from Mexico, and the church remained unfinished. When the diocese of León was established in the 19th century, the cathedral was eventually completed. Reflecting the two distinct periods of time in which it was constructed, the cathedral is largely baroque, with 19th-century neoclassical embellishments. Inside, the church's pretty nave and six chapels also have an interesting mix of decorative styles; the nave's vaulted arches show Moorish influence, while one chapel holds an art deco Christ.

Museo de la Ciudad

Just a few blocks from the main square, the Museo de la Ciudad (City Museum, Aldama 136, tel. 477/714-5022 or 477/714-0325, 9:30 A.M.–2:30 P.M. and 5–7 P.M. Tues.–Fri., 9:30 A.M.–2 P.M. Sat., US$2) is a modern two-story museum that shows ongoing exhibits of contemporary art and photography. Most exhibiting artists are local or from around Mexico.

Santuario Expiatorio del Sagrado Corazón de Jesús

Though built more recently, the soaring, neo-Gothic Santuario Expiatorio Sagrado Corazón de Jesús (Madero 721, tel. 477/714-2096, generally 8 a.m.–8 p.m. daily) is one of the most striking structures in the city. Elaborate bronze doors and beautiful stained-glass windows complement its elegant white exterior. Construction on this massive temple began in 1921 and has never officially been completed, as renovations and additions are ongoing. Inside, there more than 20 altars to visit.

SHOPPING

The city of León has been a major leather producer since the colonial era. Today, León is one of the largest shoe manufacturing centers in the world. Shopping for discount shoes and leather products is one of the major attractions of a trip to León, and there are shoe stores littered throughout the city. In the area around the *zócalo,* there are numerous small shops selling shoes and leather handbags, easily accessible to tourists in the city. For more serious shoppers, there are entire malls dedicated to leather goods.

Zona Piel

Find shoes galore in the shopping district known as Zona Piel, conveniently located in the blocks around the city's bus station. Here, you'll find several large leather and shoe malls, where literally thousands of shoe distributors sell their products at very low prices. One of the big Zona Piel shopping centers, **Plaza del Zapato** (Hilario Medina 100, tel. 477/763-3838, www.plazadelzapato.com, 10 a.m.–8:30 p.m. Mon.–Sat., 10 a.m.–6 p.m. Sun.) is a consumer shrine to footwear. Here, shops and products run the gamut. You can find everything from leather pumps and suede boots to running shoes and sandals. Many of the shops carry designer knock-offs at good prices, and there are also several children's shoe stores.

While you're there, you might as well stop into **Plaza Piel** (A. López Mateos 1509 Ote., tel. 477/763-4150, 10 a.m.–8:30 p.m. Mon.–Sat., 10 a.m.–4 p.m. Sun.), located right next door to the Plaza del Zapato. With a name that means "Leather Plaza," this mall sells a selection of locally produced shoes, as well as a large collection of other leather goods, like wallets, belts, handbags, and leather jackets.

Just down the avenue, **Plaza León** (López Mateos 1102 Ote., tel. 477/713-5695, www.plazaleon.com, 10 a.m.–8:30 p.m. daily) has a couple of nice leather shops selling handbags and clothing, as well as banks, restaurants, gift shops, and other stores.

SAPICA

If you are serious about shoe shopping or happen to be in the region during April or September, it is worth a trip to the biannual shoe festival, Salón de la Piel y del Calzado (SAPICA, Cámara de la Industria del Calzado del Estado de Guanajuato, Adolfo López Mateos 3401 Ote., Fracc. Julián de Obregón, tel. 477/152-9000, www.sapica.com). This massive shoe and leather goods exhibition is a shopper's paradise and a major business event for the city. During this four-day footwear extravaganza, the massive pavilions at Poliforum León are divided into categories like women's shoes, Western style, casual, and sport, each filled with myriad vendors. If you are looking for black stilettos, hardy hiking boots, or lightweight sandals, you will find them here. For those who are really interested in footwear, there are also daily fashion shows and speakers. Bring patience and a mood for crowds; SAPICA draws thousands of visitors daily from throughout the Bajío and beyond.

ACCOMMODATIONS

León's accommodations tend to cater to business travelers who have come to work with one of the many manufacturing plants or corporate offices in the city. Therefore, it's not surprising that there is an ample selection of chain hotels, like Holiday Inn, Radisson, Howard Johnson, and Fiesta Inn, sprinkled through the *centro histórico* and near León's convention centers.

Independently owned hotels in León tend to feel similarly impersonal, with a functional attitude and little emphasis on charm.

For low cost and convenience, you can't beat the inexpensive rooms at **Hotel Real Rex** (5 de Febrero 104, tel. 477/714-2415 or toll-free Mex. tel. 800/471-0600, www.hotelrealrex. com, US$29–40). Just off the main plaza, this big and industrial-looking hotel has 110 plain guest rooms, a lobby bar, and a very casual diner-style restaurant. Rooms aren't artfully decorated and can feel a bit worn, but they are comfortable, clean, and sufficiently spacious. They boast dark carpets, big beds, small baths with showers, and cable television.

Part of a Mexican chain of hotels of the same name, **City Express León** (Adolfo López Mateos Ote. 3002A, Fracc. San Isidro de Jerez, tel. 477/710-5900 or toll-free Mex. tel. 800/248-9397, www.cityexpress.com.mx, US$62–68) is a low-cost yet comfortable place to stay. Here, economical prices are paid out in reduced living space; in other words, rooms are very small. However, with clean and modern decor (plus amenities like cable television and air-conditioning), everything feel pared down, but not unattractive. The staff is friendly and efficient, and there is lots of parking. Rates include a small breakfast.

A more upscale establishment, **NE Hotel Nueva Estancia** (A. López Mateos 1317 Ote., tel. 477/637-0000 or toll-free Mex. tel. 800/087-7704, US$90) is one of the nicer places to stay in León. Some rooms in this all-suite hotel are of a decidedly modern design; others feel a bit more dated, with cotton bedspreads and wicker chairs. There is a swimming pool and hot tub in the courtyard for guests, as well as an Italian restaurant downstairs serving wood-fired pizzas. It is located a quick cab ride or about 15 minutes on foot from the city center, not far from the Plaza del Zapato and the bus terminal.

FOOD

If you are staying in the *centro histórico,* there are numerous casual restaurants around León's main plaza. Many are nice for a coffee and snack, though they are not necessarily culinary destinations. For a filling meal, try **Brasil 2000** (Mariano Escobedo 1008, tel. 477/715-4857 or 477/715-7850, 1:30 P.M.–midnight daily, US$10). Owned by a Rio native, this restaurant's specialty is juicy cuts of beef (this is a great region for ranching, after all). Curious carnivores can try some more unusual Brazilian cuts, or stick to classics, like the New York steak or *arrachera.* At this large, family-friendly restaurant with a very low-key atmosphere, waiters serve meat to the table from huge skewers. For a set price, it's an all-you-can-eat meat bonanza, accompanied by a salad buffet. It also has a full bar and Brazilian cocktails. A favorite with locals, this restaurant is hopping on Sunday afternoons.

You can get a nice plate of Italian food at **Frascati** (Cerro Gordo 201A, Col. Campestre, tel. 477/773-7154, www.frascatileon.com, 2–11 P.M. Mon.–Thurs., 2–midnight Fri.–Sat., 2–6 P.M. Sun., US$10), just across the street from the Plaza Mayor mall. On the weekend, the modern dining room and small bar are often filled with local shoppers; there is a view of the brick oven as you enter. Pizzas and pastas are the specialty here, though you can also order cuts of meat accompanied by french fries, if Italian isn't your thing. Vegetarians have plenty of options at Frascati (not the case in many León restaurants), including spinach ravioli, spaghetti with pesto, or mushroom pizza.

If you'd like to get a bite while shopping in Zona Piel, there is a **Sanborns** (Plaza León, López Mateos 1102 Ote., Local 3, tel. 477/713-6232, 10 A.M.–8:30 P.M. daily, US$8) in Plaza León. This famous Mexican chain of department stores and cafeterias serves traditional Mexican and international food. It is particularly well known for tasty enchiladas, as well as bottomless cups of coffee. It's a family-oriented place with not-so-spicy dishes; you'll find a range of options on the Sanborns menu, including soups, sandwiches, salads, tacos, flautas, *chilaquiles,* and desserts, as well as a full bar. Breakfasts are also tasty.

INFORMATION AND SERVICES
Tourist Information

León's tourist office, the **Oficina de Convenciones y Visitantes** (Vasco de Quiroga 101, tel. 477/763-4400 or 477/763-4401, leon@leon-mexico.com) is in a location not entirely convenient to the *centro histórico,* but it is close to the central avenue López Mateos and the shopping district. If you make your way there, they can provide maps of the city and will help you locate shopping centers.

Money

There are hundreds of banks throughout the city of León, in both the downtown district and the shopping areas. There is a **Banorte** (Av. López Mateos 13, tel. 477/716-1616 or 447/714-1312, 9 A.M.–5 P.M. Mon.–Fri.) in the *centro histórico* that has ATM machines. Tellers can change foreign currency to pesos. There is also a **Banamex** branch (Francisco Madero 125, tel. 477/716-8880, 9 A.M.–4 P.M. Mon.–Sat.) downtown with weekend hours. For shoppers, there are several banks and ATMs in Plaza León, including **Bancomer** (Plaza León, López Mateos 1102 Ote., Local A4, tel. 477/710-3900).

GETTING THERE AND AROUND
By Air

León's Del Bajío International Airport (BJX, Carretera Silao-León, Km 5.5, Col. Nuevo México, Silao, tel. 472/748-2120) is just outside the city in Silao. One of the busiest airports in the region, it has daily direct flights to and from the United States, as well as several daily flights to and from Mexico City, Monterrey, and other Mexican cities.

By Bus

León's large and busy **Central de Camiones** (bus station) is on Bulevar Hilario Medina, just off the large avenue, Bulevar López Mateos. Taking the bus to León can be rather convenient if you are going to buy shoes. Most of the major shoe outlets are located in the blocks around the terminal in the Zona Piel. If you plan to visit the *centro histórico,* you can take a taxi from the station downtown.

The first-class bus line **ETN** (Hilario Medina s/n, tel. 477/763-0779 or 477/763-0778, toll-free Mex. tel. 800/800-0386, www.etn.com.mx) has service between León and most major Mexican cities, including Guanajuato, San Miguel de Allende, Querétaro, and Guadalajara. Another first-class line, **Primera Plus** (Hilario Medina, toll-free Mex. tel. 800/375-7587), also services León.

By Taxi

There are inexpensive taxis throughout the city center, as well as taxis that will transport you from the airport to the city of León. You can flag a cab in the street or call **Servicio de Taxi Línea Dorada** (Faisán 300, San Sebastián, tel. 477/770-4050) or **Sitio Taxis Haciendas El Rosario** (Camino a la Presa s/n, Col. Haciendas El Rosario, tel. 477/717-6677 or 477/717-8877, www.paginasprodigy.com.mx/sitioelrosario) to pick you up.

THE BAJÍO

BACKGROUND

The Land

GEOGRAPHY

San Miguel de Allende, Guanajuato, and the Bajío region are located in Mexico's central highlands, known as the Mexican Altiplano. Formed by ancient volcanoes, the Altiplano extends all the way from the U.S. border to the Trans-Mexican Volcanic Belt near Mexico City. Running north to south, it has an average altitude of about 1,100 meters (3,600 feet) and is bordered by great mountain ranges on both sides.

The region known as the Bajío is a vast plain within the Mexican Altiplano, which covers the states of Querétaro and Guanajuato as well as segments of southern Jalisco and eastern Michoacán. Though the plain is situated at about 1,800 meters (6,000 feet) above sea level, the term *bajío* means "lowlands." While not technically "low," the Bajío lies below the craggy mountains of the Cordillera de Guanajuato and the Sierra Gorda, which run past the plains to the north and east, respectively. León and Querétaro are the two largest cities in the Bajío, though the region also includes the well-known colonial cities of Guanajuato, San Miguel de Allende, and Dolores Hidalgo.

There are several important water sources within the Bajío. Of particular note, the Río Laja basin covers about half of the state of

© ARTURO MEADE

Guanajuato and is the principal water source near San Miguel de Allende. The Río Laja is a tributary of the larger Río Lerma. One of the country's longest and most important watersheds, the Lerma passes along the border between the states of Querétaro and Michoacán, then passes through the state of Guanajuato on its course northward. It empties into Lake Chapala in Jalisco.

CLIMATE

The Bajío's climate is temperate, dry, and semi-arid, receiving modest annual rainfall. With very little humidity in the air, the weather can fluctuate significantly in the course of a single day. Throughout the year, evening temperatures are significantly lower than daytime temperatures; travelers should pack accordingly.

It rarely rains in the Bajío during the long dry season, which runs from October to mid-June. During summer's erratic wet season, rain typically falls during brief but furious thunderstorms in the afternoons or early evening. Thunderstorms rarely last more than an hour or two; however, their fierce downpours can cause destruction and flooding. By the end of the rainy season, the dry landscape of the Bajío is totally transformed. September and October can be particularly pleasant months to visit, when the desert blooms with wildflowers. In total, the Bajío receives somewhere around 50–64 centimeters (20–25 inches) of rain each year.

Although the Bajío enjoys a temperate climate year-round, there are distinct seasons. December and January are the coolest months, with average daytime temperatures hovering around 20°C (70°F) and nighttime temperatures dropping to around 0°C (low to mid-30s F). Evening frosts are not uncommon, with temperatures sinking below freezing on the coldest nights. Though surprisingly chilly, the winter season is very short. Spring begins as early as February, and weather is consistently warm by March. Throughout March and April, the weather is usually warm and dry, averaging 24–30°C (high 70s and 80s F), though the evenings continue to be chilly.

May is typically the warmest month in the Bajío, with temperatures reaching 30–35°C (high 80s and low 90s F). Few tourists visit the area in May, the one month of the year when the climate is uncomfortably hot. In June, the rains begin, and the temperatures drop. During the rainy months, the climate tends to be warmest in the mornings, cooling off after the afternoon showers. By September and October, the rains have begun to subside, but the climate remains pleasant, hovering around 25°C (high 70s F).

The climate is similar throughout the Bajío, though there are some regional differences. Located in a mountainous valley, the city of Guanajuato tends to be a few degrees cooler than San Miguel de Allende, whereas Querétaro may be a few degrees warmer. In the town of Santa Rosa, located in the mountains outside Guanajuato, the climate is rather chilly all year long.

ENVIRONMENTAL ISSUES

The Bajío region was sparsely populated when the Spanish settlers arrived in the 15th century. Thereafter, extensive ranching and agriculture in the region changed the quality of the land. Throughout the Bajío, there has been massive deforestation to accommodate human settlements and farming, and an overall degradation of natural plant and animal ecosystems. Due to the resulting decrease in plant cover, flood plains of the Río Lerma have suffered from severe erosion, with dramatic flooding causing a major problem during the short but intense rainy season. Deforestation has also made it more difficult for the soil to absorb rainwater, depleting the underground water table.

Human activities have polluted freshwater sources in most of Mexico, including the Bajío region. The Río Laja and especially the Río Lerma have been polluted by untreated sewage from surrounding towns and cities. The heavy agricultural, ranching, leather, paper, and petrochemical industries around the Bajío have further added to the contamination of

the land of the Bajío after the summer rains

drinking water sources. Currently, there are few water recycling or treatment programs in the region.

Water has become a particular concern for rural populations in the Bajío, especially around San Miguel de Allende. Here, semi-arid land supports a relatively large population with a very modest annual rainfall. Rapid urban growth around the city of San Miguel has created a new necessity for sustainable urban planning and resource allocation. However, there are few programs in place to ensure that water will be continue to be available for the growing populace.

Flora and Fauna

Mexico is one of the world's most biodiverse countries, encompassing a wide range of extremely distinct ecosystems, from arid desert to tropical wetland. Located in the center of Mexico, the Bajío is covered by several high altitude semi-arid ecosystems, including xeric shrubland, coniferous forest, and dry forests. Today, much of the Bajío's original flora and fauna has been affected by human development and agriculture. At the same time, ecological reserves, parks, and botanical gardens continue to protect large swaths of the region's native ecosystems and environments.

TREES AND SHRUBS

Many beautiful trees grow naturally around the Bajío region, as well as several decorative species that are common in the cities. In the Bajío's scrubland, the hardy and deciduous mesquite tree continues to flourish despite widespread deforestation for agriculture. Mesquite rarely grows taller than 8–9 meters, and can be identified by its dark bark, fringe of narrow green leaves, and thorny branches. This tree is native to Mexico and its name comes from the Nahuatl word *mizquitl*. Mesquite is particularly well known for its fragrant, hard, and slow-burning wood, which is used for charcoal grilling. Its yellow flowers are frequently used in honey production.

Huizaches (sweet acacias) are another hardy and drought-resistant tree native to central Mexico. Growing naturally around San Miguel de Allende and the Bajío, they have fluffy yellow flowers and slender green leaves, similar to the mesquite. Both *huizaches* and mesquites grow in lower-lying scrubland, with grass and underbrush rising beneath them.

Throughout the Bajío's cities, the sprawling branches of the jacaranda tree make pleasant shade throughout the year. In the spring, jacarandas become a particularly stunning aspect of the landscape during their annual bloom in March, when they explode into a canopy of purple blossoms. Though not native to Mexico (they are originally from Brazil), these tropical plants thrive in the Bajío's natural environment. Within the cities of San Miguel de Allende and Guanajuato, it is also common to see guava, orange, pomegranate, lime, and other fruit trees, which flourish in the sunny climate.

San Miguel de Allende would not be the same without the brightly hued vines of bougainvillea spilling into the alleyways and brimming over gardens. Although it is not indigenous to Mexico, bougainvillea flourishes here. In some cases, their woody trunks can be as large as trees, while their colored leaves come in a variety of hues, from magenta to orange to white. Another popular decorative plant, poinsettia, is native to Mexico. When not trimmed for a Christmas flowerpot, poinsettia will often grow rather large. The red "flower" of a poinsettia is not a flower at all; in fact, the red petals are actually the plant's upper leaves, which have a hue distinct from the lower, green leaves.

CACTI AND SUCCULENTS

A famous native of the New World, the phenomenal, water-saving cactus proliferates blithely in the low-rainfall region of the Bajío. Consumed as food, distilled for drink, candied for desserts, and artfully planted for low-water landscaping, cacti and succulents play myriad roles in the Bajío.

The large nopal (prickly pear or paddle cactus) is perhaps the most common and recognizable cactus in the region. From a central stalk, a prickly pear grows flat oblong paddles, covered in spines. Its fruit, called tuna in Mexico, is juicy and delicious. In addition, the prickly pear paddle is an easy-to-cultivate, flavorful, and highly nutritious food source. They are sold throughout markets in the Bajío, served in stews, or fried up and stuffed into quesadillas.

Also abundant in the Bajío, the agave has played a central role in traditional Mexican life for centuries. This fleshy cactus is the source of

Lush flora grows around El Chorro, the site of a natural spring, in San Miguel de Allende.

© ARTURO MEADE

agave flower at the end of its life cycle

mezcal, tequila, and pulque, three iconic beverages in Mexican culture. While all agaves have juicy leaves growing in rosettes around their central stalk, there is a wide variety within the genus. There are dozens of agave species in the Bajío, some of which grow quite large. All agaves bloom just once and at the end of their life cycle, sprouting a giant stalk and flowers, which can reach up to nine meters.

Cactus are also popular for gardens and landscaping. Often used as a form of natural fencing, the beautiful columnar organ cactus grows naturally in the region, and it can be found as far north as the United States.

BIRDS

Bird-watching in the Bajío can be interesting for both the novice and expert. There are huge populations of migrant and resident birds throughout the region. The Laja River Valley is one of the first major wetlands south of the U.S. border. Therefore, it is an important route for migrating birds, as well as home

to a surprisingly abundant supply of shorebirds and waterfowl. You may be surprised to learn that there are Mexican ducks, gulls, and grebes spotted around San Miguel de Allende. In fact, there is a large and rather noisy flock of egrets living inside the city itself, which nest at Parque Juárez and in the trees around El Chorro.

Throughout the Bajío, casual observers will notice hummingbirds, wrens, doves, woodpeckers, flycatchers, warblers, towhees, and sparrows. Even those who don't routinely look for birds will undoubtedly spot the gorgeous vermillion flycatcher, a small bird with a black back and a brilliant red chest. You can join an ecological or bird-watching tour in the countryside or around the Presa Allende (the municipal reservoir) to seek out more unusual regional species, like roadrunner.

The Bajío is also an important habitat for birds of prey, notably American kestrels, redtailed hawks, white-tailed kites, crested caracaras, and turkey vultures. In the evenings, it is not uncommon to see large white barn owls soaring over the churches in San Miguel de Allende.

MAMMALS

You are unlikely to spot any large mammals near an urban center, though field mice, squirrels, and other rodents are abundant. In the evenings, it is not uncommon to see jackrabbits or cottontails running through the grasslands outside of the cities. Other nocturnal critters will occasionally wander into the city center, including opossums, skunks, and the elegant ring-tailed cat. Although you are unlikely to catch a glimpse of them, the Bajío is also home to coyotes, gray foxes, and even bobcats.

INSECTS AND ARACHNIDS

Mosquitoes are common throughout the Bajío during the summer and fall. Although they are nuisances, most mosquito-borne illnesses have not been reported in the Bajío for many years. In addition, the Bajío makes a cozy home for

MEEP! MEEP! THE ROADRUNNER AND OTHER INTERESTING BIRDS OF THE BAJÍO

BELTED KINGFISHER

These compact water birds have a bluish-black back, a thick beak, and a large crested head on a stocky body. This bird is best known for its impressive diving abilities, splashing headfirst into the water from great heights and emerging with a fish in its beak.

BROAD-BILLED HUMMINGBIRD

This medium-sized, nectar-loving hummingbird is a dazzling emerald green, and it often nests in the trees and rooftop gardens around San Miguel de Allende. These wee creatures often consume more than their body weight in a day.

CACTUS WREN

A speckled brown-and-white bird with a distinctive white eye-stripe, the lovely cactus wren forages for food in the desert chaparral and is often at home among the spiny branches of the mesquite tree. As its name implies, this large wren may make its nest in the hole of a cactus.

CRESTED CARACARA

These large and striking raptors are found in central Mexico, though a few are spotted in the southernmost regions of the United States. Sometimes called a Mexican eagle, this impressive bird has a black back, white belly, and a wingspan over one meter.

GOLDEN-FRONTED WOODPECKER

One of several woodpeckers tapping around the Bajío, the golden-fronted woodpecker has a golden strip along the back of its neck. In addition to insects, these birds love to eat the fruit of the prickly pear cactus.

GREAT-TAILED GRACKLE

The male members of this grackle species can be distinguished by their long tails and shiny jet-black feathers. Their loud squawks can be heard in cities, where many great-tailed grackles live, and they enjoy a wide range of foods, from insects to berries.

INCA DOVE

Despite its name, this long-tailed pigeon-like dove does not live anywhere near Peru. Instead, you might see these light brown or grayish doves flitting around the Bajío.

PEREGRINE FALCON

One of the world's fastest predators, the compact and beautiful peregrine falcon has gray feathers and a speckled white or rust-colored underbelly. This falcon likes to feast on other birds, rather than rodents or insects, and they catch their unlucky prey in mid-flight.

ROADRUNNER

If you are both observant and lucky, you may catch a glimpse of the wonderful roadrunner in the Bajío countryside. A member of the cuckoo family, this large speckled bird has a feathery crest and strong legs. As in the cartoon, they are incredibly fast runners, capable of catching a snake on the ground. They thrive in semi-arid ecosystems, which are filled insects and reptiles – the roadrunner's favorite fare.

SNOWY EGRET

Few expect to find the elegant, long-legged egret – a classic water bird – in the Mexican high desert. However, the snowy egret has found a happy nesting spot in the trees around Parque Juárez in San Miguel de Allende, as well as along the shores of the city's reservoir.

VERMILLION FLYCATCHER

The small but brilliant vermillion flycatcher makes its home in the southwestern United States and central Mexico. Its plump body with red chest is a welcome sight among the green leaves of a mesquite tree, where it feasts on insects.

WHITE-THROATED SWIFT

Swift as its name implies, this high-speed bird has a black back and wings, though this species can be distinguished from other regional swifts by its white throat feathers. One of the fastest birds, it can travel at up to 320 kilometers per hour.

scorpions, spiders, cockroaches, grasshoppers, praying mantises, crickets, and beetles. While scorpions and spiders are the most universally feared, they are usually reclusive and avoid human contact.

In addition to pests, the Bajío is a good place to spot colorful dragonflies, damselflies, and dozens of butterfly species. Often, in the early spring or late fall, you can spot monarch butterflies traveling over the Bajío on their way to their winter nesting grounds in the state of Michoacán.

© ARTURO MEADE

Grasshoppers rest on a cactus.

History

EARLY HISTORY

Anthropologists believe that the first humans arrived in the Americas about 30,000 years ago, crossing a narrow land bridge over the Bering Strait from Asia. In the Bajío region, little is known about the first human inhabitants; however, archaeologists have discovered marble weapons and tools that date back to 20,000 B.C. in the state of Guanajuato. While they lived on the land for millennia, the original migrants to North America eventually died out, and were supplanted by a new wave of immigrants at the beginning of the Stone Age. These people, most likely of Asian descent, settled the entire continent, reaching all the way into the Andes Mountains of South America. As the planet began to warm, the oceans rose and the land bridge between Asia and the Americas disappeared. Thereafter, America was physically isolated from Asia and Europe.

MESOAMERICAN CIVILIZATIONS

Between 8000 and 2000 B.C. sedentary human settlements began to develop in southern Mexico, Belize, Guatemala, Honduras, El Salvador, and Nicaragua. This swath of culturally linked territory is generally called Mesoamerica, which means "middle America." Like all humans during the Stone Age, early Americans were hunter-gatherers. While the

first agricultural settlements in Eurasia date back to 6200 B.C., studies suggest that farming began around 2500 B.C. in the western hemisphere. With farming came civilizations of increasing complexity. By the time the Spanish arrived in the New World, Mesoamerica was home to some of the largest, most sophisticated, and most populous civilizations in the world.

The first great Mesoamerican culture, the Olmecs, appeared in the lowlands around the states of Veracruz and Tabasco around 1500 B.C. Little is known about the Olmec culture, though they left behind ruins of their urban centers and their famous sculptures of massive stone heads. Several centuries later, the first Maya civilizations began to flourish around the Yucatán Peninsula, Guatemala, and Belize. The Maya were great artists, astronomers, and architects who built massive pyramid-temples at the center of their cities. On the eve of the conquest, the Maya were still a populous people in Southern Mexico (as they are today), though their cities had been mysteriously abandoned in the 8th and 9th centuries A.D. To the east, the Zapotec civilization began to flourish in the modern-day state of Oaxaca.

To the north, an unknown culture built the city of Teotihuacan around 200 B.C. This massive metropolis includes two of the world's tallest pyramids. The central Mexican region was later controlled by the massive Toltec empire

THE CHICHIMECA:
ORIGINAL INHABITANTS OF THE BAJÍO

When the Spanish conquest arrived in the Americas, the regions around modern-day Mexico City were home to large sedentary populations. To the north, the land was more sparsely populated, principally dominated by nomadic tribes that were not under the control of the massive Aztec empire. As missionaries and ranchers began to settle the Bajío, they named Mexico's great central plateau El Gran Chichimeca. The name "Chichimeca" does not refer to any tribe in particular; it is a general term that the Nahuatl-speaking people of central Mexico used to refer to the nomadic tribes of the north.

Today, there is little record of the tribes that dominated Northern Mexico, nor is there a record of the languages and customs that distinguished one tribe from another. Even the number of people living in Northern Mexico then cannot be accurately determined. Based on different evidence, historians have estimated that there were between 150,000 and 625,000 indigenous people in El Gran Chichimeca, covering about 450,000 square kilometers of territory. Some of these tribes practiced modest agriculture, but most were nomadic hunter-gatherers.

Though little is known about the Chichimeca, one thing we do know is that the Spanish settlers, like the Mexica, were frightened of them. Wild and bellicose, rival tribes of the Chichimeca were often war with each other. What's more, their battle tactics were psychologically terrifying; warriors would strip down and cover themselves in full body paint, screaming as they ran in for attack. When victorious, they often tortured prisoners of war. The Spanish regarded the Chichimeca as savages, accusing them of cruelty and cannibalism in the few texts they wrote about the people. Despite their fear, the Spanish pursuit of silver and gold pushed them deep into Chichimeca territory. Hoping to settle the region, the Spanish royalty doled out many land grants during the 1540s, sending migrants and farmers to the Bajío and beyond. In addition to gold seekers,

Franciscan friars were among the first to make inroads into this vast territory, often setting up schools and churches in remote Chichimeca outposts.

For the indigenous people of El Gran Chichimeca, the introduction of mining to the northern territories was a huge threat to their way of life. When Spanish ranchers arrived, the new settlers and their animals encroached on Chichimeca land. In the early years of the silver trade, wagoners on the Camino Real let their horses and donkeys graze on Indian corn fields. In turn, Chichimeca Indians began to raid the Spanish settlements, stealing cattle, robbing stores, and attacking donkey trains headed for Mexico City along the silver route. On top of that, cattle ranches changed the quality of land and its soil (in Zacatecas, large grasslands were eventually rendered semi-arid due to extensive livestock grazing).

In the 1550s, the tribes of the Gran Chichimeca began to launch more serious attacks on the Spanish settlers, who retaliated in kind. This period of violent clashes is often called the Chichimeca War. The silver barons largely financed this war against the native people; surprisingly, they had more expendable funds than the Spanish crown. Many Chichimeca prisoners of war were enslaved after their capture. Those who lived peacefully on the land were also enslaved to work in the mines or on ranches.

It wasn't until the beginning of the 1600s that the Spanish settlers were able to dominate the tribes along the silver route. Most were killed or displaced, and those who survived began to assimilate into mestizo culture, replacing their homes in caves for straw houses in Spanish settlements. Some Chichimeca pueblos were established, but even these were eventually reduced and finally disappeared. The only Chichimeca tribe that survived was the Pames of San Luis Potosí. Zacatecos survived in small settlements until the 17th century and worked in Spanish mines and family homes as servants and slaves.

Adobe buildings in Mineral de Pozos show their age.

A.D. 800–1000. The Toltecs would eventually disperse, about a century before the Nahuatl-speaking people (often known as the Aztec) took power in central Mexico.

Until recently, there had been very little study of the pre-Columbian cultures that inhabited the Bajío region. Numerous ruins and religious sites from sedentary cultures have been discovered throughout the states of Guanajuato and Querétaro, most of which share similar architectural styles and cultural characteristics. To date, few have been opened for study (and even fewer are open for tourism). However, early studies strongly suggest that these ruins once pertained to the Toltec empire in Tula. For unknown reasons, these cultures were impelled to abandon their cities to join the people in Tula's capital city, farther south. When the Spanish arrived in the Bajío during the 16th century, there were few sedentary civilizations remaining in the region. Instead, the region was dominated by nomadic hunter-gatherer tribes, collectively referred to as the Chichimecas.

THE CONQUEST

General estimates suggest that there were as many as 30 million people living in modern-day Mexico when Christopher Columbus arrived in the New World. During the 15th century, Nahuatl-speaking people dominated Mesoamerica from the powerful tri-city alliance of Tenochtitlan, Texcoco, and Tlacopan near modern day Mexico City. Ruled by the Mexica people, Tenochtitlan was a massive city of grand pyramids and large public squares, connected by waterways and teeming with markets and activity. The Mexica were accomplished artists and thinkers, with advanced city planning and agricultural capabilities, a calendar system, and complex religious beliefs. They were also bellicose warriors, hated and feared by the other civilizations in Mesoamerica. During the 15th century, Tenochtitlan was one of the largest cities in the world—more populous than any city in Spain.

In 1519, Hernán Cortés set sail for Mexico from the Spanish colony in Cuba. Having come with the intention to secure the land for

Spain, Cortés and his soldiers initially made peaceful contact with the rulers of Tenochtitlan and were welcomed into the city by emperor Montezuma. Tensions brewed, and, after a misguided Spanish attack on Mexica nobles, the relationship soured. War between the Spanish and Tenochtitlan was inevitable.

Though the fight between the Spanish and Mexica was long and brutal, many tribes near Tenochtitlan assisted the Spanish forces in battling Tenochtitlan, which had terrorized their villages for centuries. The Spanish were further assisted by the smallpox virus, which they had unwittingly introduced to the Americas. Once infected with smallpox, thousands of native people fell sick and died, greatly weakening the Mexica's power. After numerous attempts to take the capital city, Hernán Cortés and his cavalry successfully overthrew the people of Tenochtitlan in 1521.

THE COLONIAL ERA

Shortly after Cortés's final definitive victory over the Mexica, Spanish settlement of Mexico began. Missionaries and settlers began to arrive in the New World, seeking Catholic converts and worldly fortune. The first Spanish viceroy of Mexico, Don Antonio de Mendoza, took his post in 1535. For the next 300 years, the Spanish crown would control politics, religion, and trade in the colonies.

To encourage settlement, the Spanish crown doled out land grants to Spanish settlers, authorizing them to begin farming and mining operations in the north. The Franciscans were among the first groups to settle the states of Michoacán, Querétaro, and Guanajuato, where they opened rural schools and hospitals, hoping to attract native people. In 1543, Fray Juan de San Miguel founded San Miguel de los Chichimecas on the banks of the Río Laja.

Having heard news of the conquest, the native tribes in the Bajío region were not welcoming to the Spanish settlers. The Chichimeca repeatedly attacked Spanish ranches and raided their donkey trains. San Miguel de Allende and other settlements were temporarily abandoned during a period called the Chichimec War, a protracted series of attacks against the Spanish, which ran roughly 1550–1590. Despite hostility from the native people and harsh desert conditions, the thirst for gold and silver created an incredible incentive for Spanish settlers to expand their interests in the northern region. Many Spanish landowners helped to fund the war against the native people, in the absence of sufficient support from the crown.

Despite hardship, Spanish efforts quickly paid off. In 1546, a Spanish convoy found a large silver vein in Zacatecas, and, shortly thereafter, silver was discovered in both Guanajuato and San Luis Potosí. The mining settlements required enormous resources, and, in turn, generated impressive wealth. Throughout central and north Mexico, mine owners commissioned churches and built lavish mansions, making the "silver cities" some of New Spain's most beautiful settlements. A long highway connected the northern mines to the capital in Mexico City, known as the Camino Real de Tierra Adentro (Royal Inland Route). Both San Miguel de Allende and Querétaro were important protective towns along this route, gaining incredible wealth through auxiliary industries and agriculture. Like the silver cities, they were lavishly constructed in the baroque style of the 17th and 18th centuries.

Over the course of the next century, the Chichimeca were subdued by the Spanish and the Bajío region became a prominent, wealthy, and heavily populated part of New Spain. Although the Bajío was originally divided into large haciendas, or rural estates, it eventually became more developed as the silver trade flourished. By the 18th century, immigrants from across Mexico had come to work in the mines and industries, and the Bajío became one of the most densely populated regions in the world.

Throughout Mexico, the colonial era was a time of great inequity, and the Bajío was no exception. With the incredible wealth gleaned from the silver trade and related industries, ruling families lived in lavish mansions, traveled in horse-drawn carriages, and ate food imported from Spain. At the same time, disenfranchised indigenous laborers often worked for impossibly low wages and lived in inhumane conditions.

Divided by ethnicity and heritage, colonial society was highly stratified. In the New World, full-blood Spaniards born in Spain were called *peninsulares* (for the Spanish peninsula where they were born) or *gachupines,* and they retained the highest social status. *Peninsulares* were also appointed to all of the most important political posts. Mexican-born people of Spanish heritage were referred to as criollo and, despite their common heritage, had a lower social and political standing. Mestizo people of mixed ethnic heritage held a far lower place in society, only better than the abysmal position of indigenous people and black slaves.

WAR OF INDEPENDENCE

Among the criollo population, there was already quite a bit of resentment against peninsular-born Spanish when the Bourbon kings took control of Spain in the 18th century. A self-proclaimed "enlightened despot," King Charles III made major changes to the oversight of Spanish territories in the New World. He quickly established royal monopolies on many important industries, like tobacco, ice, stamped paper, mercury (an important element for silver extraction), and gunpowder. He also declared a Spanish monopoly on profits from cockfights and outlawed church loans, a major source of credit within Mexican communities. For many—especially those in the pious Bajío region—the most outrageous blow was King Charles's expulsion of the Jesuits from Mexico in 1767.

In the Bajío, rich criollo landowners began to hatch a plan against the Spanish governors of Mexico. Independent thinkers like Juan Aldama and Ignacio Allende from San Miguel began to hold secret meetings with other conspirators, including Miguel Domínguez, the Mexican-born governor of Querétaro. Pastor Miguel Hidalgo from the small town Dolores was among the conspirators' most important allies, a beloved priest with great influence among the native and mestizo people. When Napoleon invaded Spain in 1807, the conspirators decided to exploit the Spanish weakness and plan their attack against the crown.

Originally, Aldama and Allende were selected to oversee the independence army; however, there was a change of plans when Spanish loyalists in Querétaro uncovered their plot. Alerted to the conspiracy, royalists locked conspirator Josefa Ortiz de Domínguez into a government mansion; however, she managed to get the word to Allende and Hidalgo before the Spanish forces could arrest them. With no time left, Hidalgo immediately launched the insurgency.

On September 16, 1810, Miguel Hidalgo released the prisoners from the Dolores jail and then ascended the stairs before the city's parish church. There, he gave an impassioned call to war, rousing the crowd with his famous words, *"¡Viva Mexico!"* (This is known today as *el grito.*) With a ragtag army and small cavalry, Hidalgo rode from Dolores to the settlement at Atotonilco, where he gave another call to arms. In Atotonilco, Hidalgo seized a banner from the Catholic sanctuary that bore the image of the Virgen de Guadalupe. The banner would become the official flag for the Mexican army and a symbol of independent Mexico.

Hidalgo's army met with easy success in San Miguel de Allende and Celaya but sustained major casualties in taking the city of Guanajuato. Thereafter, a major loss at Battle of the Bridge of Calderón threw the army into chaos, precipitating the upcoming 11 years of chaotic armed conflict. The following year, Miguel Hidalgo, Ignacio Allende, and Juan Aldama were ambushed and executed by royalist forces.

After the death of Hidalgo and the other army generals, José María Morelos took over as head of the army. He in turn was captured and executed. The battles continued haphazardly across the country for almost a decade until the government of Ferdinand VII was overthrown in Spain. As a result of the change in Spanish governance, Colonel Agustín de Iturbide, a fierce royalist, switched sides to join the Mexican army. With Iturbide at the

INDEPENDENT SPIRIT

During the colonial era, the Bajío region was one of the wealthiest and most influential areas in New Spain. During the early 19th century, influential landowners resisted the policy change instituted by Spain's Bourbon kings, and began to plan a conspiracy against the crown. Many of the most famous figures in the history of Mexico are from the cities of San Miguel de Allende, Dolores Hidalgo, and Querétaro. Today, you will see their names on statues, on street corners, and in public plazas throughout the region.

MIGUEL HIDALGO Y COSTILLA

The great leader of the independence movement, Miguel Hidalgo was born in Dolores, Guanajuato; the city was later renamed Dolores Hidalgo in his honor. Hidalgo was a parish priest and an incredibly popular figure with the local population. As the general of the Mexican army, he officially gave the call for the revolution to begin with his famous cry, *"¡Viva Mexico!"*

IGNACIO ALLENDE

A wealthy landowner from one of San Miguel's most prominent families, Ignacio Allende was one of the chief conspirators against the Spanish crown. A high-ranking official in the Spanish military, he hosted secret meetings at his home on San Miguel's central plaza, the *jardín*. During the war, Allende fought alongside General Hidalgo.

JOSEFA ORTIZ DE DOMÍNGUEZ

The wife of Querétaro's mayor, Josefa Ortiz de Domínguez was one of the few women to actively participate in the conspiracy. When the conspirators' plot was discovered by Spanish royalists, Ortiz de Domínguez was imprisoned. However, she was able to send news by courier to Allende and Hidalgo, sparing them arrest and saving the independence movement.

JUAN ALDAMA

When the news of the conspiracy's discovery reached San Miguel de Allende, Juan Aldama rushed to Dolores, where he informed independence leaders Ignacio Allende and Miguel Hidalgo that the plot had been uncovered. He fought in the war with Allende and Hidalgo, and today his name graces one of the prettiest streets in San Miguel, **Calle Aldama.**

JUAN JOSÉ DE LOS REYES MARTÍNEZ

Popularly known as El Pípila, Juan José de los Reyes Martínez was born in San Miguel de Allende; he worked in the mines of Guanajuato when the War of Independence broke out. He is remembered throughout the Bajío for his bravery in the battle to take the Alhóndiga de Granaditas in Guanajuato, an early and important victory for the Mexican Army.

JOSÉ MARIANO JIMÉNEZ

Though not a Bajío native (he was born in San Luis Potosí), Jiménez's legacy is closely tied to the city of Guanajuato. This leader of the Mexican Army was executed along with Hidalgo, Allende, and Aldama, and, like his fellow heroes, his severed head was suspended from a corner of the Alhóndiga de Granaditas by royalist forces.

helm, Mexico achieved independence in 1821 with the signing of the Treaty of Córdoba in Córdoba, Veracruz.

THE NEW NATION AND THE MEXICAN-AMERICAN WAR

The end of armed conflict ushered in a century of political unrest and instability in Mexico. After finally securing independence from Spain, Mexico took its shaky first steps toward establishing an autonomous nation. Both Guanajuato and Querétaro were recognized among 24 states in the First Mexican Empire, with independence leader Agustín de Iturbide acting as interim head of state.

In 1823, Antonio López de Santa Anna led a successful revolt against Iturbide's government, thereafter establishing the first Mexican republic. Again, Guanajuato and Querétaro were included among the federation of 19 states, and Guadalupe Victoria, another hero of the War of Independence, became the country's first president.

It was during this period of unrest that U.S. citizens began to settle in Texas with the permission of the Mexican government. These settlers had little interest in conforming to Mexico's laws, and when conflict between the American settlers and the government reached a head, Santa Anna sent troops to Texas. Texas briefly gained total independence; however, tensions flared when the territory was annexed by the United States. After several battles in Texas, the U.S. Army invaded Mexico from the north, marching to the capital via Puebla and taking control of Mexico City. The capital of Mexico was temporarily relocated to Querétaro. In Querétaro, Santa Anna signed the infamous Treaty of Guadalupe, which ceded half of Mexico's territory to the United States, including California, New Mexico, Arizona, Texas, and Nevada.

REFORMATION AND THE PORFIRIATO

Santa Anna was ousted after another coup in 1855. Liberal Oaxacan politician Benito Juárez became president of the republic and took the lead on a series of liberal reforms, including the abolishment of church property and the constitutional recognition of freedom of religion. Juárez's celebrated presidency was interrupted in 1860 when France invaded Mexico under Napoleon III. The French established the Second Mexican Empire, placing Emperor Maximilian I in charge of the state. In 1867, there was yet another successful upheaval by the liberals, and Maximilian was executed in Querétaro. Benito Juárez returned to the presidency, and he remained in power until his death in 1872.

Not long after Juárez's successor, Sebastián Lerdo de Tejada, had won his second election, army general Porfirio Díaz took office in a coup. A powerful leader with a strong military outlook, Díaz was both a dictator and despot;

he created a strong central government that favored foreign investment. While the country's wealth increased, social conditions for the poor only worsened under Díaz's iron-fisted control. While his legacy is controversial, Díaz did manage to keep Mexico in relative peace during his entire presidency. His rule is known as the Porfiriato.

The Porfiriato was a mixed blessing for the Bajío, where some cities flourished while others withered away in disrepair. San Miguel de Allende was all but abandoned, its churches left to crumble and its tiny population dwindling away. Guanajuato, on the other hand, continued to produce silver and received handsome gifts from the president himself. Porfirio Díaz attended the grand opening of Teatro Juárez, and he commissioned the city's beautiful municipal market in commemoration of the independence movement. The silver town of Pozos was also a favorite of the president, who renamed the city Ciudad Porfirio Díaz.

MEXICAN REVOLUTION

In response to the ongoing dictatorship of conservative leader Porfirio Díaz, wealthy politician Francisco I. Madero announced his intentions to run for the presidency. When Díaz threw him in jail, Madero helped to organize a revolution against the government, assisted by general Victoriano Huerta. The great idealist revolutionary, Emiliano Zapata, joined their efforts in the south, recruiting a troop of peasant soldiers and demanding large-scale land reform on behalf of the people.

Once Madero took the presidency, he proved to be a weak leader, uninterested in enacting the land reforms for peasants that had inspired Zapata to join him. Observing this weakness, Huerta organized a coup against Madero, taking the presidency himself after Madero was executed. Again, Mexico's famous rebel leaders joined forces. Together, Venustiano Carranza, Álvaro Obregón, Pancho Villa, and Emiliano Zapata led the revolt against Huerta's government, with additional support from the U.S. Army. They successfully toppled the regime in August 1914, with Carranza at the head of the army.

Carranza took the presidency with initial opposition from Villa and Zapata. However, he won support with the people through promises of land reform, eventually overseeing the writing of the Constitution of 1917. The new constitution was based on the Constitution of 1857, though it included many important land, law, and labor reforms. Carranza was eventually forced out of power and replaced by General Álvaro Obregón. Pancho Villa was ambushed and executed during the Obregón presidency, likely at the president's own command.

THE 20TH CENTURY

Mexico's government began to stabilize in the decades following the revolution, eventually coalescing into a single political party, the Institutional Revolutionary Party (PRI). The post-revolutionary period was a time of great progress, as the country began to flourish culturally and intellectually. During Obregón's presidency, vanguard thinker José Vasconcelos served as the Secretary of Public Education. Vasconcelos oversaw the establishment of the National Symphonic Orchestra and the Symphonic Orchestra of Mexico. He also began the Mexican mural program, through which famous painters like Diego Rivera and David Alfaro Siqueiros were commissioned to paint monumental art on the walls of public buildings. After the 1920s, the Mexican economy began to grow annually.

In 1937, Lázaro Cárdenas was elected to the presidency. He continued to reform land rights and redistribute territory as laid out in the Constitution of 1917. In a move that would serve as a model for other oil-rich nations, Cárdenas expropriated oil reserves from the private companies that had been running them. He established Petróleos Mexicanos (Pemex), concurrently founding the National Polytechnic Institute to ensure a sufficient engineering force in the country. Among other famous decisions, Lázaro Cárdenas granted exile to Bolshevik revolutionary Leon Trotsky, who lived the final years of his life in Mexico City.

Music and cinema flourished during the 1930s and 1940s, with Mexican movies outselling Hollywood films during World War II. During and after the Spanish Civil War, many European intellectuals took up residence in Mexico, adding to the thriving art and cultural community. In the 1950s, Luis Buñuel, the famous Spanish filmmaker, made some of his most influential pictures in Mexico, eventually naturalizing as a Mexican citizen.

In the second half of the century, Mexico began to depend heavily on the income from oil exports, which eventually led to a devastating economic crisis in 1982. It took more than a decade for Mexico's economy to recover. Just as it did, Mexico became a member of NAFTA on January 1, 1994, a massive free trade agreement with the United States and Canada.

The same morning that NAFTA went into effect, a small indigenous army called the Ejército Zapatista de Liberación Nacional (EZLN) took control of three cities in the southern state of Chiapas. This rebellion was small in scope but wide-reaching in consequences, inspiring widespread support for indigenous people throughout Mexico and the world. The army's leader, Subcommandante Marcos, became a national spokesman for the indigenous cause and met repeatedly with Mexican government leaders.

Government

As laid out in the Constitution of 1917, Mexico is a federal republic overseen by an elected government. Like its neighbor to the north, it is a federation of 32 individually governed states (including the *distrito federal,* or federal district), united by a national government in Mexico City.

ORGANIZATION

Mexico is overseen by a federal government, which divides into three branches: executive, legislative, and judicial. The president, elected to a single six-year term, oversees the executive branch. The Congress is divided into the Senate and Chamber of Deputies, and there is a single supreme court, with justices appointed by the president. Each of Mexico's 32 states has three representatives in the senate. Citizens elect two of the three senators, while the leading minority party appoints the third. There are 500 deputies in the Chamber of Deputies, with one representative for every 200,000 citizens. Of these, the people directly elect 300, while the other 200 are appointed by proportional representation. The federal government operates in the *distrito federal* (federal district) in Mexico City, or Mexico D.F.

There are 32 states in Mexico, each overseen by its own state government. In each state, power is also divided between the executive, legislative, and judicial branches, with an elected governor overseeing executive activities. States are independent and sovereign. Each has its own laws, though none can enact laws that contradict the country's federal constitution.

Each state in Mexico is further divided into autonomous municipalities. Municipalities are managed differently in each state; however, a municipality usually comprises a larger city and all the small towns and ranches surrounding it. In San Miguel de Allende, for example, Los Rodríguez is overseen by the municipality, even though it is about 16 kilometers (10 miles) outside the city and has almost 3,000 inhabitants.

Municipalities are run by a local government, with a *presidente municipal* (municipal president) elected democratically to a nonrenewable post. In the Bajío, a large percentage of the state and municipal divisions were laid under the Spanish viceroyalty, which divided the country into *ayuntamientos* (town councils), overseen by local governors.

Both Guanajuato and Querétaro are the capitals of their states and therefore are home to both the municipal and state government.

POLITICAL PARTIES

From the end of the Mexican Revolution until the year 2000, the Partido Revolucionario Institucional (PRI, Institutional Revolutionary Party) was the sole party in Mexican politics. Although once considered socialist, the PRI upholds more centrist views today. Their members and supporters are called *priistas.*

During its long reign over Mexico, the PRI was commonly accused of running a dictatorship. Members were also widely charged with corruption and fraud. Although the PRI had a fraught relationship with the Mexican people, it remained uncontested for most of the 20th century. In 1988, PRI defector Cuauhtémoc Cárdenas ran against the official PRI candidate but was defeated in a highly controversial election that included an unexplained glitch in the electoral system.

In 2000, President Vicente Fox Quesada was elected to the office of president under the conservative Partido Acción Nacional (PAN, National Action Party) ticket. Before his election, Fox was a prominent businessman in the Bajío and the supervisor of the Coca-Cola company in Mexico and Latin America. He represented Guanajuato in the Chamber of Deputies then served as governor of the state 1995–1999. His home and ranch are located in the community of San Cristóbal, Guanajuato. After Fox's election, the PRI underwent serious restructuring and continues to be an influential political party in Mexico.

© ARTURO MEADE

a government building in downtown Guanajuato

In 2006, Felipe Calderón, also a PAN candidate, won the presidential elections by a slim margin and amid prominent accusations of fraud from the opposing candidate, Manuel López Obrador. López Obrador is a member of the third prominent political party, the Partido de la Revolución Democrática (PRD, Party of the Democratic Revolution), traditionally the most leftist of the three major parties.

In the states of Guanajuato and Querétaro, voters tend to elect fiscally and socially conservative candidates. PAN has a loyal following in Guanajuato, home of former president Vincente Fox. Querétaro is also considered an important stronghold for the PAN, where they repeatedly receive a large percentage of votes. PAN has controlled the Querétaro government since 1997.

ELECTIONS

Elections for both national and regional posts are secret, universal, compulsory, and free. They are overseen by the Instituto Federal Electoral (Federal Electoral Institute). IFE credentials, or voting cards, are the national form of identification, so there is no need to separately register to vote. The president and senators are elected to one six-year term. State and regional elections may or may not be held concurrently with federal elections.

Economy

Mexico has a free-market economy, with energy, agriculture, manufacturing, ranching, fishing, and forestry forming the largest sectors. After Brazil, Mexico is the second largest economy in Latin America and is among the 15 biggest economies in the world. Nonetheless, the distribution of wealth in Mexico is highly uneven, with widespread poverty throughout the country.

Although Mexico's economy has grown steadily throughout the 20th century, it has suffered from intermittent crises. In 1982, the country fell into a serious recession, principally caused by poor economic policy, falling oil prices, and high inflation worldwide. Having borrowed extensively from international banks, Mexico's president, Miguel de la Madrid, was forced to reduce public spending. Economic recovery was slow, lasting almost the entire decade. In 1996, the currency was devalued.

During the worldwide financial crisis of 2009, Mexico's GDP dropped 6.5 percent, with remittances from the United States also dropping off as that country suffered economic crisis. Since the crisis, the economy has been rebuilding, with significant foreign investment during 2010.

Guanajuato contributes about 3.5 percent to the national gross domestic product (GDP), with manufacturing its largest industry. Among all states, Guanajuato's has the seventh largest economy in Mexico. Querétaro is a much smaller state, yet also a manufacturing capital. In total, Querétaro contributes about 1.8 percent to the GDP.

AGRICULTURE

Although a large percentage of Mexico's population is involved in agricultural activities, farming has slowly become less important to the nation's overall economy. Currently, agriculture accounts for just 4.3 percent of the GDP. At the same time, more than 15 percent of Mexico's people work on farms. Data suggests that at least half of Mexican farmers are subsistence farmers, principally producing corn or beans on five hectares or fewer.

With its fertile plains and large watershed,

A rancher leads a small herd of goats down a dirt road near Atotonilco.

the Bajío has traditionally been an important agricultural region in Mexico. The state of Guanajuato is the country's biggest producer of strawberries and broccoli, as well as a major producer of asparagus, rye, barley, wheat grain, alfalfa, and sorghum. Querétaro is a top producer of roses, in addition to significant crops of vegetables, grain, and meat. In both Querétaro and Guanajuato, there has been an increase the production of organic fruits, vegetables, and dairy products over the past decade. Agriculture accounts for only a small percentage of Querétaro and Guanajuato's overall economy.

MANUFACTURING

Manufacturing is a huge contributor to Mexico's economy, accounting for up to 90 percent of the country's exports and 20 percent of the GDP. Manufacturing is crucial to Guanajuato, comprising almost 24 percent of the state's economy. León, Guanajuato's biggest city, and the suburb of Silao are major manufacturing zones. Within manufacturing, metal products and machinery account for the largest manufacturing sectors countrywide, followed by food and tobacco, chemicals, petroleum products, and shoes and clothing.

ENERGY

Mexico built its first oil well in 1896. Today, it is the world's sixth largest oil producer. All natural resources, including oil, are state property, as declared by president Lázaro Cárdenas in the 1930s. Petróleos Mexicanos, or Pemex for short, is the state-run company in charge of extracting, refining, and distributing oil. Although it has faltered over the years, Pemex is the single largest source of income for the country. Mexico meets almost 90 percent of its own energy needs internally.

TOURISM

Mexico is one of the world's most popular destinations, welcoming more than 20 million visitors annually. Although Mexico is most famous for its beach resorts, cultural tourism is also a major draw in the country's colonial towns and cities. The Mexican government invests heavily in tourism, including massive international marketing campaigns designed to attract potential visitors to the country.

Tourism is vital to the Bajío's economy, especially in cities like San Miguel de Allende, Guanajuato, Tequisquiapan, and Bernal, which rely heavily on the income from hotels, restaurants, gift shops, tour operators, and other tourist-related activities. Since it was declared a United Nations World Heritage Site, Guanajuato has seen a huge increase in tourism. Today, it is one of the most popular cultural destinations in the country for both national and international tourists. Even Querétaro, a state less recognized as a tourist destination, owes 20 percent of its internal economy to tourism and related commercial activities.

RELATIONSHIP WITH THE UNITED STATES

Historically, the United States has always been Mexico's most important trading partner. That status has become even more important since the North American Free Trade Agreement (NAFTA) was inaugurated in 1994, creating a tri-lateral free trade zone between Canada, the United States, and Mexico. In the decades following NAFTA's acceptance, trade between Mexico and the United States of America tripled. (Trade ties between Mexico and Canada have also strengthened.) Today, export to the United States makes up a quarter of the Mexican GDP, though Mexico also has free trade agreements with dozens of other countries. The largest exports to the U.S. are oil, cars, and electronics.

Mexico's economy is closely linked to the economy of the United States. After NAFTA was ratified, many U.S. companies relocated their factories south of the border, creating an even larger manufacturing industry in Mexico. Some studies report that Mexico's maquiladoras, or manufacturing plants, have increased 15 percent since 1994. Although these maquiladoras were originally located along the border, León, Guanajuato, is one of the central Mexican cities that has experienced a massive increase in the manufacturing sector since NAFTA.

In addition to Mexico's trade partnership with the United States, roughly 8–10 percent of the Mexican population resides legally or illegally in the United States. Remittances from Mexicans living in the United States add up to about US$21 billion each year, the second largest source of foreign currency after energy and oil.

DISTRIBUTION OF WEALTH

Mexico is a wealthy nation with abundant natural resources and a GDP among the world's largest. Unfortunately, Mexico's wealth is not distributed evenly through its population. According to data produced by the Mexican government, 44 percent of Mexico's people live in poverty. Of those, 11.2 million people (or roughly 10 percent of the total population) are living in extreme poverty, lacking access to basic medical care or sufficient food.

Poverty varies by region. Wealth is concentrated in and around the capital, Mexico D.F., and along the U.S. border. Chiapas is the poorest and most southerly state of Mexico, where almost 77 percent of the population lives in poverty, and the annual per capita income was less than US$4,000 in 2007. The Bajío region is neither the richest nor the poorest part of Mexico. In 2007, Querétaro's per capita annual income was between US$7,000 and US$9,999, whereas Guanajuato rung in a bit lower, between US$5,200 and US$6,999 per capita annually. The national average was US$8,945.

Inflation in food and energy costs has made the effects of poverty more profound for many of Mexico's people. However, the lack of opportunities and employment for a large sector of the population makes it difficult to eradicate poverty, especially in rural areas. Social programs have lagged.

People and Culture

DEMOGRAPHY

Mexico is a large and multi-ethnic country. There are varying figures with regards to its population demographics; however, in broad strokes, the country is a mix of indigenous, mestizo, and white people. Indigenous people (*indígenas*), are direct descendants of the native people of Mexico, and many still speak native languages. According to Mexico's census data, the country's population is about 10–12 percent indigenous, though numbers vary greatly by region. The majority of Mexicans are considered mestizo, a broad term that refers to a mix of ethnic and cultural heritage, which may include white, indigenous, and African ethnicities. Most white people in Mexico are Spanish descendants, though there have also been other European migrants to Mexico over the course of country's history. Mexico is also home to small populations of Turkish, Lebanese, Chinese, Japanese, and Korean people.

About six million people in Mexico speak an indigenous language, though the vast majority of these people also speak Spanish. There are 62 indigenous languages spoken across Mexico. Relatively speaking, there is only a small indigenous community in the Bajío region. In the state of Querétaro, about two percent of the people speak an indigenous language, with the largest populations of indigenous communities concentrated in the cities of Amealco de Bonfil and Tolimán. In the state of Guanajuato, less than one percent of the people speak an indigenous language.

The vast majority of the people in Guanajuato and Querétaro live in urban environments. In both states, roughly 75 percent live in cities, with almost half of Querétaro's total population residing in the capital. These statistics reflect an overall trend in Mexico, where the majority of the population lives in overcrowded urban centers. In fact, over 50 percent of Mexico's total population resides in the country's 55 biggest cities.

EMIGRATION

Although the figures are not exact, an estimated 8–10 percent of all Mexican citizens live in the United States. Mexican emigration to the United States has a major influence on Mexico's economy and culture, especially in states where emigration is high. After oil, remittances from Mexicans living overseas account for about US$21 billion of annual income, the country's second largest source of foreign currency.

According to a study conducted by the National Institute of Statistics and Geography (INEGI) in 2000, the state of Guanajuato has one of the highest emigration rates in the country, along with the states of Zacatecas, Michoacán, and Durango. In 2000, roughly 3.5 percent of Guanajuato's population immigrated to the United States, or about 163,300 people that year. In the same year, the state of Querétaro lost about 1.8 percent of its population to emigration, or 24,700 people. By comparison, about 1.6 percent of the total Mexican population moves to the United States annually.

RELIGION

Spanish missionaries introduced Catholicism to the native population in Mexico during the 15th and 16th centuries. Missionaries were extremely active in New Spain, establishing an abundance of churches, Catholic schools, and hospitals, often with the financial assistance of wealthy Spanish nobles. The largest Catholic cathedral in the Americas is just beside the government buildings in Mexico City's central plaza, indicating the enormous importance of the church to both the state and the people.

During the early Spanish conquest, there were massive conversions among the indigenous population to Catholicism. Conversions spiked after the apparition of the Virgen de Guadalupe in Mexico City in 1531. While accepting the new religion, many indigenous communities incorporated their own religious beliefs into Roman Catholic ritual, creating some unique Catholic traditions in the New World.

Throughout Spanish rule of Mexico, the Catholic church had a major influence on governance and society. During the independence era, the image of the Virgen de Guadalupe adorned the official flag of Mexico's first national army. Catholics continued to maintain massive power in Mexico until the 1850s, when president Benito Juárez began to secularize the country's constitution and laws. Among other reforms, he limited church power and appropriated church property for the state. While the relationship between the church and government warmed after Juárez left office, anti-clerical forces gained power during the Mexican Revolution. The current Mexican constitution separates church and state. Nonetheless, the Catholic church continues to be an important part of Mexico's national identity. Almost 90 percent of Mexicans identify as Catholic.

Guanajuato and Querétaro are largely conservative and Catholic states: 95 percent of Querétaro's residents and 96 percent of Guanajuato's residents identify as Catholic,

Weddings and religious festivals are celebrated with dancing paper dolls, called *mojigangas*.

© ARTURO MEADE

and, as a result, Catholicism is a big part of civic life in central Mexico. Foreigners from any background will quickly be introduced to myriad Catholic holidays, often celebrated with rich tradition and pageantry. The Holy Week festivities in San Miguel de Allende, for example, are among the country's most beautiful and well attended. Every town celebrates its patron saint's holiday with enormous fanfare and parties. Religion also plays an important role in personal and family life, with milestones like baptism, confirmation, weddings, and funerals celebrated in the Catholic tradition.

Although church and state are separate in Mexico, the predominantly Catholic outlook of the Mexican populace is nonetheless reflected in state policy. Over the years, family planning has been adopted throughout Mexico's public health organizations; however, abortion is illegal in both Guanajuato and Querétaro. In Guanajuato, there has been a great deal of

HELPFUL SPANISH-ENGLISH COGNATES FOR TRAVELERS

As an English speaker, you may know more Spanish vocabulary than you think. Spanish and English share hundreds of cognates – words with a similar spelling and meaning. Many words have an easy-to-recognize English equivalent, with the Spanish word taking an o, a, or e on the end. In other cases, the -tion ending in English is replaced by the -ción ending in Spanish. Sometimes, it is just the pronunciation that changes, as some Spanish and English words are exactly the same!

Cognates are especially helpful for travelers to Mexico, where words are constantly incorporated from English (computadora for computer is a good example). If you start paying attention, you are likely to see many words and phrases you understand. As you brush up your español, here are some cognates that may be useful during your travels in the Bajío:

aeropuerto: airport	**hospital:** hospital
artista: artist	**hotel:** hotel
auto: automobile	**local:** local
balcón: balcony	**mapa:** map
banco: bank	**medicina:** medicine
computadora: computer	**menú:** menu
consulado: consulate	**monumento:** monument
costo: cost	**nacionalidad:** nationality
declaración: declaration	**periódico:** periodical, or newspaper
delicioso: delicious	**persona:** person
desierto: desert	**plaza:** plaza
doctor: doctor	**rancho:** ranch
dólares: dollars	**romántico:** romantic
familia: family	**taxi:** taxi
festival: festival	**teléfono:** telephone
gasolina: gasoline	**turista:** tourist
historia: history	**visa:** visa

FALSE COGNATES
Before you get carried away, remember that there are a few words that have deceptively similar spelling in Spanish and English, yet different meanings. Tuna refers to the fruit of the prickly pear, not the fish. Librería is not a library, but a bookstore. A library is a biblioteca. Fútbol is a true cognate if you are British; for Americans, the translation is soccer.

media attention surrounding several young women who were imprisoned for seeking illegal abortions.

LANGUAGE

Spanish is the language most commonly spoken in Mexico, including San Miguel de Allende, Guanajuato, and the Bajío region. In addition to Spanish, English is widely spoken throughout the Bajío, particularly in San Miguel de Allende, where there is a large and influential English-speaking expatriate population. In San Miguel, most restaurant menus, publications, and advertisements are printed in both English and Spanish. There are also several English-language newspapers and publications.

The Arts

A major cultural destination, the Bajío is an excellent place to immerse yourself in Mexico's artistic and cultural heritage. It's home to several large universities, numerous museums and galleries, and a large population of artists and writers, and there are ongoing cultural events and exhibitions throughout the region.

VISUAL ARTS

After the conquest, Mexican artistic traditions were closely tied to Spanish aesthetics and to the activities of the Catholic church. The colonial cities of San Miguel de Allende, Guanajuato, and Querétaro are excellent places see and learn more about early colonial art and architecture in Mexico. Made wealthy by the booming silver trade, the Bajío region attracted master painters, sculptors, and artisans to assist with the building and decoration of Catholic chapels during the 17th and 18th centuries.

In particular, Guanajuato's churches contain a wonderful collection of colonial painting, including many works by 18th-century master Miguel Cabrera. (While some visual artists from the colonial era are well known, a large number of the existing paintings are unsigned.) After being inducted into the United Nations World Heritage program, Guanajuato undertook a massive restoration project of cultural heritage. Unfortunately, many churches in the Bajío were sacked or destroyed over the course of history. However, there are original altarpieces, retablos, paintings, and sculpture remaining among the rebuilt interiors of many churches in the Bajío.

While there were some very talented artists in New Spain, it wasn't until after the Revolution of 1910 that the arts began to express an original and distinctly Mexican character. In the post-revolutionary era, the Mexican government promoted varied cultural and artistic programs, including the famous public mural project, overseen by the Secretary of Education, José Vasconcelos. The muralists, along with other vanguard thinkers of the post-revolutionary era, brought worldwide renown to Mexico's artistic scene. Diego Rivera, one of the most prominent Mexican muralists, was born in the city of Guanajuato; his childhood home is a museum dedicated to his work, as well as the work of his contemporaries.

San Miguel de Allende held a modest and yet important role in the great intellectual and artistic achievements of the early 20th century. All but abandoned during the late 19th century, San Miguel became a retreat destination for artists, thinkers, and musicians from Mexico City during the 20th century. In 1937, Peruvian writer and art historian Felipe Cossío del Pomar visited San Miguel de Allende. The following year, Mexican president Lázaro Cárdenas granted Pomar the funds he needed to open a fine-art school in one of San Miguel's abandoned convents. Both Mexican and American artists came to study and teach at this school, including (for a brief time) the famed muralist David Alfaro Siqueiros. Though it would go through several incarnations, Cossío de Pomar's art school is still open today as the Instituto Allende.

Since the early 20th century, San Miguel de Allende has maintained a strong affinity with the visual arts, widely recognized as an artists' community. It is a wonderful place to see or make art. There are numerous privately owned galleries in town, most featuring local artists. While San Miguel is perhaps the most well known destination for contemporary art in the Bajío, visitors will be pleased to find several interesting museums and gallery spaces in both Querétaro and Guanajuato.

MUSIC AND DANCE

Mexico's unique musical traditions have their roots in the 16th century, when traditional European composition and instruments mixed with Mesoamerican musical traditions. The result was a wide range of *sones* (musical genres), most of which are also accompanied by traditional dance. Music and dance traditions are popular throughout Mexico. In any of the Bajío's cities, visitors may have the opportunity to see a traditional music or dance performance

Children join in the festivities during the Día de San Miguel Arcángel.

© ARTURO MEADE

in one of the city's public squares. Querétaro occasionally hosts performances by Mexico's Ballet Folklórico, a traditional dance troupe from Mexico City.

Mexico's most well-recognized musical ensemble, the mariachi band, dates back to 18th-century Jalisco. Dressed in two-piece *charro* suits and *corbatin* bow-ties, mariachi bands usually feature an impressive lineup of violins, trumpets, guitars, and *jaranas* (a large five-string guitar). Mariachis play traditional Mexican ballads, often singing the chorus in unison. In central Mexico, mariachi music is a fixture at special events, like weddings or birthday parties. However, it is not necessary to await a special event to enjoy mariachi; on any night, you can commission a tune from the mariachis waiting in the central plazas of Guanajuato or San Miguel de Allende.

Some of the most famous names in Mexican music and cinema are originally from the Bajío region, and they are honored in their home towns. In the 19th century, Juventino Rosas, a famous band leader and composer of Otomí descent, was born in the small town Santa Cruz de Galeana (today, Santa Cruz de Juventino Rosas). Following the Revolution of 1910, the great singer and songwriter José Alfredo Jiménez was born in Dolores Hidalgo. Today, Jiménez is remembered as one of the greatest creative minds of his generation. Jiménez's contemporary, Jorge Negrete, was a native of the neighboring city of Guanajuato, later to become one of Mexico's most cherished singers and actors during the Golden Age of Mexican cinema.

LITERATURE

Mexico's writers have made a significant contribution to literary traditions in Spanish, including several noted authors from San Miguel de Allende and the Bajío region. Although poems, stories, and legends were passed down orally before the Spanish arrived in the New World, historians point to the descriptive chronicles of the conquest (written by Hernán Cortés, as well as other Spanish and indigenous writers) as the true birth of Mexican literature. These accounts have been incredibly important to anthropologists' understanding of Mexico's native cultures.

After the conquest, Mexico made a distinguished contribution to literature during the colonial era. Baroque poet Sor Juana Inez de la Cruz holds a hallowed place in Spanish literary history, along with her contemporaries, dramatist Juan Ruiz de Alarcón and writer Carlos de Sigüenza y Góngora. (Sor Juana's image is well known to any Mexico tourist, as it adorns the 200-peso bill.) During the 19th century, Mexican writers contributed to the Spanish Romantic Movement and, later, to modernism. In San Miguel de Allende, Ignacio Ramírez (also known as "El Nigromante," or The Necromancer) was a celebrated poet, journalist, and political thinker of the 19th century, as well as a noted atheist.

During the 20th century, Mexico's national character was more strongly reflected in its literary traditions. Writers like Rosario Castellano and Juan Rulfo began to describe a distinctly Mexican environment, exploring the country's mixed identity and heritage. By the second half of the 20th century, Mexico's diverse writers had become highly recognized and widely translated, including Carlos Fuentes, Elena Poniatowska, and Laura Esquivel. In the 1990s, Octavio Paz was the first Mexican to win the Nobel Prize in literature.

In addition to Mexican authors, many foreign authors have lived in and written about Mexico. English writers Graham Greene and D. H. Lawrence both wrote novels based on their experiences in Mexico. Beatnik poet and novelist Jack Kerouac lived in Mexico City (and is rumored to have visited San Miguel de Allende), while Chilean writer Roberto Bolaño ably described youth culture in Mexico City in his novel *The Savage Detectives*. Colombian Nobel laureate Gabriel García Márquez has resided in Mexico City for decades.

ESSENTIALS

Getting There

BY AIR

Two major airports service the Bajío region, the Del Bajío International Airport (BJX) in Silao and Querétaro International Airport (QRO) in Querétaro. If you are traveling to San Miguel de Allende or Dolores Hidalgo, either airport is appropriate. If you are traveling to Querétaro, choose QRO, while visitors to Guanajuato should choose BJX. Both airports are equipped with customs and immigration offices, but these offices only handle arrivals and departures from the country, not resident or tourist visas.

BY BUS

Mexico's extensive and efficient bus service makes it easy to travel between cities. The Bajío is serviced by several first-class bus lines, which have extensive routes in the region, as well as connecting service throughout the country. The most prominent bus lines servicing the Bajío are ETN (toll-free Mex. tel. 800/800-0386, www.etn.com.mx) and Primera Plus (toll-free Mex. tel. 800/375-7587, www.primeraplus.com.mx). Both companies allow you to make reservations over the phone, online, or at one of their ticket sales desks at the bus station.

In most cases, it is better to make your own bus arrangements than to rely on a travel agent, unless the travel agent is an authorized point-of-sale for the bus company. From Mexico City, buses to the Bajío arrive and depart from Mexico Norte, one of four bus terminals in the capital.

Bus travel is comfortable and efficient, and departures and arrivals are almost always on time. First-class buses are equipped with bathrooms and occasionally offer a snack and beverage to passengers. Because buses are incredibly popular in Mexico, it is a good idea to book bus tickets in advance, especially during a holiday weekend. Holiday weekends can also cause a bit of delay on popular bus routes, particularly those buses heading to and from the beach or Mexico City.

BY CAR

Driving to the Bajío region has been popular with U.S. visitors for many decades. In just one long day from the Texas border, you can reach the Bajío from the United States. Driving in Mexico is usually comfortable and easy, with a circuit of well-maintained toll highways running across the country. With a good map and some basic safety precautions, tourists can travel by road to the Bajío and have the benefit of a car to use while visiting the region.

Car Permits

All foreign residents bringing a car into Mexico must request a temporary import permit from the customs office at the border. The permit is good for 180 days. Thereafter, the car must be returned to the United States. Alternatively, the car's temporary import permit may be renewed locally if the car's owner has an FM3 or FM2 resident visa. All cars brought into Mexico from the United States or Canada must be returned with the import permit sticker still attached to the windshield.

Car Insurance

All foreign vehicles must be insured in Mexico. Fortunately, Mexican auto insurance is inexpensive and widely available. You can pre-register for insurance via the Internet, or you can sign up for insurance at one of the many insurance agents located along the U.S.-Mexico border. U.S. automobile insurance is not valid in Mexico.

Choosing Safe Routes

Widespread violence related to the drug trade along the U.S.-Mexico border has made travel through the northern regions more precarious than it was in the past. Throughout the north and around the city of Monterrey, there have been an increased number of illegal roadblocks and car-jackings. While drivers should certainly be aware of the hazards of driving through Northern Mexico, many Americans and Canadians continue to drive through Mexico with little problem.

To ensure your safety on the road, travel only during the day. Whenever possible, choose to drive on a toll road rather than a free highway. Toll roads are well maintained, well lit, and patrolled by police. On most Mexican toll roads, the toll also includes insurance coverage while you are on the highways. Most toll booths will accept bank cards as well as cash, but look out for the signage as you approach.

Mexican toll roads are patrolled by **Los Ángeles Verdes** (Green Angels), a fleet of emergency responders and road mechanics operated by the Mexican Secretary of Tourism. The Green Angels can offer tourist information for visitors, assist with medical emergencies, and attend to mechanical problems 8 A.M.–6 P.M. daily. Dial 078 from a telephone to reach the Green Angels.

Driving Safety

Automobile accidents are the number one cause of death for American tourists in Mexico. Drivers should always remain alert on Mexico's highways, where inexperienced drivers, big trucks, and rampant speeding make accidents unfortunately common. Stay alert and drive defensively.

On highways, faster traffic travels in the left lane and slower traffic travels in the right lane. Often, a slower car will put their driver's side turn signal on to indicate that it is safe to pass. The passing car will then put on its driver's side blinker and pass to the left. Do be aware that a driver's blinker can also indicate the intention to turn to the left, rather than safety to pass. Always use precaution when passing slower cars.

Highway Information

Guia Roji (www.guiaroji.com.mx) publishes the best road maps of the Mexican highway system. They sell a countrywide atlas, city maps, and highly detailed maps of Mexico City. Their valuable flipbook atlas, *Por Las Carreteras de Mexico,* is published annually and contains maps of every state highway and many cities. Guia Roji has an Internet store. In addition, their road atlas is sold in many gas stations and convenience stores across Mexico.

You can get updated information about Mexico's highways at the government's Caminos y Puentes Federales (www.capufe. gob.mx) website, including toll costs for each highway and road conditions.

Getting Around

Walking is the most popular mode of transportation for most Bajío tourists. In the pretty and compact *centro histórico* of most colonial cities, you can easily visit most major sights on foot. When you need wheels, there are several other options.

BY BUS

While national bus lines are efficient and comfortable, intercity buses can be rather baffling—and rather noisy! In the cities of the Bajío, most buses do not run on exact schedules, nor are there published route maps for tourists. In most cases, learning to use the bus systems in a city comes down to trial and error.

In San Miguel de Allende or Guanajuato, the majority of sights are located in the city center and do not require bus travel. If you would like to take a bus to a neighborhood or sight outside the city center, head to one of the city's larger bus stations. Each bus will have its destination posted in the window. When in doubt, you can always ask the bus driver where the bus is headed. When you get on, you pay the driver directly for the cost of your ticket, unless the driver indicates that you should sit down (someone may then pass through the bus to collect your fare).

In every major Bajío town, there are buses from the first-class bus terminal to the city's

© ARTURO MEADE

Frequent first-class bus service makes travel in the Bajío easy.

downtown district. Look for the buses marked Centro.

BY CAR

Driving a car around the Bajío region is generally safe and easy. In particular, drivers in San Miguel de Allende are courteous and cautious.

the Mexican highway as it cuts through Guanajuato State

Big cars and SUVs can be more difficult to navigate through the city's narrow streets, but otherwise, the biggest nuisance is drivers stopping to talk to their acquaintances in the middle of a busy street. Don't get exasperated; in a few weeks, you may find yourself doing the same.

Foreign plates are not uncommon in the Bajío, and they rarely warrant extra attention from cops. As long as you have your paperwork in order, you will rarely have problems with law enforcement.

BY TAXI

There are inexpensive taxis circling throughout San Miguel de Allende, Guanajuato, and other cities in the Bajío. Taxis are not metered, charging a flat rate for travel around town. More outlying neighborhoods may cost more than a trip within the city center. To be sure, ask the price of the ride when you get in. It is safe to hail taxis in the street, though you can also call a cab if you are in a more remote location.

Visas and Officialdom

ENTRY REQUIREMENTS

To enter Mexico, every foreign citizen must have a valid passport and an official permit to travel, or tourist card. Note that residents of the U.S. and Canada can no longer travel to Mexico with their birth certificate and photo ID. Today, all travelers must present a valid passport, including children. (When leaving Mexico, non-Mexican children must be accompanied by both parents or carry an official letter from the absent parent authorizing them to travel.) In Mexico, you will pass through immigration at your final destination, not your first port of entry. You can find more information about tourist cards, non-immigrant visas, and immigrant visas at the Instituto Nacional de Migración website (National Immigration Institute, www.inm.gob.mx).

If you are arriving in Mexico by airplane, you will be directed to immigration and customs checks on the ground. If you drive into Mexico, it is your responsibility to locate the immigration office closest to the border crossing and complete the necessary paperwork.

Most immigration offices are open 24 hours a day and, in most cases, the immigration office is just a few yards from the border checkpoint. Note that some immigration offices are farther from the border.

TOURIST CARDS

Every foreign visitor must have a permit to travel in Mexico. Visitors from most countries will be issued a temporary permit, or tourist card, at the point of entry. Technically called the Forma Migratoria Múltiple (FMM), tourist cards are good for up to 180 days of travel in Mexico. If you are arriving in Mexico via airplane, the flight staff will usually provide the FMM form to fill out while in the air, which will then be validated and stamped by an immigration official on the ground. On the form, you need to list the address where you will be residing in Mexico or the name of a hotel. The cost of the visa is included in the taxes and fees of your airfare. If you are traveling to Mexico by car and intend to visit the Bajío, you will need to stop at an immigration office at the border to request your FMM and pay the fee, about US$25.

After you have received your stamped form from immigration, keep it in a safe place until your return. You will be asked to return the form when you leave the country. If you lose the form, you will be required to pay a fee at the airport.

RESIDENT VISAS

Foreigners who wish to reside in Mexico may apply for a resident visa either at a Mexican consular agency in their home country or at an official immigration office in Mexico. The vast majority of foreign residents choose the latter, initially entering the country with a tourist card and processing their resident paperwork once in Mexico. All visa applications for residents of San Miguel de Allende and Guanajuato are processed at the Instituto Nacional de Migración in San Miguel de Allende. There is a separate immigration office in the city of Querétaro, which serves immigrants and visitors in that state.

There are two types of resident visas, the FM3 and the FM2. FM3s are long-term nonimmigrant visas, meaning the visa holder does not intend to naturalize. Even so, there are pathways toward citizenship for FM3 holders. These visas are renewed annually. An FM2 is an immigrant visa, intended for people who plan to permanently reside in Mexico. Most foreign residents in Mexico have FM3 visas.

There are several types of FM3s, which afford different rights to the visa holder. People who would like to live or retire in Mexico using their savings or foreign income are called *rentistas*. Their visa application process is rather straightforward. To apply for an FM3, *rentistas* must provide a passport, proof of residence (such as an electricity bill in your name), and proof that you have sufficient funds to reside in Mexico, usually through three months of bank statements (the amount considered the acceptable minimum monthly income changes each year). Qualified professionals, artists, or investors may also apply for the right to legally participate in lucrative activities, such as giving art classes or opening a business. To apply for an FM3 with work benefits, you must provide proof of your skills and be sure to file taxes with the Mexican government every year.

In the case that you are offered a job in Mexico, your employer must sponsor your FM3 application. In most cases, employment visas are only extended to foreigners who have special skills not generally available within the local population. For example, native speakers of a foreign language, like English or French, can seek employment as language teacher. If you receive an FM3 through your employer, the paperwork is nontransferable. If you leave your current job, your next employer must sponsor the visa's extension.

STUDENT VISAS

If you will be studying in Mexico for longer than six months, you can apply for a student visa at the Mexican consulate near your home. To apply, students must present a valid passport, a letter of acceptance from the school where they will be studying, proof of a minimum monthly income, and a certificate of health.

CUSTOMS
Basic Allowances
Customs *(aduana)* allows visitors and residents of Mexico to bring personal effects into the country, as well as duty-free gifts valued at no more than US$300. Personal effects may include two photographic or video cameras and up to 12 rolls of film, up to three cellular phones, and one laptop computer. The full list of permitted items is available at the Administración General de Aduanas website (Customs Administration, www.aduanas.gob.mx). Most animal-derived food products are not permitted, including homemade foods, pet food or dog treats, fresh or canned meat, soil, or hay. Other food products are permitted, including tobacco, dried fruit, coffee, and fruit preserves. There are severe penalties for carrying firearms to Mexico.

If you are arriving by air, you will be given a customs declaration form on the airplane and will pass through the customs checkpoint right after immigration. You may choose to have your luggage reviewed by customs; otherwise, customs checks are performed by random selection. After collecting your luggage, you will be directed to a stoplight and asked to press a button. If you get a green light, you can pass. If you receive a red light, customs officials will open your luggage to inspect its contents. In larger airports, luggage is often passed through an X-ray machine, and passengers may be asked to open their luggage if a possible contraband item is detected.

If you are entering Mexico by car or on foot at a border crossing, you will be asked to choose the voluntary review line or the "nothing to declare" line. If you choose to declare nothing, you must come to a full stop at the border and wait to receive a red or green light. If you receive the red light, customs officials will ask you to pull over and they will check the contents of your car, including the trunk.

Pets
Dogs and cats may enter Mexico with their owners. To be admitted, a pet needs a certificate of health issued by a licensed veterinarian, as well as a proof of vaccination against rabies and distemper, administered at least 15 days before entering the country. Double-check that all your pet's information, including name and address, is correctly noted on the forms. If you have all the paperwork, you will receive a Certificado de Importación Zoosanitario for the animal, which has an associated cost of about US$110. Both cats and dogs may be given a physical exam at the border, especially if they appear sick. Sick animals may also be detained at the border.

More unusual animals like lizards or rabbits can also be imported to Mexico, but owners should check with customs and immigration officials to determine what paperwork is necessary before making the trip.

Cars
If you are driving your car to the Bajío region from the United States or Canada, you must acquire a temporary import permit. You can apply for a permit at the Vehicular Control Module desk at the customs and immigration offices at the border. To apply, you must present proof of citizenship (a passport), an immigration form (a tourist card or resident visa), a valid registration for your car, the leasing contract (if the car is rented), a driver's license, and an international credit card or debit card in the driver's name. Bring two copies of each document, as well as the original. You will be charged the cost of the permit (about US$27).

Your temporary import permit includes a sticker, which must be affixed to your car's windshield, just above the rearview mirror. Do not remove that sticker until you are returning the car to the United States and are in the presence of a customs agent at the border. If you bring a car into Mexico, you are not permitted to sell that car in Mexico and it must be returned to its country of origin. If you have a resident visa, your car is legal in Mexico for as long as your visa is valid. However, the car's temporary permit must be renewed at a local transit office every six months. If your car's permit is not valid, the car can be confiscated by Mexican authorities.

To expedite the approval process, you can request a permit for your car via the Internet. You can find the complete guidelines for Internet applications at the customs *(aduana)* website (www.aduanas.sat.gob.mx).

EMBASSIES AND CONSULATES

All foreign embassies are located in the capital in Mexico City. Most embassies are near the city center, with the majority of embassies concentrated in the Polanco and Cuauhtémoc neighborhoods, including the United States Embassy (Paseo de la Reforma 305, Col. Cuauhtémoc, tel. 55/5080-2000), Canadian Embassy (Schiller 529, Col. Bosque de Chapultepec, tel. 55/5724-7900), Australian Embassy (Ruben Dario 55, Col. Polanco, tel. 55/1101-2200), and the British Embassy (Río Lerma 71, Col. Cuauhtémoc, tel. 55/1670-3200). If you have trouble with the law while you are in Mexico, or your citizenship papers have been lost or stolen, you should contact your embassy right away.

If you are traveling in the Bajío region, there is a U.S. Consular Agency in San Miguel de Allende (Plaza las Golondrinas, Hernández Macías 72, Int. 111 and 112, tel. 415/152-2357, consuladosma@gmail.com, clancyek@state.gov, 9 A.M.–1 P.M. Mon.–Thurs.). The consular office is a branch of the U.S. Embassy in Mexico City and can assist with lost or stolen passports, apostilles (certificates of notarization authenticity), and other services. For all other nations, the closest field offices are in the capital.

POLICE

Protección Civil (Civil Protection) is the local police force. They respond to emergencies, break-ins, or other complaints within the municipality. Around town, you may see Civil Protection officers in blue fatigues patrolling the streets in cars or on foot. In addition, *transitos* (transit cops) patrol the roadways around town. They are principally involved in preventing traffic infractions, like speeding, and assisting at the scene of accidents. Throughout Mexico, calling 066 will summon emergency services.

In addition to city police, there are Policía Federal (Federal Police) patrolling the intracity highways. Their territory may include major ring roads around town, as well as larger avenues in big cities like Querétaro. In recent years, the Federal Police have been more involved in anti-drug activity throughout the country, though most tourists will only notice them on the highways. Federal Police can be helpful in the case of a roadside emergency or accident.

Mexico has developed a bad and not undeserved reputation for police corruption. The famous *mordida* (bribe) has become so legendary that many people reach for their pocketbook as soon as they hear police sirens behind them. Visitors to the Bajío can expect a rather different set of circumstances. While police corruption is widespread in many Mexican states, Guanajuato and Querétaro's police are usually honest and will rarely pull over a tourist in search of a bribe. In the case that you have been extorted or harassed by a police officer or any other official, it is necessary to note the officer's name, badge number, and patrol car number in order to make a complaint.

Food

One of the world's great cuisines, Mexican food is diverse and delicious. Typical dishes can be as simple as a quesadilla (a warm tortilla wrapped around melted cheese) or as elaborate as a *mole negro* (a Oaxacan sauce prepared with dozens of hand-ground ingredients). Eating well is enjoyed throughout Mexico, where cities are packed with food stalls, bakeries, fruit stands, markets, restaurants, and cantinas.

BASICS

Since the pre-Columbian era, corn, squash, chile peppers, and beans have formed the base of the Mexican diet. In addition to these key staples, Mexican food makes ample use of other native American foods, including tomatoes, green tomatoes, avocados, potatoes, prickly pear cactus, chocolate, and turkey. In the 15th century, Spanish settlers introduced new culinary techniques to Mexico, along with new ingredients like wheat, onions, rice, cheese, chicken, pork, and beef. Throughout the country, European traditions began to fuse with indigenous recipes. The result was a new and wholly original cuisine.

A staple at most Mexican meals and a key ingredient in many traditional dishes, tortillas are round flatbreads made of corn or wheat flour. A warmed tortilla wrapped around seasoned meat or vegetables is a taco. A tortilla filled with melted cheese is a quesadilla. In addition to tortillas, corn flour is used to make a variety of flatbreads. *Sopes* are thick corn discs, served with beans, sour cream, and salsa, whereas *huaraches* are torpedo-shaped flatbreads. Gorditas, a specialty of the Bajío region, are thick corn flatbreads griddled and stuffed with cheese, meat, or other fillings.

Beyond tortillas and other flatbreads, corn is an essential ingredient in many traditional foods, which may have roots in the pre-Columbian era. One of the oldest and most popular foods in the Americas, tamales are made of corn masa (dough) steamed in a corn husk or banana leaf and stuffed with chile peppers,

meat, cheese, or sweet ingredients. Pozole, a hominy soup, is another corn-based dish with pre-Hispanic origins.

Chile peppers are fundamental to the Mexican palate. Salsa, a sauce made of ground chile peppers and condiments, is served as an accompaniment to almost every meal in Mexico, formal or informal. There are many types of salsas, from the ubiquitous *salsa verde* (made with green tomatoes and chiles) to *pico de gallo* (a fresh salsa of chopped tomatoes, onion, and serrano chile peppers).

Chile peppers are used to season meat, beans, and sauces, or are served whole and stuffed with cheese. There are hundreds of varieties of chile pepper cultivated in Mexico, as well as a range of dried chile peppers produced from these crops. Some chile peppers are incredibly hot, while others are mild but flavorful.

Like chile peppers, many varieties of beans

gorditas, quesadillas, and tamales for sale in Tequisquiapan

© ARTURO MEADE

cultivated and prepared in Mexican cooking. Beans are generally served as a side dish to a meal or as a soup. In addition to beans, rice is a common accompaniment to a meal.

Mexico has a large ranching industry, with a variety of meats and cheeses produced throughout the country. Pork and chicken are popular, and Northern Mexico is known for its large ranches of grass-fed beef. Traditional cuts include the lean *arrachera* and *norteña.*

Mexico also produces several varieties of cheeses, including *panela* (a smooth, low-fat fresh cheese) and *cotija* (a dry and salty cheese used for crumbling on top of dishes). Mennonite communities in the north of Mexico make *queso chihuahua* (Chihuahua cheese), which resembles a mild cheddar. In the Bajío region, look out for *queso ranchero* (ranch cheese), a fresh and salty cheese that can be crumbled on top of beans or folded into quesadillas.

Thanks to long and abundant coastlines, fish and shellfish are popular at Mexico's beach resorts, as well as across the country. Shrimp cocktail is particularly beloved by the local crowd, as are breaded and fried fish steaks. Common fish include red snapper, dogfish, and tilapia.

MEALTIMES

Mexicans typically eat three meals each day. Breakfast *(desayuno)* is usually a light morning meal, often accompanied by hot chocolate or coffee. A larger breakfast or brunch is called *almuerzo,* typically eaten a bit later than a regular breakfast. *Almuerzo* is usually more substantial than a typical breakfast.

The *comida* is the midday meal, usually eaten around 2 P.M. The *comida* is traditionally the largest and most important meal of the day. A traditional *comida* begins with soup, followed by a pasta or rice course, and finally, a main course, served with tortillas or a basket of *bolillos* (white rolls). The Bajío region remains fairly traditional with regards to mealtimes. Families usually eat *comida* together, and many small businesses close 2–4 P.M. to accommodate the afternoon meal.

Dinner is eaten late in the evening and is usually a lighter meal than lunch. Traditional dinners include tamales with *atole,* sweet breads with milk or coffee, or tacos. In big cities like Querétaro or tourist towns around the Bajío, going out to dinner at a restaurant is a common activity.

EATING OUT

From casual *fondas* to fancy sit-down restaurants, eating out is popular with tourists and locals in the Bajío. Eating out can begin quite pleasurably at breakfast, when typical Mexican restaurants will offer a wide selection of sweet and savory dishes. A common breakfast food, tamales are often featured on a morning menu, along with an assortment of egg dishes, enchiladas, pancakes, and even grilled meat. Among the most popular breakfast plates, *huevos rancheros* are two fried eggs served atop toasted tortillas and bathed in a semi-spicy red sauce. *Chilaquiles* are fried or baked tortillas bathed in red or green salsa, smothered in cheese and cream, and served with a fried egg or chicken. Certain tacos are also considered breakfast food. Notably, *barbacoa* (pit-steamed lamb) and carnitas are generally consumed in the morning or during an early lunch *(almuerzo).*

During the lunch and dinner hours, most Mexican restaurants serve an assortment of traditional dishes, including *antojitos* or *entradas* (appetizers), *sopas* (soups), main plates, and dessert. While every restaurant has a different menu, many serve a range of typical Mexican dishes, like guacamole (mashed and seasoned avocado), chile relleno (a cheese-stuffed and deep-fried poblano pepper), or enchiladas (stuffed tortillas bathed in salsa), often served on a plate accompanied with rice, beans, and tortillas. In addition to restaurants, informal eateries and roadside stands sell finger foods like tacos, quesadillas, gorditas, tamales, fresh fruit, and tortas.

When eating out, it is typical for a meal to be served with salsa and tortillas. Some restaurants will serve *bolillos* (white rolls) in lieu of tortillas, but you can always ask for tortillas if you prefer them. Generally, the Bajío's cuisine

informal eateries, or *fondas*, outside the Mercado Hidalgo in Guanajuato

is not as spicy as what you'd find in other parts of Mexico. In San Miguel de Allende, in particular, food is generally served mild, and even salsas on the table will not always be hot. If you want some kick, ask for *salsa picante.*

REGIONAL FOOD

Mexican food is highly regional and surprisingly diverse. For example, the north of Mexico is known for its cuts of meat and flour tortillas, Baja California is famous for battered fish tacos, and Oaxaca is the capital of spicy mole sauces. Although it is an important agricultural center, the Bajío has never distinguished itself as a culinary destination. Nonetheless, the Bajío has a small menu of regional dishes to offer the visitor, as well as ingredients (like nopal) that are produced locally and consumed more widely here than in other parts of Mexico. Notably, *enchiladas mineras* is a hearty dish of tortillas rolled around cheese, covered in a mild chile sauce, then smothered in fried potatoes and carrots. On top of that, Bajío restaurants will often prepare traditional food from other

states, giving the visitor an opportunity to sample some of Mexico's most iconic dishes.

Some of Mexico's most interesting culinary traditions can be found in the southern states of Veracruz, Puebla, Oaxaca, and Yucatán. If you are interested in trying specialty foods, look out for popular Mexican dishes like *cochinita pibil* (shredded and seasoned pork from the Yucatán), *mole negro* (a chocolate-based sauce from Oaxaca), and *chiles en nogada* (a poblano chile pepper stuffed with almonds, raisins, apples, dried fruit, cinnamon, and meat, then bathed in a creamed walnut sauce).

DRINKS

Delicious, cheap, and refreshing, *aguas frescas* or *aguas de fruta* are a cheap and ubiquitous beverage throughout Mexico. Usually, these drinks are made with fresh fruit, water, and sugar, blended together with ice and then strained. The most popular *aguas* include tamarind, mango, lime, lemon, fruit, piña colada, *jamaica* (hibiscus), and *horchata* (rice water with cinnamon). Fresh juice is sold at informal

¡POR TODO MAL, MEZCAL!

A cousin to tequila, mezcal is a distilled spirit made from the heart of the maguey plant. A smooth yet potent drink, mezcal is produced throughout Mexico, using various types of maguey cactus. By contrast, tequila is produced with blue agave (a specific type of maguey) and must be made in the state of Jalisco. In fact, tequila could be considered a subset of the maguey-based spirit, mezcal. Like tequila, mezcal is usually served straight and sipped, accompanied by salt and lime or orange slices. If you like tequila and have never tried mezcal, it is worth a taste.

Mezcal is produced throughout Mexico, usually in small batches at family ranches. Varieties of mezcal from the state of Oaxaca are particularly well known, and many present a smoky flavor that comes from roasting the maguey leaves before distillation. In recent years, producers in Oaxaca and around the country have begun to bottle and export the spirit. However, it is still largely a cottage industry, produced in small batches and often bottled in recycled tequila bottles.

Mezcal is also produced in small batches throughout the state of Guanajuato. Guanajuato's mezcal has rather different characteristics than Oaxacan mezcal, usually taking on a more flowery or perfumed aroma. In ad-dition, Guanajuato's producers often mix the liquor with water, giving it a smoother taste and lower alcohol content than the extremely potent Oaxacan version. (A special note to the squeamish: The famous worm found at the bottom of a bottle of Oaxaca's *mezcal de gusano* is never included in Guanajuato's variety.)

Mezcal is produced in small towns throughout the Bajío, including the small town of Santa Rosa near Guanajuato. However, the most famous mezcal from Guanajuato is made in the town of Jaral de Berrio (www.jaraldeberrio.com), which is in the northeast corner of the state. Lovingly referred to as JB, mezcal from this producer is served in bars and cantinas throughout the Bajío (ask for the house mezcal in any bar and JB is likely what you'll get). Mezcal fanatics can also pick up a bottle for themselves, if they are willing to make the trek out to this teensy town. Bottles are sold in the strangely magnificent former hacienda in Jaral, off a dusty road off the highway from San Felipe, Guanajuato, to Villa de Reyes, San Luis Potosí. To get there, head north on Highway 51 from Dolores Hidalgo and then take the small state highway toward Villa de Reyes before entering down-

---

stands in the morning, as are *licuados* (shakes made with milk, sugar, and fruit).

Both coffee and chocolate are cultivated in Mexico and widely consumed as hot beverages. A popular option at many casual *fondas* and restaurants, *café de olla* is filtered coffee mixed with cinnamon and *piloncillo* (unrefined sugar). *Atole* is another popular beverage for the morning or evening, a hot drink made of corn starch and sweeteners, often served alongside tamales.

Corona is one of the world's most popular beers, and one of a ubiquitous roster of national brews. Most Mexican beers are, like Corona, light lagers, though León and Negra Modelo are both amber colored. Though Mexican beers are often served with a lime in foreign countries, they are rarely embellished in Mexico. If you like the lime taste, you may want to try a *michelada,* a savory beer served with a mix of lime juice, salt, Worcestershire sauce, and hot sauce.

In addition to beer, Mexico is famous for its tequila, a distilled liquor made from agave cactus. Tequila is popular throughout Mexico, served straight or in Mexico's famous cocktail, the margarita. When ordering a fine tequila, it is best sipped slowly sipped from a tall shot glass, rather than downed in a single gulp. *Sangrita* is a popular chaser for tequila,

Small-batch mezcal is made in the small town of Jaral de Berrio, Guanajuato.

town San Felipe. It's quite a trek, so take a map and company if you are making the drive for the first time.

When raising your glass of mezcal in a toast, you may feel inspired to utter the popular Mexican saying *"¡Por todo mal, mezcal! ¡Por todo bien, también!"* ("For everything bad, mezcal! For everything good, too!").

made of tomato juice and spices. A cousin to tequila, mezcal is a spirit made from distilling maguey cactus. Unlike tequila, mezcal can be produced in any region and is gaining popularity throughout Mexico, as well as overseas.

Recently, vineyards in Baja California, Coahuila, and Aguascalientes, among others, have begun to produce nice wines. Liquor stores in Mexico and most restaurants serve Mexican wines.

DESSERTS

The most ubiquitous Mexican dessert is the famous flan, a thick egg custard. On the street, you'll often find ice creams *(nieves)* for sale in cups or cones. *Nieves* are made from cream or water base, and often incorporate fresh tropical fruits like mango or coconut. In addition to *nieves, paletas* (popsicles) made from real fruit, sugar, and milk are sold in small shops or street corners throughout the country. A popular treat in San Miguel de Allende, churros are deep-fried pastry sticks doused in sugar and cinnamon.

MARKETS

Since the pre-Columbian era, Mexicans have bought the majority of their food in markets *(mercados)*. In Mexico, markets are the best place to buy fresh produce. Vendors often display their produce in artfully arranged piles and may offer you a chance to sample their product. In addition to fruit stands, food markets can be a good place to buy inexpensive grains and legumes, like dried beans, rice, hibiscus, lentils, and garbanzos, as well as Mexican cheeses and dairy products. Adventurous eaters may want to try some of the food prepared at a market's *fonda* (food stall).

Many visitors believe that bartering for a lower price is customary in Mexican markets; this is not necessarily the case in the Bajío. Most Bajío merchants will offer a reasonable price for their goods, and it is not necessary (and sometimes rude) to bargain. This is especially true for foodstuffs, which are often very inexpensive to begin with. However, if you are buying in bulk, a merchant may offer you a lower rate for the entire lot.

A vendor at Querétaro's Mercado de la Cruz sells squash flowers, corn, and herbs.

Conduct and Customs

GREETINGS

When meeting someone for the first time or greeting acquaintances in Mexico, it is customary to make physical contact, rather than simply saying hello verbally. A handshake is the most common form of greeting in Mexico. Between male and female friends, or between two women, Mexicans will often greet each other with a single kiss on the cheek. Male friends may also give each other a quick hug. The same gestures are repeated when you say good-bye. When greeting a group of people, it is necessary to greet and shake hands with each person individually, rather than greeting the group together.

When speaking to an elder or to someone with whom you will have a professional relationship, it is customary to use the formal pronoun *usted* instead of the informal *tú*. Spanish language classes will often spend quite a bit of time explaining the difference between *usted*

and *tú*, though most English-speaking tourists find themselves baffled by the distinction. Err on the side of caution by using *usted* when speaking to most people you don't know well or anyone older than you.

MANNERS

Mexicans are generally very polite when interacting with people they do not know well. In the Bajío region, good manners are still practiced and appreciated. Most Mexicans are approving of those who make an effort to be polite, yet forgiving of foreign tourists who aren't familiar with the country's customs.

When you sit down to eat in Mexico, it is customary to wish other diners *"Buen provecho"* before you start eating. *Buen provecho* is similar to the well-known French expression *bon appetit,* and generally means, "Enjoy your meal." In small towns and even big cities, it is not uncommon to greet other diners when you enter a restaurant, or to wish them a *buen provecho* when you enter or are leaving. Likewise, it is common courtesy to make eye contact and greet the salesperson when you enter a store. Commonly, Mexicans will say *disculpe* (forgive me) before asking a question of a salesperson or waiter.

When greeting someone, it is common practice to speak to that person using a polite title, such as señor for a man, señora for a married or older woman, and señorita for a young woman. When speaking with a professional, Mexicans may also use the person's professional title, such as *doctor* or *doctora* (doctor), *arquitecto* (architect), or *ingeniero* (engineer). The title *licenciado* or *licenciada* is often used to address a college graduate, as a term of respect. In addition, the term *maestro* (master) can be used when addressing a skilled tradesman or a teacher.

On San Miguel de Allende and Guanajuato's narrow sidewalks, two pedestrians cannot always fit side-by-side. Step into the street to allow someone else to pass, especially when that person is elderly. If you have to squeeze past someone, you can say *"con permiso,"* which functions like "excuse me" in English.

PUNCTUALITY

The famous Mexican penchant for putting things off until mañana (tomorrow) does have an element of truth. Time is a bit less structured in Mexico, and it is common practice to arrive a bit tardy for a social engagement. In a professional setting, however, punctuality is required.

TIPPING

In a restaurant, it is customary to tip the server 10–15 percent on the bill, though foreign tourists are generally expected to tip toward the higher end of that scale. In San Miguel de Allende, it is customary to tip 15–20 percent of the bill at a restaurant, especially in a sitdown restaurant. In bars, a 10 percent tip is

standard. Though sometimes a customer may choose to leave a bit more or less based on the quality of the service, tipping is obligatory. European tourists who do not tip at home should be prepared to conform to Mexico's tipping standards.

In most cases, it is not necessary to tip a taxi driver when traveling within city limits, though tipping is always welcomed. If a taxi or shuttle service is taking you to the airport or to another city, a tip is customary and can be given at the passenger's discretion. Likewise, tour guides and transport services can be tipped at your discretion; in most cases, around 15 percent is appropriate. At service stations, a small tip of about 5–10 percent is customary for gas station attendants (all gas stations are full service in Mexico). It is customary to tip porters at an airport or hotel between US$5–10, depending on the size of your load.

DRINKING LAWS

Throughout Mexico, the legal drinking age is 18. Although it is not legal to drink on the street, you may see people take drinks outside during citywide parties. Drinking and driving is a serious offense in Mexico, though it remains a huge problem on the road. Dry laws *(ley seca)* are sometimes enacted on election days or, occasionally, during major holidays, like Independence Day (September 16). In that case, liquor stores and bars may close early (or not open at all). The decision to enact dry laws is up to each municipality.

SMOKING

In 2008, smoking indoors at both restaurants and bars was prohibited throughout Mexico. While the law is heavily enforced in Mexico City, you may find less stringent standards in the Bajío. Usually, restaurants do not allow their customers to smoke in enclosed spaces (patios are still fair game), but some bars and music venues may be more lenient.

Tips for Travelers

OPPORTUNITIES FOR STUDY

The Bajío is an excellent place for beginners to learn Spanish. Not only is the region friendly and safe, but there are many language schools in Guanajuato, as well as several schools in San Miguel de Allende. A few language schools offer U.S. or foreign college credit for class work through cooperative programs with universities overseas.

In addition to Spanish-language programs, San Miguel de Allende is a great place to take art classes. Many working artists in San Miguel de Allende give classes in disciplines like watercolor, ceramics, oil painting, printmaking, and jewelry-making. There is also the well-reputed Centro Cultural Ignacio Ramírez, where students can take classes in a variety of disciplines (though the school does not confer certificates or degrees). The Instituto Allende confers undergraduate degrees in art to Mexican students; its master of art (MFA) program is internationally accredited and attracts students from the United States.

Students who plan to take classes in Mexico for six months or less can use a standard tourist visa while they are attending classes. If you will be studying for more than six months at an accredited school, it may be easier and more efficient to apply for a student visa. Student visas can be processed either at a Mexican consulate overseas or at a local immigration office in Mexico.

OPPORTUNITIES FOR WORK

Many foreigners work and own businesses in the Bajío. Both Guanajuato and San Miguel de Allende boast numerous American- and Canadian-owned restaurants, bars, galleries, bookshops, and boutiques, as well as a smattering of business owners from Europe and Asia. Mexico will extend self-employment benefits to FM3 visas holders who wish to open their own business or to give classes legally. In many cases, it is easier to open your own business or

© ARTURO MEADE

Many U.S. and Canadian expats have found employment in Guanajuato and other parts of the Bajío.

give independent classes than to find employment through another source. To be eligible for this visa, foreigners must have proof of foreign income.

Foreigners may be employed by a Mexican- or foreign-owned business; however, foreign employees must be sponsored by their employer, who will assist with the visa application process at immigration. In most cases, Mexico will extend employment visas to foreigners with special skills that are not available within the local population. For example, native speakers of English can seek employment in a bilingual school. In order to be eligible for an employment visa, foreigners must present all necessary documentation for a tourist visa, as well as documentation of their skill, such as a university diploma or a certificate in teaching English as a second language. In most cases, a school or other business that routinely employs foreigners will be familiar with the visa application process.

OPPORTUNITIES FOR VOLUNTEER WORK

There are many opportunities for rewarding volunteer work in the Bajío, whether you like working with people, animals, or the environment. Several U.S. universities operate rural assistance programs for college-age volunteers, and there are several summer programs operated by international charities, such as Amigos de las Americas. In addition, many Bajío nonprofit organizations welcome part-time volunteers. Volunteers in Mexico are expected to maintain their legal status but do not need to apply for special visa. For students, several of Guanajuato's Spanish-language schools operate volunteer programs at local charities, which can be an excellent way to learn more about the local culture and continue improving your Spanish skills.

Note that the Mexican constitution prohibits foreigners from participating in political activities, including demonstrations. Breaking this law can result in deportation. If you are volunteering in Mexico, refrain from attending political demonstrations.

ACCESS FOR TRAVELERS WITH DISABILITIES

The Bajío can be a difficult place for travelers with disabilities, most especially those with limited range of movement. Colonial cities of the Bajío were built hundreds of years ago, and their streets are often narrow and paved with stone. There are very few sidewalk ramps or even elevators in the colonial towns of San Miguel de Allende and Guanajuato. The situation is changing, but slowly. If you are in a wheelchair or have trouble walking, the easiest place to visit is Querétaro, where the city center is flat and most sights are at ground level.

That said, Bajío residents are friendly and courteous, and most are willing to lend a hand

as necessary. Many senior citizens with limited range of movement are able to comfortably visit San Miguel de Allende, while many others make their home there.

TRAVELING WITH CHILDREN

San Miguel de Allende, Guanajuato, and the Bajío are comfortable places to travel with your family. On the whole, Mexico is a family-oriented society, in which children are well-loved members. There are plenty of family-friendly activities in the region, like horseback riding, and children are generally welcomed in stores and restaurants. If you are planning to stay in a hotel with your children, be aware that some bed-and-breakfasts in the Bajío do not allow children under a certain age.

Many foreign children live in San Miguel, mostly from the United States and Canada. In San Miguel de Allende, there are several bilingual schools, as well as English-language schools. Over the summer, there are several day camps for local and international kids, as well as Spanish classes for children at local language schools. The library and municipal government often host events and movies for children in San Miguel de Allende; however, most of this programming is in Spanish.

Remember that, like adults, children must have a valid passport to be admitted to Mexico, even if they are accompanied by their parents. In order to combat child trafficking and kidnapping, Mexico requires that both parents accompany a non-Mexican minor when leaving the country. If one or both parents are absent, the child must be accompanied by an official letter of consent authorizing the child's travel plans.

TRAVELING WITH PETS

Once across the border, dog lovers will meet many like minds in Mexico, where pets are popular and beloved parts of the family. At the same time, traveling with a pet can be more complicated, especially if you are planning to stay in hotels. Few inns or bed-and-breakfasts welcome pets, so you should make reservations

KID-FRIENDLY SAN MIGUEL

With its bright colors, festive atmosphere, and kid-friendly attitude, San Miguel can be a wonderful place to visit with the family. If you are bringing your tots to San Miguel, here are some ways to spend your time.

LEARN

At the **Biblioteca de San Miguel de Allende,** a nonprofit cultural center and library, kids can find books in English and Spanish, or participate in one of the many children's programs or movies (often in Spanish). For teenagers, MexArt offers art and dance summer programs at **Casa Crayola,** and many of San Miguel's language schools welcome kids during the summer.

SEE

San Miguel de Allende is a wonderful place to introduce children to Mexican culture. For a diverting look into the history of Mexican toys, take the family to **La Esquina: Museo del Jugete Popular Mexicano,** which features a wonderful collection of antique handmade toys, like rocking horses, whistles, and dolls. Kids can pick out their own classic toys in the museum gift shop.

EXPLORE

It's easy to imagine life on the range when surrounded by vast plains and towering cactus. Ford streams and explore canyons on a horseback ride with **Coyote Canyon Adventures** or head out for an off-road mountain biking excursion with **Bici-Burro.** Teenagers can take an ATV tour of the surrounding countryside or buzz around town on a rented four-wheeler.

PLAY

In the *plaza principal,* or **jardín,** life recalls an older and more wholesome era, where throngs of kids bounce balls along the cobblestones, long lines await the ice cream vendor, and police officers on horseback snap photos with wee ones. In **Parque Juárez,** there is always a crowd of tots on the playground in the afternoon.

SWIM

There is no better place to spend a summer afternoon than at one of the many swimming spots around town. With a spring-fed Olympic-sized swimming pool and huge lawns, **Taboada** is an excellent place to pack a picnic lunch and spend a day with the kids. For water slides and big swimming pools, take the family to **Xote,** on the highway toward Dolores Hidalgo.

EAT

Children are generally welcomed in San Miguel restaurants, and there are several places that are particularly family friendly. Live music, solicitous service, and cheesy pizza make **Mama Mia** a good choice for kids, while the varied menu and tasty fries at **Hecho en Mexico** are guaranteed to please younger palates. Get double scoops of the flavorful ice cream on San Miguel's street corners, or take a trip to Dolores Hidalgo, where *nieves* are served in wacky flavors like shrimp or avocado.

SLEEP

Not all bed-and-breakfasts in San Miguel de Allende accept children, so parents should check the hotel's policy before making reservations. Fortunately for families, there are numerous places great for kids, boasting big grounds and private pools. **Rancho Hotel Atascadero** has tennis courts, pools, and gardens, as well as larger suites that accommodate the kids in loft beds.

It can be difficult traveling with pets in the Bajío.

warrants any special attention from locals, and most people treat women with respect. Hundreds if not thousands of women travel unaccompanied to San Miguel de Allende each year, and even more foreign women live alone in town. At the same time, a woman traveling alone in the Bajío region should exercise sensible precautions, especially at night.

SENIOR TRAVELERS

The Bajío region, especially San Miguel de Allende, is a welcoming place for older travelers. The cobblestone streets and many hills in San Miguel can make the city a bit more challenging to traverse on foot. All visitors to San Miguel must be careful not to twist their knee or ankle on the uneven streets. Beyond these small problems, many senior travelers have a comfortable and rewarding experience in the Bajío.

GAY AND LESBIAN TRAVELERS

Despite its reputation as a very conservative and largely Catholic region, people in the Bajío are socially tolerant and accepting. Gay and lesbian travelers are unlikely to experience discrimination from locals, especially in larger cities. In the cosmopolitan small towns of San Miguel de Allende and Guanajuato, the population is markedly more open-minded than the Bajío's conservative reputation would lead you to believe. There is a relatively large and visible gay population in San Miguel, made up of both local and foreign residents. While public displays of affection between same-sex couples are relatively uncommon, gay couples will rarely experience negative commentary from locals.

for yourself and your pet in advance. If you have trouble locating a pet-friendly hotel, consider a rental house or apartment, which may have a more liberal pet policy.

Pets are generally not permitted in the coaches of Mexico's bus lines, though hardy canines may travel in the luggage compartment below the bus. Many rental car companies and tour operators will permit an animal in their vehicles, though they may charge an additional fee. Travelers should check individually if they plan to bring their dog or cat on the road.

WOMEN TRAVELING ALONE

The whole Bajío region is generally safe for solo female travelers. A lone female rarely

Health and Safety

There are few serious health and safety risks for visitors to the Bajío. With sensible precautions, visitors can enjoy a safe and comfortable trip to the region.

DOCTORS AND HOSPITALS

Most people traveling to Mexico for a short trip will not need to visit a doctor or hospital. However, those coming to Mexico for an extended stay may need or want to seek medical care. There are plenty of doctors, dentists, and hospitals in San Miguel de Allende, Guanajuato, and the Bajío, many of which have extensive experience working with foreigners. It is usually easy to locate competent, English-speaking doctors in the Bajío.

In almost all cases, Mexican doctors and hospitals do not accept U.S. insurance. Medicaid is also not accepted in Mexico. If you will be in Mexico for an extended period and are concerned about health care, you can explore the options for international coverage. Fortunately, if you have to pay out of pocket, medicine in Mexico tends to be far more inexpensive than in other developed countries; in many cases, tourists can pay for their medical exams, associated lab tests, and prescription medication out of pocket. Hospitals will usually accept cash and credit cards, though private doctors are usually cash-only.

PRESCRIPTIONS AND PHARMACIES

Visitors to Mexico are permitted to carry prescription medication for a pre-existing conditions among their personal affects. They can bring no more than three months' worth of medicine with them, and it should be accompanied by documentation from a doctor. (There can be strict penalties, including incarceration, for tourists who are suspected of drug abuse.) Most common over-the-counter medication is available in Mexico. Drugs in Mexico are regulated and safe; there are also generic brands.

If you need to purchase medication while you are in Mexico, you can visit a doctor who will write you a prescription. Most Mexican pharmacies do not ask for prescriptions for the majority of medications, with the exception of certain oft-abused substances. However, it is usually a better idea to get a prescription for medication, as the brands may differ in Mexico and there can be penalties for those carrying medication without a prescription. Prescription medication is often a bit cheaper in Mexico than in the rest of North America or Europe. If you would like to purchase prescription medication to take home from Mexico, the rules for export depend on your home country.

Many pharmacies *(farmacias)* are open 24 hours a day, while others close in the evening. In smaller towns like San Miguel de Allende and Guanajuato, there is always at least one pharmacy open through the night to attend to emergencies.

COMMON CONCERNS
Altitude Sickness

The Bajío's elevation is 6,500 feet (2,000 meters), and, for some visitors, the altitude may require a short adjustment period. Altitude sickness, though rarely serious, can include symptoms like shortness of breath, dizziness, headaches, and nausea. If symptoms are severe or persist past a few days, see a doctor.

Gastrointestinal Distress

Some tourists experience gastrointestinal distress when traveling in Mexico for the first time. Changes in the food you eat and the water you drink, changes in your eating and drinking habits, and a new overall environment can cause unpleasant diarrhea, nausea, and vomiting. Because it often affects Mexico newcomers, gastrointestinal distress is called *turista,* which translates to "tourist" (it's also known as "traveler's diarrhea" in English). In many cases, *turista* can be effectively treated with a few days of rest, liquids, and anti-diarrhea medication, such as Pepto Bismol,

HIGH LIFE: PREPARING FOR THE BAJÍO'S ALTITUDE

Situated atop a wide plain in the central Mexican plateau, the Bajío region doesn't feel like the mountains. There are no pine trees and granite peaks, just sun and cactus. However, at almost 2,000 meters (6,500 feet), San Miguel is as high as Lake Tahoe, California. In some cases, tourists forget that they are at altitude and may blame that queasy feeling on last night's tacos.

Altitude sickness can affect both young and old people, even those who are in good physical shape. Symptoms may include nausea, dizziness, loss of appetite, and fatigue. Keep an eye out for altitude sickness and take a few simple steps to increase your body's chances of a smooth acclimation.

DRINK LOTS OF WATER
Bodies tend to lose water more quickly at higher altitudes. Stay hydrated throughout your trip.

LIMIT COFFEE AND COCKTAILS
It's best to avoid drinks that can dehydrate you, especially alcohol and caffeine.

DON'T PUSH IT
Take it easy during your first few days in the Bajío. Let your body adjust to the altitude before heading off to a horseback riding adventure or a hike in the countryside.

EAT LIGHT
Doctors recommend avoiding heavy foods when you first arrive at a higher altitude. Have smaller meals and stick to lighter foods, like carbohydrates.

STAY ALERT
Altitude sickness is rarely serious; however, if symptoms don't improve after a day or two, see a doctor.

Kaopectate, or Imodium. Although you cannot necessarily prevent *turista* from striking, you will have a better chance of faring comfortably through your vacation if you eat and drink in moderation, get plenty of sleep, and stay hydrated. Many visitors to the Bajío do not experience any stomach discomfort.

More serious gastrointestinal problems can also occur in Mexico, though less frequently. If you are experiencing serious nausea, vomiting, and diarrhea, consult a doctor who can test and treat you for parasites or other gastrointestinal maladies.

Water Quality
Mexican tap water is treated; however, it is nonetheless considered unsafe for drinking. Bottled water is readily available throughout Mexico and, like any bottled beverage, is safe to drink. If you will be staying in Mexico for an extended period, you can purchase large plastic jugs of purified water to be delivered to your home. You can also make tap water safe for drinking by boiling it for several minutes to kill any bacteria or parasites. Most grocery stores sell droplets to sterilize fruits and vegetables; these can be use to purify water, though the flavor may be affected.

Most Mexicans do not consume tap water and therefore do not serve it in their restaurants. In the Bajío, ice is almost always made with purified water. Likewise, coffee, lemonades, and other drinks are almost always made with purified water.

Food Safety
When eating raw fresh vegetables and some fruits, it is common practice to disinfect them before consumption. In some cases, leafy vegetables may contain residual bacteria from watering or handling. For raw consumption, supermarkets sell several varieties of food sanitizer, the most common of which are made with chloride bleach or colloidal silver. If you

plan to cook your vegetables, you do not need to disinfect them; the heat will kill any potentially harmful substances.

Some visitors experience gastrointestinal distress after consuming raw vegetables, including shared salsa on the table in restaurants. If you are in the Bajío for a short vacation, you may want to err on the side of caution and avoid raw vegetables, or only consume vegetables that have been sterilized. There is always more risk associated with food stands located outdoors or in marketplaces, where hygiene is more difficult to maintain. Some people consume street food with no incident; others become ill after eating in markets or on the street. Use your discretion and introduce new foods into your diet slowly.

Infectious Disease

H1N1, or swine flu, was a major health concern in Mexico in the spring of 2008. There were more than 250 cases in the state of Guanajuato, with more than 50 confirmed cases in San Miguel de Allende. Since then, news of H1N1 has disappeared from the region. You may still notice hand sanitizers at the entryway in restaurants, and, of course, it is always best practice to wash your hands before eating. However, H1N1 is no longer a major health concern in Mexico.

Hepatitis A is more common in developing nations than in the first world. It affects the liver and is contracted from food or water infected with fecal matter. Vaccines are available to protect against hepatitis A infection. Symptoms may resemble the flu, though they are severe and may last several months.

There has been a recent surge in the number of cases of dengue fever in Mexico, though it remains a very limited problem in the center of the country. In the Bajío, there were a few cases reported in León, Guanajuato in 2007. Nonetheless, the government has launched an extensive campaign against mosquito proliferation, which includes periodic check of residences and their water storage systems, as well as occasional insecticide spraying. The only

way to prevent dengue infection is to avoid mosquito bites.

Creepy Crawlers

Mosquitoes are a common nuisance during the summer months, especially close to bodies of water or large gardens. Most serious mosquito-borne illnesses (such as malaria or dengue) are unusual in the Bajío region. However, their itchy bites make this pest a serious nuisance.

Scorpions live in the Bajío, and they occasionally turn up indoors. In most cases, scorpion stings are painful but not fatal. The exception is in and around the city of León, where a highly venomous scorpion can be found. Under any circumstance, consult a doctor if you are stung by a scorpion. Most scorpions are reclusive and avoid human contact. To avoid encountering them, shake out your shoes in the morning before you put them on, and use care moving bookcases or other furniture with its back to the wall.

Spiders are also common in the Bajío, including the poisonous black widow. Black widows are shiny black with a red hourglass on their abdomen. Like scorpions, black widows are generally reclusive. They may hide in wood piles, fields, or quiet corners. Though they rarely kill healthy adults, they can be a risk to children, the elderly, or pets. If bitten by a black widow, consult a doctor.

CRIME

The Bajío is a relatively safe region where violent crime is uncommon. The most common crimes in the Bajío are petty theft and break-ins. Nonetheless, visitors should take the reasonable precautions they would take when visiting any foreign country. Avoid traveling alone at night, don't carry excessive amounts of money in cash, and remain aware of your surroundings.

Over the past five years, there has been a rise in drug-related violence throughout Mexico. Although San Miguel de Allende and the Bajío region have not been caught in much crossfire (and tourist areas are rarely targeted in violent attacks), visitors should take the time to familiarize themselves with the political and social situation in modern Mexico. On that note, it is better to avoid consuming illegal drugs in Mexico, even in areas where drug violence is not a problem.

In the case that you have been arrested for a crime in Mexico, contact your embassy. International law requires that the Mexican government contact a foreigner's embassy at their request. However, foreign citizens may still be tried and held accountable under Mexican law for any crimes committed in Mexico.

Information and Services

MONEY
Currency

Mexico's currency is the peso. However, in San Miguel de Allende, many shops, hotels, and even some restaurants will accept U.S. dollars. In most cases, a shop will list both prices, though, on occasion, you will see prices listed simply in dollars; both currencies are denoted with a $ sign. Clearly, the arrangement can lead to confusion for San Miguel's shoppers, who aren't sure if an item is surprisingly cheap or incredibly expensive. (Restaurant menu prices are almost always listed exclusively in pesos.)

Exchanging Money

For most visitors to the Bajío, the most common and efficient way to change money is by using a foreign bank card at an ATM at a bank or credit union. Banks and credit unions generally offer the day's best exchange rates (often posted at the bank's entrance). Most international bank cards are accepted at Mexican banks, though it is always advisable to call your bank at home before attempting to withdraw money or use a credit card in a foreign country. When using your ATM card, always choose an official bank. Recently, there have been reports that ATM and credit card numbers have been stolen and used for illicit withdrawals in Mexico.

You can also change foreign currency to pesos at a *casa de cambio* (exchange house). There are *casas de cambio* in the *centro histórico* in both San Miguel de Allende and Guanajuato.

Be aware, however, that the Mexican government is attempting to reduce crime and fraud by limiting the amount of money that a customer can change in a single day. If you might need a large sum of money, plan ahead or use travelers checks.

Travelers Checks and Credit Cards

Mexico is still a largely cash culture. Across Mexico, credit cards are not generally accepted for smaller purchases, like a cup of coffee or a souvenir. When accepting a credit card, merchants must pay a percentage of their sales to the bank and are therefore reluctant to use cards for smaller items. (In some cases, merchants will give you a discounted price if you pay with cash or, conversely, charge you a bit more if you pay with a card.) Some hotels and restaurants do not take credit cards, especially those of the budget variety. At the same time, credit cards are widely accepted for large purchases, at gas stations, in shops, and in upscale restaurants. To rent a car, a credit card is required.

Travelers checks are an alternative to cash and can be useful in situations where you need to change a lot of money on a single day. The drawback is that travelers checks cannot be changed everywhere and may not be accepted at restaurants or shops in Mexico. There are American Express representatives in most main tourist centers. In addition, most travelers checks can be changed in many Banamex branches.

THE BAJÍO BY THE NUMBERS

TIME ZONE
San Miguel de Allende, Guanajuato, and the Bajío fall within the same time zone as central standard time in the United States, six hours behind Greenwich mean time. Since 1996, all Mexican states except Sonora have participated in **daylight saving time,** though clocks may not fall back or spring forward on the same weekend as in the U.S. and Canada.

ELECTRICITY
Like the United States and Canada, Mexico uses 110 volts 60 cycles. It can be useful to bring a socket adapter, since many Mexican outlets only allow for a two-prong plug.

WEIGHTS AND MEASURES
Mexico uses the metric system for all measurements, including temperature, distance, weight, and volume.

CLIMATE
Average high temperatures range 21-29°C (70-85°F) year-round. Average low runs 7-14°C (44-58°F).

POPULATION DISTRIBUTION
In the states of Guanajuato and Querétaro, 70 percent of the population lives in cities; 30 percent is rural.

COMMUNICATIONS AND MEDIA
Mail and Shipping Services
The Mexican post office will ship letters, postcards, and packages to any location in the world. They offer insured as well as expedited shipping services.

In addition, many major shipping companies offer shipping services in Mexico, including Estafeta, DHL, RedPack, UPS, and FedEx.

Internet Access
Mexico is wired. Internet cafés are scattered throughout the center of any large or medium-sized city, including Guanajuato, San Miguel de Allende, Dolores Hidalgo, and Querétaro. You may find fewer services in very small towns like Pozos. Otherwise, getting connecting is rarely a problem. Those who travel with their laptop will also find an increasing prevalence of wireless service in cafés or public libraries, as well as in hotels.

Newspapers, Radio, and Television
Large media conglomerates control the majority of Mexico's communication channels. Televisa Group is the largest and most powerful media company, operating several television stations, newspapers, and radio stations. In addition to privately owned stations, the government runs two public television stations, available on a limited basis throughout the republic.

For current events, there are both local and national newspapers and news magazines. In the Bajío, there are several papers published in the cities of Guanajuato, Celaya, León, and Querétaro, which cover local news and politics. In addition, national dailies are distributed in all of the Bajío's major towns, including the Mexico City papers *El Universal, Reforma,* and *La Jornada.*

TIME ZONE
San Miguel de Allende, Guanajuato, and the Bajío are on central standard time. Along with every state except Sonora, the region participates in the national daylight saving time (DST) program. Usually, DST begins in the spring and terminates in the fall, roughly around the same time as in the United States, though rarely on the exact same date.

RESOURCES

Glossary

adobado chile seasoning or marinade
aduana customs
aeropuerto airport
agave large Mexican succulent plant
agave azul blue agave, used in tequila production
agua water
aguas frescas or aguas de fruta cold fruit drink
alebrije hand-painted copal wood animals and figurines from Oaxaca.
almuerzo meal eaten around midday
andador pedestrian walkway
antigüedades antiques
antojitos snacks or appetizers
arquitecto architect
arrachera Mexican skirt steak
arte art
artesanía traditional handicraft
atole a sweet and hot beverage made with corn flour
autobus bus
autopista highway
ayuntamiento town council
azulejo tile
Bajío a geographical region that encompasses the states of Guanajuato and Querétaro, as well as segments of the states of Jalisco and Michoacán.
Ballet Folklórico a traditional Mexican dance troupe from Mexico City
banco bank
barbacoa pit-cooked lamb
biblioteca library
bolillo white roll

bomberos firefighters
botana appetizer
buen provecho an expression used to say "enjoy your meal"
burro donkey
caballo horse
café coffee
café con leche coffee with milk
café de olla boiled coffee with unrefined sugar and cinnamon
caldo broth
caldo tlalpeño chicken and chipotle soup
calle street
callejón alley
callejonadas the city of Guanajuato's famous traveling minstrel shows
calzada road
camión bus
cantina traditional bar or drinking establishment
capilla chapel
carnitas braised pork
carretera highway
casa house
casa de cambio exchange house
casita small house
castillo castle
catrina skeleton figurine or drawing dressed as an aristocrat; originally invented by artist José Guadalupe Posada
cempasuchil marigold
centro histórico historical district
cerveza beer
chal shawl
charro traditional Mexican cowboy or horseman

Chichimeca A name used by the Spanish during the early colonial era to describe the nomadic tribes of Northern Mexico

chilango Mexico City resident

chilaquiles fried tortilla strips bathed in salsa, cream, and cheese

chiles en nogada poblano pepper stuffed with meat, dried fruit, and nuts, covered in creamed walnut sauce, and sprinkled with pomegranate seeds

chiles rellenos stuffed chile peppers

chipotle a smoky dried chile pepper, derived from fresh jalapeño pepper

chorro spring

churro a tube-shaped sweet bread, deep fried and dusted in sugar

clínica clinic

cochinita pibil Yucatecan style pulled pork

comida the large midday meal in Mexico, typically eaten around 2 P.M.

comida corrida an economical, set-price lunch served in restaurants

concha a sweet roll topped with sugar

convento convent

corregidor magistrate, in the colonial era

correo postal service

corrida de toros bullfight

cotija a variety of aged Mexican cheese

consulado consulate

criollo a term used in New Spain to describe a Mexican-born person of Spanish descent

Cruz Roja Red Cross

cuaresma Lent

cuatrimoto ATV vehicle

cultura culture

cumbia a traditional musical style from Colombia

desayuno breakfast

Día de los Muertos Day of the Dead

distrito federal federal district, Mexico City

dulces sweets

dulces típicos traditional Mexican sweets

El Gran Chichimeca In the colonial era, the name give to the Northern Mexican region, including the Bajío, by Spanish settlers

embajada embassy

enchiladas mineras cheese-stuffed tortillas in *guajillo* sauce with sautéed potatoes and carrots

enchiladas verdes stuffed tortillas bathed in green salsa

enmoladas tortillas in mole sauce

entrada appetizer

equipal traditional wood and pigskin furniture style from Jalisco

escuela school

español Spanish

farmacia pharmacy

feria fair

festival festival

fiesta party

fiestas patrias patriotic holidays

flan egg custard dessert

flauta deep-fried and stuffed tortilla, topped with cream and salsa

FM2 immigrant visa

FM3 non-immigrant resident visa

fonda casual restaurant

gachupín Spanish person

galería gallery

gomita gum drop

gordita stuffed corn cake

gringa a flour tortilla filled with melted cheese and meat

gringo American

guanabana soursop, a tropical fruit

guayaba guava

guisado stew or side dish

hacienda estate

hojalatería tinwork

horchata traditional drink made with ground rice, sugar, and water

huarache torpedo-shaped corn flatbread

Huasteca Mexican region comprising northern Veracruz, southern Tamaulipas, a portion of San Luis Potosí, and the Sierra Gorda in Querétaro

huevo egg

huevos a la mexicana eggs scrambled with tomato, onion, and chile pepper

huevos rancheros fried eggs in tomato-chile sauce

huipil traditional women's tunic from Southern Mexico

huitlacoche corn fungus

iglesia church

indígena indigenous person, or indigenous (adj.)

ingeniero engineer

instituto institute

jamaica hibiscus

jamoncillo flavored milk-fudge

jarciería shop selling home and cleaning products

jardín garden

joyería jewelry

Las Mañanitas Mexico's birthday song

lavandería laundry

La Vía Dolorosa Stations of the Cross

ley seca dry law

librería bookstore

licenciado college graduate

licuado milkshake or fruit shake

longaniza a type of sausage

maciza in carnitas, pork shoulder or leg

maestro master; teacher

maguey large succulent plant common in Mexico

majolica tin-glazed pottery, originally from Italy

mañana tomorrow; morning

manta lightweight cotton fabric frequently used in traditional Mexican clothing

mantilla lace or silk scarf

maquiladora manufacturing plant

mariachi a traditional Mexican music ensemble

menudo beef stomach soup

mercado market

mesquite mesquite tree

mestizo a person of mixed ethnic heritage

mezcal distilled spirit made from the maguey plant

mezcal de gusano mezcal distilled with the maguey worm

michelada beer served with lime juice, salt, hot sauce, and Worcestershire sauce

migajas pork drippings

migración immigration

milagritos small tin ornaments

mixiote lamb steamed in agave leaf

mole flavorful sauce made of ground nuts and spices

mole negro ground sauce made of chocolate, nuts, and spices from the state of Oaxaca

momia mummy

montalayo lamb stomach

mordida literally, bite; slang for bribe

museo museum

Navidad Christmas

nevería ice cream parlor

nieve ice cream

norteño northern

novena nine days of prayer or worship

órgano organ

oro gold

Otomí indigenous ethnic group of central Mexico

palenqueta honey-covered disc of nuts or seeds

paleta popsicle

pan bread

pan de dulce sweet bread

panela a variety of fresh cheese

panteón cemetery

papadzules Yucatecan tacos stuffed with hard-boiled egg

papel picado decorative cut-paper adornments

parque park

parroquia parish

partido political party

Partido Acción Nacional National Action Party

Partido de la Revolución Democrática Party of the Democratic Revolution

Partido Revolucionario Institucional Institutional Revolutionary Party

pascua Easter

pasilla a mild but flavorful dried chile pepper

pastor taco preparation using chile pepper and spices

Pemex Petroleos Mexicanos (Mexican Petroleum)

peña rock

peninsular colonial era term for a person born in Spain

peso Mexico's currency

petate woven rush mat

picadillo spiced ground beef

pico de gallo salsa made of chopped tomatoes, onion, cilantro, and chile peppers

pipián a sauce made of ground pumpkin seeds and spices

plata silver

plaza plaza or public square

plaza de toros bullring

plazuela small plaza

poblano from the state or the city of Puebla

Porfiriato Historical period during the presidency of Porfirio Díaz

posada inn

pozo well

pozole hominy soup

presa reservoir

presidente municipal municipal president

priista member of the PRI political party

Protección Civil Civil Protection, or police

pueblo small town

pulque alcoholic drink made from fermented maguey sap

puntas de filete beef tips

querétense something or someone from Querétaro

quesadilla a warmed tortilla stuffed with cheese

queso cheese

queso de tuna prickly pear cheese, a regional sweet

queso fundido melted cheese

ranchera musical style from Northern Mexico

raspado shaved ice

rebozo shawl

reggaeton modern musical style based on reggae

rentistas FM3 visa designation for foreigners who live but do not earn money in Mexico

requesón ricotta-style cheese

restaurante restaurant

retablo devotional painting

río river

salsa roja condiment made with red tomatoes and chile peppers, or red chile peppers

salsa verde condiment made with green tomatoes, chile peppers, and spices

sangrita a tomato-based chaser for tequila

santa escuela a Jesuit school in the colonial era

Semana Santa Holy Week

señor Mr.; sir; man

señora Mrs., madam; woman

señorita Miss; young woman

serape traditional Mexican wool shawl or cloak

serrano variety of green chile pepper

siesta nap

sombrero hat

sopa soup

sopa azteca tortilla soup

sope thick, round corn-based flatbread

surtido mixed

taco seasoned meat or vegetables enclosed in a warm tortilla

tacos dorados deep-fried tacos

talavera hand-painted majolica-style pottery from Puebla, Mexico

tamal tamale, or steamed corn cake (plural: tamales)

teatro theater

templo temple, church

Tenochtitlan Capital city of Mesoamerica at the time of the Spanish conquest

tequila a Mexican distilled spirit made from blue agave

tintorería dry cleaner

tlayuda a large Oaxacan tortilla stuffed with beans and cheese

torta hot sandwich served on a white roll

transito transit

tranvía trolley

tú you, informal

tuna prickly pear fruit

turismo tourism

turista tourist or traveler's diarrhea

universidad university

usted you, formal

verano summer

viceroy colonial governor

Viernes Santo Good Friday

vino wine

vino tinto red wine

visa visa

xoconostle sour prickly pear fruit

zapote sapodilla, a tropical fruit

ABBREVIATIONS

Col. *colonia* (neighborhood)

esq. *esquina* (corner)

Gto. Guanajuato (state of Guanajuato)

IMN: Instituto Nacional de Migración (National Institute of Immigration

nte. *norte* (north)

ote. *oriente* (east)

PAN Partido Acción Nacional (National Action Party)

pp *por persona* (per person)

PRD Partido de la Revolución Democrática (Party of the Democratic Revolution)

PRI Partido Revolucionario Institucional (Institutional Revolutionary Party)

prol. *prolongación* (prolongation, usually of a city street)

pte. *poniente* (west)

Qro. Querétaro (state of Querétaro)

s/n *sin número* (without number)

Spanish Phrasebook

Your Mexican adventure will be more fun if you use a little Spanish. Mexican folks, although they may smile at your funny accent, will appreciate your halting efforts to break the ice and transform yourself from a foreigner to a potential friend.

Spanish commonly uses 30 letters – the familiar English 26, plus four straightforward additions: ch, ll, ñ, and rr.

PRONUNCIATION

Once you learn them, Spanish pronunciation rules – in contrast to English – don't change. Spanish vowels generally sound softer than in English. (*Note:* The capitalized syllables receive stronger accents.)

Vowels

a like ah, as in "hah": *agua* AH-gooah (water), *pan* PAHN (bread), and *casa* CAH-sah (house)

e like ay, as in "may:" *mesa* MAY-sah (table), *tela* TAY-lah (cloth), and *de* DAY (of, from)

i like ee, as in "need": *diez* dee-AYZ (ten), *comida* ko-MEE-dah (meal), and *fin* FEEN (end)

o like oh, as in "go": *peso* PAY-soh (weight), *ocho* OH-choh (eight), and *poco* POH-koh (a bit)

u like oo, as in "cool": *uno* OO-noh (one), *cuarto* KOOAHR-toh (room), and *usted* oos-TAYD (you); when it follows a "q" the **u** is silent; when it follows an "h" or has an umlaut, it's pronounced like "w"

Consonants

b, d, f, k, l, m, n, p, q, s, t, v, w, x, y, z, and ch pronounced almost as in English; **h** occurs, but is silent – not pronounced at all.

c like k as in "keep": *cuarto* KOOAR-toh (room), Tepic tay-PEEK (capital of Nayarit state); when it precedes "e" or "i," pronounce **c** like s, as in "sit": *cerveza* sayr-VAY-sah (beer), *encima* ayn-SEE-mah (atop).

g like g as in "gift" when it precedes "a," "o," "u," or a consonant: *gato* GAH-toh (cat), *hago* AH-goh (I do, make); otherwise, pronounce **g** like h as in "hat": *giro* HEE-roh (money order), *gente* HAYN-tay (people)

j like h, as in "has": *jueves* HOOAY-vays (Thursday), *mejor* may-HOR (better)

ll like y, as in "yes": *toalla* toh-AH-yah (towel), *ellos* AY-yohs (they, them)

ñ like ny, as in "canyon": *año* AH-nyo (year), *señor* SAY-nyor (Mr., sir)

r is lightly trilled, with tongue at the roof of your mouth like a very light English d, as in "ready": *pero* PAY-doh (but), *tres* TDAYS (three), *cuatro* KOOAH-tdoh (four).

rr like a Spanish r, but with much more emphasis and trill. Let your tongue flap. Practice with *burro* (donkey), *carretera* (highway), and Carrillo (proper name), then really let go with *ferrocarril* (railroad).

Note: The single small but common exception to all of the above is the pronunciation of Spanish

y when it's being used as the Spanish word for "and," as in "Ron y Kathy." In such case, pronounce it like the English ee, as in "keep": Ron "ee" Kathy (Ron and Kathy).

Accent

The rule for accent, the relative stress given to syllables within a given word, is straightforward. If a word ends in a vowel, an n, or an s, accent the next-to-last syllable; if not, accent the last syllable.

Pronounce *gracias* GRAH-seeahs (thank you), *orden* OHR-dayn (order), and *carretera* kah-ray-TAY-rah (highway) with stress on the next-to-last syllable.

Otherwise, accent the last syllable: *venir* vay-NEER (to come), *ferrocarril* fay-roh-cah-REEL (railroad), and *edad* ay-DAHD (age).

Exceptions to the accent rule are always marked with an accent sign: (á, é, í, ó, or ú), such as *teléfono* tay-LAY-foh-noh (telephone), *jabón* hah-BON (soap), and *rápido* RAH-pee-doh (rapid).

BASIC AND COURTEOUS EXPRESSIONS

Most Spanish-speaking people consider formalities important. Whenever approaching anyone for information or some other reason, do not forget the appropriate salutation – good morning, good evening, etc. Standing alone, the greeting *hola* (hello) can sound brusque.

Hello. *Hola.*
Good morning. *Buenos días.*
Good afternoon. *Buenas tardes.*
Good evening. *Buenas noches.*
How are you? *¿Cómo está usted?*
Very well, thank you. *Muy bien, gracias.*
Okay; good. *Bien.*
Not okay; bad. *Mal* or *feo.*
So-so. *Más o menos.*
And you? *¿Y usted?*
Thank you. *Gracias.*
Thank you very much. *Muchas gracias.*
You're very kind. *Muy amable.*
You're welcome. *De nada.*
Goodbye. *Adios.*
See you later. *Hasta luego.*

please *por favor*
yes *sí*
no *no*
I don't know. *No sé.*
Just a moment, please. *Momentito, por favor.*
Excuse me, please (when you're trying to get attention). *Disculpe* or *Con permiso.*
Excuse me (when you've made a boo-boo). *Lo siento.*
Pleased to meet you. *Mucho gusto.*
What is your name? *¿Cómo se llama usted?*
My name is . . . *Me llamo . . .*
Do you speak English? *¿Habla usted inglés?*
Is English spoken here? (Does anyone here speak English?) *¿Se habla inglés?*
I don't speak Spanish well. *No hablo bien el español.*
I don't understand. *No entiendo.*
How do you say . . . in Spanish? *¿Cómo se dice . . . en español?*
Would you like . . . *¿Quisiera usted . . .*
Let's go to . . . *Vamos a . . .*

TERMS OF ADDRESS

When in doubt, use the formal *usted* (you) as a form of address.

I *yo*
you (formal) *usted*
you (familiar) *tú*
he/him *él*
she/her *ella*
we/us *nosotros*
you (plural) *ustedes*
they/them *ellos* (all males or mixed gender); *ellas* (all females)
Mr., sir *señor*
Mrs., madam *señora*
miss, young lady *señorita*
wife *esposa*
husband *esposo*
friend *amigo* (male); *amiga* (female)
sweetheart *novio* (male); *novia* (female)
son; daughter *hijo; hija*
brother; sister *hermano; hermana*
father; mother *padre; madre*
grandfather; grandmother *abuelo; abuela*

TRANSPORTATION

Where is . . . ? *¿Dónde está . . . ?*
How far is it to . . . ? *¿A cuánto está . . . ?*
from . . . to . . . *de . . . a . . .*
How many blocks? *¿Cuántas cuadras?*
Where (Which) is the way to . . . ? *¿Dónde está el camino a . . . ?*
the bus station *la terminal de autobuses*
the bus stop *la parada de autobuses*
Where is this bus going? *¿Adónde va este autobús?*
the taxi stand *la parada de taxis*
the train station *la estación de ferrocarril*
the boat *el barco*
the launch *lancha; tiburonera*
the dock *el muelle*
the airplane *avión*
the airport *el aeropuerto*
I'd like a ticket to . . . *Quisiera un boleto a . . .*
first (second) class *primera (segunda) clase*
round-trip *ida y vuelta; viaje redondo*
reservation *reservación*
baggage *equipaje*
Stop here, please. *Pare aquí, por favor.*
the entrance *la entrada*
the exit *la salida*
ticket *boleto*
the ticket office *taquilla*
(very) near; far *(muy) cerca; lejos*
to; toward *a*
by; through *por*
from *de*
the right *la derecha*
the left *la izquierda*
straight ahead *derecho; directo*
in front *en frente*
beside *al lado*
behind *atrás*
the corner *la esquina*
the stoplight *la semáforo*
a turn *una vuelta*
right here *aquí*
somewhere around here *por acá*
right there *allí*
somewhere around there *por allá*
road *el camino*
street; boulevard *calle; bulevar*
block *la cuadra*

highway *carretera*
kilometer *kilómetro*
bridge; toll *puente; cuota*
address *dirección*
north; south *norte; sur*
east; west *oriente (este); poniente (oeste)*

ACCOMMODATIONS

hotel *hotel*
Is there a room? *¿Hay cuarto?*
May I (may we) see it? *¿Puedo (podemos) verlo?*
What is the rate? *¿Cuál es el precio?*
Is that your best rate? *¿Es su mejor precio?*
Is there something cheaper? *¿Hay algo más económico?*
a single room *un cuarto sencillo*
a double room *un cuarto doble*
double bed *cama matrimonial*
twin beds *camas individuales*
with private bath *con baño*
hot water *agua caliente*
shower *ducha*
towels *toallas*
soap *jabón*
toilet paper *papel higiénico*
blanket *cobija*
sheets *sábanas*
air-conditioned *aire acondicionado*
fan *abanico; ventilador*
key *llave*
manager *gerente*

FOOD

I'm hungry *Tengo hambre.*
I'm thirsty. *Tengo sed.*
menu *carta; menú*
order *orden*
glass *vaso*
fork *tenedor*
knife *cuchillo*
spoon *cuchara*
napkin *servilleta*
soft drink *refresco*
coffee *café*
tea *té*
drinking water *agua pura; agua potable*
bottle of water *botella de agua*

bottled carbonated water *agua mineral*
bottled uncarbonated water *agua sin gas*
beer *cerveza*
wine *vino*
milk *leche*
juice *jugo*
cream *crema*
sugar *azúcar*
cheese *queso*
snack *antojito; botana*
breakfast *desayuno*
lunch *almuerzo*
daily lunch special *comida corrida* (or *el menú del día* depending on region)
dinner *comida* (often eaten in late afternoon); *cena* (a late-night snack)
wine list *lista de vinos*
the check *la cuenta*
tip *propina*
eggs *huevos*
bread *pan*
salad *ensalada*
fruit *fruta*
mango *mango*
watermelon *sandía*
papaya *papaya*
banana *plátano*
apple *manzana*
orange *naranja*
lime *limón*
fish *pescado*
shellfish *mariscos*
shrimp *camarones*
meat (without) *(sin) carne*
chicken *pollo*
pork *puerco*
beef; steak *res; bistec*
bacon; ham *tocino; jamón*
fried *frito*
roasted *asada*
barbecue; barbecued *barbacoa; al carbón*
spicy, hot *picante*

SHOPPING
money *dinero*
money-exchange bureau *casa de cambio*
I would like to exchange travelers checks. *Quisiera cambiar cheques de viajero.*
What is the exchange rate? *¿Cuál es el tipo de cambio?*
How much is the commission? *¿Cuánto cuesta la comisión?*
Do you accept credit cards? *¿Aceptan tarjetas de crédito?*
money order *giro*
How much does it cost? *¿Cuánto cuesta?*
What is your final price? *¿Cuál es su último precio?*
expensive *caro*
cheap *barato; económico*
more *más*
less *menos*
a little *un poco*
too much *demasiado*

HEALTH
Help me please. *Ayúdeme por favor.*
I am ill. *Estoy enfermo.*
Call a doctor. *Llame un doctor.*
Take me to ... *Lléveme a ...*
hospital *hospital; sanatorio*
drugstore *farmacia*
pain *dolor*
fever *fiebre*
headache *dolor de cabeza*
stomachache *dolor de estómago*
allergy *alergia*
burn *quemadura*
cramp *calambre*
nausea *náusea*
vomiting *vomitar*
medicine *medicina*
prescription *receta*
antibiotic *antibiótico*
pill; tablet *pastilla*
aspirin *aspirina*
ointment; cream *pomada; crema*
bandage *venda*
cotton *algodón*
sanitary napkins *toallas*, or use brand name, e.g., Kotex
birth control pills *pastillas anticonceptivas*
contraceptive foam *espuma anticonceptiva*

condoms *preservativos; condones*
toothbrush *cepilla dental*
dental floss *hilo dental*
toothpaste *crema dental*
dentist *dentista*
toothache *dolor de muelas*

POST OFFICE AND COMMUNICATIONS

long-distance telephone *teléfono larga distancia*
I would like to call ... *Quisiera llamar a ...*
collect *por cobrar*
station to station *a quien contesta*
person to person *persona a persona*
credit card *tarjeta de crédito*
post office *correo*
general delivery *lista de correo*
letter *carta*
stamp *estampilla, timbre*
postcard *tarjeta*
aerogram *aerograma*
air mail *correo aereo*
registered *registrado*
money order *giro*
package; box *paquete; caja*
string; tape *cuerda; cinta*

AT THE BORDER

border *frontera*
customs *aduana*
immigration *migración*
tourist card *tarjeta de turista*
inspection *inspección; revisión*
passport *pasaporte*
profession *profesión*
marital status *estado civil*
single *soltero*
married; divorced *casado; divorciado*
widowed *viudado*
insurance *seguros*
title *título*
driver's license *licencia de manejar*

AT THE GAS STATION

gas station *gasolinera*
gasoline *gasolina*

unleaded *sin plomo*
full, please *lleno, por favor*
tire *llanta*
tire repair shop *vulcanizadora*
air *aire*
water *agua*
oil (change) *aceite (cambio)*
grease *grasa*
My ... doesn't work. *Mi ... no sirve.*
battery *batería*
radiator *radiador*
alternator *alternador*
generator *generador*
tow truck *grúa*
repair shop *taller mecánico*
tune-up *afinación*
auto parts store *refaccionería*

VERBS

Verbs are the key to getting along in Spanish. They employ mostly predictable forms and come in three classes, which end in *ar, er,* and *ir,* respectively:
to buy *comprar*
I buy, you (he, she, it) buys *compro, compra*
we buy, you (they) buy *compramos, compran*
to eat *comer*
I eat, you (he, she, it) eats *como, come*
we eat, you (they) eat *comemos, comen*
to climb *subir*
I climb, you (he, she, it) climbs *subo, sube*
we climb, you (they) climb *subimos, suben*

Here are more (with irregularities indicated):
to do or make *hacer* (regular except for *hago,* I do or make)
to go *ir* (very irregular: *voy, va, vamos, van*)
to go (walk) *andar*
to love *amar*
to work *trabajar*
to want *desear, querer*
to need *necesitar*
to read *leer*
to write *escribir*
to repair *reparar*
to stop *parar*

to get off (the bus) *bajar*
to arrive *llegar*
to stay (remain) *quedar*
to stay (lodge) *hospedar*
to leave *salir* (regular except for *salgo*, I leave)
to look at *mirar*
to look for *buscar*
to give *dar* (regular except for *doy*, I give)
to carry *llevar*
to have *tener* (irregular but important: *tengo, tiene, tenemos, tienen*)
to come *venir* (similarly irregular: *vengo, viene, venimos, vienen*)

Spanish has two forms of "to be":
to be *estar* (regular except for *estoy*, I am)
to be *ser* (very irregular: *soy, es, somos, son*)
Use *estar* when speaking of location or a temporary state of being: "I am at home." *"Estoy en casa." "*I'm sick." *"Estoy enfermo."* Use *ser* for a permanent state of being: "I am a doctor." *"Soy doctora."*

NUMBERS

0 *cero*
1 *uno*
2 *dos*
3 *tres*
4 *cuatro*
5 *cinco*
6 *seis*
7 *siete*
8 *ocho*
9 *nueve*
10 *diez*
11 *once*
12 *doce*
13 *trece*
14 *catorce*
15 *quince*
16 *dieciseis*
17 *diecisiete*
18 *dieciocho*
19 *diecinueve*
20 *veinte*
21 *veinte y uno* or *veintiuno*
30 *treinta*
40 *cuarenta*

50 *cincuenta*
60 *sesenta*
70 *setenta*
80 *ochenta*
90 *noventa*
100 *ciento*
101 *ciento y uno* or *cientiuno*
200 *doscientos*
500 *quinientos*
1,000 *mil*
10,000 *diez mil*
100,000 *cien mil*
1,000,000 *millón*
one-half *medio*
one-third *un tercio*
one-fourth *un cuarto*

TIME

What time is it? *¿Qué hora es?*
It's one o'clock. *Es la una.*
It's three in the afternoon. *Son las tres de la tarde.*
It's 4 A.M. *Son las cuatro de la mañana.*
six-thirty *seis y media*
a quarter till eleven *un cuarto para las once*
a quarter past five *las cinco y cuarto*
an hour *una hora*

DAYS AND MONTHS

Monday *lunes*
Tuesday *martes*
Wednesday *miércoles*
Thursday *jueves*
Friday *viernes*
Saturday *sábado*
Sunday *domingo*
today *hoy*
tomorrow *mañana*
yesterday *ayer*
January *enero*
February *febrero*
March *marzo*
April *abril*
May *mayo*
June *junio*
July *julio*
August *agosto*
September *septiembre*

October *octubre*
November *noviembre*
December *diciembre*
a week *una semana*
a month *un mes*

after *después*
before *antes*

Courtesy of Bruce Whipperman,
author of Moon Pacific Mexico.

Suggested Reading

HISTORY AND CULTURE

Brading, David. *Miners and Merchants in Bourbon Mexico*. Cambridge, U.K.: Cambridge University Press, 2008. Widely recognized as one of the preeminent scholars of early Guanajuato and the Spanish colonies, David Brading offers a fascinating look at life in colonial Mexico.

Coe, Michael D. *From the Olmecs to the Aztecs*. London: Thames and Hudson, 2008. Yale anthropologist Michael D. Coe has written extensively about Mesoamerican civilizations. In this volume, he introduces the great cultures of pre-Columbian Mexico.

Collier, George. *Basta: Land and the Zapatista Rebellion in Chiapas*. Oakland, California: Food First Books, 1994. An excellent introduction to indigenous communities and the 1994 Zapatista uprising in Chiapas.

De las Casas, Bartolomé. *Short Account of the Destruction of the Indies*. London: Penguin Books, 1992. A Dominican friar and humanitarian, de las Casas recounts his first-hand observations about Spanish abuse of indigenous Americans during the colonial era.

Franz, Carl, and Lorena Havens. *The People's Guide to Mexico*. Emeryville, California: Avalon Travel Publishing, 2006. A cultural handbook to travel in Mexico, the *People's Guide* offers hard-won and well-placed advice for adventurous Mexico travelers.

Kennedy, Diana. *My Mexico*. New York: Clarkson Potter/Publishers, 1998. More anthropological tome than practical cookbook, this book offers detailed regional recipes from across Mexico, accompanied by the author's personal observations and stories.

Krauze, Enrique. *Mexico: A Biography of Power*. New York: Harper Perennial, 1998. A general history of Mexico, written by one of the country's preeminent intellectuals.

Riding, Alan. *Distant Neighbors*. New York: Knopf, 1984. Though written in the 1980s, this book still offers a current perspective on the differences between U.S. and Mexican culture with incredible accuracy.

Womack, John. *Emiliano Zapata and the Mexican Revolution*. New York: Vintage, 1970. An exhaustive and well-researched history of the great hero, Emiliano Zapata, written by Harvard's Mexico expert, John Womack.

SAN MIGUEL DE ALLENDE AND THE BAJÍO

Cohan, Tony. *On Mexican Time: A New Life in Mexico*. New York: Broadway Books, 2000. Cohan's best-selling memoir vividly recounts his first years of life as an expatriate in San Miguel de Allende.

Dean, Archie. *The Insider's Guide to San Miguel*. Self-published, 2009. You will have to seek out this classic guide to San Miguel de Allende in one of the city's local bookshops or buy it online (www.thesanmiguelguide.com). It offers a comprehensive and annotated list of restaurants, hotels, and other businesses in San Miguel.

De Gast, Robert. *Behind the Doors of San Miguel de Allende.* Petaluma, California: Pomegranate Communications, 2000. De Gast's followup to his successful photography book about San Miguel shows you the courtyards and gardens behind the town's distinctive doorways.

De Gast, Robert. *The Doors of San Miguel de Allende.* Petaluma, California: Pomegranate Communications, 1994. A wonderful photographer and writer, Robert de Gast captures the unique culture and color of San Miguel through photos of its beautiful doorways.

Schmidt, Carol, and Norma Hair. *Falling...in love with San Miguel: Retiring to Mexico on Social Security.* Laredo, Texas: Salsa Verde Press, 2005. Two women frankly and humorously recount their joyous adjustment to expatriate life in San Miguel de Allende. It's more memoir than handbook.

Internet Resources

SAN MIGUEL DE ALLENDE
Falling in Love with San Miguel
http://fallinginlovewithsanmiguel.com
San Miguel residents and co-authors of the book *Falling...in love with San Miguel* have a wonderful and well-maintained website about life in the city, including a blog, photos, local recommendations, practical advice, and a message board.

Portal San Miguel
http://portalsanmiguel.com
If you want to keep your finger on the pulse of San Miguel de Allende, check out this local blog, which offers restaurant and gallery reviews, updated event listings, and links to local business.

San Miguel de Allende Official Site
www.sanmiguelallende.gob.mx
The official website of San Miguel de Allende offers information about the city and city services, like education and the police force, in Spanish.

The Little Schools
www.littleschoolssma.com
This website offers a directory of artists, chefs, personal trainers, yoga instructors, and other professionals who give individual and group classes in San Miguel de Allende.

This Week in San Miguel
http://thisweekinsanmigueldeallende.com
Want to know where the party is this weekend? Here's an updated and comprehensive online calendar of classes and events in San Miguel de Allende, including a small city guide.

GUANAJUATO
Festival Internacional Cervantino
www.festivalcervantino.gob.mx
The official site for Guanajuato's renowned annual Cervantino festival offers programming information and a gallery of photos from previous years.

Guanajuato Official Site
www.guanajuato.gob.mxpr
The official website of Guanajuato's state government offers general information about state programs, as well as links to tourist information.

Vamos a Guanajuato
www.letsgoguanajuato.com
www.vamosaguanajuato.com
The Guanajuato government offers an

introduction to the state's most popular tourist destinations, including photo galleries, hotel listings, and descriptions of the major sights and attractions.

QUERÉTARO
Travel Querétaro
www.queretaro.travel/english

Maintained by the Querétaro state government, this informative website details major sites in Querétaro, lists upcoming events, and offers maps, photo galleries, and cultural articles. The Spanish version contains more detailed content than the English version.

MEXICO
Mexconnect
www.mexconnect.com

Mexconnect features hundreds of articles on Mexican travel, food, history, and culture from independent contributors across the country. It also has advice about relocation and visas.

People's Guide to Mexico
www.peoplesguide.com

Authors of the *People's Guide to Mexico* offer practical advice, a travel blog, articles, and links in complement to their popular guidebook about Mexican travel.

Solutions Abroad
www.solutionsabroad.com

For those considering relocating to Mexico, this Mexico City–based website offers advice about visas, employment, education, and other pertinent topics.

U.S. Embassy in Mexico
http://mexico.usembassy.gov

The United States Embassy offers recent Mexico related news, travel advisories, and information about their citizen services.

Index

List of Maps

Acknowledgments

Much love and many thanks to Arturo Meade, whose photographs, wisdom, and sensibility are woven throughout this book and without whom I may never have finished the research! Warmest thanks to Marie Moebius for her ideas, generosity, and invaluable help with research, and to Alicia Wilson Rivero for feeding me, tracking down the last-minute details, and imparting her many spirited opinions. I am grateful to José E. Guitérrez Tobias and Pedro Sánchez for sharing their extensive knowledge of San Miguel's traditions and holidays. To Carmen Meade, Gabriela Gonzalez Meade, Brian Care, Eric Arbanovella, and the many other people who took the time to write me back, answer my phone calls, and share their opinions: Thank you. I am very grateful for the help and encouragement I received from Grace Fujimoto and Leah Gordon at Moon, as well as from Lucie Ericksen and Mike Morgenfeld. Finally, I would like to thank Brucine, Francis, and Amy Doherty, who help me in everything I do.

www.moon.com

DESTINATIONS | ACTIVITIES | BLOGS | MAPS | BOOKS

MOON.COM is ready to help plan your next trip! Filled with fresh trip ideas and strategies, author interviews, informative travel blogs, a detailed map library, and descriptions of all the Moon guidebooks, Moon.com is all you need to get out and explore the world—or even places in your own backyard. While at Moon.com, sign up for our monthly e-newsletter for updates on new releases, travel tips, and expert advice from our on-the-go Moon authors. As always, when you travel with Moon, expect an experience that is uncommon and truly unique.

KEEP UP WITH MOON ON FACEBOOK AND TWITTER
JOIN THE MOON PHOTO GROUP ON FLICKR

MAP SYMBOLS

▓▓▓ Expressway	【 Highlight	✗ Airfield	⚓ Golf Course
─── Primary Road	○ City/Town	✈ Airport	🅿 Parking Area
── Secondary Road	◉ State Capital	▲ Mountain	⬟ Archaeological Site
═══ Unpaved Road	⊛ National Capital	✦ Unique Natural Feature	⛪ Church
‑‑‑‑‑ Trail	★ Point of Interest		⛽ Gas Station
·········· Ferry	• Accommodation	🗟 Waterfall	Glacier
══ Railroad	▼ Restaurant/Bar	▲ Park	Mangrove
▓▓ Pedestrian Walkway	■ Other Location	🚩 Trailhead	Reef
▥ Stairs	Δ Campground	🎿 Skiing Area	Swamp

CONVERSION TABLES

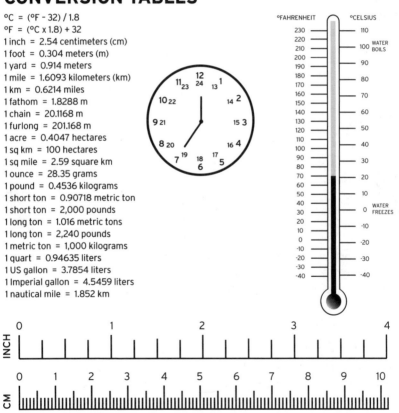

°C = (°F – 32) / 1.8
°F = (°C x 1.8) + 32
1 inch = 2.54 centimeters (cm)
1 foot = 0.304 meters (m)
1 yard = 0.914 meters
1 mile = 1.6093 kilometers (km)
1 km = 0.6214 miles
1 fathom = 1.8288 m
1 chain = 20.1168 m
1 furlong = 201.168 m
1 acre = 0.4047 hectares
1 sq km = 100 hectares
1 sq mile = 2.59 square km
1 ounce = 28.35 grams
1 pound = 0.4536 kilograms
1 short ton = 0.90718 metric ton
1 short ton = 2,000 pounds
1 long ton = 1.016 metric tons
1 long ton = 2,240 pounds
1 metric ton = 1,000 kilograms
1 quart = 0.94635 liters
1 US gallon = 3.7854 liters
1 Imperial gallon = 4.5459 liters
1 nautical mile = 1.852 km

°FAHRENHEIT °CELSIUS

WATER BOILS — 100 / 210
WATER FREEZES — 0 / 30

MOON SAN MIGUEL DE ALLENDE, GUANAJUATO & THE BAJÍO
Avalon Travel
a member of the Perseus Books Group
1700 Fourth Street
Berkeley, CA 94710, USA
www.moon.com

Editor: Leah Gordon
Series Manager: Kathryn Ettinger
Copy Editor: Deana Shields
Graphics and Production Coordinator: Lucie Ericksen
Cover Designer: Lucie Ericksen
Map Editor: Mike Morgenfeld
Cartographers: Chris Henrick, Kaitlin Jaffe
Indexer: Deana Shields

ISBN: 978-1-59880-897-1
ISSN: 2161-9514

Printing History
1st Edition – October 2011
5 4 3 2 1

Text © 2011 by Julie Doherty Meade.
Maps © 2011 by Avalon Travel.
All rights reserved.

Front cover photo: Day of the Dead decorations around the Parroquia de San Miguel Arcángel, San Miguel de Allende © Raymond Klass/ DanitaDelimont.com
Title page photo: the massive dome of the Templo de la Inmaculada Concepción, San Miguel de Allende © Arturo Meade
Other front matter photos: pages 4-6, 7 top, 9 top-left, 10 left, 11, 13, 14, 16-18, 20-24: © Arturo Meade; pages 7 bottom, 9 top-right & bottom, 10 right, 12, 15, 19: © Julie Doherty Meade

Printed in Canada by Friesens

KEEPING CURRENT

If you have a favorite gem you'd like to see included in the next edition, or see anything that needs updating, clarification, or correction, please drop us a line. Send your comments via email to feedback@moon.com, or use the address above.